Once upon a time in Papunya

VIVIEN JOHNSON has an extensive body of work relating to the artists of Papunya Tula and how the movement they started in 1971 has influenced the rest of the Western Desert and eventually all of Aboriginal Australia. Her pioneering books, including the monumental *Lives of the Papunya Tula Artists*, and her work on Indigenous cultural and intellectual property rights have had wide social impact. Her last appointment was as a Global Professor at the University of New South Wales. Vivien was also founding Editor-in-Chief of the *Dictionary of Australian Artists Online.*

Once upon a time in Papunya

Vivien Johnson

NEW SOUTH

A New South book

Published by
University of New South Wales Press Ltd
University of New South Wales
Sydney NSW 2052
AUSTRALIA
www.unswpress.com.au

First published 2010

10 9 8 7 6 5 4 3 2 1

National Library of Australia
Cataloguing-in-Publication entry
Author: Johnson, Vivien
Title: Once upon a time in Papunya/by Vivien Johnson.
ISBN: 978 174223 007 8 (pbk.)
Subjects: Bardon, Geoff, 1940–2003
Papunya Tula Artists Pty. Ltd.
Art, Aboriginal Australian.
Aboriginal Australians – Northern Territory – Papunya – Painting.
Painting, Aboriginal Australian – Northern Territory – Papunya.
Painting, Aboriginal Australian – Northern Territory – Western Desert.
Art, Australian – 20th century.
Art and mythology.
Dewey Number: 709.0110994291

Cover design Jenny Grigg
Text design Jenny Grigg, Avril Makula and Di Quick
Printer Ligare

This book is printed on paper using fibre supplied from plantation or sustainably managed forests.

Contents

Acknowledgments

Special thanks to my friends and colleagues John Kean, Jeremy Long and Fred Myers for reading some of the draft chapters and for their supportive and helpful comments; Sotheby's Australia for their generous support in supplying images; all the artists of Papunya Tula, past and present; Alison Anderson; Linda Anderson; Dorn Bardon; Geoffrey Bardon; Philip Batty; Roger Benjamin; Diana Calder; Wally Caruana; Francesca Cavazzini; Jack Cooke; John Corker; Diane de Vere; Bob Edwards; Peter Fannin; Fred Friis; Christine Godden; Iris Harvey; Ian Howard; Mr and Mrs WL Jackson; Michael Jensen; Tim Johnson; Richard Kelton; Kate Khan; RG (Dick) Kimber; Tim Klingender; Graeme Marshall; Vincent Megaw; Michael Jagamara Nelson; Laurie Owens; Stephen Oxenbury; Zena Pearlstone; Hetti Perkins; Charlotte Phillipus Napurrula; Long Jack Phillipus Tjakamarra; Cara Pinchbeck; Clifford Possum Tjapaltjarri; Arnold Probin; Richard Probin; Sarita Quinlivan; Alison Reid; Murphy Roberts Tjupurrula; Roxana Roman; Nicolas Rothwell; Judith Ryan; Luke Scholes; Glenn Schwinghammer; Carmel and Rod Sears; Billy Stockman Tjapaltjarri; Paul Sweeney; Charlie Tjapangati; Turkey Tolson Tjupurrula; Grenville Turner; Penny Tweedie; Anthony Wallis; Ellen Waugh; Andy Weislogel; Bobby West Tjupurrula; Margie West; Simon Wheeler and *The Ithaca Journal*; John and Barbara Wilkerson; Daphne Williams; Centre for Cross-Cultural Research, Australian National University; College of Fine Arts, University of New South Wales; the staff of Papunya Tula Artists Pty Ltd; Anna Lee my physiotherapist; and Museums and Art Galleries of the Northern Territory; Araluen Art Centre; Wollongong City Gallery; Art Gallery of New South Wales; National Gallery of Victoria;

Queensland Art Gallery; National Museum of Australia; Art Gallery of South Australia; Australian Museum; and the National Gallery of Australia.

Every effort has been made to ensure the early Papunya boards reproduced in the book are all 'unrestricted' images and thus suitable for reproduction and distribution in Australia or anywhere else. I am deeply grateful to the senior cultural authorities from Papunya, Kintore and Kiwirrkura, who inspected the images of early Papunya boards reproduced in this book and cleared them for possible publication.

Introduction

Search for 'Papunya, Northern Territory' on Google Earth and you will see a huge circle, pierced on the right-hand side by the dirt road from Alice Springs 260 kilometres away to the south-east and on the left by another heading west 300 kilometres to Kintore, just inside the border with Western Australia. Inside this circle is the huddle of buildings comprising the remote Aboriginal community of Papunya. Only the Phillipus compound sits outside the circle, off to the north-west in the direction of Kalipinypa and other sites in the country of its patriarch, Long Jack Phillipus Tjakamarra, all but last of the founders of the famous Papunya Tula Artists company which started here almost forty years ago.

If you look more closely, you can see four giant U-shaped tracks coming off the circle to the north, south, east and west. They're hard to see because nothing has ever been built along them. After the torrential summer rains of 2009–10 in Central Australia, some of the heaviest since the incredible downpour of 1971–72, they have almost disappeared under a blanket of invasive buffel grass, at least from the air. On foot, though, they are still easy to find and follow. Every morning when I'm in Papunya, I take the one to the south, entering near the football oval, passing through a stand of mulga trees and emerging not far from the wide, sealed road to the airstrip, one of the most tangible achievements of the

Northern Territory Emergency Response (or 'Intervention'), as a huge sign alongside it proclaims.

No-one knows who graded these U-shaped tracks, but to Papunya's Aboriginal residents, the design of their road system represents, not a mini-Canberra in the desert, but the underground chambers of the sacred Honey Ant 'Boss' whose massive petrified body nestles alongside their community. Once upon a time, these hills – one small and two larger – variously known to the locals as Papunya Tula, Warumpi and Tjupi, were the site of a great gathering of Honey Ant ancestors from across the Western Desert:

> The Honey Ant Dreaming is very important to all Centralian tribes, and from the Luritja point of view centres about Yuendumu, Mt Allan and Napperby Station areas (250–300 kilometres north-west of Alice Springs). From key sites over this large tract of land, the mythological Honey Ants travelled south-west to the Papunya area where they met with Honey Ants from the far west Pintupi fringe country near the Ehrenberg Range. After this great meeting, some of them returned to their homes, but others remained to live 'everywhere' along the mythological travelling routes and neighbouring country.[1]

Mirroring this ancient gathering of Honey Ant ancestors, Papunya at the beginning of the 1970s brought together more than a thousand people from several different language groups in a government settlement originally built to accommodate only half that number. Tensions were aroused by the high levels of disease and death, which provoked suspicions of hostile sorcery from other groups. It was a nightmare for the settlement authorities, on top of the health problems and the sheer pressure such a large population put on resources. But from an Aboriginal perspective, this large and unusually cosmopolitan setting also presented an opportunity for exchanges of ritual knowledge and experience which Geoffrey Bardon, the 'sensitive' art teacher who arrived in Papunya settlement at the start of the 1971 school year, was able to help them direct into artistic expression.

The thousand or so small panels now known as the 'early Papunya boards' were painted at Papunya between mid-1971 and the end of 1972. They were the work of a group of Aboriginal men resident at the settlement. Some of the men were in their twenties, but the core group of twenty or thirty were much older, senior initiated law men in their own society, custodians of a vast network of significance and interconnection which for millennia had bound together the peoples of the Western Desert across linguistic and geographical distances as 'one country'. These men made history by their decision to paint about that world. They were the first of their people to inscribe their culture in permanent images based upon their own visual traditions. At the end of 1972 the painters formed an artists' company, Papunya Tula Artists, and from those first images went on to make their mark in the stubbornly Eurocentric world of contemporary Australian art. Like their ancestral Honey Ants, the painting movement they started spread 'everywhere' in an explosion of artistic creativity still reverberating across Indigenous Australia – and the world.

Geoffrey Bardon's name, like Papunya's, is synonymous with the birth of Western Desert art. His story of the beginnings of that art movement – how he arrived at Papunya Aboriginal settlement in Central Australia at the beginning of 1971, how his enthusiasm for traditional Western Desert designs galvanised the senior men to paint the now-famous Honey Ant Mural on the wall of the Papunya Special School and set the painting movement in motion – has been told and retold so often that it almost has the force of a Dreaming narrative itself. Certainly it dominated the rest of Geoffrey Bardon's own life. His elegiac writings, most recently his 527-page magnum opus, *Papunya: A Place Made After the Story* (published posthumously in 2004), describe in loving and extraordinary detail the events of 1971 and 1972. So why do we need another book about the early Papunya boards?

For me, the sudden surfacing of the early Papunya boards in the late 1990s in massed hangings on the walls of Australia's auction house previews was a revelation. For decades I had been researching the history and repercussions of Western Desert art. Here at last was the opportunity to explore the pre-history of Papunya Tula Artists for which I had waited so long. Bardon's 1991 *Papunya Tula: Art of the Western Desert* was still in print, but the reappearance of hundreds of the boards opened up a new way of seeing the beginnings of Western Desert art – through the prism of the visual statements of the artists themselves. My approach would be that of a detective, gathering and sifting the evidence, including personal testimonies, but relying wherever possible on the facts to unravel the mystery of the origins of these early works. At that point, nothing seemed more critical than the principal exhibits.

The contribution of the auction houses was not limited to enticing these long-lost paintings out of the woodwork. They also spotlighted the position of these re-emerged boards in an historical sequence of early Papunya boards. Media-driven scandals about 'fake Aboriginal art' in the mid- to late 1990s spawned the mania for ironclad provenance, which in turn inspired the increasingly thorough work of the auction houses in authenticating the paintings. From this emerged another significant fact. A surprising number of the early boards still bore stock numbers which could be used to establish the order in which the works had been painted. If all the early Papunya boards with Stuart Art Centre consignment numbers could be arranged in chronological order, the development of the painting language of Western Desert art over its seminal period would be laid bare – or so I imagined.

True, half the paintings were still missing. The Stuart Art Centre archive, to which I had access for two fascinating weeks in 2000 at the Art Gallery of New South Wales, was fragmentary and incomplete. But it was obvious from the beginning that it would not be possible to make any kind of sense of the paintings without some reference to the events that had shaped them – and to the men who had painted them. Had Bardon not said that the paintings reflected precisely the circumstances in which they were produced? When I factored in my own detailed research into the lives of the artists[2] and the information I had about what was happening in Papunya with the painters during the early months of the painting enterprise, things began to fall into place.

Bardon's account of the period immediately after the painting of the Honey Ant Mural in mid-1971 on the Papunya School wall describes a series of separate painting groups among the men, based on friendship, tribal affiliations, kinship, even occupations around the settlement. It became apparent from close examination of the paintings from the earliest consignments that each of these groups had worked collaboratively and had generated among themselves a range of styles and techniques. These separate discoveries were brought together when the settlement authorities allowed the painters to take over a disused storage room at the eastern end of the old Papunya 'town hall'.

This huge, curved, corrugated iron structure – like a giant humpy – was the 'Great Painting Room' that Bardon's writings have made vivid in his readers' imaginations as the place where the early Papunya boards were created. As a sustained endeavour prolonged over many months, the Great Painting Room was an even more remarkable collective achievement than the more famous Honey Ant Mural. Here men of different countries and languages and vastly different experiences worked alongside one another, sharing their Dreamings as they observed one another's work and listened to its songs, bound together by the awesome responsibility they also shared of being the first to bear witness to their cultural heritage in this permanent 'whitefella' medium.

It was a radical step, so radical that it is doubtful that its implications were fully grasped by the painters, many of whom were Pintupi newcomers to the Papunya settlement, generally despised by the rest of the population for their lack of sophistication in the ways of the colonisers. By providing the Pintupi with a situation in which the immediacy of their experience of culture and country became their remarkableness and their strength, the Great Painting Room turned this situation on its head. In an atmosphere charged with joy and inspiration, the 'painting men', as they were known around Papunya at the time, produced some of the most remarkable visual statements ever to come out of this country.

Many of the paintings display a fineness of execution and detail which none of those present attained again, although they scaled other artistic heights. The appearance of such sophisticated artistry in the work of painters who had come out of the desert just a few years before they picked up their paintbrushes only makes sense if we recognise that there were also within this founding group individuals with refined painting skills – men like Kaapa Tjampitjinpa, who was chosen by the guardians of the Papunya Honey Ant Dreaming to lead the team assigned to paint the Honey Ant Mural because of his acknowledged mastery of 'European' brushwork. He was a practising artist in a western sense before Geoffrey Bardon arrived in Papunya. Bardon acknowledged Kaapa's importance to the beginnings of Western Desert art, saying:

> The painting movement was built around this man's compulsive will and extraordinary ability to paint.[3]

The early Papunya boards are unique, not only as the first works of the Western Desert school of painting, but also in their frequent depiction of elements of the secret/sacred ritual world of initiated men. Bardon spoke often in his writings of his repeated counsel to the painters that they produce only innocuous 'children's versions' of their Dreamings. But they appear not to have understood him, or if they did understand, not to have heeded his advice. Once they realised that these basically uncensored depictions of the men's ceremonial world could cause serious offence to members of related Aboriginal groups with shared authority in these Dreamings when their existence became known outside Papunya, the painters took steps to modify the content of their work and eliminate (for the most part) these elements.

But what about the paintings that had already gone out into the world? From the 1970s to the early 1990s, most of the 1971–72 works disappeared from sight, so that the problem of what to do about the controversial disclosures contained in some of the early paintings also disappeared. The comparatively few early Papunya boards that had entered public collections in Australia were kept under wraps by curatorial staff aware of their potentially controversial nature. Only those paintings considered devoid of controversial elements or that had been cleared for exhibition by the artist or other appropriate cultural authorities were placed on public display. However, the reappearance since the mid-1990s of so many of the early Papunya boards at auction has meant that this issue was bound to resurface.

In their enthusiasm to sell off the boards to cashed-up overseas clients, the art auction houses had become involved in a tense stand-off with a bureaucracy and Minister empowered by the *Protection of Movable Cultural Heritage Act 1986*, whose 1999 amendments had brought the early Papunya works under its protection, to thwart this ambition by refusing to let the boards leave the country. In 2000 I was offered a part in this drama. As an 'expert examiner', I was called upon to assess the cultural significance of early Papunya boards coming up for export. I regarded such an intervention as urgently necessary. The minutely detailed first inscriptions of the cultural traditions of the Western Desert peoples in these early Papunya boards were being treated as highly priced commodities that could simply be sold to the highest bidder. How could this be happening without reference to the contemporary custodians? It was as if this priceless cultural heritage belonged to no-one. Why was it being left to expert examiners such as me – who, however knowledgeable, were outsiders to Western Desert culture – to try to deduce what the boards might mean to their rightful custodians within that culture? Why not just ask them? It sounds so simple, yet when the government bureaucrats finally agreed to a process of community consultation about the cultural significance of the boards, the results were far more disconcerting than I had anticipated.

In some ways, the story of the early Papunya boards is an art mystery. Not a 'whodunit'; more a 'why-did-they-do-it?'. If the early Papunya boards, or at least those that depict too explicitly things that are supposed to be men's secret business, are so 'dangerous', why were they created in the first place? Why did the men paint those paintings which would turn out to be, in Dick Kimber's dramatic phrase, 'a cross that they now bear'?

By the end of this story we may be closer to understanding some of the who, how, when and even why of these enigmatic objects. But precisely *what* they are may continue to elude non-Indigenous and maybe even most Indigenous understandings, especially now that the individuals who created them are for the most part no longer able, if they were ever willing, to shed any light on the matter. But whatever they are and however they came to be, they *did* come to be. They are in the world and we must find ways to deal with this – ways that include the rights of those who created them. And the rights of their descendants, the contemporary inheritors and guardians of the inner meanings the boards encode and disclose, which the original artists also inherited down through the generations. Like the peripatetic Honey Ant ancestors for whom they are named, the early Papunya boards continue to dispense knowledge and power, for they too are part of the Dreaming.

1

The School of Kaapa

Kaapa Mbitjana Tjampitjinpa was not the kind of individual the Welfare Branch ordinarily singled out for anything – except maybe disciplinary action. On at least one occasion the settlement authorities tried to expel him from Papunya as a 'troublemaker'.[1] He was a drinker and, by reputation at least, a cattle duffer[2] and grog runner.[3] He refused to stay docilely around the settlement performing the menial tasks to which the administration assigned all able-bodied men if they wanted to receive the meals prepared daily in the Papunya kitchens and served in the communal dining room. He was forever running off to visit relatives in Yuendumu or Napperby or into Alice Springs on some nefarious errand or other. Kaapa has been described as 'possibly the greatest wheeler-dealer of all time',[4] but there was something roguish and lovable about his 'wickedness' that enabled him to badger people – especially whitefellas – into doing things for him.

No doubt that was why Jack Cooke, District Welfare Officer for the Southern Division (Central Australia), was barrelling along the bitumen towards Alice Springs that winter's day in 1971 after a routine inspection visit to Papunya settlement with half-a-dozen of Kaapa's paintings on the back seat of his car. Perhaps Jack Cooke had something of the larrikin about him too, because he took Kaapa's paintings and entered them in the upcoming Caltex/Northern Territory Art Award. He later remarked with evident pride that this was the first time an Aboriginal artist had been entered in what was typically a display of conservative, white, Territorian art. The winner was to be announced at a function at the Alice Springs Golf Club on the night of 27 August 1971. Jack Cooke was in the audience that night. As he remembered it over thirty years later, the judge's decision 'knocked the Alice Springs artistic community right back on their backsides'.[5]

'The winner is …' Jo Caddy, Adelaide painter and judge of the Award, hesitated over a name whose correct pronunciation would still defeat most European tongues. '… Karpa Jambajimba, for his painting …' Another pause, while she struggled with one of those Aboriginal place names which generations of European explorers had carelessly overwritten with the names of colonial administrators and English lords, '… *Gulgardi*'.[6] Twenty years later, Jack Cooke still remembered what Jo Caddy had said about Kaapa when he came up to collect his prize. Whatever else it symbolises, the term 'boards' refers to this defining moment:

> This old man is a true artist. He took what he found, an old piece of waste lumber he located in a rubbish tip and the dregs of some paint he found lying around the settlement and made art out of it.[7]

In its coverage of the story a few days later under the page 3 headline 'Aboriginal artist shares rich prize', the *Centralian Advocate* ignored this remark. It preferred to appease the wounded artistic egos of its white readership by quoting Jo

Caddy's explanation for her decision to acquire *Gulgardi* and a group of Top End bark paintings for the Araluen Trust:[8] that 'they might not be around in such numbers in years to come'.[9] Although this prediction proved spectacularly wrong,[10] for the painter of *Gulgardi*, the announcement was a moment of unadulterated triumph, when his art found legitimacy in the eyes of the whitefellas. Kaapa Mbitjana Tjampitjinpa had shown the scornful settlement authorities who sacked him from his job picking up papers around the Papunya Special schoolyard for the crime of stealing paintbrushes,[11] that he really was an artist, in fact the 'number one' artist. His idea of paintings about tribal culture and ceremony had received the first public sign of the recognition and acclaim that a few decades later would be literally worldwide.

Those six paintings that emerged from Papunya in July or August 1971 are the starting-point of this story. The award-winning *Gulgardi*'s inclusion among the six is crucial, and not only because Kaapa's win (and the substantial prize money that went with it) helped to galvanise the artists into the outpouring of creativity that produced the early Papunya boards. It also enables us to determine the timing of Jack Cooke's trip into Alice Springs with the paintings, which must have been in late July or August 1971 so that *Gulgardi* would be delivered in time for the judging. It was Papunya Tula's longest-time supporter, Dick Kimber, an Alice Springs high school teacher at the time, who first recounted the Jack Cooke episode in the essay 'Papunya Tula Art: Some Recollections August 1971 – October 1972', which he wrote for the catalogue of the 1986 *Dot and Circle* exhibition mounted by the

Flinders University Art Museum. *Dot and Circle: A Retrospective Survey of the Aboriginal Acrylic Paintings of Central Australia*[12] was a key early scholarly publication on the painting movement. It included not only Kimber's invaluable essay but also an excerpt from Geoffrey Bardon's by then out-of-print 1979 publication *Aboriginal Art of the Western Desert*,[13] and contributions from Janet Maughan, Rodney Morice, Andrew Crocker and JVS Megaw, as well as the first appearance of Pat Hogan's name in the literature of the movement. Her 'Notes and Inventory for the Early Consignments of Pintupi Paintings' listed the contents of nineteen consignments of paintings delivered to her Stuart Art Centre by Geoffrey Bardon 'between Show day in Alice Springs in 1971 (generally July) and Yuendumu Sports Day 1972 (August)'.[14]

As the only eyewitness account of the first few months of the painting movement (apart from Bardon's) by an interested and meticulous observer, Kimber's writings on this period have been enormously influential. This includes his dating of Jack Cooke's trip into town as *October* 1971, at least a month *after* Geoffrey Bardon's delivery of the first consignment of paintings to the Stuart Art Centre:[15]

> Jack Cooke, Assistant Director of the then equivalent to the Federal Department of Aboriginal Affairs, had been one of the few people highly impressed by the art and its potential for sales that would assist the Aboriginal people. In October 1971 he brought six paintings into Alice Springs – wonderful works with minutely detailed human figures and ceremonial regalia painted against black backgrounds. They were sold on the instant.[16]

The Araluen Trust acquired *Gulgardi* under the terms of the Award, but the other five paintings were indeed 'sold on the instant'. The competition judge Jo Caddy purchased one titled *Goanna Corroboree at Mirkantji*, and her friend Helen Brown who had accompanied her from Adelaide for the Award bought two more, both untitled at the time. The Alice Springs Town Council bought a work titled *Corroboree at Waru* from an exhibition of Award works mounted at the local high school. Kimber purchased the sixth painting. It was included in *Dot and Circle* as the first work in the exhibition, reproduced on page 58 of the catalogue as 'An October 1971 work believed to be one of the first paintings offered for sale in Alice Springs'.[17]

Knowing Kimber's interest in Aboriginal art, Jack Cooke contacted him to tell him about the paintings and Kimber photographed some of them on the lawns of the old Department of Aboriginal Affairs (Welfare Branch) building:

> Jack gave me permission to take them out into the sunlight to photograph them. I placed them on the ground along the base of one side of the building, took the photographs, then returned them to Jack's care.[18]

Gulgardi was not among the slides Kimber took that day; Cooke must have contacted him *after* he delivered the painting to the Award. If it had been, Kimber might have realised his error in ascribing these events to October, several months after the Award. But 'October 1971' was what he had written on the box of slides. What could it refer to if not when he took the photos? The answer is as simple as I suspect most solutions to the chronological mysteries of this history would be if one could only stumble across them: he was broke at the time – mainly from the expense of paying off the painting he had purchased – and could not afford to have the slides developed until October 1971![19] And why does it matter? Because if those paintings came into town in July or August rather than October, that makes them the first six paintings to come out of Papunya.[20]

In October 1989, eighteen years (and three months) after she bought the paintings and one month before Kaapa's death, Jo Caddy's friend Helen Brown sold the two paintings she had bought at the time of her visit to Alice Springs for the 1971 Art Award to the Art Gallery of South Australia for what would today be considered extremely modest prices: at $7000 and $5000 they cost the Gallery somewhat less than they would have paid for a contemporary Papunya Tula canvas at that time. One of these works so exactly fits Kimber's description in his *Dot and Circle* essay of the paintings Jack Cooke delivered to Alice Springs that his later recognition of it as the very painting this description was based upon will come as no real surprise.

But it would be another seven years before these two paintings went on public display, in the 1996 *Dreamings of the Desert* show of the Gallery's entire collection of Western Desert art, and another six years after that before Kimber finally saw an image of them in the catalogue of this exhibition. I showed it to him in a café in Alice Springs where we had met to discuss the chronology of events in those early months of the movement, particularly the timing of Jack Cooke's arrival in Alice Springs with the paintings in the light of what Cooke had told me about entering *Gulgardi* in the Caltex/Northern Territory Art Award when I visited him in the Adelaide Hills in April 2002. Kimber instantly recognised one of the paintings which Jo Caddy's friend had purchased in August 1971 as the one he had photographed on the Department of Aboriginal Affairs lawns and on which he had based his *Dot and Circle* report. 'That's the one!' he exclaimed,[21] pointing to the expressive ceremonial figures kneeling by the ground mosaic.

Another nine years later, when Dick Kimber put the painting he had purchased up for auction in Sotheby's second Important Aboriginal Art auction in July 1998, it was acquired (for $85 000) by the John and Barbara Wilkerson Collection.[22] Renamed *Mikanji*,[23] it next appeared in the catalogue of the *Icons of the Desert* exhibition of this collection and was once again described (quoting Kimber) as 'an October 1971' work.[24] On the basis of this mistaken chronology, *Icons* curator Roger Benjamin represented the painting in his catalogue essay as 'an aesthetic advance on the July–August works by Kaapa Tjampitjinpa, who had won the Caltex Art Award with *Gulgardi* on August 27 1971':

> In comparison with such works, Kaapa has avoided the use of perspective and literal figures of men participating in ceremony. In *Mikanji* Kaapa provides a symmetrical schematisation of the ceremonial scene. 'Realistic' figures are replaced by U-signs placed around a central sand mosaic partitioned off by large ceremonial objects.[25]

Benjamin's observations may well be apt, but the timing is crucial because between August and October when these 'aesthetic advances' supposedly occurred, Kaapa would have been exposed to Geoffrey Bardon and his criticisms of the European influences in his paintings as he worked with Billy Stockman and Long Jack Phillipus at the back of Bardon's classroom. Bardon's 2004 account gives September 1971 as the date Kaapa 'joined our painting group'.[26] So in August or July when Jack Cooke was in Papunya being humbugged by Kaapa to take his paintings into town for him, Kaapa was still working independently of Bardon. And this matters because it means that the developments Benjamin sees in *Mikanji* were, every bit as much as *Gulgardi* itself, the product of an artistic practice based upon Aboriginal traditions which existed in Papunya prior to and independently of the painting group that gathered around Geoffrey Bardon. And the leader and main exponent of that pre-Bardon practice was Kaapa Tjampitjinpa, whose authorship of the six paintings Jack Cooke brought into town that day Kimber omitted to mention in his *Dot and Circle* essay. In recognition of Kaapa's authorship of most of the known paintings (but certainly not all)[27] in the style of miniaturised depictions of ceremonial grounds, objects and performances on plain backgrounds that characterised the paintings produced in this independent practice, I have christened it the 'School of Kaapa'.

When Ron Radford, then Curator of Contemporary Australian Art at the Art Gallery of South Australia, argued in favour of the acquisition of Helen Brown's paintings that they would fill a gap in the Gallery's otherwise unusually representative collection of Western Desert art in being both works by Kaapa Tjampitjinpa *and* examples of the 'very earliest type' of Papunya paintings, he was more accurate than he knew. Only since the late 1990s, thanks in part to the auction houses' tireless promotion of the hundreds of early Papunya boards passing through their hands, has it become obvious that the half-dozen paintings Jack Cooke brought into town and Kimber saw and described were not at all typical of the painters' work over the first two years of the movement – not even of Kaapa's.

In those days no-one really knew what early Papunya paintings looked like. In the absence of the vital information that Kaapa Tjampitjinpa had painted 'most if not all' of the works answering Kimber's description in the *Dot and Circle* essay, that description came to represent all the early Papunya works produced over the first two years of the movement, which people had not seen and could at that stage only imagine. It was all they had to go on. But it was a confabulation to cover the huge gaps that then existed in the historical record of the origins of Papunya painting. What Radford probably meant by the 'very earliest type of Papunya painting' was all the early Papunya boards produced in the Bardon years – 1971–72. The Gallery still lacked a Kaapa Tjampitjinpa from any period of the movement or any works from 1971 to 1972, and Radford saw Helen Brown's paintings as a way to plug two significant gaps in one fell swoop. He was based in Adelaide and one of the small band of Papunya enthusiasts at that time, so he would have seen Kaapa's painting in the *Dot and Circle* exhibition and presumably read Kimber's description of 'minutely detailed human figures and ceremonial regalia painted against black backgrounds'. If he did somehow put two and two together, it was not the first – or the last – time he would secure remarkable desert paintings for the national collection by acts of prescient curating.

Kimber did mention that Kaapa had painted 'most if not all' of those six paintings in his notes in the 1998 Sotheby's sales catalogue for *Mikanji*. Nevertheless, the misconception still persists that his description applies to the very earliest works by the group around Geoffrey Bardon rather than to the independent practice of the School of Kaapa. As we shall see in the next chapter, realistic scenes of the ceremonial life were not at all typical of the earliest paintings from Bardon's group, much less archetypal. They were also quite unlike the paintings Kaapa himself produced once he joined the group of 'painting men' around Geoffrey Bardon. Paintings like the six Jack Cooke brought into Alice Springs in July or August 1971 are actually extremely rare.[28] In a sense this group of paintings were some of the *last* to be painted in the pre-Bardon style.

Kaapa Tjampitjinpa

Who was this man Kaapa? How had he come to be a practising artist in a western sense before Geoffrey Bardon set foot in Papunya? Born in the mid-1920s at the Emu Dreaming site of Altijira, west of Napperby station, Kaapa Tjampitjinpa was the eldest son of a man known disparagingly to some whitefellas as 'Mad Jack'. Perhaps Kaapa inherited from his father the flamboyant personal style that the settlement authorities found so disconcerting. In Aboriginal terms, Kwalapa Tjangala was a man of ritual substance, being 'Boss' for the site of Warlugulong, his birthplace and the source of the great ancestral bushfire later represented in his son's paintings – and made famous in monumental works[29] by his nephews Tim Leura Tjapaljtarri and Clifford Possum Tjapaltjarri. Tim and Clifford were the sons of Kwalapa's sisters Margie Long Nangala and Long Rose Nangala. Billy Stockman was adopted into Clifford Possum's family as a baby after his mother, another of Kwalapa's sisters, was killed in the 1928 Coniston massacre.

The slaying of prospector Frederick Brookes in a dispute at the native well now known as Brookes Soak brought to a head tensions over resources that had been simmering since the early years of the 20th century. The granting of pastoral leases to the west of Alice Springs, including Coniston where these events took place, meant systematic European incursions onto these lands. An orgy of indiscriminate retaliatory slayings of Aboriginal people across the region was unleashed by the discovery of Brookes' body stuffed down a rabbit hole. Though their lives were profoundly disrupted by these traumatic events, some Aboriginal people were able to reach an accommodation with the pastoralists which permitted them to remain in contact with their homelands. Napperby station, where Kaapa's family moved early in his childhood, was one such place.

Here Kaapa spent the rest of his boyhood, living off the land with his extended family on a diet that included European rabbits as well as goannas, and the occasional 'killer' (beef). His constant companion was Dinny Nolan, the son of Kwalapa's brother Palapanda Tjangala. Throughout their lives Dinny and Kaapa remained close. Kaapa would often call upon Dinny to confirm his stories of their boyish escapades. These included one hilarious tale where they killed a bullock and buried it in the ground to avoid detection by an enraged station owner – only to be summarily ordered off 'his' land, an irony in which Kaapa took particular delight:

> We was youngfellas – not youngfellas, big boys, and we had spear – y'know, we wasn't very good – we try and kill'm bullock – silly people. But we been kill'm. And then that whitefella he come round with a motor car and that bullock he been hiding – in the ground, under the ground. That whitefella been say – fat bloke from the station – 'You lot better get out my land'.[30]

Kaapa, Dinny, Tim, Clifford and Billy were all part of the younger generation of Anmatyerr tribesmen who had grown up on the stations. As young, uneducated, Aboriginal men in Central Australia, their only employment prospects were as cheap labour for the cattle industry. The life had its satisfactions, despite the economic exploitation. They were living on or near their own lands and they had escaped the deadening influence of the missionaries at settlements like Hermannsburg and Haasts Bluff. In the words of Sir Paul Hasluck (who did not particularly approve of the pastoralists' approach):

> The pastoralists did not believe in teaching the black anything except the job he wanted him to do, and on many stations there was a decided prejudice against the mission-trained boy. He was regarded as 'spoilt'. Perhaps the general attitude of the station owner or manager might be summarised as follows: ... don't interfere with their tribal life. Allow them to live as far as possible in their natural conditions.[31]

Later, 'experimenting with turning traditional art into a commercial form – paintings on flat surfaces'[32] came easily to men like Kaapa and his cousins who had not been cowed by the mission experience into secretiveness about the ceremonial life and boldly decided to make it the subject of their paintings.

'Working that *idea* ...'

Napperby station's owner was also notoriously antagonistic to anthropologists, so these young men also escaped the attentions of the steady stream of amateur and professional anthropologists eager to record the ceremonies and esoteric knowledge of the men of the Western Desert tribes, and often to remove their sacred objects to ethnographic museums and departments of anthropology for purposes of study. However, as initiated men working across the area west of Alice Springs, they would have been aware of the Europeans' interest in such matters. Certainly they were aware of the tourists' fondness for 'Aboriginalia' which they carved in the stock camps after work. As Dick Kimber noted in his essay 'Recollections of

Papunya Tula 1971–80', DD Smith of the adjacent Mt Allan station promoted the production of painted wooden plaques for the tourist trade and was, in Kimber's view, a formative influence on the symmetry later found so often in the paintings of Anmatyerr artists like Kaapa, Tim Leura and Clifford Possum:

> It is a traditional feature, and in part had been developed as a result of requests for earlier works in wood: the late D.D. Smith, owner of Mt Allan Station, on which all of the men had worked, had promoted the production of very symmetrical ovate painted wooden plaques, and an opposing paired snake and goanna in relief about a central wooden pole which were much in demand by tourists. The origin of these items, in turn, goes back to interests by the Hermannsburg missionaries from about the 1920s and, I believe, also to the practice of the whittling of wood by stockmen, Afghan cameleers and other bush workers.[33]

They were all skilled woodcarvers. Tim and Clifford were already renowned in Central Australia when Bardon arrived there in 1971 for their beautifully painted and at times eerily realistic carvings of lizards and snakes. Carving was also Kaapa's first artistic medium. ('Kaapa' could even be an Aboriginalised spelling of 'carver', pronounced with a strong Anmatyerr accent.) In 2009 the National Museum of Australia acquired a boldly carved and painted lizard by Kaapa at auction. Its gaping mouth, lined with red teeth, is as startling as the artist's signature on a piece of disposable 'tourist art'. It says much for Kaapa's artistic ambitions.

One of Clifford Possum's carvings can be dated back to at least the mid-1960s. When he saw it again in the 1990s, he commented that he had done the piece 'before I had children' (his eldest daughter Gabriella Possum Nungurrayi was born in Papunya in 1965). Like most carvings to come out of Central Australia in those times and these – and for that matter most paintings – it is unsigned. It had belonged to a woman called Laura Ulcoq who lived in Papunya until the early 1970s with her parents and knew its authorship. In a letter in which she enclosed photographs of the pre-1965 sculpture, Laura recalled that:

> Around the time Albert Namatjira was painting, Clifford, his brother Tim Leura and fellow tribesman Kaapa all tried their hand at watercolour painting but when they couldn't get the hang of it they decided to return to their old style of painting their dream stories instead.[34]

The reference to Albert Namatjira puts the date when these three artists began experimenting with watercolour landscapes in the Hermannsburg style he famously invented back to at least 1959.[35] In that year, in the confines of the Papunya settlement, Albert Namatjira served out his sentence for supplying a relative with the liquor that Namatjira's Australian citizenship allowed him to buy but not to share with others who were still legally 'wards' of the state. Namatjira did his last paintings in Papunya shortly before his death. His famous utility truck inscribed with the words 'Albert Namatjira Artist Alice Springs' was a familiar sight around the settlement for years afterwards.

But Clifford Possum, Tim Leura and Kaapa had also known Albert Namatjira when he was in his prime. Clifford Possum recalled meeting him at Glen Helen station in the early 1950s:

> I seen him Namatjira – he been livin in Glen Helen – that tourist mob – Glen Helen Gorge – I got him from Namatjira's son – he gave me watercolour – I start painting boomerang – and then ukutukutu [women's dancing board]. I start painting – I been doing carving and sell'm. I been

getting good money – from tourist people you know – yeah – I been doing watercolour with the boomerang – use'm them kangaroo, them euro, them tjampi [grass] them watia [trees].[36]

Noting the young man's skill in decorating his carvings, Namatjira asked Clifford Possum (as perhaps he also asked his brother and cousin, but both died with this part of their personal stories unrecorded):

> 'You want to learn watercolour painting, carry on my work?' But I said, 'No, No. I do it my way. Carving – start from carving.'[37]

Though he denied it when interviewed by CAAMA[38] in 1988 ('I don't do landscape paintings'), Clifford Possum may also have 'tried his hand' at painting Namatjira-style watercolours. His older brother Immanuel Rutjinama used to say that it was he who introduced Clifford Possum to painting, with the watercolours he once gave him when he was staying at Napperby. In any case, Clifford had quickly abandoned landscape, deciding 'No, he wanted his traditional designs'.[39] There are no paintings in the Hermannsburg style known to be by Tim Leura, but techniques like the washes of colour he uses to create atmospheric effects of mist and smoke in so many of his early paintings in the Papunya style indicate his exposure to the Namatjira School.

Kaapa definitely painted watercolours in the Hermannsburg style. A couple of his landscapes have surfaced at auction, most recently *Hermansberg* [*sic*] *Watercolour Untitled*, which Mossgreen auction house sold for $7170 to the National Museum of Australia in late 2009 from its Fine Early Aboriginal and Oceanic Art auction. Kaapa's work in the School of Kaapa style carries over the delicate intensity and mastery of European brush method[40] found in the best work of the Hermannsburg painters. His artistic journey would take him a long way from the decorous watercolour landscapes of Arrente country that won his mentor fame and fortune in the 1940s and 1950s, but for those like Kaapa who took up their paintbrushes after Albert Namatjira, his brilliant, trailblazing career was what had made an Aboriginal artist something to be. In fact, what finer occupation was there in Aboriginal Central Australia of those times for an intelligent man with imagination and independence of spirit?

Clifford Possum was reputedly an excellent horseman, and in 1971 when Geoffrey Bardon came to Papunya, he was still working at Narwietooma station where he held the position of head stockman until 1978, painting only during his 'holiday time' visits to Papunya. But Kaapa had always disliked the hard, dangerous and underpaid life of the Central Australian stockman. By the late 1950s, he was living at Papunya and working on the construction of the settlement. Jeremy Long, who was Superintendent at Haasts Bluff in this period, remembered him well:

> There weren't a great number of Napperby people there, but they had a significant impact. Kaapa was there – he may occasionally have done some work, but I wouldn't have thought he was doing much. He was a smart cookie – he got money from gambling. The people who were working, as soon as they got paid there would be gambling. Kaapa was the sort of character people regarded as a 'bad influence'. He was enterprising, not taking any nonsense from the whites – much more sophisticated than most.[41]

Like other 'unenthusiastic stockmen' (to use Long's description) who had ended up at Papunya in the 1960s, Kaapa had found himself a wife there. To support his growing family, he supplemented the meagre 'training allowance' paid by the settlement authorities (or what he could make by gambling for others') with the income from his art:

> Apparently Kaapa was the first to begin this form of painting, and did so, in fact, prior to Geoff Bardon coming to the fore. Kaapa didn't paint as we know the art now, but combined realism (as done by the Hermannsburg Arandas) with the symbols … With a bit of imagination, one could almost follow the transition from Albert Namatjira, Otto Pareroultja, Kaapa to Anatari [*sic*] No. 3. They would certainly make an interesting display, placed side by side.[42]

Kaapa himself, when asked more than fifteen years after these events, how painting had started up at Papunya said: 'Before the painting, we been thinking about it. We been working that *idea* – everybody.'[43] He did not elaborate on what exactly the idea was, except to say: 'We been start first making out of wood – snake and little goanna, not perentie [large, goanna-like lizard], small one. Old people too. *And then we like to try to do painting.*' But when the interviewer concluded: 'So it was your idea, you mob?', Kaapa said with breathless emphasis: '*Yuwai yuwai*' [Yes yes], adding: 'Geoff Bardon, he was at the school – old men working at school painting – Tjala Tjukurrpa [Honey Ant Dreaming] on the wall.' According to Johnny Warangkula's son Mike, his father often hung out with Clifford Possum, Tim Leura and Kaapa in a tent they had pitched on the lee side of Warumpi Hill some distance from the settlement. Perhaps it was here the *idea* was hatched.

According to Geoffrey Bardon's account, the Pintupi farm-workers had been coming to his flat after work since April, and Billy Stockman and Long Jack Phillipus began painting behind a barricade of desks at the back of his classroom after the mural project, but it was not until September that Kaapa joined them there. Bardon did not meet Tim Leura or Clifford Possum until the second year of the movement. It was in February 1972 that Tim Leura, whom Bardon says he had met for the first time only three weeks before, introduced his 'brother' Clifford to the kindly and enthusiastic patron of their art as 'such a good painter and wood carver' that he couldn't 'beat him'.[44] Tim Leura was living in Papunya with his wife Daisy Nakamarra and their young family and may still have been doing stockwork – but as we shall see he also painted and took his paintings into town to sell them himself. The Anmatyerr stockmen were, as Bardon remarked 'the most independent men in the community',[45] but though the Tjapaltjarri brothers were among the 'very last' to join Bardon's group of painters, they were not the last to begin painting in Papunya, but in fact some of the very first.

The first Papunya paintings

Jack Cooke vividly remembers the first time he saw a Papunya painting. It was hanging on the wall of the Papunya canteen. It was 'lemony yellow', with a 'bit of a mixture of styles: part Albert Namatjira gum trees, a goanna, and a bit of Aboriginal dot style painting'.[46] What he found most striking about it was that it was painted on 'a piece of junk timber. There was still a cleat which he [the artist] hadn't bothered to remove, nailed on with a couple of brads.'[47] When Cooke inquired who had painted it, he was referred to Kaapa, who at that time could be found in the vacant old settlement office, working on his latest painting. In this 'squat unimposing building',[48] with a plaque on the outside announcing that Papunya settlement had been officially opened on 1 October 1960 by Sir Paul Hasluck, the Federal Minister for Territories, Kaapa Mbitjana Tjampitjinpa had established his 'studio'. No trace remains today of the building. Even in 1971 it had been abandoned by the white administration. Kaapa and his associates painted on the floor of an enclosed verandah or in an inside room, out of sight not only of women and children but also of the settlement authorities. For this, Kaapa at least had his reasons. There were school slates along with the scrap wood and masonite, fibro, old bits of packing cases, cupboard doors, cement sheets and pieces of cardboard lined up round the walls of the space for the men to paint on, and the lime green, orange and turquoise which figure somewhat garishly on some of the paintings brought out by Jack Cooke probably came from what the children had left lying around the schoolyard. Iris Harvey, legendary proprietor of the Arunta Bookstore on Todd Street in Alice Springs, who told me she recalled the painting on which Dick Kimber based his *Dot and Circle* description 'as if it were yesterday', particularly remembered the 'large green snake' – and also remembered wishing it had been in ochre colours.[49] But as Jo Caddy pinpointed in her speech at the Caltex Art Award, the genius of the School of Kaapa was in working with whatever was at hand.

Everyone knew Kaapa, who had been in Bardon's words 'a most enterprising and independent artist in the traditional manner before my arrival in Papunya'.[50] He was a familiar face hawking his paintings around the staff area of the settlement with the watercolourists Joshua Ebatarinja and Albert Namatjira's son Keith who were residents of Papunya at that time, and Nosepeg Tjupurrula who used to sell artefacts.[51] The Papunya canteen was evidently an outlet for the work of Kaapa and other artists working independently in Papunya prior to Bardon's role as their benefactor and 'agent'. The words 'PAPUNYAH [*sic*] STORE / PAPUNYAH / VIA ALS' were written in charcoal on the back of one of the paintings Helen Brown bought, indicating that it too had once been offered for sale at the Papunya canteen. Community stores in many Western Desert communities continue to serve this role, nowadays often in competition with community-owned art enterprises.

Though only a handful of their painted carvings seem to have survived (or at least been identified as theirs) from all their years of pre-Bardon production, Tim Leura Tjapaltjarri and Clifford Possum Tjapaltjarri frequently joined their cousin Kaapa in his studio/headquarters. Jack Cooke remembered seeing Clifford Possum there, working on what he described as 'his grotesque statues', and Billy Stockman Tjapaltjarri too. A 1972 carving attributed to Billy Stockman is depicted in Bardon's *Papunya Tula: Art of the Western Desert* (1991). Bardon says he commissioned it from Billy as a present for his father. He noted that Kaapa had finished dotting the tail when Billy Stockman grew 'weary of the big job'. Clifford Possum, however, had a different reaction when he saw the image. He said that it was basically his carving, left behind unfinished when he returned to Narwietooma station. We should expect collaboration to be part of the artistic practices of the School of Kaapa. Though its founders were familiar with the European-influenced landscape tradition of Namatjira and his followers, the School of Kaapa was a wholly Indigenous initiative. Although most of the paintings that left Kaapa's studio had Kaapa Tjampitjinpa's name on them, others too tried their hand at the style.

An untitled work attributed to Kaapa in the Museums and Art Galleries of the Northern Territory collection perfectly matches Jack Cooke's description of the painting he saw in the Papunya canteen. In the water-damaged bottom left-hand corner is a delicate Namatjira-style depiction of a desert oak with a strikingly realistic goanna image poised beneath it. It was one of fifteen early Papunya paintings collected by Welfare Branch officers that were donated to the Museums and Art Galleries of the Northern Territory after Cyclone Tracy by the Department of Aboriginal Affairs (which in 1973 took over the Welfare Branch for which Jack Cooke worked). Though the Museum has no date or documentation for the painting, its meticulous detail leaves little doubt that it was painted by Kaapa around the same time as the other six paintings we have been considering in this chapter, with which it properly belongs. It is, in a way, the missing link between them and Kaapa's watercolour landscapes in the developmental sequence Roy Monks described from Namatjira through Kaapa to Anatjari No. 3. It begins in the left-hand corner as a landscape but as the eyes move across to the right it mutates into a graphic depiction of a ceremonial scene in the unmistakable style of the School of Kaapa.

The first School of Kaapa painting I saw was *Corroboree at Waru.*[52] It was in the main banking chamber of the old ANZ bank in Alice Springs when I went to Central Australia to look for the Papunya painters in 1980. When I asked what the first paintings had been like, Andrew Crocker, the Secretary/Art Supervisor of Papunya Tula Artists, told me to go down Todd Street and look at the paintings on display in the bank. Hung high up near the ceiling, in a jumble of paintings packed in like an auction preview gone mad, it was a striking image with a strange perspective instantly identifiable as a ceremonial ground. In 1991 the Alice Springs Town Council (who owned the art collection displayed in the bank) donated this work with the rest of its collection of early Papunya boards to the Araluen Art Centre, but for years none of these paintings were put on display in the new gallery premises on Larapinta Drive. *Corroboree at Waru*'s whereabouts came to light in 1999 when it was mistaken for *Gulgardi* and exhibited as the painting which had won Kaapa the 1971 Caltex/Northern Territory Art Award in the *Papunya Tula Artists: Twenty-Five Years and Beyond* retrospective organised by Flinders University Art Museum in 1996.[53]

In 1999 I still had not laid eyes on the real *Gulgardi,* but if I had had the opportunity of examining *Corroboree at Waru* under this misnomer, I might have been surprised at the judge's choice of such an unlikely looking prizewinner, especially given how controversial her decision was likely to be. But I was overseas during the Flinders retrospective, and it was not until April 2001, in the course of documenting Araluen's collection of early Papunya boards, which were still stored in a back room, that I had an opportunity to examine *Corroboree at Waru* at close range. Its yellow background is roughly applied with the brush strokes on the left-hand edge running horizontally and on the right-hand side running vertically. If this is the work of an experienced watercolour painter, it is very carelessly done. It looks to have been applied by someone not familiar with paint, who did not anticipate the reading of a horizon out of the direction of his brush strokes. The way the design elements are squeezed along the bottom edge of the board and the shaky tentative brushwork also suggest an inexperienced artist. It is hard to believe the concentric circles on it are the work of a man who according to Bardon could draw freehand better circles than a compass – with his eyes closed![54]

The real *Gulgardi* is painted on a battered piece of plywood that looks as if it was once a cupboard door. It comes complete with rusty nails and holes where the door handle was attached. Its background is a light grey wash applied very smoothly as to brushwork, though unevenly as to density, so that occasionally darker patches show through. Evidently the pale plain backgrounds were giving the artist coverage problems due to the sheer lack of materials. Darker, denser colours for the backgrounds may originally have represented a solution to this problem at a time when paint was scarce. Kaapa's sure, fluid hand is discernible everywhere, from the red and yellow ochre border with fine white dots along the inner rim, to the lithe, lifelike figure in elaborate corroboree paint and headdress kneeling at the top centre. The design of the painting is balanced and, like most of Kaapa's subsequent work, symmetrical as to the elements arranged between this figure and the large ceremonial pole that runs along the base of the painting. Three concentric circles with white dotted rims, the outside two in yellow and black and the central one in white, red and black, are evenly placed between two U-shapes in red and black at the ends representing seated figures. On either side of the central circle are smaller ceremonial poles flanked with arcs that may be boomerangs or body paint. Finely painted wallaby or kangaroo tracks coming in from the top and bottom corners weave symmetrical paths around the inside of the U-shapes. Delicate red spirals are placed symmetrically around the central vertical axis. The markings on the ceremonial poles are apparently the tracks of a lizard and its dragging tail. The painting seems to represent an episode in the Warlugulong story Kaapa inherited from his father, possibly the ritual kindling of the great bushfire which engulfed the ancestral Lizard Man's sons. The painting shows typical Kaapa formality. The concentric circles are tightly controlled, and respond to each other with force. They are closely related to the adjacent objects, forming an integrated geometric whole.

Gulgardi is not signed, but then few early Papunya works are. The lack of a signature is remarkable only because many of Kaapa's works, including the watercolour landscape mentioned earlier and the red-mouthed goanna carving, do have signatures. The two paintings bought by Jo Caddy's friend are also signed, in paint, with the name 'Koyaa' in shaky, white, painted lettering at the centre bottom of one painting and just to the left of centre bottom on the other. Kaapa's grasp of written English was minimal – his signature was a design motif approximating the written version of his name rather than its literal transcription. *Corroboree at Waru* is signed too – twice. On the front of the painting in the bottom right-hand corner, where you would expect to find the signature on a painting in the European tradition, the word 'Karpa' is neatly written in red textacolour or biro in a hand which looks far more familiar with the act of writing than the hand which inscribed 'Koyaa' on the other works.

On the basis of this 'signature', the painting was catalogued on its arrival at Araluen as the work of Kaapa Tjampitjinpa. A hessian-backed frame, of the kind Pat Hogan used to get done for all the Stuart Art Centre works (perhaps they used the same framer, who never deviated from this popular 1970s look), for thirty years concealed the inscription on the back of the painting, which states in carefully painted, small, white lettering with black shading added: 'Fraser Daneil Janda-Jimba of Yuendumu Settlement'. The words are written along lines which were painted in first for the purpose and framed within a rectangular shape drawn in with the same black and white paint. This is no quick labelling job by an outsider hurriedly carrying out Kaapa's commission: that might much more readily be concluded of the red textacolour inscription on the front. Who was Fraser Daniels? Could he have been the painter of *Corroboree at Waru*?

Fraser Daniels was Kaapa Tjampitjinpa's brother. He was many years younger than Kaapa and used to hang out with Kaapa's eldest son on his visits to Papunya. The misspelling of 'Daneil' and the spelling of the skinname as 'JandaJimba'[55] suggest that the ascription on the back at least is his work. This is how a young boy attending the school at Yuendumu would have been taught to write his name in the 1960s. The painting might have been a gift from his older brother – Hogan's notes on the Stuart Art Centre consignments indicate such transactions were not unheard of, at least among Bardon's group of artists. The painting is not as finely or as confidently executed as *Gulgardi*, but Kaapa may not have been himself that day. There are stylistic differences too: for example, the use of western perspective and the asymmetry of *Corroboree at Waru*, but these may not be decisive either. It may be a transitional work where Kaapa was still making compositional decisions based on his experience as a watercolourist rather than the plane view and Anmatyerr principle of symmetry that inform his later work. *Gulgardi* may well have been a watershed in this process. But these differences also indicate the possibility that Fraser Daniels tried his hand at a few paintings while on a visit to Papunya. If *Corroboree at Waru* is Fraser Daniels' work, there is enough of his older brother in it to conclude that it was painted with Kaapa at his shoulder keeping a sharp eye on the proceedings – or perhaps painting beside him. Perhaps they worked together; Kaapa was certainly not averse to assistance on his paintings in later years.

The untitled Darwin Museum work contains all the same elements as *Corroboree at Waru* (and its sister work *Goanna Corroboree at Mirkantji*, the painting which Jo Caddy bought at the time of the Caltex/Northern Territory Art Award): the snake, the goannas, the upstanding spears, the ceremonial poles, with the addition of a strange ritualistic construction and two ceremonial figures kneeling beside an oval-shaped ground painting. It is also signed 'Karpa' in the bottom right-hand corner, possibly by the same person who signed the front of *Corroboree at Waru* (my guess is Jack Cooke). This time there can be no question from the masterly brushwork that the work is definitely Kaapa Tjampitjinpa's. A third concentric circle with centrally planted upstanding spears which appears to have been added as a device for linking the figures to the ceremonial pole with fine, fluid, wavy lines shows a lighter touch and may be the work of someone else – perhaps this part of the painting was executed by Tim Leura or Clifford Possum, whose ceremonial figures the ones in this painting resemble rather more than the strikingly realistic muscular physique of the corroboree man of *Gulgardi.*

The motif of two corroboree figures kneeling beside a ground painting recurs in the Art Gallery of South Australia piece, although in this work they are placed on either side of a scaled-down ceremonial pole, rather than at right angles to one another as in the Darwin Museum work. Their body paint is curious – as if someone had added underpants. I was once told that this wearing of 'underpants' was a sign a painting was intended – and thus presumably suitable – for general exhibition. But as we shall see, there are no certainties on this score.[56]

The second Kaapa work acquired by the Art Gallery of South Australia from Helen Brown is the one work in the group of six brought into town by Jack Cooke that does *not* fit Kimber's description. There are no ritualised figures, ceremonial grounds, regalia and poles – or realistic snakes and goannas. It is on a plain black background with a motif like a stylised spinal cord through the centre in orange and lime green. The designs on either side appear to be derived from the body paint of the ceremonial figures which, in effect, they have replaced. Only the palette and the circumstances of the painting's arrival in Alice Springs suggest its contemporaneity with the other Art Gallery of South Australia work. Only Kaapa's distinctive brushwork and the signature 'Koyaa' identify it as his work alongside the other paintings in the group. How do we explain this painting's appearance at this point in Kaapa's development?

Could Geoffrey Bardon's famous 'intervention' in the painting of the Honey Ant Mural have been enough to produce this dramatic change?

> 'Are these ants proper Aboriginal honey ants? Nothing is to be whitefella.' 'Not ours', he said, 'Yours.' 'Well paint yours,' I said – 'Aboriginal honey ants.'[57]

In his several accounts of the incident, Bardon identifies Kaapa's response to his criticism of the 'realistic illustrations of honey ants and birds, similar to the European manner'[58] in the second version of the mural as a 'deciding moment'. Kaapa consulted with his co-muralists Bill Stockman and Long Jack Phillipus, then took up his brush and painted the honey ant design with travelling marks around it. Geoffrey Bardon comments:

> This was the beginning of the Western Desert painting movement, when, led by Kaapa, the Aboriginal men saw themselves in their own image and

before their very eyes, on a European building. Something strange and marvellous was set in motion.[59]

I will have more to say about the Papunya School mural project in chapter 4.[60] In the context of the School of Kaapa, however, the mural is significant because it brought Kaapa and Geoffrey Bardon together, although the real beginning of their remarkable collaboration, which brought the desert art movement to life, was still a little way off. In this famous exchange, Kaapa was exposed to Bardon's criticisms of the European influence in the style he had evolved while working independently, although since it occurred towards the end of the mural project, it is not certain that it took place before Jack Cooke took Kaapa's paintings into town. But even without this direct exposure Kaapa was certainly astute enough to know about Bardon's interest in 'correct Aboriginal design'.[61] It is equally certain that Kaapa was his own man and doubtless mindful of the fact that the 'European elements of realism when depicting goannas, honey ants or kangaroos' to which Bardon objected helped make his work saleable to tourists. This would explain why in July or August 1971 he was still painting independently in his old style and selling these paintings through the Papunya canteen. As Bardon tells it, Kaapa held back from actually joining the painters working with him until the first sales of paintings in September 1971 had demonstrated their saleability and indeed the better money to be made from works in Bardon's preferred style.

In the meantime, it appears from the Jack Cooke six that Kaapa had been working on some experiments of his own in the new style back at the headquarters of the School of Kaapa. How could a 'true artist' resist? The left-hand section of the other Kaapa work the Art Gallery of South Australia acquired from Helen Brown is divided off from the rest of the painting by three sinuous lines and also consists entirely of 'correct Aboriginal designs': a pattern of concentric circles and lines of travel flanked by smaller circles and kangaroo tracks above a set of three concentric circles surrounded by U-shapes and more smaller circles.

In a 1987 interview with John Kean, who co-managed Papunya Tula in the late 1970s, Kaapa gave the following answer when asked why he had changed his early style:

JK: The early paintings were very different. You put in like men sitting down and different things.
K: Yuwai yuwai [Yes yes]. Then we changed again.
JK: How did you get the idea to change the paintings?
K: Little bit dangerous.
JK: So what did you do with those dangerous ones?
K: Cover'm up again (*his voice drops to an inaudible whisper*). Nobody see this way. Now we do like this one – palya [good].[62]

This is curious, given his assurances to Dick Kimber when the latter enquired about the secret/sacred aspect of *Mikanji*.[63] The secret/sacred controversy, which had such a decisive impact on the development of a secularised painting language for Western Desert art, will be considered in more detail in following chapters. For the moment, however, we will simply consider whether the works described in this chapter as the final expressions of the School of Kaapa could have been the source of the later censure of the Papunya painters by their neighbours and countrymen for revealing too much detail about the ceremonial sphere in their paintings. It does seem unlikely, if only because those paintings disappeared so quickly into public and private collections for decades before any of Kaapa's countrymen could have seen them – except in the very unlikely event that they went along to the Caltex/ Northern Territory Art Award. The fact that several of the paintings we have been considering were displayed in the Papunya canteen might suggest they would have found nothing to upset them in these paintings if they had – but then again, that might be why Kaapa was so eager to get the paintings away into Alice Springs with Jack Cooke …

For some reason, possibly Kaapa's dress sense: suit coats held together with safety pins over his bare chest when I knew him, a 'walking swag' in Geoffrey Bardon's evocative description, I am reminded here of what Johnny Rotten said in response to Malcolm McLaren's grandiose claims on behalf of the Sex Pistols. Rotten insisted he was a musical anarchist but not a revolutionary. Kaapa had a punk-like disdain for the rules and regulations which the white authorities attempted to impose upon him and he was undoubtedly an artistic revolutionary – but does that make him a cultural delinquent?

One of the last known paintings in the classic style of the School of Kaapa is the work of Tim Leura, and strangely enough it is called *A Joke.* It was sold at Sotheby's 2001 Aboriginal Art auction as one of a group of seven early Western Desert paintings from a private Canadian collection. It is painting No. 5 from the eighth consignment to the Stuart Art Centre, which places it early in 1972, more than six months after the events being considered here. Tim Leura's explanation of the painting to Hogan when he brought it into her gallery may have been designed to obscure its secret/sacred references. But perhaps it was also a parable for the fate of the original artistic venture of Kaapa, himself, and the absent Clifford Possum:

> One fella A is laughing at fella B for starting party too soon. Third fella (tracks around centre) is still away catching kangaroo.[64]

When Clifford Possum did arrive, he produced for Geoffrey Bardon's startled gaze the flawless *Emu Corroboree Man* – a kind of latter day School of Kaapa masterpiece with its ceremonial figure, leg cocked in the motion of the dance, superbly executed line work, background infilling and a nod to the emerging 'dot' style. Despite his reservations about 'decoration associated with "illustrations" concerning mythology',[65] Bardon was sufficiently impressed by the artist's 'exceptional skill and confidence'[66] to commission another one like it. Bardon spoke of his reservations about the work's 'questionable secrecy' to Larry May, an American traveller who purchased the painting from him in May–June 1972 and took it to Texas for thirty years before it returned to Australia to be exhibited for the first time in Clifford Possum's 2003–04 retrospective (with the artist's blessing).

Perhaps this is why another painting almost identical to Clifford Possum's was produced 'unknown to me [that is, Bardon] at the time'.[67] When it surfaced at auction in the wake of the Clifford Possum retrospective, I thought at first it might be a forgery, although there was no reason to suspect the former Welfare Branch officer who claimed to have bought it from the artist in the 1970s but was now uncertain of his identity. It was subsequently sold at Sotheby's as Untitled (Rainmaker Bird Ceremony), attributed to Tim Leura Tjapaltjarri, although according to a diagram in Bardon's 2004 book it is titled *Emu Ceremonial Dreaming* and is the work of Long Jack

Phillipus – unless Tim Leura produced yet another near identical painting. This is not as unlikely as it may sound, based on the following note by Bardon:

> Unknown to me at the time, Long Jack Phillipus working in close proximity to Clifford Possum Tjapaltjarri, also produced an Emu Dreaming as did Tim Payungka Tjapangati, Bill Stockman Tjapaltjarri and Tim Leura Tjapaltjarri.[68]

The most remarkable thing about all these paintings is that none of these painters usually painted Emu Dreamings, during Geoffrey Bardon's time or at any other in their long years with Papunya Tula Artists. When Tim Leura and Clifford Possum used the Emu story on the large *Warlugulong* canvases of the mid- and late 1970s mentioned earlier, they were careful to make their annotator Dick Kimber aware that they had no direct authority over this element of the paintings, but needed the permission of the Tjampitjinpa owners of the Dreaming for its inclusion. It strikes me that the identity of the Emu Corroboree Man can be none other than the man who started the party in Tim Leura's parable: Kaapa Mbitjana Tjampitjinpa, whose borning place was the Emu Dreaming site of Altijira and who often referred to himself as 'Emu Man'. Surely all of these paintings were painted in a kind of homage to the man still known among all the painters of Papunya Tula as 'the first artist'?

There is no sign that Kaapa himself painted again in the School of Kaapa style. However, in the large canvas *Trial by Fire*, painted by Tim Leura Tjapaltjarri in 1975 and recently unearthed in the vaults of the National Museum of Australia,[69] we see its continuing influence, at least in the work of Kaapa's associates. Apart from human figures, there are the skeletons which haunt the paintings as they did the life of Tim Leura, whose air of profound melancholy struck many who knew him even more than his 'drop-dead gorgeous' looks. The soulful skeletons also made a reappearance in the final decade of his brother Clifford Possum's artistic output, at first as the tragic sons of Lungkata devoured by the fire from Warlugulong, but later transformed into the Goanna brothers who fought and killed one another, and eventually into dead spirits at Napperby, where the story of Kaapa and his cousins began:

> We three start painting: Tim Leura, Kaapa Tjampitjinpa, Clifford. Before everybody. This is in Papunya – and outside from Papunya. First on art board and on carving.[70]

2

'So Beautiful'

Pat Hogan would later recall the memorable moment when Geoffrey Bardon delivered the first consignment of paintings from Papunya to her Stuart Art Centre with the words: 'They were so beautiful!'[1] But vivid as her memory of the paintings may have been, she must have been mistaken in claiming that it was Alice Springs Show Day, which in those days fell in late July, when she took delivery of them.[2] For one thing, Bardon's writings consistently cite September 1971 as the date when he took the first fifty paintings into Alice Springs to sell.[3] Nor were the paintings Bardon delivered to Pat Hogan the first he had brought into town to sell. The Stuart Art Centre was located on faraway Larapinta Drive across the railway line, attached to the Stuart Caravan Park that Hogan helped her husband run before she branched into Aboriginal art. Her gallery did not even have a display window. Bardon was looking for an outlet that matched his own aspirations for the paintings – as well as the painters' desire for the best possible return for their labour. His first stop, he said, was the home of Rex Batterbee, by then an old man, though still dealing in the watercolour landscapes of the followers of his protégé Albert

Namatjira, for whom he, like Bardon now with the Papunya painters, had worked as a disinterested 'agent'. But Batterbee was out of town when Bardon called in with the paintings, so he took that very first shipment down to Iris Harvey, who ran a large stationery supply shop which also sold art materials. The fate of the paintings Bardon left with Iris Harvey is not known: none acquired from this source have come to light to give her name a place in the history of the early Papunya boards. In this account, therefore, the first consignment of paintings to Pat Hogan's Stuart Art Centre is taken to represent the first works by Bardon's group of painting men to come on the market in Alice Springs.

Could Pat Hogan have confused the first consignment with the half-a-dozen School of Kaapa paintings Jack Cooke had brought into town, whose date of arrival in Alice Springs we saw in the previous chapter was some time before the Caltex Art Award, possibly July 1971? There is nothing to connect those paintings to the Stuart Art Centre, not even – as we shall see – any stylistic resemblance, though there was a close connection between Kaapa's win in the Art Award and Hogan's interest in the paintings. That is how Hogan's friend, Laurie Owens, who became settlement Superintendent at Papunya in July 1971, remembered the sequence of events:

> When Kaapa won the Caltex Prize in Alice Springs, that raised a few eyebrows – particularly Pat Hogan, who became involved at that time – in tune with Jo Caddy's interest. She saw it as very important to give the artists incentive and return for their work – wanted the work in her gallery, gave generous space, contributed to the cost of framing.[4]

When I asked Geoffrey Bardon about the date of the first consignment to the Stuart Art Centre, citing the chronological inconsistencies I had turned up, he couldn't help me with a precise date. He did volunteer that July was definitely too early. He remembered that it had been the day of an election – and that his decision to take some works into town and try to sell them was a reaction to the explosion of interest in painting set off by Kaapa's Art Award win.[5]

The paintings Pat Hogan received in that first consignment came with explanatory diagrams in Geoffrey Bardon's hand on special roneoed letterhead with the name of the Papunya Art and Craft Council and the symbol for a star: a concentric circle surrounded by dots, which had first excited his interest in the traditional design motifs as 'simplifications of perceived objects'.[6] This was the insignia of the Papunya artists co-operative[7] established under the auspices of the Papunya Special School to support the painters in their work. The co-op was formed in September – or in some accounts October[8] – 1971, with Head Teacher Fred Friis, Geoffrey Bardon and Deputy Head Teacher Geoffrey Lawson as the directors and Obed Raggett, Geoffrey Bardon's assistant in the art room, as executive negotiator and translator.[9] Given the presence of those special letterheads in the Stuart Art Centre Archive for paintings in the first consignment, it is improbable that the consignment left Papunya before these arrangements were in place, that is, several months *after* Pat Hogan's recollection of its arrival in Alice Springs.

Pat Hogan was the first of the private dealers in Western Desert art, but at a time when there was no other outlet for the painters' work in Alice Springs. Today there is a vast army of private dealers, and they are as little liked by those working on the communities with the artists as it seems Hogan was by Bardon – and for essentially the same reason: that their inroads pose a threat to established harmonious working relationships with the artists. Whatever Hogan's faults, researchers of the Western Desert art movement owe her a debt of gratitude for her meticulous application of the first numbering system for the paintings. The Stuart Art Centre consignment lists provide a chronological ordering of more than half the painters' total production over Geoffrey Bardon's time in Papunya. As he says:

> In addition to the six hundred-odd paintings I had sold in Alice Springs [to Hogan's gallery], I had sold about three hundred to various interested persons and, by a sort of default, built a personal collection of more than a hundred paintings. This meant that about a thousand paintings had been produced to date, in defiance of the Commonwealth policies that were destroying Aboriginal culture. I felt I was making a point about the esteem owed to Aboriginal culture, yet I was undermined by bureaucrats and art dealers.[10]

Hogan's 'Notes and Inventory for the Early Consignments of Pintupi Paintings'[11] listed the contents of each consignment by the artists and the number of paintings by each of them it contained. This information was based on the Stuart Art Centre stockbook entries, which assigned each painting by each artist a number within the consignment. Thus 1CON1 identifies the first painting of the first consignment, and so on. Hogan understood the value of this information; on the Stuart Art Centre documentation that went out with each painting, she informed the buyer:

It is important that this label should never be destroyed. The evidence it bears of the registered stock number may, in future, prove to be of very great value for the purposes of identification and authenticity.[12]

If only she had *dated* each consignment as it came in, the task of fitting the hundreds of other unnumbered paintings sold by Bardon or by the artists themselves in Papunya or Alice Springs into the chronological sequence provided by the consignment lists would have been relatively straightforward. Bardon could often supply a month or at least the time of year for paintings he sold and many of the purchasers were visitors to Papunya, who recalled the timing of their visits to the settlement. However, the consignments are undated, and it takes some fancy detective work to unravel the conflicting strands of Hogan's, Bardon's and Kimber's testimonies. At least Hogan's dating of the nineteenth and final consignment to Yuendumu Sports Day in August 1972 accords more or less with the time of Bardon's departure, although chaos reigned for a period thereafter. During this so-called 'interregnum' period (August–November 1972), Hogan seems to have simply added any new paintings onto the end of the nineteenth consignment. According to her 'Notes' in *Dot and Circle*, the nineteenth consignment originally contained forty-seven paintings, but works numbered in the four hundreds have since turned up at Sotheby's and elsewhere. By the end of 1972 Peter Fannin, Bardon's friend, fellow teacher and flatmate at Papunya, was installed as the first manager of the painters' company, Papunya Tula Artists Pty Ltd. He soon established a new system for numbering stock, to which the company still adheres today.

The first consignment

Amazingly, given how many paintings from the Stuart Art Centre consignments are still unaccounted for, and all the gaps in the chronological sequence of paintings produced in Papunya over 1971–72, the very first painting of the very first consignment can be positively located, attributed and annotated. For almost thirty years, *Sandhills and Clouds* by 'Mick Jabaljara', that is the late Mick Namarari Tjapaltjarri, hung on the storage racks of the Museum and Art Gallery of the Northern Territory in Darwin after it was purchased from Pat Hogan's Stuart Art Centre as part of a group of 105 early Papunya works by the Museum's foundation Director Colin Jack-Hinton in late 1971 or early 1972. Painted in enamel house paints in a stark palette of red and white on a black background, it is a simple design of three wavy lines joined by horizontal bars with crescent shapes down the outsides, the wavy lines depicting sandhills and the crescent shapes clouds. There is no controversial imagery or subject matter and no plain dark background. The painting is dotted – all over.

How can this be? The Papunya painters' progression from undotted to dotted surfaces and from controversial to uncontroversial subject matter has been repeated endlessly in books and catalogues on Western Desert art from the mid-1980s onwards.[13] The 'dot screen' – so the story goes – came later, as a means of covering over the secret/sacred elements of the imagery so as not to give offence to the painters' neighbours and kinsfolk across the rest of Central Australia. From this act of self-censorship, the core visual language of circles, lines, U-shapes, tracks and dotted backgrounds that dominated the language of Aboriginal art for the rest of the century was formed. Plausible as this developmental progression sounds, when we examine the evidence of the paintings themselves, a more complex and interesting story of the beginnings of Western Desert art starts to emerge. Not only, as we have seen in chapter 1, were the first paintings to come out of Papunya *not* the work of Bardon's painting group, nor did the first works this group produced look anything like most people's idea of a very early Papunya painting, if *Sandhills and Clouds* is at all typical of the paintings in the first consignment.

The paintings that have come up at auction from this consignment suggest that *Sandhills and Clouds* is typical. An untitled painting by Johnny Warangkula, with the artist's name and the consignment number '1' written on the back[14] (although apparently no painting number) was sold in Sotheby's June 1996 Fine Aboriginal and Contemporary Art auction.[15] The background is dotted – very unevenly; the work predates the distinctive effects of 'tremulous illusion' (to use Geoffrey Bardon's felicitous phrase) with which Johnny Warangkula so brilliantly transcended his difficulties with neat brushwork. It may also predate the more familiar representation of the important Rain Dreaming site of Kalipinypa as two concentric circles representing waterholes joined by wavy streams depicting running water, which is ubiquitous in the work of Walter Tjampitjinpa from the outset.

This is the design of *Water Dreaming at Kalipinypa* by Walter Tjampitjinpa which according to its entry in Sotheby's *Aboriginal Art* 2000 sales catalogue is painting No. 18 of the first Stuart Art Centre consignment. Its annotation on the Papunya Art and Craft Council letterhead gives no information as to the locale represented in the painting, whose title is based on the familiarity to contemporary audiences of the classic Kalipinypa motif. It too is painted in red, black and white enamel house paint. Long Jack Phillipus has confirmed that Kalipinypa was the subject of a painting by him (also painted with red, black and white house paint enamel) whose design is strikingly similar to the untitled first consignment work by Johnny Warangkula. According to Long Jack, the larger concentric circle depicts the main waterhole at Kalipinypa and the parallel straight lines to the sides show the different run-off channels.[16]

Kingsley Tjungurrayi's *Storm*, sold at Sotheby's 1998 Important Aboriginal Art auction and now in the John and Barbara Wilkerson Collection,[17] bears the Stuart Art Centre stock number 1CON10 on the reverse. Wavy streams of lightning are set against a background featuring Bardon's favourite star symbol. It, too, is completely infilled with dots and devoid of imagery referring to the ceremonial life and painted with the same red, white and black enamel house paint found in Mick Namarari's *Sandhills and Clouds*. Yet another painting from the first consignment, also by Johnny Warangkula, came to light when it was purchased with several other early Papunya works by the National Gallery of Victoria in the late 1980s from Pat Hogan's personal collection. She gave it the title *Dingo Puppy Story* (although it is more likely its subject was also Kalipinypa) and identified it as the first painting by Johnny Warangkula she saw. It also is devoid of ceremonial imagery, dotted all over and painted in red and white house paint on a brown ground.[18]

The use of house paint scavenged from around the settlement seems a reliable indicator that a painting occurs very early in the chronological sequence, before the poster paints mixed with PVA glue with which Geoffrey Bardon supplied the painters from the school art supplies became available. Why else would the painters have needed to forage for art materials? Importantly, and unlike the later consignments, the paintings in the first consignment were selected from what the painters had produced up to that point, not necessarily in the order of production. The house paint palette establishes priority over works using the 'art room' palette, and deflects the explanation that Bardon simply selected the works with the most innocuous imagery for the first consignment.

On the evidence so far, it seems that in the group of painters around Geoffrey Bardon, an initial period of uncontroversial imagery and dotted infilling *preceded* more controversial stylistic developments. But five paintings are hardly sufficient basis for generalisation, given the total of twenty-nine works in the first consignment. Where are the others? With most early Papunya boards, this is a question to which only time, assisted by the auction process, might one day provide an answer, but for another dozen works from the first consignment, an answer is potentially available. Like *Sandhills and Clouds*, they were part of inaugural Director Colin Jack-Hinton's initial purchase for the Museum in Darwin, comprising more than half the works from the first three consignments and, at least according to Pat Hogan's stocklist in the Stuart Art Centre Archive,[19] including a total of thirteen paintings from the first consignment. It might sound like the answer to a researcher's prayers, but like so much else in this story, the group of early Papunya paintings formally acquisitioned by the Museums and Art Galleries of the Northern Territory on 13 March 1972 raises more questions than it answers.

Just how many paintings were there in that first purchase? In Pat Hogan's *Dot and Circle* list of the nineteen consignments she received from Papunya up to July 1972 she says: 'Of the first three consignments, *seventy-eight* [author emphasis] paintings went to the Museum and Gallery in Darwin under the auspices of Colin Jack-Hinton'.[20] But 105 early boards were accessioned, that is, formally registered as part of its collection by the Museum in March 1972. Where did the extra twenty-seven paintings come from? This might be the moment to draw attention to another discrepancy, between the number of paintings Geoffrey Bardon says he brought in to the Stuart Art Centre on that first trip (fifty) and the number Pat Hogan listed in the first consignment in the Stuart Art Centre stock-book (twenty-nine). Is Bardon's figure just a rough estimate, or did Hogan only catalogue twenty-nine of the paintings and leave the other twenty-one uncatalogued? Did she later decide to 'throw them in' with the Jack-Hinton deal in the interests of making the Museum's collection of the 'very earliest works' as substantial as possible? Most of the 105 paintings in Darwin came with annotations, but for about twenty the record says 'no data'. Yet Jack-Hinton's comment in Sotheby's June 1997 *Important Aboriginal Art* sales catalogue on six paintings he bought for himself at the same time (paintings that had lost their attached documentation) suggests that he would not have considered undocumented works suitable for the Museum's collection: 'that seemed to have reduced their ethnographic, but certainly not their artistic significance'.[21] Maybe Jack-Hinton paid Iris Harvey's stationery supply shop a visit and bought up what she had left of the very first shipment of paintings from Papunya – this would at least explain why they have never surfaced anywhere else.

These questions might be answered by consulting the information on the backs of the paintings in the Darwin Museum, were it not that most of them have for the past thirty-eight years (1972–2010) remained in the frames in which they arrived from Alice Springs, which conceal the stock numbers written in chalk or textacolour on the backs of them. Nor did whoever originally registered the paintings for the Museum note down the vital clues to their location in the consignment lists from the Stuart Art Centre labels that should have accompanied them to Darwin.[22] The label miraculously still clinging to the back of its frame provided this information about *Sandhills and Clouds*, but it remains – for now – maddeningly uncertain *which* of the other 104 other works that were formally acquired by the Museum on 13 March 1972[23] might be those other twelve works.

However, if the 1971–72 Jack-Hinton purchase is examined for works using the same palette of red, white and black (or occasionally brown or beige) enamel house paint characterising the first consignment paintings identified so far, something rather interesting emerges. There are four paintings in the enamel palette by Mick Namarari, two by Long Jack Phillipus, one by Johnny Warangkula, three by Mick Tjakamarra, four Walter Tjampitjinpas and one Kaapa Tjampitjinpa. According to the Stuart Art Centre stockbook, these numbers almost *exactly* correspond with the numbers of paintings from the first consignment by each of these artists sold to the Darwin Museum. Four were by Mick Namarari, one by Long Jack Phillipus, one by Johnny Warangkula, three by Mick Tjakamarra, three by Walter Tjampitjinpa and one by Kaapa Tjampitjinpa.[24] Can it be coincidence that all share this palette – and the simple, uncontroversial designs and all-over dotting of other works so far identified from the first consignment? Alas, until the Museums and Art Galleries of the Northern Territory staff complete their conservation work on the paintings and the results are made available, there can be no certainty on this score. But they *would* have looked 'beautiful' together, the shared palette effecting an aesthetic unification, just as the classic Papunya Tula palette of red ochre, yellow ochre, black and white (and what could be mixed from these colours) did for Papunya Tula paintings from the mid-1970s well into the 1990s.[25] If they are the Darwin 105's other twelve first consignment works, then they too share the innocuous subject matter and all-over dotting of the other works considered.

The Old Pintupi

However, the really interesting question here is not when the first consignment arrived at Pat Hogan's gallery or which paintings in Colin Jack-Hinton's purchase for the Museum came from it, but why were the first consignment painters painting such innocuous imagery – especially in light of the far weightier subjects many of them were representing by the time of the second consignment? At least there is no uncertainty about who the *painters* represented in the first consignment were. According to the Stuart Art Centre records, the twenty-nine paintings in the first consignment were painted by eight men: Kaapa Tjampitjinpa, Billy Stockman Tjapaltjarri, Mick Wallankarri Tjakamarra, Long Jack Phillipus Tjakamarra, Johnny Warangkula Tjupurrula, Walter Tjampitjinpa, Mick Namarari Tjapaltjarri and Kingsley Tjungurrayi. What do these men have in common that might explain their initially restricting themselves to 'easy' subjects?

Not quite everyone in the first consignment did stay with 'easy' subjects. There is a Kaapa work painted in red, white and black enamel house paint on a beige background that sounds innocuous enough in the Museum catalogue's description of it as 'Toothache in rocks. Old people put them in ground. Painting also depicts a big snake.' However, this might not be entirely accurate as an account of its symbolism. And *Snake Story*, the only Billy Stockman in the first consignment, which was *not* included in the Darwin Museum purchase and which has not yet been located, appears in a slide and a diagram in the Stuart Art Centre Archive to have a plain black background, to include a depiction of a ceremonial object and not to be painted in house paint. If we leave these two former members of the School of Kaapa out of the equation for the moment, our task will be greatly simplified. Because the other six painters represented in the first consignment all had in common, not just long exposure to Europeans, but to a particular kind of European.[26] Unlike Kaapa and Billy Stockman's experiences with the laissez-faire pastoralists, they had been exposed to the proselytising of the Lutheran missionaries of Hermannsburg and Haasts Bluff – for most of their lives.

Johnny Warangkula was perhaps twelve or thirteen years old when light planes, probably those of the Mackay Exploring Party conducting an inland aerial survey in May or June 1930, flew over his family's lands. An animated raconteur, he loved acting out the story of his family hiding in the trees in fear of 'mamu' (devils), talking really quickly in a mixture of broken English and Pintupi-Luritja that would have been almost incomprehensible without his expressive hand and body movements – and sound effects. The family's fears soon faded when they met the members of the Mackay party at their base camp at Ilpilli on the eastern fringes of Pintupi territory and received presents of food and clothing. Just a few months later, in August 1930, Pastor Albrecht and a group of Aboriginal missionaries from Hermannsburg made their first journey by camel to minister to the 'western tribes'. They were met by a group of Aboriginal people at Ilpilli whose 'headman' Kamutu Tjungurrayi was wearing the gifts from Donald Mackay: 'a pair of new trousers and a new shirt, which he had put on in a hurry – back to front'.[27] Johnny remembered this meeting for his first taste of flour, which initially he had taken for ashes, but eagerly ate as hot damper served with treacle. Hoping to find more of this food and water at Hermannsburg, Kamutu and the other members of his group soon afterwards joined earlier Pintupi migrants to the east. The evangelical patrols continued, ranging widely across the far western lands as far north as Pikilyi in the Southern Warlpiri (Ngaliya) lands, and to Ilpilli in the Ehrenberg Ranges. In 1931 a party of four Aboriginal evangelists, one of whom was Albert (later Namatjira), went out and stayed at both these places. Johnny remembered them encouraging people to come in to the Hermannsburg mission with promises that if they became Christians 'noone will go hungry or die for want of water'.[28]

Drawing on these repeated friendly contacts, the missionaries and researcher Ted Strehlow were able to arrange for ninety Warlpiri, Pintupi and others to be camping in the area of Mt Liebig for the convenience of the Adelaide University expedition that included Norman Tindale, which established a base camp there, eager to study the 'Pintubi social framework'. This was in 1932, the year Long Jack Phillipus was born at Kalipinypa, north-east of present-day Kintore. His mother and father were recorded in the genealogies Tindale collected, as were his close countrymen from the Mt Morris area, 'Namarare' (Mick Namarari) who was recorded as a 'little child' and 'Waralngola' (Johnny Warangkula) who was estimated to be 'about fifteen'. Also recorded at Mt Liebig was Walter Tjampitjinpa, then a young man of marriageable age, having come in to Hermannsburg with a party of young men and boys who arrived at the mission in 1923 and stayed. In 1936 he married a Pintupi woman, Ngalunta Napangati, who had run away from her promised husband at Yarakula and taken refuge at Hermannsburg. In 1971 Walter Tjampitjinpa was the most senior custodian of the Kalipinypa Water Dreaming and thus entitled to authorise its representation, just as Mick and Bert Tjakamarra and Tom Onion had authorised the painting of the Honey Ant Mural. Walter, Long Jack Phillipus, Johnny Warangkula and Mick Tjakamarra all painted versions of the classic Kalipinypa motif in the red, black and white first consignment palette.[29]

Not long after their encounter with the researchers at Mt Liebig, Johnny Warangkula's family took up residence at the mission, as did the parents of Mick Namarari, who had guided the missionaries to Ilpilli in 1932. Mick attended Hermannsburg mission school until he was eleven, when the family went to live in the area around Haasts Bluff, 40 kilometres to the south of present-day Papunya. Long Jack Phillipus was a young man by the time his family came in to live at Haasts Bluff in 1957, but his Pintupi mother and his subsequent marriage to Kamutu's daughter Suzette Long Napaltjarri ensured his close connection to the Pintupi immigrants. He was sufficiently affected by his contacts with the missionaries to become a staunch Christian, and was ordained in later life as a Lutheran pastor. Long Jack's family joined large numbers of Pintupi, Warlpiri and other tribespeople who had taken up residence in the area around Haasts Bluff after a government-sponsored permanent ration depot and trading post for dingo scalps was established there by the Lutheran missionaries in 1941. In that year the federal government declared the Haasts Bluff area, including Papunya and effectively to the Western Australian border, a permanent Aboriginal Reserve. In the late 1950s, the entire Haasts Bluff Aboriginal population of four hundred people was moved en masse to Papunya because of problems with the water supply.

In Papunya in 1971, these men – Johnny Warangkula, Mick Namarari, Long Jack Phillipus and Walter Tjampitjinpa (and Kingsley Tjungurrayi, who was also originally from Ilpilli but had spent enough time in the east to identify as Luritja) – were part of the group within the settlement population who called themselves the Old Pintupi[30] to distinguish themselves from the so-called New Pintupi in terms of the length of their exposure to Europeans and their ways. They were proud of their sophistication in the ways of Europeans – and well able to understand what it meant to be an artist from their contact with the cottage craft industries of the Hermannsburg missionaries and the brilliant career of Albert Namatjira, who in 1931, as the evangelist Albert, had first encouraged their families to embark on the great adventure of the journey east, before himself embracing this profession. Jeremy Long, who was Superintendent at Haasts Bluff from 1957 to 1959, reflected on the impact of the mission experience:

What I think people are overlooking – because most of us are more or less pagans – is the influence of church and missionaries. There was the ban on ceremonies at Hermannsburg – I never saw an important ceremony at Haasts Bluff – only very public affairs. By contrast in the summer of 1960/61 driving back to Yuendumu, there were initiations going on – openly, I was taking photographs. The extrovert and confident Warlpiri, taking over the world. The bloke driving with me said to turn off – there was a camp, wandered through the bush a bit, and there was this big initiation going on, people from Jay Creek, Hermannsburg. But this didn't happen under the aegis of the church. I think the people at Haasts Bluff had been hit by this, all the early contacts with Hermannsburg missionaries and evangelists who came out doing the contact thing through the thirties – and there wasn't much reason to change. The missionary at Haasts Bluff was in the big house, there were government people there too, but the missionary was central. I thought it was pretty surprising that these people once at Papunya should be the ones to start painting traditional ceremonial designs – because they were so secretive before. What makes them come out and start showing themselves?[31]

Part of the answer to this question may lie with the only first consignment painter we have not yet considered, a man who was in his own gentle way as canny as Kaapa at getting whitefellas to do things for him, and who, from the moment Kaapa handed him that little scrap of paper with the design for the Honey Ant Dreaming Mural sketch to present to Geoffrey Bardon that winter's night in 1971, was the undisputed 'Boss' of the Papunya painting movement: Old Mick Tjakamarra.

The grey eminence

The presence of Mick Tjakamarra within the earliest group of painters was crucial. Without his blessing as one of the last surviving elders of his generation of the Kukatja tribe, one of the senior traditional owners of the ground on which everybody else at Papunya stood, the painting enterprise would have been a social impossibility for the artists. He and his brother Bert were (with Tom Onion) the senior 'kutungulu' (managers) for the site of Tatata where the Papunya Honey Ant Dreaming originated. The significance of this became apparent to Bardon during the negotiations for the mural, which was not simply a statement of the ongoing survival of Indigenous traditions for the benefit of the whitefellas. It was also a reminder to out-of-area residents of Papunya of the landowners' ongoing ritual authority over this place. Kaapa Tjampitjinpa was following correct cultural protocol when he said in his 1987 interview with John Kean that it was Mick and his brother Parta (Bert Tjakamarra) who created the mural – with himself and his team of painters merely their helpers:

> JK: Who were the first blokes who worked on the Tjala Tjukurrpa [Honey Ant Dreaming mural]?
> K: Old Mick and Parta [Mick Wallankarri Tjakamarra and his brother Bert Tjakamarra] first and we second – we helping. And that old Tjampitjinpa – dead fellow, and them olden people. Tjala travelling this way – right through.[32]

Mick also had a great love of painting – unlike his older brother Parta (Bert) Tjakamarra and Tom Onion Tjapanangka, who rarely if ever painted themselves, Mick moved rapidly from supervisor of the younger men in the Tjala Tjukurrpa (Honey Ant Mural) project to one of the group of painters and continued his prolific output well into his eighties. In the process he put the weight of his personal authority behind the painting enterprise – and perhaps gave these men the courage to take their first tentative steps along a path whose dangers they may not have foreseen. Bardon found Mick and Walter (the 'old Tjampitjinpa' Kaapa mentions) 'in no way friendly' when he came upon them painting down at the old settlement office with Kaapa in the early days of his acquaintance with the men, before the mural project commenced. They were 'courteous' in spite of their 'apparent reservations' and gave him the impression 'that they wondered why I was interested in them'.[33] They were also probably sizing him up, to see how he could be useful to them.

I remember having the same experience the first time I met Old Mick. On my first visit to Papunya in July 1980, he was the first person through the door of the artists' house, seemingly within minutes of the Papunya Tula Artists' vehicle driven by Andrew Crocker pulling into the driveway. I usually put parentheses around the 'Old' by which so many of the original Papunya artists are known, as a reminder that they were not always so, that their lives had spanned childhood, youth, young adulthood and middle age before this epithet became applicable. But Old Mick was *so* old even then that it did almost seem that he always had been. Certainly he'd been the oldest person around by a considerable margin for as long as most of Papunya's residents could remember. The first thing he said to me (and the second and third, because I found it difficult to grasp his meaning, speaking as he always did in a quavering, almost shrieking, falsetto) was 'Cuppa tea?'. Other artists began arriving with their paintings and sat silently around the room with the cups of tea Old Mick had indicated I should make for them too, while he presented me and my then husband with his introductory lecture for newcomers to their community. I understood little of it. But I could not help noticing the way all the men deferred to him when he took over the storytelling from each of them as they provided Andrew Crocker with the annotations for their paintings. And how they came in on the cue of his wild, high, starting notes to the songs of their Dreamings in the paintings. The last thing he said to me on that visit and every other time I visited Papunya for another sixteen years until it finally came true, was that he wouldn't be there next time I came.

Mick was born in the very early years of the 20th century, and over his exceptionally long life had acquired an encyclopedic knowledge of the Dreaming and the authority among his countrymen that went with it. His varied and extensive contacts with Europeans were reflected in his exceptionally good English. He was more at his ease in conversation with Europeans than most of the younger men in the painting group. He had been a police tracker for twenty years, lived at Hermannsburg mission, and worked as a stockman at Glen Helen station, another of the early pastoral properties where the local Aboriginal population had reached a mutually acceptable arrangement with the leaseholder. Mick might have known Tim Leura and Clifford Possum and their cousin Kaapa from the time they spent at Glen Helen with Albert Namatjira, whose career as an artist he would also have observed there – and at Hermannsburg and later Papunya. He also knew Obed Raggett, who was the son of Fred Raggett, one of the white stockmen at Glen Helen. Obed was born and grew up at Hermannsburg, where Pastor Albrecht described him as the most intelligent of all his pupils. Obed was ritually tied to Old Mick as owner of the Papunya Honey Ant Dreaming[34] for the correct performance of whose ceremonies Mick was responsible. From his position as Bardon's classroom assistant and translator in the Papunya Special School he was ideally situated for his role as a key facilitator of the painting movement – and as Old Mick's eyes and ears.

There is one more piece to the puzzle of the first consignment, before moving on to the second: what was happening in the studio that the school yardmen Bill Stockman and Long Jack Phillipus had set up at the back of Geoffrey Bardon's classroom behind a barricade of tables, chairs and sheets of masonite? After Kaapa joined them in this space, the group responsible for most of the works in the first consignment continued to work in the old settlement office, where the house paint was presumably kept for communal use. There are thirteen works attributed to Long Jack Phillipus in the 1971–72 Darwin purchase, only two of which use the red, black and white house paint palette, the only two of his with background dotting. He may have painted them during a visit with Kaapa to his old studio. The other eleven Long Jack works in the Darwin 105 are all set on plain backgrounds of red, black or yellow and shades of beige and grey like the School of Kaapa in the powder paints mixed with PVA that Bardon supplied and several depict 'corroboree men' in the manner of Kaapa and his associates. We will come to these, several of which are second consignment works, in a moment. Then there is Billy Stockman's *Snake Story*, described earlier in this chapter (see pages 55–56). If it was painted at the back of Geoffrey Bardon's classroom where Billy Stockman usually worked, it shows that Billy Stockman and Long Jack Phillipus had been influenced by Kaapa's arrival in this space. Suddenly their works more closely resembled the School of Kaapa style than what was being produced concurrently by the group now working at Kaapa's old studio. And what of Kaapa himself?

There is no way yet of knowing which of the five Kaapas in the Darwin 105 is the one Kaapa painting sold to Darwin from the first consignment. However, we do know what became of another of the three Kaapas that were in the first consignment. *Wild Potato Story*, the twenty-fourth painting of the first consignment, was one of fifteen works in the Department of Aboriginal Affairs collection donated to the Darwin Museum in 1975 after Cyclone Tracy. The collection comprised items collected by welfare officers from the 1960s till 1974: perhaps *Wild Potato Story* was one of Jack Cooke's purchases. From three small concentric circles through its centre, the roots and tubers of the wild potato plant branch off to the sides of the painting. It is so strikingly *un*like Kaapa's previous work that one is almost inclined to dispute its attribution. However, another explanation of this painting's anomalous appearance in terms of Kaapa's known work is possible – and much more interesting.

It is very similar as a representation of the 'Yala' motif to painting No. 49 from the second Stuart Art Centre consignment, namely, the iconic *Yala Dreaming*, attributed to Billy Stockman Tjapaltjarri, one of the best known of all the early Papunya works. The evidence of artistic influence between the painter of *Yala Dreaming* and Kaapa Tjampitjinpa in *Wild Potato Story* is very strong. Not just the yams, but the yellow backgrounds of both paintings and the red and black of their concentric circles. Assuming from its location in the first consignment that it was painted first, Kaapa's *Wild Potato Story* must be the precursor of this famous work. Does it also mark the point at which Kaapa left the group working in the old settlement office and joined Billy Stockman Tjapaltjarri and Long Jack Phillipus Tjakamarra in their 'studio' in the barricaded section at the back of the Papunya School art room? Both works are painted in the powder paint mixed with PVA glue that replaced enamel house paint as the painters' medium once they made the move to Bardon's classroom. Was *Wild Potato Story* Kaapa's first painting for Geoffrey Bardon?

The second consignment

Yala (Wild Potato) Dreaming is probably the best known painting of the second consignment to the Stuart Art Centre, indeed of all the early Papunya boards from 1971. It is a lyrical portrayal of one of the staple foods of the Western Desert peoples. Across a plain, bright yellow background reminiscent of the School of Kaapa, yala roots and tubers dance in black and red with amazing grace and lightness of touch. Its fame rests partly on the fact that after more than ten years it is one of the few early Papunya works other than Johnny Warangkula's *Water Dreaming at Kalipinypa* 1972 to break the

$200 000 barrier at Sotheby's.[35] The first mystery surrounding this inspired rendition of the bush potato motif is why Colin Jack-Hinton did not purchase it with the other 105 he acquired for the Darwin Museum in late 1971 or early 1972. By the time he made his appearance in Alice Springs, it might already have been sold to the private collection in Queensland from which it was later resold at Sotheby's. However, given that there is no buyer listed in the Stuart Art Centre stockbook against this painting, it seems more likely that Pat Hogan put it aside along with some other 'very special' paintings for her personal collection and was only later induced to part with it. Either way, it is difficult to avoid the implication that, despite the historical significance of the works in the Darwin 105, they are unlikely to have been the very best pieces on offer in terms of artistic quality. This conclusion has been borne out time and again by the extraordinary works that have emerged through the auction process between 1995 and 2010 from the private collections of those who were on the scene in 1971–72 with eyes to see.

The second and more intractable mystery surrounding *Yala Dreaming* is its attribution to Billy Stockman. *Yala Dreaming* featured on the merchandise produced by the Art Gallery of New South Wales for the *Papunya Tula: Genesis and Genius* retrospective in 2000, as well as in advertisements for the exhibition and its catalogue as a Billy Stockman. The painting's attribution to Billy Stockman has remained unchallenged through more than ten years of heavy exposure. Yet Pat Hogan's stockbook lists it as the work of Billy Stockman's fellow yardman at Papunya School and pioneer painter, Long Jack Phillipus. An explanatory diagram of the painting by Geoffrey Bardon in the Stuart Art Centre Archive also identifies it as the work of Long Jack Phillipus. How did

Sotheby's come to attribute it to Billy Stockman? They did not have direct access to the Stuart Art Centre stockbook in 1998. Is the most obvious explanation for the discrepancy – that whoever looked it up for them simply made a mistake – the correct one? Or is there another piece of documentation in which Billy Stockman is given as the creator of the work? As it happens, there is.[36] The painting was sold in Sotheby's 1998 Important Aboriginal Art auction – as a Billy Stockman – with an accompanying diagram, this time in Pat Hogan's hand, on which *two* artists' names are written: 'Billy Stockman' and, across the top of the diagram, 'Johnny Warangula'!

Billy Stockman is renowned for his later paintings of Bush Potato (that is, Yala) Dreamings, but the distinctive element of these portrayals is his depiction of the feathery petals of the yam flower. There are some paintings from 1972 by Billy Stockman with realistic images of yam plants rather than the stylised rendering of *Yala Dreaming*, but none of the four second-consignment paintings by Billy Stockman in the Darwin Museum's collection, including one titled *Little Yam Dreaming*, look anything like *Yala Dreaming*.

Though he is not as famous for it as Billy Stockman, Long Jack Phillipus has also painted many Yala Dreamings over the years and – more to the point – he usually portrays the Bush Potato Dreaming after the manner of *Yala Dreaming*, with ovoid-shaped tubers branching off the roots of the plant. Long Jack also painted the School of Kaapa–influenced works (mentioned earlier) in the Jack-Hinton purchase on the same bright yellow background as *Yala Dreaming*. Except for the two 'old settlement office' works, all Long Jack Phillipus' works from this early period are set on plain backgrounds of red, white, black or yellow and shades in between, and the forms are illuminated at the edges by deftly placed, regularly sized, white dots – as in *Yala Dreaming.* Another Long Jack work in the Darwin 105, *Water and Lightning Story*, has dark oval shapes representing 'big cliffs' set in a complex network of fine, curving lines representing rain and lightning, executed with a delicacy of touch similar to the painter of *Yala Dreaming.*

In the end, who painted what matters less than what can be learnt about the early Papunya painters from carefully examining their work in an attempt to answer such questions. Over the next fifteen years of the painting movement (until female relatives began to assist some of the older artists with the background infilling of dots), the distinctiveness of each artist's dotting style remained a reliable indicator of the authorship of paintings by the Papunya Tula artists. In this very early phase of the movement, when the artists were working closely together to develop an expressive form based on their inherited visual language and were often strongly influenced by one another's design motifs, signature dotting can be critical for attributions. In the case of *Yala Dreaming*, the attribution error – if it is one – could go unnoticed because the styles of Billy Stockman and Long Jack Phillipus have many similarities at a macro level. They were painting alongside one another and were both influenced by the third member who had joined their group at the back of Geoffrey Bardon's classroom at around this time – Kaapa Tjampitjinpa, who may originally have devised this way of representing the wild potato. As for Johnny Warangkula …

The second consignment of early Papunya boards to the Stuart Art Centre comprised sixty paintings and included works by all eight artists from the first consignment, along with four who were not: Charlie Tarawa Tjungurrayi, Tutuma Tjapangati, Uta Uta Tjangala[37] and Tim Payungka Tjapangati.[38] These four men had also had extensive mission-based contact with whitefellas, unlike members of the painting group who do not figure until later in the Stuart Art Centre consignment lists. A double-sided Emu Story[39] painting in the Darwin 105 painted in the same red, black and white enamel house paint that was used earlier as a marker of first consignment works confirms Charlie Tarawa's connection to what I have called the 'old settlement office crew'. He was the younger brother of Kamutu Tjungurrayi, the man who donned Donald Mackay's shirt and trousers back-to-front to meet with the missionaries.

Kamutu and his group arrived from the Pintupi lands in the early 1930s and settled first at Hermannsburg and then at Haasts Bluff. Charlie Tarawa was a close countryman of Mick Namarari and Johnny Warangkula, with whom he also shared the experience of growing up under the missionary gaze. He was well known to all members of the old settlement office crew from years of co-residence at Haasts Bluff. Bardon said in his first book that he had 'adopted the position of spokesman for the younger Pintupi men, since Mick Numieri and Old Walter Tjampitjinpa had almost no conversation'.[40] 'Wadama', as he was known to his countrymen, played a crucial role in the later Pintupi migrations east, along with his friend Nosepeg Tjupurrula. During World War II, these two young men's travels took them to Alice Springs, where they were recruited to a military convoy heading to Wyndham. Here they witnessed the Japanese bombing of northern Australia in March 1942 – and doubtless regaled their compatriots with some extraordinary stories after their return to Haasts Bluff when the war ended.

Charlie subsequently worked as a dogger based at Haasts Bluff, travelling by camel train on long journeys westward to the Pintupi homelands hunting for dingo scalps, which the missionaries traded for rations. Sometimes he brought people back with him to visit relatives who had already migrated east. Uta Uta Tjangala and Tutuma Tjapangati both visited Haasts Bluff by this means in the 1940s. Tutuma was another enterprising early immigrant to Hermannsburg who subsequently acquired his own camels and travelled extensively in southern Pintupi (Winanpa) country across the border in Western Australia and around Lake Hopkins where his traditional lands lay. Later these two men often painted together under the school classrooms, bonded by shared country and life experience.

Uta Uta had returned to the Pintupi homelands after his initial visit to Hermannsburg with Charlie Tarawa in the 1940s. In those days the missionaries did not distribute rations to able-bodied men, and living independently off his own country probably seemed a more attractive option than settlement life under these conditions. But in 1954, the Northern Territory Administration, which had previously funded the ration depot at Haasts Bluff out of an interest in attracting the Pintupi's eastern neighbours, the Kukatja/Luritja, away from Alice Springs, assumed direct responsibility for Haasts Bluff. The same year, Harry Giese was appointed Director of Welfare in the Northern Territory. Convinced that Aboriginal people would gradually abandon their old life and settle down, working to produce their own food in new ways, Giese set about building up the settlements. As part of the transformation of Haasts Bluff from a Lutheran mission outpost into a government settlement under the direct control of the Northern Territory Administration, money was invested in a cattle station that provided stockwork for the men and fresh meat for the settlement. In 1956 when Charlie Tarawa's dogging party met Uta Uta out on their shared country near the Western Australian border he was able to report that Haasts Bluff was now a significantly more attractive proposition than when Uta Uta had last visited:

> There were rations for all, not just for the old and infirm and women and children; there was work and a small cash wage for all who wanted work; free issues of clothing and blankets were made regularly; and the growing cattle herd provided fresh meat every week for all.[41]

The response was apparently instantaneous: 'Two men walked quickly to summon others camped farther south, west of Lake Macdonald, and together the camel team and nine families set off for Haasts Bluff'.[42] Several people turned back at the Ehrenberg Ranges and one woman died just 20 kilometres from their destination, but Uta Uta was among the thirty-four people who successfully made the epic journey from their homelands across hundreds of kilometres of country in high summer in Central Australia accompanying Charlie Tarawa's camel team, to reach Haasts Bluff just before Christmas 1956.

According to Jeremy Long, the settlement manager had immediately blamed the understandably poor physical condition in which they arrived for an outbreak of pneumonia which had actually preceded their arrival. As we will see shortly, the 'bush Pintupi' were often used as scapegoats for settlement ills. Uta Uta returned to the Kintore Range area in July 1958 with Jeremy Long and a month later undertook the long walk back to Haasts Bluff. In 1971 he was working as a gardener at Papunya School, a position from which he would have observed, if not participated in, the mural project. He was also connected to Billy Stockman Tjapaltjarri through the latter's marriage to Yintinaka, the daughter of another older brother, Yatapayi, who died in the 1950s.

Though much younger than Uta Uta Tjangala, Charlie Tarawa and Tutuma Tjapangati, Tim Payungka Tjapangati shared their sense of adventure and love of travel. He and his family had been into Haasts Bluff to collect rations during Timmy's childhood. After his father died, his adoptive fathers took him back to the Pintupi homelands and further south to their own country. He was one of those who had turned back from the 1956 migration east at the Ehrenberg Ranges, but he travelled in to Haasts Bluff with Jeremy Long's 1957 Welfare Branch patrol to visit his mother, who had been among the group who came in with Charlie Tarawa the previous year. Timmy checked out Alice Springs before returning to Pintupi country with Jeremy Long the following year. Soon afterwards he arrived at Haasts Bluff, having walked in with Uta Uta and his young family. Timmy learnt some English and more about whitefella ways during a spell in Warrabri settlement, where he was sent by the government after killing a man in a fracas at Papunya in 1959. He also picked up some Warlpiri during this visit, which would later be important for communication between the Pintupi and Warlpiri members of the painting group.

As some of the most recent arrivals among the Pintupi group, and some of the last Pintupi to come in to Haasts Bluff, Uta Uta and Timmy Payungka were located socially somewhere between the well-established Old Pintupi and the newest Pintupi arrivals at Papunya in the 1960s. In Bardon's account of the early painting groups around the settlement, both men usually painted at Bardon's flat with the group of New Pintupi farmworkers who will appear in our story with the third consignment. Uta Uta and Tim Payungka's inclusion in the second consignment reflects the relative precocity of their engagement with European culture compared with many of their countrymen in the painting group whose first contacts with Europeans dated from the 1960s.

Pat Hogan found the second consignment to the Stuart Art Centre noteworthy, not for the presence of *Yala Dreaming*, but for its inclusion of 'Kaapa's first medicine painting'.[43] Hogan does not indicate what she means by this terminology – or more precisely what the painters meant in describing their work in these terms. It is of some importance, however, for all the second consignment painters except Mick Namarari, Johnny Warangkula and Kingsley Tjungurrayi contributed works to the consignment whose title and/or annotation identifies them as 'medicine stories'. Hogan sold the work she called 'Kaapa's first medicine painting' to an Alice Springs doctor in 'late 1974', telling him it was 'a very special one' and also one in a series of eight medicine paintings which Kaapa had produced around this time. It was sold for a six-figure sum in Sotheby's 2007 Important Aboriginal Art auction as *Medicine Painting* 1971, and it is, in the doctor's words, 'incredible'. In the lower right-hand quadrant of the painting a corroboree man in direct lineage from the *Gulgardi* figure and full ceremonial attire is shown kneeling astride a concentric circle, leaning slightly to one side as if swaying in the motion of the dance. The rest of the painting is covered in detailed and meticulous symmetrical patterning based on the traditional visual language of the Western Desert peoples. According to the 'cost price' column in her stockbook, Hogan paid the artist

$20 for this work, which was very large by 1971 standards (91.5 x 61 cm). It is hard to understand why Kaapa would have accepted such a trifling amount for what he might justifiably have considered one of his finest paintings. It is light years away from the sparse elegance of *Gulgardi*, but the sheer ambition of the work has all the hallmarks of an artist supremely confident of his powers. He was 'on a roll', drawn into the orbit of Geoffrey Bardon, whom this work may have been designed to impress, by the attraction of a ready supply of materials and the hopes raised by the first sale of paintings in Alice Springs of a steady outlet for his work. But perhaps he cared about none of this – his acceptance of the $20 tends to suggest as much – and simply gave himself over to the exhilaration of painterly discovery, or to something else entirely. Bardon was not the only man at the inception of the painting movement with a mission. Bardon wrote that 'Along with sacredness and secrecy, Kaapa threw his traditions to the winds',[44] but maybe he was deliberately painting up a storm, with every intention of riding the whirlwind.

Almost as extraordinary as the painting was the information contained in an annotated diagram on Papunya Art and Craft Council letterhead by Geoffrey Bardon provided to the purchaser, in comparison with which the revelations of the School of Kaapa works considered earlier in chapter 1 appear decidedly tame. It must be assumed that Bardon's annotation is a transcription of what Kaapa told him at the time the work was painted – and the shock of this sort of in-depth explanation of the graphic elements can readily be imagined. What can be discussed here is the concentric circle at the centre of the painting, glossed as a 'Dreaming waterhole – not real water but part of an olden time story'. In Kaapa's insistence on this point there is a statement of the transcendence of the elements of European landscape in his previous works in favour of spelling out his relationship to the land through the historical narratives of Western Desert culture. This trajectory is already implicit in *Gulgardi*'s title and subject matter, but *Medicine Painting* gains cultural authority from being expressed in the visual language of the titleholder.

The effect of Kaapa's *Medicine Painting* on the artists alongside whom he was presumably working when he painted it is immediately obvious. The kneeling ceremonial figures in Billy Stockman Tjapaltjarri and Long Jack Phillipus' School of Kaapa-style paintings[45] in the Darwin 105 owe a clear debt to Kaapa's in this painting – or to *Gulgardi*. Other artists were also affected. In both of Walter Tjampitjinpa's *Medicine Story* paintings in the Darwin 105[46] there are kneeling figures that also recall Kaapa's corroboree man. Charlie Tarawa's *Medicine Story* paintings in the Darwin 105[47] are of particular interest as the first inclusion of ceremonial objects and references to the secret ritual world of the men in a painting from outside the School of Kaapa and its heirs at the old settlement office.

The innocuous bush tucker and water paintings which characterised the first consignment are still represented in the second, for example *Yala Dreaming*, but they are overwhelmed by paintings which feature just the kind of explicit representations of ritual matters with which the early Papunya boards have long been associated. With the significant exception of Mick Tjakamarra, who in his wisdom anticipated the strategy later adopted by the rest of the painting group to mask the ceremonial forms on his *Medicine Story*[48] painting by submerging them in the background dotting, all these works are painted on plain backgrounds, also after the manner of *Gulgardi* and the School of Kaapa. What was it that transformed the abstract iconography of bush tucker, landscape and water that characterised the earliest paintings from *Sandhills and Clouds* to *Yala Dreaming* into the full-on ritual world of the medicine paintings?

One obvious answer, derived from tracking the spin-offs of the ceremonial figure in *Medicine Painting* (which is in turn a reworking of the *Gulgardi* figure), is the influence of Kaapa Tjampitjinpa. If it *was* Kaapa's arrival in the art room which produced the dramatic alterations in the themes of Long Jack Phillipus and Billy Stockman's paintings at this time, it may not have been long after this that the other members of the group were evicted from the old settlement office and joined him there, judging by the pervasive imagery of the kneeling ceremonial figure. No wonder the men felt uneasy working at the back of Bardon's classroom, if they were painting such things with only a flimsy barrier of desks to shield their work from the sight of the women and the uninitiated.

But of course it is not that simple. Anthropologist Fred Myers and Jeremy Long have suggested that a series of AIAS[49]-sponsored trips to sacred sites to perform and film ceremonies in May 1969 (Yumari), August–September 1970 (Yaru Yaru) and August 1972 (Mitukatjirri) had a formative influence on the painting movement by 'chang[ing] their perceptions of how white people regarded their cultural traditions'.[50] Uta Uta Tjangala was one of two principal performers in the Yina (Old Man) Dreaming rituals filmed at Yumari rockhole in May 1969 on the first of these expeditions, and *Pintubi Revisit Yumari* featuring his performance may well have been shown to the participants when the AIAS team returned in late 1970 for the second trip to Yaru Yaru. Turkey Tolson, interviewed in 2000 for the catalogue of *Papunya Tula: Genesis and Genius*, may have been referring to these events – or to other ceremonial activities from which the figure of the ceremonial man kneeling by the ground painting with upraised arms derived – when he said that the timing of Geoffrey Bardon's arrival in Papunya had been 'good', because 'we had a big ceremony before he got there ... all the tjilpi [old men] in one place, big mob of old men teaching us. Not only Pintupi; there was Warlpiri, some Arrente.'[51] The Yumari story is part of a vast storyline extending as far east as Mt Liebig, a key site in the recent Pintupi migrations. As with the Honey Ant Mural and the Kalipinypa paintings from the first consignment, was it a matter of choosing a Dreaming subject in which many of the painters had rights, one which the senior custodians, namely Uta Uta and Charlie Tarawa, were on hand to sanction?

As already suggested, the medicine painting genre would have appeared alarmingly controversial to Geoffrey Bardon. Whether in response to his anxiety over the symbolism of these paintings or for reasons of their own, the painters began to provide explanations which avoided alluding to any subject matter that might trouble their kindly patron. Uta Uta Tjangala's *Bush Tucker*[52] from the Darwin 105 is an example. The long, ovoid shape which dominates the painting is said to be 'a big bag which contains meat and bush tucker for a ceremony'. The yellow circles at the end of the stalk-like projections along its length are glossed as 'big bags to cover up private parts'. In countless portrayals over the years by Uta Uta of the Yumari story he made famous, these elements have been identified as the Old Man's testicles 'gone walkabout' – part of the painful torment he endures for a sexual liaison with his strictly forbidden mother-in-law relation and a distinctively Western Desert metaphor for male impotence. The dominant themes of the medicine paintings partake of both the painters' worlds and are exactly the sort of things which might be presumed to concern a group of old men (which, notwithstanding the presence of a few younger men, most of the artists were when painting started up at Papunya in 1971): death, loss of virility, access to women in the ritual context and the initiation of young men – all central to men's experience of old age in traditional Western Desert society.

Uta Uta is holding up his painting *Bush Tucker* in that marvellous photograph of Geoffrey Bardon and the painters outside the old Papunya Town Hall which housed the legendary Great Painting Room. The photo captures the spirit of the early painting movement and also provides one of the few pieces of hard evidence about the relationship between the Stuart Art Centre consignments and the sequence of events. Fred Friis, who took the photo, left Papunya School at the end of 1971 and was replaced by the less sympathetic Terry Parry, so the photo must have been taken in 1971. It is evidently not the dead of winter: Geoffrey Bardon and most of the painters are wearing shorts and shirts. They are proudly holding up their work – either the paintings they are currently working on, or completed works which have not yet been consigned to the Stuart Art Centre, several of them clearly recognisable from the Museums and Art Galleries of the Northern Territory's first purchase of early Papunya paintings. In that frozen moment are brought together the production of these works, the timing of the second or third consignment to the Stuart Art Centre, the Darwin Museum's initial purchase of early Papunya boards and the painters' accession to the Great Painting Room, which was to transform yet again their artistic practice.

3

The Pintupi Factor

Years before anyone put paintbrush to 'board', Papunya was one of the most publicised Aboriginal settlements in Australia. Its proximity to Alice Springs relative to other large Aboriginal settlements and hence easier accessibility for short-term visitors like journalists may have contributed to its notoriety, but essentially it had the fascination of the exotic. For the press, the sixty-seven people who arrived in Papunya between 1962 and 1966 straight from the desert were the so-called 'lost tribe' of the Pintupi, the last of their people to abandon the nomadic lifestyle of their ancestors and their homelands in the Gibson Desert straddling the Northern Territory/Western Australian border, bounded by the Ehrenberg Ranges to the east, the gravel plains beyond Jupiter Well to the west, Lake Mackay to the north and the Walter James Range to the south. For countless generations, this had been Pintupi country, and while they remained upon it they were of course anything but 'lost'. But they were cut off from their relatives and countrymen by the vast expanse of uninhabited territory that now stretched between them and the settlements in the east. And, after eight years of drought conditions, Papunya, with food and water laid on, may have sounded like a nice place – for a visit. For the young men, it was like the adventures of Nosepeg and Charlie Tarawa in the 1930s and 1940s[1] all over again. The older people were reportedly less eager to experience the white men's world, but perhaps they knew in their hearts that there were not enough people left in the desert now to meet the needs of their social order. Initiations and suitable marriage partners were becoming more and more of a problem.

While the reasons for the Pintupi exodus are probably unknowable forty years after the event, Pintupi comments confirm both that they were the helpless victims of interfering whites and that they went willingly, rushing 'like perishing bullocks to water'.[2] In *The Flaming Desert*, botanist Peter Latz puts forward the intriguing suggestion that, even without the drought, rapid ecological change to their lands might have meant the Pintupi were living a very hard life on their country, much harder than their ancestors had:

> Early on, when I first went out to some of the harshest areas of these deserts, I was amazed at the location of many of their native wells. How did they know to dig for water just there, I wondered, one particular spot of many possible ones, in this seemingly god-forsaken bit of country. The answer, I now realise, is pretty straightforward. Sometime in the past, many of the well sites were waterholes, which have since been covered by sand. And of course this sand is now occupying vast areas, which in the past supported a much more varied and richer population of plants and animals (including plenty of kangaroos).[3]

Perhaps a comment[4] from Jeremy Long, that the Pintupi had no means of making an informed judgment about the course of action they were embarking upon, is most apposite. What is certain is that the departure from their lands of some of the last Pintupi people still living in the Gibson Desert and their subsequent arrival in Papunya between 1962 and 1966 was a crucial factor in the emergence of the painting movement in 1971.

The Pintupi patrols

In July 1957, a cavalcade of vehicles laden with fuel, water, food and expertise headed west from Mt Doreen station under the leadership of Ted Evans, the Chief Welfare Officer of the Northern Territory, accompanied by Jeremy Long, then a cadet patrol officer. This was the first Welfare Branch patrol to the Pintupi lands: appointment of patrol officers had been government policy since the war years, but resources had been lacking – perhaps because their function of mediating contacts between Aboriginal people living on their lands and settler culture was basically inconsistent with the centralising aims of the government settlements.

The area in which the first 1957 patrol sought to make contact with previously uncontacted Pintupi people was not a Welfare Branch responsibility at the time, but concerns had been expressed about the condition in which the 1956 Pintupi immigrants had arrived at Haasts Bluff[5] and it had been reported that some Pintupi people were using the bores along the western fringes of Mt Doreen station because their own lands were in the grip of drought. However, like most political about-faces, this solicitous intervention in the lives of the inhabitants of the western lands was sparked by a media furore. Young Rupert Murdoch, then owner of the *Adelaide News*, had debunked a Western Australian Parliamentary report on 'starving natives' on the reserves in neighbouring Western Australia,[6] stirring up a storm of public protest and concern that made nervous bureaucrats in Darwin suddenly keen to satisfy themselves about the wellbeing of the people on the Northern Territory side of the border in light of the ongoing rocket testing out of Woomera.

With the help of their Pintupi guides,[7] the party located a total of forty-four people in the vicinity of Lake Mackay, about half of whom had had no previous contact with Europeans. All those contacted by the patrol were judged to be in good health, with adequate food and plenty of water following the heavy rains which had replenished their dwindling supplies during the party's month-long journey. The pastoral or mining potential of the regions traversed being judged 'almost negligible' by the experts accompanying the patrol, the Welfare Branch officers recommended that the area should be declared a reserve. The Branch would then be responsible for control and supervision of any further contact between these people and the outside world. For this purpose annual patrols to the Lake Mackay area were also recommended.

In late October 1957, another Welfare Branch patrol led by Jeremy Long, with earlier Pintupi immigrants Nosepeg Tjupurrula and Tapatapa Tjangala as guides, set out from Haasts Bluff, this time to the Kintore Ranges, 20 kilometres inside the Western Australian border, in order 'to ascertain the number and condition of the Pintupi inhabitants'[8] in that region. This was the patrol which took Timmy Payungka Tjapangati[9] back to Haasts Bluff to visit his mother. He was taken on as a guide to lead the party to Yumari, thereby circumventing the officers' instructions that there were to be 'no lifts' provided back to the settlements. However, this may not have been the message communicated by their Aboriginal guides, who may have encouraged the people to come in, apparently believing that this was what was expected of them. Jeremy Long's report to the Welfare Branch reiterated the need for extension of reserve lands to protect their remaining inhabitants from 'unhelpful contacts' and noted that they appeared well able to support themselves, though 'they are gratified to have the Government take an interest in them'. He also recommended the sinking of bores in Pintupi country to provide a reliable water supply, concluding that:

> such improvements will serve not merely the 200 or so that are nomadic in the area now but also the Pintupi who make up the bulk of the population of Haasts Bluff. Though a generation is growing up that has no first hand knowledge of the Pintupi tribal lands, the adults do not like living at the settlement and are keen to return to their own country if the Administration would assist them to live there and develop it.[10]

In September 1959, the recommended enlargements to the reserve area were declared, but the hopes of the Pintupi (first raised by the Aboriginal evangelists in the 1930s), that facilities like those they had heard about at Haasts Bluff would one day be provided for them on their own lands, would not be realised for another generation.

The Northern Territory Administration promulgated a policy of non-interference with the Pintupi, while another Commonwealth authority, the Weapons Research Establishment (WRE), constructed more roads through their territories, along which more families were soon 'footwalking' their way to the government settlements in the east. The newest and finest of these was Papunya, built in the late 1950s with local Aboriginal labour to accommodate more than four hundred people who were trucked across from Haasts Bluff in 1959. Several more patrols went out along the new roads into the Pintupi heartlands with the objective of making contact with any remaining residents. The July 1962 patrol brought Yala Yala Gibbs and his family back to Papunya with them so that his young son Mawitji (Morris) could receive treatment for burns, but apart from medical evacuations, non-interference remained the rule. To Jeremy Long, however, it seemed that 'most, if not all, of these people intended to move in to Papunya'.[11] One man, John Tjakamarra, was so upset when his request for a lift was refused that he angrily hurled a stick at the side of the car as they drove away. Looking back, they could see the group moving behind them in the direction of Papunya.

Yala Yala Gibbs, who had been returned to the desert after his son's health improved, was among a group of Pintupi who walked into Papunya in July 1963. So were his pregnant wife Nyingura Napurrula and their son Morris and George Tjungurrayi's sister Nancy Nungurrayi. Freddy West Tjakamarra met a mapping party in 1961 and then a Welfare Branch patrol in 1962, and arrived in Papunya with his two wives and two children in August 1963 after walking east as far as Wili rockhole and getting a lift in from the manager of the Haasts Bluff cattle station. A number of the people who walked in to Papunya between 1962 and 1963 were ferried back to their country by Welfare Branch and WRE patrols – or returned the same way they had come. But they went only to gather up their relatives and begin the long march back east.

Anticipating their intentions, and remembering the state of the 1956 arrivals at Haasts Bluff, approval was granted for a Welfare Branch–WRE–Western Australian Department of Native Affairs patrol. In April 1964 Welfare Branch and WRE officers brought forty-two people into Papunya, including Kenny Williams' mother Ngata Nungurrayi, Yumbuluru (Yumpululu) Tjungurrayi, Yanatjari (Anatjari No. 1)

Tjampitjinpa and Kayi Kayi Napangati, all of whom had been contacted by the 1962 patrol. John Tjakamarra reached Papunya in another WRE vehicle just before the truck bearing his countrymen and women. Another patrol in August 1964 collected more people, who were reportedly camped as close to the sides of the road as the dry conditions would permit, in expectation of the trucks that would carry them to Papunya. Anatjari ('No. 3') Tjakamarra was among a group of seventeen people who walked out to the road from west of Lake Macdonald and were picked up by a WRE patrol officer and brought into Papunya in July 1966. This brought to 160 the number of Pintupi immigrants since 1956, among whom were many of the founders (and some later famous names) of the Papunya Tula Artists company.

The 'Untouchables'

Initially, the problems of adjustment to settlement life proved almost insurmountable for many of the new arrivals from the west. Nothing was as they might have imagined it when they set out on their epic journey. The plentiful supplies of whitefella food they had been led to expect could only be accessed in the communal dining room, which at Papunya and all other government settlements had replaced the old 'copper' and ration store system[12] that had operated at Haasts Bluff. Meals were served on plates, to be eaten with knives and forks, under the supervision of white staff charged with 'encouraging the adoption of table manners as well as European foods'. The settlement manager had the job of guarding the door to stop people, with plates of food stuffed down their dresses or dripping out from under hats, trying to take food back to their camps.[13] People ignored tables and chairs and squatted on the floor in the old way, trying to eat the stew served up to them. According to Jeremy Long, who led the April 1964 patrol that had ferried forty-two people into the settlement, it was 'a disaster': 'They were shoved into the kitchen eating stew – there's no escaping the horror of the dining room'.[14]

The system was finally abandoned in 1969 when the Training Allowance Scheme was introduced and a cash store opened to enable residents to have at least some measure of independence in the conduct of their daily lives. The institutionalisation must have been excruciating for people whose previous lifestyle had given them a rare measure of personal autonomy within their own strict laws. The ridicule of the rest of the settlement population, Aboriginal and non-Aboriginal alike, must also have been hard to bear. A District Welfare Officer sent to Papunya to observe the situation in 1964 reported that the Pintupi 'appear to be despised by the majority of Papunya people who openly laugh at them and "rubbish" them rather than making any attempt to help them'.[15] Laurie Owens, Papunya Superintendent from July or August 1971, described them as the settlement's 'Untouchables'.[16]

Then there was 'work'. Under the 1953–57 Welfare Ordinance, whose introduction Director of Welfare Harry Giese regarded as an important step in implementing the government's assimilation program, 'Aborigines have to be trained in the first instance to work, and then to recognise traditional European incentives to do so'.[17] Arnold Probin arrived in Papunya in 1960, about six months after the settlement opened, to take up the position of Farm Manager. He stayed on as Settlement Manager till 1973, with the task of putting the able-bodied Aboriginal men to work as a condition of receiving food from the settlement's communal kitchen and dining room. He had nearly two hundred men to occupy until lunchtime – once the food was served, people declined to work for the rest of the day. The various farm projects Probin supervised over the years included raising donkeys, a piggery, citrus gardens, vegetable gardens and turkeys. The New Pintupi, whom Probin referred to as the 'strays … collected up' every winter by Jeremy Long's Welfare Branch patrols out west, presented particular problems. According to Probin, 'they had no idea'.[18] He recalls giving people a branch to drag back and forth, and men wheeling wheelbarrows upside down. Any job would do – learning to labour rather than useful work was the object of the exercise. They were allocated to outdoor work – mostly as farmworkers, though some less volatile individuals were assigned to tending the grounds of the Papunya School and other settlement buildings.

In response to the Pintupi's difficulties, Harry Giese announced plans in May 1964 for 'a chain of bores west of Papunya (which) will assist the newcomers to move back and forth from their "countries" as they wish'.[19] But the institutionalised eating arrangements, which he himself had introduced, could not accommodate groups who wanted to live outside Papunya. With increasing desperation, the Pintupi continued to request it. But thirteen investigational drillings in the Ehrenberg Ranges failed to find suitable water and plans to allow the Pintupi to camp at some distance from Papunya in the direction of their country did not bear fruit until the late 1960s. In 1968 two hundred Pintupi people moved to Waruwiya bore, 56 kilometres to the west, but inside a year the group returned to Papunya because of problems with the water supply and an ominous spate of accidents. In 1970 another outstation with a special school for the Pintupi children was established at Alumbara bore, 15 kilometres west of Papunya. The population expanded rapidly to three hundred, but an incident in which the Pintupi residents fought white staff and police reinforcements to prevent the arrest of a youth accused of theft curtailed this experiment also. They later told the court that they were afraid the boy would be shot, since one of the staff had threatened to use the rifle he carried. The Pintupi were summarily trucked back to the main settlement, and the following year Papunya's police station, the first on an Aboriginal settlement in the Northern Territory, was opened at a cost of $125 000 – denying the Aboriginal residents access to a sacred tree connected to the Papunya Honey Ant Dreaming which was enclosed within the barbed wire compound.

So, for the entire eighteen months that Geoffrey Bardon was in Papunya, from January 1971 to July 1972, so were all the Pintupi. By June 1973 they were gone again, to Yai Yai, 40 kilometres west of Papunya. Had they not been at Papunya, the dynamics of the painting group would have been radically different. To the mix of ex-stockmen, traditional Kukatja landholders of the Papunya area, and their long-lost countrymen the Old Pintupi, some of whom had lived their whole lives in the area of Haasts Bluff, the 'wild Pintupi' brought an acute longing for the country for which those accustomed to settlement life also pined. Pastor Albrecht, from the Hermannsburg mission, tells an illuminating tale about a young man who accompanied the first evangelical patrol to the western lands in 1931:

> The night before we reached Meranano's home area, we had a rather peculiar experience. Sitting around the camp fire at night, Meranano got up and walked away from us. Then we heard in a plaintive voice: 'Pikilli, Pikilli' repeated many times. After a while the young man returned to our camp with a painful expression on his face. He had been overcome by sheer homesickness, now that we had come so close to his 'home'.[20]

Having made the journey across the vast expanse of uninhabited territory that stretched between their homelands and the settlements to the east, the Pintupi then grieved for their homelands. Painting offered them not only an escape from the daily humiliations of life at Papunya as the wild Pintupi, but also a way of channelling this 'worry for country' into paintings about the stories and ceremonies that bound them to it. In the process, they became artists. As Arnold Probin said: 'All my gardeners turned into artists. I couldn't believe it!'[21]

The third consignment

The third consignment that Geoffrey Bardon took to the Stuart Art Centre consisted of forty-one works, with paintings by Walter Tjampitjinpa, Mick Wallankarri Tjakamarra, Johnny Warangkula and Mick Namarari of the old settlement office crew and by Charlie Tarawa, Tim Payungka and Uta Uta Tjangala. It also marked the first appearance on Pat Hogan's stocklists of members of the New Pintupi group.

The first painting in the consignment was by Anatjari 'No. 3' Tjakamarra,[22] who was working alongside Uta Uta Tjangala as one of the Papunya School gardeners at the time when the painting movement began. It is a network of circles and connecting lines and quite unlike the works considered so far in this account. The annotation supplied with the painting when it was purchased from the Stuart Art Centre by the Museums and Art Galleries of the Northern Territory explains that it is an account of 'a journey somewhere in Western Australia past waterholes and camp sites' and 'a map, without any representational details' which must be filled in by 'each man ... actually tell[ing] the story himself'. Perhaps Anatjari was thinking when he painted it of pre-contact times and his travels over immense distances with his brother Tjampu, which took them as far north as the Pollock Hills and as far north-east as the Kintore Ranges. Or perhaps he was thinking of the journey which had brought him to Papunya just five years earlier. Anatjari Tjakamarra was among the last people to leave the Pintupi homelands, in the group of seventeen whose long march from the remote south-west corner of Pintupi territory ended beside the road where they were picked up and transported into Papunya. The line which cuts through the centre of the painting could be that road, cutting though the heartlands of the artist's country.

According to Dick Kimber, the key influences on Anatjari's work were 'to do with secret-sacred men's activities, highly demanding, prolonged over several years, and only also endured and carried out by two other middle-aged Pintupi men at the time – and, as far as I know, by no-one else since then'.[23] This 'ritually very correct, conservative man, with a great concern for country' went on to become 'the most precise of all Pintupi, indeed all Papunya Tula, artists in the mid '70s',[24] but as yet there is not much sign of this. In both composition and execution, this work – perhaps his first – is very like a painting by his close kinsman and countryman, John Tjakamarra, reproduced in Geoffrey Bardon's *Aboriginal Art of the Western Desert* under the title *Man's Corroboree* as an example of 'an early work painted on my verandah when the men were just starting to show me what they could do, and it has a wonderful strength through simplicity'.[25]

Bardon characterised John Tjakamarra's painting as 'concentric circles connected by a linear maze' – a description equally applicable to Anatjari's, and to the works of the six other New Pintupi artists included in the third consignment: 'Tommy No. 4', 'Ronnie', 'Darkie', Anatjari No. 1, Charlie

Tjakamarra, and George Tjapaltjarri. None of these last four names appears again in the Stuart Art Centre consignment lists. To judge from their works, which were all included in the 1972 Darwin purchase, they were no less accomplished than the artists who did continue painting in this very early period. All except the mysterious Darkie later appeared on the books of Papunya Tula Artists. Collectively they define another distinctive group style that emerged in the time before the artists came together in Bardon's Great Painting Room. Though it temporarily vanished when the painters moved soon afterwards to a communal working space, it re-emerged in classic forms in the Pintupi large grid-and-circle canvases of the late 1970s and early 1980s when these artists were painting regularly for Papunya Tula Artists. Anatjari (No. 1) Tjampitjinpa was one of the company's most consistent painters in this style until his death in 1999.

Ronnie Tjampitjinpa emerged in the 1980s as one of Papunya Tula's leading artists, pioneering a new style of bold, scaled-up linearity in Kintore men's[26] painting and was hailed by some as the 'King of Kintore', but he was a shy young man in his late twenties when he painted the three entries for 'Ronnie' in the third consignment stocklist.[27] Bardon does not mention George (Nyunmul-nga) Tjapaltjarri (these days better known as 'Dr George'), who would have been in his early thirties when he painted the third consignment work that bears his name, his only contribution to the early Papunya boards. Tjapaltjarri remembers that he started out helping the old men in West Camp – the name given to the Pintupi camps on the western side of the settlement in the direction of Pintupi country. He struck Jeremy Long as a 'youngish bachelor, very lively and extroverted ... the sort of person who was really keen to see the world' when Long brought him into

Papunya from the desert in 1964. Perhaps Tjapaltjarri was too busy seeing the world or qualifying as a 'ngangkari' (Aboriginal doctor or 'clever man') – or both – to settle into being an artist at this early stage of his life. He returned to painting only later in the history of the movement.

Bardon did remember Tommy No. 4, but only as a young man who occasionally painted with the group. It seems he was referring to Dr George's older brother, Tommy Lowry Tjapaltjarri, who, though he painted for Papunya Tula Artists during the 1980s until his death in 1987, created less than a dozen works in the seminal Papunya period. His *Water Story*[28] painting acquired by the Darwin Museum as part of the 1972 purchase is a sophisticated and idiosyncratic variant of the circle-and-line mazes of his compatriots. Charlie (Ward) Tjakamarra, who was probably about the same age as Tommy Lowry, arrived in Papunya from the desert in September 1964, brought in by one of the WRE patrols. He subsequently moved west to Balgo in the Great Sandy Desert, a community notorious in those days for its disapproval of the Papunya painting movement, and did not resume painting till he moved to the Papunya Tula–serviced community of Kiwirrkura, in the mid-1980s. The presence of these younger men in the group, though it was short-lived or intermittent, contradicts the widespread assumption that all those painting at Papunya in 1971 were old men.

Darkie Tjapaltjarri was not a young Pintupi man, but an old Warlpiri one, though he had a reputation for wildness and never wore European trousers. But he died in 1968 and the works attributed to him in the third consignment are almost certainly by his son-in-law Turkey Tolson.[29] Though his name does not appear anywhere in the Stuart Art Centre consignment lists, Turkey repeatedly affirmed his participation in the early years of the painting movement. For example, in the interview he did for the *Papunya Tula: Genesis and Genius* catalogue, he said that he had first painted for Bardon 'little ones, boards. Not canvas, boards. Couldn't try making big ones. I'd make all the rubbish ones.'[30] In 1971 Turkey Tolson would have been in his twenties. He was a leading exponent throughout the late 1970s and 1980s of the classic Pintupi grids of circles and connecting lines. These two third-consignment works would thus be his first paintings, and the only ones he painted so early in the movement. Why would he have produced just these few paintings and then have stopped? Perhaps the increasingly controversial subject matter of the paintings after the third consignment made him hesitate. Decades later he spoke to me in tones of strong condemnation of this next phase of the painting movement.[31]

One of the most remarkable paintings in the third consignment is by Charlie Tarawa Tjungurrayi, whose loquacity alone made him stand out among his perennially silent Pintupi countrymen. But as this painting shows, his artistic vision even at this early stage of the movement was also very distinctive. Sotheby's gave it the title *Fear* when it was auctioned in its 2001 Aboriginal Art sale. According to the annotation, the red cruciform shape at the bottom of the painting is the 'fright' one feels when the spirits of the dead appear. Few other works address the emotional dimension of a Dreaming narrative so directly. The star-shaped motifs are the 'spirit fingers of the dead'. Alternating bands of black and white through the centre of the painting are the icy winds which are the breath of the spirits of the dead ('Kurumbas'). As senior custodian of the site of Tjitururrnga depicted in *Fear*, Charlie Tarawa had the authority to be expansive about its esoteric meanings. Towards the end of his painting career, he created a small number of white impasto-style paintings to which he apparently 'attributed exceptional importance',[32] in which the application of thick white paint with the look of the white pipe clay used in the ceremonial context is very similar to *Fear.* This kind of thick, loose, impasto brushwork is rarely found in early Papunya works. Charlie Tarawa's re-invention of this technique in the late 1980s was subsequently taken up by several senior Papunya Tula painters.[33] *Fear* prefigures both this influential development in Charlie Tarawa's later style and the widespread adoption of its technique of 'atechnical' linework that has become one of Papunya Tula Artists' trademark styles since the 1990s.

Mysteries of the fourth consignment

The great storm centre of Kalipinypa was responsive to the artists' evocation of its power in many of their paintings. The summer of 1971–72 was one of the wettest on record with water flowing in 'rivers up to 30 kilometres wide' where usually only scattered waterholes and dry creekbeds were to be found. As Bardon commented: 'The Water Dreaming was the first convincing theme and apparent obsession in the Papunya movement'.[34] Such compelling evidence of the efficaciousness of the painting men's work would soon inspire weightier subject matter. But its first effect was to prevent the paintings getting out. Hogan reported in her *Dot and Circle* article that the fourth consignment of paintings to the Stuart Art Centre 'did not arrive owing to the rain'.[35] Or did it?

Although the lack of a separate listing in the Stuart Art Centre stockbook might suggest otherwise, the fourth consignment did arrive. As Hogan explained in her *Dot and Circle* listing of the consignments, 'one must accept that Consignment 5 contains both 4 and 5. This is important to realise as it makes some paintings in lot 5 earlier than others.'[36] According to her *Dot and Circle* inventory, the thirty-six identified paintings in this consignment were the work of just four artists: Charlie Tarawa Tjungurrayi, Long Jack Phillipus Tjakamarra, Uta Uta Tjangala and Walter Tjampitjinpa. Another twelve were 'unidentified'. However, when we examine the list of the fifth consignment paintings in the Stuart Art Centre stockbook – from which it has thus far been assumed that Pat Hogan's consignment summaries were compiled, it contains *ninety-four* paintings, which are attributed to *eleven* different artists.[37] The seven artists whose names do *not* appear in Hogan's *Dot and Circle* summary of the fifth consignment are Kaapa, Johnny Warangkula, Mick Namarari, Anatjari Tjakamarra, Tim Payungka and Billy Stockman – all artists who had already figured in the first three consignment lists – plus one name not so far seen in this account, that of 'Timmy Japaljarri Madgera'.

The simplest explanation of the discrepancy between these two different versions of the fifth consignment is that the *Dot and Circle* summary refers to the original fifth consignment before its amalgamation with the fourth. But quite a few questions remain unanswered. What source *did* Hogan use to compile her *Dot and Circle* summaries of the consignments if not the Stuart Art Centre stockbook? And what happened to the twelve 'unidentified' works referred to in the *Dot and Circle* account of the original fifth consignment? And why were so many paintings labelled 'unidentified'? There was nothing like this in the first three consignment lists, and there is nothing comparable to it again until the eighteenth consignment. What happened at the time of the fourth and fifth consignments that so many paintings seem to have arrived at the Stuart Art Centre without markings or identification? And how did the paintings finally reach the Stuart Art Centre?

The answer to this last question for at least one painting is provided by a diagram[38] in one of Hogan's sketchbooks in the Stuart Art Centre Archive which identifies a painting by 'Timmy Leura' to which Hogan gave the title *Wild Peanut Story* as the twelfth painting of the fourth consignment. The design appears to be an Anmatyerr variant of the Pintupi site network and at the bottom of the page is written 'Brought to Gallery by Tim'. *Wild Peanut Story* may not survive, but other paintings have turned up with fourth consignment stock numbers, raising questions like: Why the *twelfth* painting? Had eleven other paintings already been brought into the gallery by 'Timmy Leura' and other artists? Or were they part of a load which Jack Cooke recalls Nosepeg Tjupurrula taking into town one time with 'all these paintings thrown on the back of a Toyota with swags, dogs, families'?[39] Or was Hogan working to a list generated in Papunya when the fourth consignment was originally assembled?

We'll never know, but the most intriguing mystery of the fourth/fifth consignment is soluble from the evidence of the extant paintings: its inclusion of Timmy Madgera Japaljarri (that is, Tim Leura Tjapaltjarri). From Hogan's reference to him as 'Timmy Leura' on the *Peanut Story* painting annotation, it seems that she knew who he was. But did Bardon, according to whose account Tim Leura did not join the painting group until February 1972? Could Bardon have confused the artist's name with his language group ('Madgera/Mangera' could be an attempt at a phonetic rendering of 'Anmatyerr') and not realised that the man he met in February 1972 had been a member of the painting group for several months? Or perhaps he wasn't, but was following the practice of the School of Kaapa and working independently, bringing his paintings into the Stuart Art Centre himself to sell? Four paintings by Tim Leura Tjapaltjarri which have surfaced with fifth consignment stock numbers, all of them originally part of the fourth consignment, go some way towards answering these questions.

In *Yam Story (Nighttime)* by Tim Leura,[40] four ovoid shapes with markings so delicate as to be almost imperceptible are arranged diagonally around the central concentric circle. Four 'ceremonial sticks', greatly simplified and stylised, radiate out from the centre between them. A series of small oval shapes at opposite corners of the painting are pieces of snake ready to be eaten at the ceremony. Yam plants represented by concentric circles, with realistic leaves and branches, are also shown against a velvety black background dotted with yam flower 'stars' and denoting the night sky against which ceremonies are held. It was suggested earlier that dark backgrounds might have been a solution to problems of coverage with lighter colours experienced by the School of Kaapa painters due to shortage of materials, but they are also an implicit reference to the spiritual realm, the 'night-time' of the painting's title, to which the ceremonies belong. A similar fifth consignment painting by Tim Leura, *Rainmaker Bird Story*, sold at Sotheby's June 1998 Important Aboriginal Art auction, is also small and painted with skill and care rather than painterly finesse. Sotheby's assertion that *Rainmaker Bird Story* is one of Tim Leura's very first paintings seems equally applicable to *Yam Story (Nighttime)*.

Two other paintings by Tim Leura from the fifth consignment present a dramatic contrast in terms of both composition and execution to these two exquisitely understated works. *Story of Young Men after Initiation* was presented to the Araluen Arts Centre in 1991 through the Alice Springs Town Council by Jock Nelson, Mayor of Alice Springs from 1971 to 1973. *Children's Ceremonial Snake Dreaming* was purchased from the Pat Hogan Collection by the National Gallery of Victoria in the late 1980s. Both are beautifully detailed depictions of scenes from the ceremonial life. *Children's Ceremonial Snake Dreaming* in which 'two totemic ancestors' are represented both by the U-shapes depicting their seated figures at the head of their sacred boards, and as realistic figures in bodypaint who appear to be looking up at the viewer from the ceremonial ground, is particularly dramatic. Both these paintings are uniquely Tim Leura's – but also unmistakably in the lineage of the School of Kaapa.

From the evidence of these four paintings, it appears that when Tim Leura joined the group of painters working with Bardon, he continued painting in the earlier style while simultaneously coming under the influence of the artistic discoveries of the other painting men, perhaps in those works produced under Bardon's eye. Since Tim Leura does not seem to have been personally acquainted with Bardon at this point, Kaapa himself may have passed on to his younger cousin the reservations which the helpful school teacher held about certain aspects of the School of Kaapa style. But *Tim Leura came into the group at a different moment from Kaapa* – a moment which followed the ritually weighty preoccupations of the medicine painting phase reflected in the works of the second consignment and also included the experience of working alongside the otherwise outcast New Pintupi. Formerly cloistered at Bardon's flat, the evidence of the paintings points to the Pintupi men now having taken their places alongside the Anmatyerr ex-stockmen, Old Pintupi and local Kukatja landholders in the luminal space of the Great Painting Room. In *Yam Story (Nighttime)* and *Rainmaker Bird Story* – smaller, superficially less ambitious works – instead of attempting to depict the ceremony using European-style figuration, Tim Leura encodes its meaning and regalia through a process of abstraction and stylisation to create a 'wholly Indigenous' way of representing the ritual life of initiated men. The peoples of the Western Desert believe that their ancestors reside in their designs, at least when activated by the appropriate songs. The painters apparently incanted these as they worked on the creation of what was essentially *a religious object*, a new way within their own culture, of representing the sacred. These were some of the first tentative steps along a dangerous new path in the Papunya painters' artistic journey.

4

The Problem of Secrecy

Thirty early Papunya boards accessioned by the Museums and Art Galleries of the Northern Territory on 5 July 1974[1] are of particular interest to this story. These paintings made up an exhibition organised by the Department of the Interior called *Wailbri and Pintubi Art: An Exhibition of Traditional Aboriginal Art from the Wailbri and Pintubi Tribes of Central Australia*, which opened its national tour[2] at Farmer's Blaxland Gallery in Sydney on 20 September 1972. *Wailbri and Pintubi Art* was not the first exhibition of early Papunya paintings. Geoffrey Bardon and Tim Leura Tjapaltjarri had travelled to Sydney in the 1972 May school holidays and put up a selling exhibition of between twenty and thirty works on the first floor of David Jones' George Street department store. That was the first commercial exhibition of Papunya paintings, but the paintings in *Wailbri and Pintubi Art* were painted quite some time before them. Twenty-six of the paintings were from the fifth consignment to the Stuart Art Centre, which according to the chronology established so far dates them from late 1971.[3] The visual evidence indicates that this consignment may have been the first whose contents emanated from the

Great Painting Room. We do not know what became of the paintings in the David Jones' selling exhibition or (with one or two exceptions) what they looked like. But we do know what the paintings in *Wailbri and Pintubi Art* were and where they are. Every single one.[4]

For two years, those thirty paintings toured venues around Australia, eventually arriving back in Central Australia in late August of 1974, at the Residency Art Gallery in Parsons Street in the centre of Alice Springs. The exhibition's opening at the Residency brought some of the earliest Papunya paintings for the first time into wide public exposure in Alice Springs. The result was explosive to say the least. Rocks and spears were thrown at the building by incensed tribesmen. Under a page 2 headline – 'Sacred paintings cause closure' – the *Centralian Advocate* reported on 5 September 1974 that an exhibition of 'Pintubi art' that had opened at the Residency Museum and Art Gallery the previous Wednesday had been closed by the weekend, and replaced with a display of Arrente watercolour landscapes. The closure followed the discovery that many of the paintings in the exhibition 'were sacred to the Aborigines and considered "taboo" to women and children'. Residency curator Mr Keith Williams had informed the *Advocate* that the Museum and Art Gallery was aware that 'six or seven' paintings were considered sacred, but had believed that this significance 'had worn out'. However, when it was realised that 'many elders still respected the significance of the paintings, it was decided they should be removed'. The decision to close the exhibition had been made by Dr Colin Jack-Hinton, Director of the Museums and Art Galleries of the Northern Territory.

Mr Roy Monks of the government-funded Centre for Aboriginal Artists and Craftsmen in Alice Springs had told the *Advocate* that the paintings depicted items and events including tjurungas (sacred objects), ritual killings and ceremonial headdresses, which although familiar to Aboriginal men, should never be seen by women or children. According to Monks, there had been complaints from Aboriginal women who had attended the exhibition in Canberra that the paintings were 'offensive' to women. In his opinion, a 'dangerous' situation could develop if they were viewed by those not entitled under Aboriginal law to do so. If a young uninitiated man saw these depictions, 'physical harm' could result. It was Monks' view that the painters had not intended when they painted these things that women and children should see them.

The shutting down of the exhibition just days after it had opened sent shockwaves through the then small world of desert art. Ever since they were removed from the walls of the Residency, those thirty paintings have resided on the storage racks of the Museum and Art Gallery of the Northern Territory in Darwin, along with another 170 works from 1971 and 1972 that this institution's far-sighted inaugural Director also acquired around the time of their creation – about a decade before any other public collecting institution in Australia (or anywhere else) began purchasing Papunya paintings, and more than twenty-five years before most of them began acquiring early Papunya boards – at hundreds and thousands of times their original prices.

The disturbance at the Residency is widely credited in the literature with causing the Papunya painters to censor overt depictions of secret/sacred materials in their work, replacing them with the all-over dotted backgrounds that became the hallmark of Papunya painting for the next quarter of a century. This is only partially true. An earlier public disturbance over an Aboriginal art display at the 1972 Yuendumu sports weekend may also have triggered modifications in the painters' symbolism and subject matter. Moreover, as we saw in chapter 2, the paintings comprising the first consignment to come out of Papunya from the group around Geoffrey Bardon were uncontroversial in style, so the painters were not so much inventing a completely new style of painting as reverting to their original uncontentious one. Nevertheless, the Residency incident is a key public episode in the local history of the Papunya painting movement, on a par with Kaapa Tjampitjinpa's win in the Caltex/Northern Territory Art Award in August 1971, and the question of why those particular paintings should have been so offensive to Aboriginal eyes repays closer scrutiny.

The book I set out to write on the early Papunya boards almost a decade ago took inspiration from the auction houses' ever closer attention to provenance and particularly to the Stuart Art Centre consignment numbers on the backs of many of the early paintings. I had the idea of using these numbers to sort the early boards into chronological order and from this produce a scholarly analysis of the artistic development of the founding Papunya Tula artists. To this end, I assembled a database of over one thousand early Papunya boards, gathered from public galleries and museums, auction catalogues and private collections. Although chapter 3 concludes with a discussion of Tim Leura's *Yam Story (Nighttime)* from the mysterious fourth consignment as the creation of 'what is essentially a religious object', or at least 'a new way of representing the sacred', I did not yet see this finding as the starting point for the story which will unfold in the rest of this book. Up to this point, I was systematically examining the consignments in chronological order. Chapter 4 opens with the paintings in *Wailbri and Pintubi Art* because they almost all came from the next consignment after the ones I had already considered. Conversely, most of the extant paintings identified as being from the fifth consignment happened to have been in this exhibition.

However, once I started to explore some of the questions which the so-called Residency incident involving these paintings suggested to me – questions like what was it about those particular paintings that made them so offensive to Aboriginal eyes? – I came face to face with a burning issue. I had known for a long time about the problem of secrecy with the early boards and had referred to the Residency incident in numerous catalogue essays I had written about the painting movement, but I had never actually confronted its implications before in my own work. Over the twenty years of my ongoing relationships with the Papunya Tula artists thus far (from 1980 to 2000), the early Papunya boards had been quite simply out of sight and mind. Not only for me, but for the painters themselves, and for the emerging audiences for contemporary desert acrylic paintings. But now I began to ask myself whether it was proper, from the perspective of the artists and their culture, for a white woman to be looking at the kind of paintings that had caused the 1974 disturbance – much less publishing images of them in a book. It took me a long time to find the answers to these questions and longer still to be able to live with them. In the meantime – in part because of the expertise I had developed through building and populating my database – I found myself caught up in the processes by which the destiny of the early Papunya boards was even then being decided. For years I wrestled with the issues, finally deciding to change direction and to write about the recent history of the early Papunya boards, a history in which I was now implicated, however powerlessly. My purpose was no longer a stylistic analysis of the early painting boards but to wrest the boards back from their emergent status as aesthetic objects of desire and icons of the cool half-million into the realm of cultural values and historical significance.

But before moving on to these more contemporary events, let's return to the *Wailbri and Pintubi Art* exhibition and its significance for this story. It revolves not only around the issue of secrecy – which was there well before the Residency incident, but also around what was happening in Papunya when the early boards were created.

'One hurrying European with no anthropology'[5]

Geoffrey Bardon's first encounter with the problem of secrecy – of the men painting things that should not be exposed to public display – came at the very beginning of his story. The Honey Ant Mural at Papunya School with which the painting movement began in his account faced onto the school playground where its exposure to women and children was clearly inescapable. Despite the negotiations with local elders that had gone on beforehand, there were still issues about whether the painters had breached rules of disclosure. The realistic whitefella image of a honey ant which Geoffrey Bardon famously requested Kaapa change to 'blackfella' honey ants had itself replaced the 'hooks' and 'double hooks' of an earlier version after unnamed tribal authorities had declared the mural in its original form 'unsafe'. As Bardon describes the incident in his 2004 book, the photographing of three schoolgirls in front of the first version of the mural ('with no danger really to anybody'[6]) sparked off the controversy:

'This changed quite soon, and within days; somehow, the Ceremonial Men or Women did not think that the mural was safe and were not happy with it; it was reorganised showing a European ant, quite clearly, and also the profile of a European bird'.[7] In the third and final version of the mural, the whitefella elements of the European honey ant and bird were replaced by paired U-shapes in black with an orange circle inside, which were apparently acceptable to everyone. In his 1991 account, Bardon did not mention the trouble over the first version, only the replacement of the whitefella elements by 'blackfella honey ants', when he described the mural's completion to the satisfaction of everyone as a seminal moment.

In retrospect, the significance of this moment lies not only in the replacement of a whitefella honey ant by a blackfella one, but also in the replacement of design elements that were unacceptable to the Ceremonial Men or Women because 'unsafe', with something that was both 'wholly Indigenous' and acceptable to those cultural authorities. In his 2004 book, Bardon explains that reaching such a compromise was his objective with the painting movement generally. In the first of several discussions in his last book on the problem of secrecy, recalling his 'insistence, even ... pleading' with the men to paint 'children's' stories rather than the 'powerful' stories, he says:

> I was seeking after a brotherhood and sisterhood of meanings, a making of peace between the controversial and the non-controversial among all four tribal groups but always, if possible, while seeking out and asking the painters for an intelligibility in what they did.[8]

These 'powerful stories' were a source of tension from the beginning. Because of them, Bardon says, 'there was always a feeling among the men that, as with the Honey Ant Mural, there could be unwelcome revelations, or tribal rivalry or discontent, even government complaints, because of what was shown'.[9] Perhaps it was, as Fred Myers has suggested, a 'creative tension',[10] but Bardon's attitude to the 'powerful' in their work was also a source of tension between him and the painters. They were, he says, 'aroused and concerned'[11] by his repeated requests to them not to paint anything secret.

Bardon first put forward the idea of 'painting specifically and in detail for the children'[12] in July 1971, when he requested from the painters 'children's stories' for use in his teaching and as a community collection. The men apparently approved of the idea of a collection of paintings for the school that would remain in the community and produced works that were suitable for this purpose, but continued also to produce works 'not for viewing by children'. Bardon says that up to December 1971 he was mesmerised by 'the great first climactic articulation of the painting men's creativity'[13] and focused on helping them to develop their own story representations to the exclusion of any whitefella influences, but also that:

> time and again I was uncertain about the rules of secrecy, men wishing to paint 'powerful' stories to please, though they were in no hurry for me to understand any inner meaning of the representations.[14]

In January 1972, before he returned to Papunya after the school holidays, Bardon went to see Jennifer Isaacs, the research officer in charge of Aboriginal arts for the Australia Council for the Arts. In her 'Epilogue: Encounters with Geoff Bardon' in Bardon's magnum opus, she recalls the moment when Bardon walked into her Sydney office with a group of boards 'covered in a finely painted but hitherto unknown hieroglyphic form of communication'.[15] She recognised immediately 'that the men were also showing in this new art form representations of bull-roarers, "tjurunga", and the webbed fibre structures which if shown to women could result in traditional punishment of a very severe kind. It was amazing art and also fraught with danger.'[16] Isaacs says she was unprepared for the 'furore' that erupted over the idea that the Australia Council for the Arts might support Bardon and the painters. 'People in Alice Springs and elsewhere ... cryptically suggested' that a 'painting fever' in Papunya could 'possibly end in loss of life, or at the very least, in Aboriginal behaviour that could not be controlled'.[17]

The source of these comments may have been Dick Kimber, who had first raised the idea that the paintings were 'potentially dangerous' after seeing Kaapa's work in the School of Kaapa style at the Caltex Art Award in August 1971. He was worried enough to write to his friend Bob Edwards, at that time Curator of Anthropology at the South Australian Museum but soon to be Director of the Aboriginal Arts Board of the Australia Council. Kimber also brought up his 'perceptions of the potential problems' with Geoffrey Bardon when they first met in late November or early December 1971. The conversation was an amicable one, with Kimber commenting as well on the art's appeal and helping Bardon with his application for assistance to the Australia Council. Kimber may also have been the source of Isaacs' startling suggestion concerning the real significance of many of Bardon's 'children's paintings': that they were 'devised by the men to in fact teach him Aboriginal law as one would a novice'.[18]

This does not apply to the second set of images of 'Children and Family Dreamings' that Bardon commissioned from the painters when he returned from his summer holidays.

They were exhibited in the Alice Springs Show in July 1972,[19] where Dick Kimber saw them and noted in his journal simply: 'Some absolutely excellent Pintupi paintings in the major art display', with no mention of any concerns about the paintings' content.[20] Bardon later used these paintings as the basis of both his films and his first books on the early years of painting at Papunya, so that he could not be reproached with placing contentious images in circulation through what he might later publish about the movement.

However, Isaacs' view is supported by Dick Kimber. Explaining the production of restricted imagery by the painters, he says that Bardon was 'clearly treated in many ways as a first-stage initiate, a *maliera*'.[21] If this was indeed the painters' intention, Bardon seems to have been completely oblivious to it. He 'considered these secrets unimpressive and of little consequence in the actual capacity for design, and … did not wish to know these secrets or the connected anthropology'.[22] However, the difficulties which he repeatedly acknowledges in verbal communication with the painters might have made even such a radical misunderstanding possible:

> I could not impart a sophisticated argument for or against the use of the material in a certain way, since for the most part my Pintupi was not up to it … and perhaps even with my interpreters my many requests [to paint uncontroversial material] simply did not get through.[23]

Both Isaacs and Kimber put forward other complementary explanations of why the men were doing paintings whose content seemed to make them so restricted for viewing. Kimber points out that the paintings were not, initially at least, for sale to the general public but for Bardon's own collection, and that as the school art teacher with an interest in traditional art, the painters almost certainly 'viewed him as requiring special instruction so that his teaching accorded with the community's desires'.[24] Isaacs suggests that:

> The men were also signalling their status and identity as much to each other as they were making statements to white people. They were … 'rattling spears', jockeying for position and status … The jockeying is hinted at in Geoff Bardon's account – for example, in the disapproval of Uta Uta's inclusion of sacred images by other artists not from his group.[25]

There may be truth in all these suggestions.

Another suggestion I find very plausible is that Geoffrey Bardon might inadvertently have *asked* the painters to produce works like these.[26] Because of his lack of the local languages, Bardon was forced to rely on a minimal vocabulary and the constant repetition of his desire for work that was 'strong' and 'real' may have unintentionally encouraged the very secret/sacred subjects he was so anxious for the painters to avoid. Perhaps his requests for the 'real' meant to the painters 'powerful' designs and content. His acknowledgment of the men 'wishing to paint "powerful" stories to please' seems to indicate that in this and other cross-culturally ambiguous terms like 'cheeky' (that is, 'dangerous') that he used in an attempt to communicate what he wanted from the painters, Bardon might not have been careful enough in what he wished for.

In one of his last statements about the problem of secrecy, Geoffrey Bardon says he has 'no doubt' that 'if what had been painted was unwelcome for the painters or anyone else that the paintings would not have been made'.[27] Papunya in his time was 'a truly violent place', and 'if the paintings had been so dangerous I feel that men would have been killed, yet I have no knowledge of this happening'.[28] Rather, the painters painted as they wished, 'I suppose because they had become free men in an otherwise brutal and degrading environment, free perhaps in a sense unknown to them before or since'.[29] Bardon's belief that the tribal authorities in Papunya must have sanctioned what was being painted but that at the same time a space of freedom had somehow opened up for the painters during his period in Papunya resonates with the only explanation I have heard from one of those directly involved: Long Jack Phillipus Tjakamarra's assertion that on the one hand 'They got a right' and on the other 'We didn't think'.[30]

Colliding cultures

From Geoffrey Bardon's point of view, the secrecy issue was perhaps the least of his problems during his time at Papunya. His tribulations with the settlement authorities because of his activities with the painting men easily preponderate over this issue in his various published accounts.

> I did not underestimate [the superintendent's] threat to prevent me selling the work. The Aboriginal culture, to my mind, was being terminated and this new achievement had to be brought to the attention of the nation. I was away by 5.30 [am] and I felt as though I was running guns through some kind of frontier or security force. I saw the ambitions of the superintendent and the racist police as provocative, and I sensed a certain danger in the whole enterprise.[31]

At first, it seems, everyone was happy with the final version of the Honey Ant Mural. Well not quite everyone. District Welfare Officer Jack Cooke called it 'eyebrow-raising' – but then, as his role in the 1971 Caltex Art Award showed, that was the way he liked things. Dick Kimber has described Cooke as 'one of the few people highly impressed by the art and its potential for sales that would assist Aboriginal people'.[32] Cooke was probably responsible for purchasing many of the thirty paintings of the *Wailbri and Pintubi Art* exhibition. Laurie Owens, Superintendent of Papunya from July or August 1971, described the mural to me as a 'very happy thing' and 'an incredible moment that Geoff orchestrated'.[33] But both Cooke and Owens gleefully recounted the outburst and intrusion of a minister from the Uniting Church in Alice Springs. This is Owens' version:

> It nearly blew me over when the Reverend came out and said: 'There's been a very bad situation created here'. He had set up a Centre for Aboriginal Development in Alice Springs with grants – he was very friendly with the people from the Office of Aboriginal Affairs. He was very much the watchdog on what happened in Aboriginal communities. He made great efforts to create good understanding of Aborigines in the general community in Alice Springs through this Centre – in that regard he was very valuable. But the Honey Ant Dreaming Mural – this had been done and apparently nobody had consulted him about it. I'm quite sure that Geoff Bardon did consult adequately with the men, but the Reverend felt outraged and wanted to get his oar in and make everyone feel very embarrassed. He said: 'This is most improper. The elders haven't been consulted. This is almost sacrilegious if not blasphemous in fact. Who did this? Who instigated this?' I had to go to a meeting of the community – the Reverend came out from Alice Springs, held court and said: 'This is a very bad affront to the elders and should never have been allowed to happen'. I think Geoff copped some opprobrium from that.[34]

The Reverend is not the first and won't be the last whitefella to believe his 'special' relationship with Aboriginal people entitles him to act as their gatekeeper in this manner and to attempt to sabotage others' good works if they have not been included in them. If Bardon was aware of this intervention, he does not mention it. But he writes at length about his problems with other interfering whitefellas including, later on, both Cooke and Owens. He says Jack Cooke advised him, towards the end of his time in Papunya, to 'discontinue my "unilateral contact with private persons concerning matters on an Aboriginal reserve"'.[35] And Laurie Owens was the Superintendent of Papunya who in Bardon's 1991 account first made the 'scandalous and vicious' allegation that Bardon was 'trafficking in Aboriginal paintings'.[36] Owens denied any recollection of this when I raised it with him in our interview:

> Not in my mind. I always thought of Geoff as the person who could really keep the impetus of the thing going. I can't in any instance think of any criticism of him from that viewpoint. There was concern that he was sometimes very volatile and unstable, but he certainly wasn't under any personal attack from me – or Jack Cooke.[37]

In an April 2002 interview at his home in the Adelaide Hills, Cooke told me that 'there was no attempt to wipe out Aboriginal culture. It was encouraged.' As evidence he cited the government's support of the Yuendumu Men's Museum which had opened in 1971, the same year painting began at Papunya. The opening had been attended by the notorious Mr Harry Giese, Director of Welfare in the Northern Territory and chief enforcer of the government policy of assimilation. Misunderstandings, it seems, were not confined to relations between Aborigines and Europeans in Papunya.

Bardon freely acknowledged his limitations in communicating with the painters, but Cooke and Owens' denials of any evil intent towards Bardon or Aboriginal culture raise the possibility of a different kind of cultural clash, which may have had a bearing on Bardon's difficulties with other white staff at Papunya. Not all the European staff in Papunya had problems with Bardon, of course. He had the friendship of his flatmate Peter Fannin, who helped the painters and eventually took on the job of running the artists' company Papunya Tula Artists in late 1972, when it became clear that Bardon would not return to Papunya. Throughout his first year in the settlement Bardon also had the unfailing support of Fred Friis, the Head Teacher of Papunya Special School, who originally counselled him to consult with the most senior Aboriginal men in the community about the school mural. Friis told me the mural idea had come up as a way of 'getting respect' from the community for the school buildings after the school library had been burnt out three times by local vandals.[38] He remembered the telegram he received before the start of the 1971 school year to tell him that 'a new art teacher was coming'. And he remembered the day Geoffrey Bardon arrived in Papunya and refused the offer to join the drinking session at the superintendent's house. He commented wryly that 'Geoff's time in Papunya might have been very different if he had accepted that beer'.[39]

'Refuse to drink with them and you immediately became a mortal enemy.'[40] Like *Wake in Fright*'s school teacher protagonist John Grant, Bardon seems to have found in Papunya his own menacing 'variation of hell'[41] in his fraught interactions with his fellow non-Indigenous resident staff. Unlike Grant, however, he also found a kind of redemption through his relationships with Papunya's Aboriginal residents, most particularly his painting men – although he did not find the deliverance which Grant finds at the end of the novel and left

Papunya and the Territory in 1972 in a state of despair and nervous collapse.

> The racism, the casual paternalism and self-righteousness of the white man's law were all of a pattern with heavy drinking and an intellectual dishonesty; many of these white people of my experience were seemingly a detritus of our culture, yet they held great power over the lives and destinies of the Aboriginal people at Papunya settlement, and as I was to find out, it was they who prevailed.[42]

Even without his rejection of the mateship represented by that beer, Geoffrey Bardon's art school background would have been enough to get many of his co-workers at Papunya offside. When he arrived in Papunya in 1971 he had his Teacher's Certificate from the NSW Department of Education, but was still finishing his Diploma of Art (Education). During 1971, over the same period the Papunya painting movement was literally being born at the back of Bardon's classroom, he satisfactorily completed his 'prescribed project' for the award. Now in the possession of his wife Dorn, the certificate is signed by John Coburn as Head of the National Art School and WE Hart as Principal of the Teachers' College and dated 31 December 1971. When I knew him later in his life, Bardon was an erudite and charming man, with a wide knowledge of western culture, who could cite ancient historians, legal precedents, educational theories and off-colour jokes with equal flair, but in his earliest writings on the art movement he sounds rather like a typical art school graduate, all high-seriousness, captivated by the art theories of his day.

Ellen Waugh, who was Geoffrey Bardon's art theory lecturer in the mid-1960s when he was studying to become an art teacher at Alexander Mackie Teachers College,[43] remembers him as a quiet, thoughtful, young man who kept to himself, like other mature-age students in her course 'Teaching Methods for Art History'.[44] Unusually in the 1960s (indeed, until the last decade or so in most teacher art education courses), Waugh began her account of Australian art with Aboriginal art, following her parents' keen interest in the subject. She also covered the progressive art theorists of the day, who were beginning to advance the novel idea that art was a cognitive and symbolic, not merely an aesthetic, activity. These days a remarkably astute octogenarian, Waugh even remembered that Bardon drew her attention in Herbert Read's classic *Education Through Art* to a footnote which referenced Viktor Lowenfeld's 1939 publication, *The Nature of Creative Activity*,[45] as the source of the division of humanity into haptic (relating to touch) and visual artistic types popularised by Read. Bardon subsequently applied this theory to the painting men:[46]

> Aboriginal temperament has a predilection to the sensitivity of touch. This is a *haptic sensation, a physical quality and tactile* [Bardon's emphasis], different entirely from the visual sensation in eyesight.[47]

Hapticity was *the* fashionable concept in relation to 'art of other cultures' in progressive art educational circles at that time. It led Bardon to 'see' things in the painters' work and, indeed, in the children's drawings in the sand that others did not read into them (though Bardon was forced by the secret/sacred controversy to acknowledge that 'Clearly there is a consciousness of the visual element, by practical necessity, and implied by the rules of visual secrecy').[48] Pursuing this idea of touch as the authentic Indigenous artistic modality, Bardon ranked the various groups of painting men in terms of their differential exposure to European culture, ranging from the 'universally haptic' 'bush Pintupi' through to the Anmatyerr/Aranda, who 'can even be described as primarily visual painters'.[49] This was one of the very few hierarchies at Papunya settlement that placed the New Pintupi at its apex. The eagerness of the New Pintupi, otherwise generally despised and derided in Papunya, to grasp the opportunity Bardon and the painting movement presented to demonstrate to their Old Pintupi countrymen and to the worldly-wise Anmatyerr, Luritja, Kukatja, Arrente and Warlpiri ex-stockmen who made up the rest of the painters at Papunya the sophistication of their knowledge of their own culture may have been the spark which ignited the painting movement. It may also have had something to do with the secret/sacred controversy – Isaacs' 'rattling spears' hypothesis.

Lowenfeld's views are reminiscent of some currently fashionable theories of Indigenous art, although these days they are traced to late 20th-century poststructuralist philosophers like Deleuze rather than to Read or Lowenfeld. Such a mindset, for all that it inspired and shaped Bardon's involvement with the painting movement, might well have alienated the hard-drinking men of the Territory. Recognising a sensitive soul, they tormented him in ways only possible in so isolated a context. But concepts like hapticity are also integral to the very specific *art theoretical* meaning that Bardon attached to the concept of assimilation. In *Aboriginal Art of the Western Desert*, Bardon made explicit his views on the way the haptic sensibility of the painting men was being overwhelmed by the dominant European visual mode, which as far as he was concerned was 'an alien language as much as the spoken languages'.[50] What Bardon opposed in the Papunya regime was the imposition of what he regarded as an alien 'way of seeing'. That was why he insisted that in the paintings produced under his eye there was to be 'Nothing whitefella'. As he put it: 'I wanted to see indigenous art. That was the size of my mission.'[51]

The received history that the painting movement began as an heroic struggle against the brutal agents of an assimilationist regime determined to crush Aboriginal culture and especially the painting movement as a defiant expression of its survival, is ironic in that what Bardon seems to have meant by assimilation had little to do with the official assimilation policies of the day. As Jack Cooke observed, official policies actually favoured the continuance of Aboriginal culture, especially in the economically productive forms represented by the painting movement. Bardon's clashes with minor officials in Papunya may, in this sense, have been less about policy than about personalities. Or about the country/city divide in mainstream Australian culture, which is also one of the underlying themes of *Wake in Fright*, with Bardon conspicuously a member of the metropolitan elites. Or about personal power – resentment by the settlement administrators of the challenge to their authority which Bardon's intense and productive friendships with the painters gave him in the politics of settlement life. He also interfered in very practical ways with the men's performance of their duties – to reiterate Arnold Probin's comment: 'All my gardeners turned into artists – I couldn't believe it!'

Bardon's accounts differ on exactly when and exactly who, but all his statements of his difficulties with the settlement authorities come down to the central accusation that he was 'trafficking in paintings from an Aboriginal reserve'. These allegations were apparently made casually and certainly never proceeded with, presumably because their effect of traumatising and intimidating Bardon had already achieved their objective of weakening his position at Papunya.[52] Bardon took them very seriously indeed – they precipitated the pre-dawn escape from Papunya in his pale blue Kombivan laden with its precious cargo of 'hundreds' of paintings that is described earlier.[53]

Something that happened in Papunya while Bardon was away in Sydney for the 1971–72 summer break suggests what the settlement authorities were really on about. They were not trying to crush Aboriginal culture or stop the painting movement – they were trying to take control of it:

> Patricia Hogan had sealed her sole agency aspirations in writing with the former superintendent in January 1972 and was now, with the new superintendent, moving to take over the painting movement at Papunya.[54]

Hogan's initiatives may have included the *Wailbri and Pintubi Art* exhibition, or at least the sale of those thirty paintings to Jack Cooke or other officers from the Department of the Interior, and Colin Jack-Hinton's purchase of what remained in Hogan's storeroom from the first three consignments of paintings to the Stuart Art Centre. Bardon does not mention either of these developments anywhere in his writings. It was Hogan who had accompanied Jack-Hinton on his first visit to Papunya in 1970 as inaugural Director of the Museums and Art Galleries of the Northern Territory, a visit she probably arranged through her friendship with the settlement Superintendent Warren Smith (another hard-drinking Territorian). During this visit, Jack-Hinton was reportedly 'dazzled' by:

> a magnificent work, composed of designs drawn in the sand and decorated with multi-coloured rocks, pebbles, ochres, feathers and plant material.

> The men all appeared to be working independently of, and without communicating with each other, but the result was a completely cohesive work.[55]

He had witnessed the construction of a traditional ground painting. Perhaps it was 'native telepathy' he saw in action, but more likely it was a well-planned performance for the benefit of a visiting dignitary. But there is no doubting either the foresight of the 'important ceremonial leaders' who would have organised such an event in setting out to impress their visitor, who twelve months later became the first public patron of their art – or the benign attitude of the settlement authorities to such public expressions of Aboriginal culture.

A year later, Pat Hogan contacted Jack-Hinton in Darwin with news of an exciting development at the settlement. A young teacher by the name of Geoffrey Bardon had arrived in Papunya at the beginning of the new school year and begun encouraging those same 'important ceremonial leaders' to paint their traditional designs on boards, pieces of linoleum, in fact anything that was available. She invited Jack-Hinton to come down and see for himself. By the time he responded to her invitation, presumably while Bardon was away in Sydney for the holidays, at least three consignments of paintings from Papunya had been delivered to her gallery. Jack-Hinton says he acquired 'virtually everything available'[56] for the Museum, apparently recognising immediately the historic importance of the boards. He was evidently sensible of the artistry of the works as well as the importance of their being held by a public institution so that they would be available in the future for purposes of study, and also accessible to the artists and their descendants. No other cultural collecting institution in Australia at the time shared his vision.

Colin Jack-Hinton's name crops up repeatedly in the history of the early Papunya boards, notably as the man who stepped in to quell the 1974 disturbance at the Residency by pulling the plug on the *Wailbri and Pintubi Art* exhibition and returning the paintings to his Museum in Darwin. I never met him, though he lumbered by me in the corridor of the Museum and Art Gallery of the Northern Territory in Darwin in 2001 when I was there to work on their collection of early boards. I did not know it was him (I thought it was George Chaloupka, another friend of Pat Hogan) and, by the time I realised who it had been, he had left the building. He died in 2006 at the age of seventy-three. One of his obituarists described him as a 'dangerous man to meet after a certain hour of the day' on account of his fondness for 'cool drinks', but all of his friends and acquaintances paid tribute to his creativity and his wide-ranging mind. He started the Museum with 'impossibly deficient' funds in the old Darwin Town Hall and was someone in every way 'larger than life'.

He was also the man charged with implementing the new arrangements for the 'preservation of Aboriginal objects' following a damning report by a Select Committee of the Legislative Council of the Northern Territory appointed in November 1964 to investigate whether any amendment of the *Native and Historical Objects and Areas Preservation Ordinance 1955* was 'necessary for the preservation of Aboriginal objects as defined by that Ordinance'.[57] The main aim of the Ordinance, which came into effect in the Northern Territory on 24 August 1957, was to stop the looting of Aboriginal sacred and ritual objects for the trade in these things, although its definition of 'prescribed objects' was far broader than this. It included carvings, paintings 'or other representation relating to the aboriginal natives of Australia which is of ethnological or anthropological interest or value'.[58] The Ordinance had prohibited the removal from the Territory of such objects without first obtaining the consent in writing of an authorised officer.[59] The Select Committee took nine months to reach its conclusion that 'the Ordinance might as well never have been passed'.[60] It accused the Welfare Branch of the Northern Territory Administration of 'gross neglect and maladministration'.[61]

Given this history, it is somewhat mysterious that the Ordinance was introduced at all. The trade in tjurungas which it was primarily designed to stamp out had been going on since the 19th century. Perhaps what the framers of the Ordinance objected to was not so much the trade itself as the reduction of its objects to the level of 'commodities for tourists'.[62] This had occurred since the 1930s, following concerted attempts especially by the Lutheran missionaries to undermine Aboriginal religious practices.[63] By 1933 tjurungas were being openly traded in the Hermannsburg store for 5 shillings each[64] and the young men of Hermannsburg were manufacturing replicas for the tourist trade in Alice Springs.[65] The policy of what later became known as assimilation had its origins in this era in the perception that 'Aboriginal society was breaking down, tradition and tribal discipline were weakening and Aborigines themselves were being attracted more and more towards the ways of the white man'.[66] The idea was not to force Aboriginal tribespeople to become 'ordinary Australians' so much as to facilitate what was regarded as an inexorable process.

The man usually regarded as the policy's architect, though it had already been in place for two decades when he took charge as Minister of the Interior in 1951, was Sir Paul Hasluck. In common with other progressive thinkers of the day, he held the 'liberal' view that in light of this breakdown of their own society 'the Aborigines should not be treated as though they were criminals or lunatics and shut away from the rest of society but should be regarded as part of the whole Australian community'.[67] As he later wrote of his pre-war involvement with Aboriginal issues: 'As I saw things at that time, the chief difficulty was not one of racial dissimilarity but of social acceptability … I did not think this required the abandonment of all aboriginal tradition and custom.'[68] Events post-war would prove that the policy-makers' assumptions about the imminent demise of Aboriginal culture and society were ill-founded. By the 1970s tjurungas were no longer openly traded to tourists in Alice Springs and in the coming years they would be used in land claims under the Northern Territory Land Rights Act as proof of a local group's ownership of particular territories. The large rents in the fabric of Aboriginal tradition so evident in the 1930s were being repaired and by the mid-1980s sober and scholarly voices like historian CD Rowley's spoke optimistically of Aboriginal 'recovery'.[69]

The Select Committee's report had denounced the removal of tjurungas from the Territory on the grounds that 'Each stone represents a small part of a much larger story and it is part of the religious upbringing of an Aboriginal that he is instructed in the interpretation of parts of the story'.[70] Its main recommendation was for the repeal of the Ordinance and its replacement by a museum controlled by an independent board of trustees whose prime purpose should be the 'collection and preservation of material related to the history of the Northern Territory and the culture of its Aboriginal inhabitants'.[71] It further recommended that funds be provided to create a repository for the museum's collection. However, since the Select Committee's investigations had demonstrated that the effectiveness of official policy depended on its agents, the report also recommended 'the employment of staff capable of carrying out the trustees' objectives'.[72]

Jack-Hinton's role as Museum Director gave him the responsibility for 'approvals for restricted good export permits' for materials potentially '*sacred or highly significant traditional*' in type. According to a printed circular issued in April 1974 and headed 'Export of Aboriginal Artefacts', he took a different view on 'modern artefacts made on Missions and Reserves', to which no restrictions had applied under the old Ordinance:

> some material which Aboriginal craftsmen and artists are capable of producing and which is being produced today may well be, and sometimes is, of a sacred or highly significant traditional type.
>
> It is intended for the moment and as a short term measure that material which is to be exported albeit regarded by Missions and Settlements in the past as 'modern' because it is recently produced will be checked by the Director of the Museums and Art Galleries.[73]

Interestingly, about one-sixth (thirty-seven) of the more than two hundred early Papunya boards in the Darwin Museum's collection have the word 'Restricted' attached to their catalogue information. It is too late to ask Jack-Hinton if he was responsible for these notations, but he certainly took on the responsibility of personally checking out all recently created work coming out of missions and settlements before it left the Territory. Could this explain the 'scandalous and vicious'[74] accusations that confronted Geoffrey Bardon when he returned to Papunya at the beginning of the 1972 school year after a long break in Sydney? Especially as the man who had the authority to issue restricted good export permits for

Aboriginal paintings to leave the Territory and also to determine what was and what was not a 'restricted good' was none other than Pat Hogan's friend, drinking buddy and recent visitor, Colin Jack-Hinton. The difference between Bardon and Hogan was that Hogan had Jack-Hinton's authorisation.

The existence of the Ordinance, but more particularly its replacement by Colin Jack-Hinton as Museum Director as a more effective way of ensuring the active enforcement of its objectives of preserving Aboriginal cultural materials in the Territory, strongly suggests that wiping out Aboriginal culture was not the aim of the government policies of the day. So does prime minister Billy McMahon's April 1971 announcement to a meeting of Aboriginal Affairs ministers of the various states and territories of his government's objective that Aboriginal Australians be assisted to 'preserve and develop their culture – their languages, traditions and arts'.[75]

McMahon's principal adviser on Aboriginal affairs was 'Nugget' Coombs, who preferred the UN term 'integration' to the current terminology of 'assimilation' because it seemed to imply that people could still be who they were while becoming full citizens of the Australian nation. Coombs was not the only influential policy-maker who believed that the chief obstacle to the acceptance of Aboriginal people was the attitude of non-Aboriginal Australians towards them. The possession of a vibrant, living culture as demonstrated in their art, it was believed, would help to make them 'socially acceptable'. What Geoffrey Bardon was doing with the painting men at Papunya was *precisely* what assimilationist policies proposed: treating Aboriginal people as Australian citizens with the same rights as other Australians to engage in commercial activities, to be artists, to sell their work on the open market. It was not the objective of the Papunya authorities to obstruct such an enterprise or any other 'socially acceptable' expression of Aboriginal culture, notwithstanding the banal cruelties and disrespect for Aboriginal people that were part of their daily dealings and that so distressed the sensitive Geoffrey Bardon.

> Why would they have been trying to stop it? By that time for ten years the officials had been saying traditional culture is good. Often they'd say, 'It's going to be like the Scots and their kilts and bagpipes' and so on – but basically like us. But they'd been supporting the Arnhem Land art industry for a decade or more – all trying to sell the idea of Aboriginals as nice people and worth knowing. The school was there to educate the children and there is no getting away from the horror of the kitchen/dining room – a terrible mistake. But there was nothing else, nothing comparable to the cultural pressures applied by the church and the missionaries to change what goes on in people's heads.[76]

The *Wailbri and Pintubi Art* exhibition was a perfect example of these policies in practice. Its national tour was organised by the Department of the Interior, the department responsible for administering the Australian government's policies of assimilation at settlements like Papunya at the time the early boards were produced. According to the introductory statement in the exhibition catalogue:

> This exhibition of a new art form developed at the Papunya Settlement in the Alice Springs region of the Northern Territory has been mounted by the Department of the Interior to show the significance of Aboriginal art and to encourage an appreciation of the culture on which it is based.[77]

The catalogue essay stressed the paintings' importance as a 'means of communicating with people of European descent' for people whose 'very limited English vocabulary' had previously prevented their making themselves understood 'to any great depth'. The essay names the Stuart Art Centre as the 'retail outlet' for the painters' group, and although there is no mention of Papunya Tula Artists as its name (presumably because this was prior to its formation), there is no sign of antagonism towards or exclusion of Bardon. Far from attempting to obscure his role in the establishment of the art movement, the writer introduces the paintings as the result of 'Geoff Bardon, a talented young artist' having taught the 'Wailbri' and 'Pintubi' tribesmen 'how to reproduce their sand drawing art form on board using commercial paints'. The exhibition's disastrous finale was as traumatic for those who espoused the value of the paintings as emissaries for Aboriginal people and culture as it was for the painters themselves. Perhaps more so, since by that time the painters were already grappling with the issues it raised for them.

Damage control

Dick Kimber's essay 'The Politics of the Secret in Contemporary Western Desert Art' was published in 1995,[78] the year the run on the early boards started at the auction houses. It appeared in an obscure *Oceania* monograph, which those responsible for the Sotheby's promotional exercise may not have seen, but it is essential reading for an understanding of the events which originally led to the seclusion of the early Papunya boards. It offers first-hand testimony, drawn from Kimber's journal notes of the time and his memory, by the 'only person – apart from the artists themselves – to have witnessed the acting out of the "politics of the secret" over the period that I consider crucial – 1971 to 1978 inclusive'.[79] It also confirms Geoffrey Bardon's assertion there was not much ado about the issue in his time, in that the first public expression of concern about the subject matter of the paintings occurred *after* his departure from Papunya in July 1972. Until then, as Kimber comments: 'Aboriginal people in general, as well as the wider European public probably did not even know that the works existed'.[80]

On the first or second weekend in August 1972, at the Yuendumu sports festival, 'a dramatic event occurred'.[81] In addition to events like fire-making, spear- and boomerang-throwing and of course football, that year the festival featured a display of Aboriginal arts and crafts, including 'a solitary painting by late Winanpa artist, S.L.Tj.'. Among the crowds of Aboriginal people who gathered for this occasion were 'a sizeable number of very tradition-oriented, middle aged to senior Pitjantjatjara men from Docker River', renowned for their strictness in upholding the law:

> As soon as the Pitjantjatjara men saw S.L.Tj's painting there was angry uproar. The painting was perceived as a serious transgression, revealing to the uninitiated, secret-sacred aspects of men's law.[82]

The painting was quickly removed before more than a few people had seen it, and the tensions aroused were allayed by 'ritual meetings' between Pintupi, Winanpa and Pitjantjatjara men throughout the weekend. But according to Kimber, the damage was done. The fact that the protest had been made by these strongly traditional men meant that all the painters at Papunya now had to come to grips with the issue.

Kimber was so troubled about the secrecy issue that he declined an offer to take on the job of co-ordinator of the newly incorporated Papunya Tula Artists, thinking 'no art (no matter how aesthetically pleasing) was worth the possible risk to people's lives'.[83] However, production of the paintings and the problems with them continued and 'it was obvious that something had to be done'. Only the artists could determine what was to be done about their current art practice. But even if they resolved their problems with the Pitjantjatjara, there was still the question of the paintings beyond their direct control, which already loomed as a danger:

> In the meantime they were all faced with the problem that hundreds of their paintings were held by a private gallery owner in Alice Springs and, through the intermittent interest of a federal government officer [Cooke], were also held by the Department of Aboriginal Affairs in Alice Springs.[84]

Apart from its inaccurate description of the exhibition as 'a display of Pintupi art',[85] Kimber considered the *Centralian Advocate*'s report on the Residency incident a 'fair summary of the problems'. But he is at pains to stress that it was not the media coverage or the helpful suggestions of 'coordinators and other interested people' but the artists themselves who initiated and determined the necessary action to heal the breach with their neighbours and countrymen and women first exposed in Yuendumu two years earlier. Before and during his employment by Papunya Tula Artists from May 1976 until May 1978, Kimber worked with the artists to assist them as they addressed problems over the depiction of secret and sacred imagery with senior men from a wide range of culturally related groups at communities across the Western Desert. The process involved 'thousands of hours of work, thousands of kilometres of travel (in all, more than a year)'.[86] Kimber highlights as the most significant figure throughout the whole course of action Winanpa statesman and one of Papunya's leading identities, Nosepeg Tjupurrula, whom he describes as 'certainly the most significant ritual leader throughout the period from the 1950s to the late 1970s'[87] and 'a master of protocol in all Law matters'.[88] Kimber's concern in the essay is to provide information 'without betraying trust and sensitive details'[89] by discussing any details of travel, traditional meetings or other matters of association. As far as he is aware, the resolution of all the major problems created by the showing of the art was achieved at this time. These events he says, 'also signalled the conclusion of an era, begun with the first works in 1971, in which the secret-sacred and the new art form co-mingled uneasily'.[90] However, this did *not* mean that the display of certain of the early works was no longer controversial.

The Residency incident had dramatically illustrated 'the existence of sizeable collections of early works which could offend by public display' as an ongoing problem. Kimber said that between 1975 and 1977, one of the artists' principal strategies for dealing with controversial disclosures in the paintings was 'to ensure that the art was always displayed at places distant from Central Australia'.[91] I shall call this the 'safety of distance' solution to the problems of secrecy. Initially the painters' concept of a safe distance was Adelaide but as more and more traditionally oriented Aboriginal people from Central Australia began travelling there for health, education and other reasons, the eastern capitals of Melbourne and Sydney became the preferred 'safe' destinations. The program of international touring exhibitions organised by the Aboriginal Arts Board was even more popular.[92]

At a meeting of the Aboriginal Arts Board in Shepparton, Victoria, on 5–7 October 1974, Director Bob Edwards tabled a report that 'a display of Pintupi/Warlpiri art in Alice Springs had caused offence to many Pitjantjatjara people'. The minutes record that 'The Board was not encouraging the display of early work done by the Warlbiri people. The Director undertook to fully investigate the matter and report back to the Board.'[93] A week later, Peter Fannin, Art Organiser for Papunya Tula Artists, sent a letter to Bob Edwards headed 'Secrecy'. He began by setting out the results of a discussion of 'the matter of secrecy ... with the Pintupi artists by resident linguist Ken Hansen in 1971/72' which explained their faith in the 'safety of distance' in terms of their theory of sickness as caused by 'mamu' (evil spirits). As Fannin explained, citing the authority of anthropologist Annette Hamilton's work in the late 1960s on 'socio-economic factors in the health of the Pitjantjatjara', only initiated men were believed to be strong enough to resist the sickness-causing mamu entering their bodies on contact with sacred objects or designs. Away from tribal country (in Alice Springs, for example) 'the associated *mamu* were unlikely to be present'.[94]

Fannin's letter also reported that consultations had occurred in the previous year after Pitjantjatjara complaints about *Wailbri and Pintubi Art* when it was shown in Canberra in 1972. Kaapa Tjampitjinpa, whom Fannin describes as 'chief protagonist for revelation', was involved in these discussions and in a subsequent discussion with Tim Leura and interpreter Jim Lester (who had been initiated and trained in Aboriginal law near Oodnadatta) at which Fannin was also present:

> After discussion in Luritja, Jim gave me to believe that the difficulty had been resolved. One agreement was not to show string crosses, even when they appear in the design being presented. A frequent theme from Papunya men was that their ceremonial practice differs from that of the

more southerly groups. The difference seems to lie in a wider distinction between a representation of a sacred object, and the sacred object itself. Jim says the southern people are prepared to accept this. There may still be some contention where a shared dreaming is concerned.

Fannin relayed the estimation of Centre for Aboriginal Artists and Craftsmen personnel Machmud Mackay and Roy Monks that 'special precautions' should have been exercised in displaying the paintings in Alice Springs. But 'the organisers seem to have been unwilling to do this,[95] and instead withdrew the paintings all together'. But, Fannin stressed, 'I have no direct knowledge of the incident'. As the disturbance in Canberra suggests, the 'safe distance' solution was only putting off problems that would have to be faced in the long run. But Fannin's principal concern was that the artists should not see the Board as dictating what they should paint. In his view, 'the matter can only be resolved by tribal Aborigines. It is a complex issue. Discussion must be leisurely. Competent interpretation is essential.'[96]

The Pitjantjatjara law men behind the complaints about *Wailbri and Pintubi Art* were simultaneously involved in legal action against Rigby, the publishers of CP Mountford's 1976 magnum opus *Nomads of the Australian Desert*. They wanted the book withdrawn from sale and Mountford charged with 'breach of confidence' for publication of images of sacred objects used in secret ceremonies. Rigby immediately withdrew the book and said it was 'conscious that Aboriginal people have begun to object to some pictorial treatments' and had 'eliminated pictures we thought objectionable' but 'unfortunately, it would seem there were some subtleties in the situation which weren't apparent to white people'.[97] Rigby was also Geoffrey Bardon's publisher for *Aboriginal Art of the Western Desert*, his first account of the beginnings of the painting movement, which finally appeared in 1979, delayed perhaps by the aftershocks of the Mountford controversy. Both books had received financial support from the Aboriginal Arts Board – the Board was to have received all royalties earned by *Nomads of the Australian Desert* to establish a fund to assist Aboriginal writers. The Pitjantjatjara law men were marshalling their forces to indict one of the Board's projects for betraying their secrets, even as the Board stepped up as the financial mainstay of their neighbours apparently engaging in deliberate disclosure of similar knowledge about their own traditions.

One can imagine the Board's dismay at the convergence of controversies and its desire to buy time until the dust cleared from the Mountford case and the Papunya initiative could be coolly assessed. In September 1974 Bob Edwards had written to Dick Kimber to say that he shared his concerns 'about the possibility that some if not all the art was sacred' and had 'long-standing reservations about the whole exercise'. At the same time, he considered it a 'good thing to keep the art alive, the artists occupied in a traditional activity and an independent income going back into the Papunya and Yai Yai communities'.[98] Edwards' plan for 'stimulating the work while the other aspects of the project can be worked out', involved the Aboriginal Arts Board becoming the main 'customer' for Papunya art, deliberately acquiring most of the production and placing the paintings either 'out of sight in museum reserve collections' or sending them overseas 'where they can be exhibited without fear of being seen by the Aboriginals concerned'.[99]

From late 1974, the Aboriginal Arts Board purchased most of Papunya Tula's stock and sent hundreds of works to overseas exhibitions, many of them never to return. Without the Board's financial support, Papunya Tula Artists would not have survived the decade. The art galleries weren't interested in the large, loosely painted canvases that the Papunya painters were now producing using the pared-down vocabulary of design elements acceptable to their kinsfolk and neighbours across the region. The museums at least recognised the quality of innovation in these paintings in their dismissal of them as not 'traditional' enough for their collections. But the art movement was fading for lack of the recognition needed to build a local market. Finally, in the early 1980s, a few imaginative curators did include some of the large, late 1970s canvases in displays of contemporary art and after a decade of neglect and dismissal Papunya Tula Artists began finally to establish a market for its sales. Only then did other Central Australian Aboriginal communities, long intimidated by the climate of fear that had followed the controversy over the secret/sacred revelations in early Papunya paintings, start painting themselves,[100] using their own versions of the modified traditional painting language originally devised by the Papunya artists to cope with the problem of secrecy. One unintended side-effect of this problem was that Papunya Tula Artists had a virtual monopoly of the market – such as it was – and the lustre of a decade's precedency on the rest of the now-booming desert art movement.

Start'm off Kaapa Tjampitjinpa, and someone, might be Johnny W, and Long Jack Phillipus and me [Billy Stockman] start, and then Wadama [Charlie Tarawa Tjungurrayi], and Yala Yala Gibbs and John Tjakamarra. Just start off. Not really good. We never know what way we going to fix it all that painting y'know. Same colour – we never know which way to fix it everything. Some put wrong thing too – not wrong stories, but wrong way. Because never know which way them paintings going – that's why we been doing that. Me and Tim Leura, we went to the Arts Board, we went to Canberra, and we sort'm out that thing. We been talking – we been doing that one too quick – too quick we been making them cos we never know about that one. But this time we know now, and we gotta sort'm out all that we been doing in the first place. All that painting got to go overseas, another place, and we can do proper painting then. We come back and we been talking to all the artists – painting mob: We got to do right thing, we don't do anything stupid way, we do right way. That's why I been talking, that's why we doing them now. After that we don't touch anything, don't do anything wrong or somebody might come from another place he might talk or something –[101]

Coming from seclusion

By the 1980s, it seemed to me, the early Papunya boards were hidden away, for all the world like the sacred objects forbidden to the sight of the uninitiated that their name, notwithstanding its resonance with 'old piece(s) of waste lumber',[102] also evokes. Apart from one remarkable painting by Johnny Warangkula, the Museums and Art Galleries of the Northern Territory kept its two hundred-odd early Papunya works out of sight in storage until well into the 21st century. A magnificent collection of ninety-seven works from the first two years of the painting movement, put together by Papunya Tula Artists and now known as the Papunya Permanent Collection, ended up at the Australian Museum in Sydney in 1983. The Permanent Collection was intended for the National Gallery of Australia by those, including Dick Kimber, who parcelled them up and sent them off to the Aboriginal Arts Board for safe-keeping in the late 1970s, but the National Gallery refused the offer, saying that they did not have the storage space for such a large number of works. The Australian Museum was also in no hurry to display the treasures that had fallen into its lap. No early Papunya paintings[103] were included in *Dreamings: The Art of Aboriginal Australia*, the first major exhibition of Aboriginal art to tour the United States since the 1950s, which featured acrylic canvases from Papunya Tula and Warlukurlangu Artists of Yuendumu. By the end of the decade Ron Radford at the Art Gallery of South Australia was beginning to build a small collection of early boards, notably the two School of Kaapa works purchased in 1989. But these two works were not exhibited until 1996, the Gallery perhaps still shy about displaying a painting that looked so like the works presumed to have caused so much trouble in the 1970s on account of their unacceptable revelations about the secret/sacred:

> The earliest paintings from Papunya were on dark plain backgrounds with prominent foreground elements consisting of realistic depictions of shields, spears, axes and, in particular, sacred objects – bull-roarers, *tjurunga*, and string emblems, all of which are used in secret initiation and other ceremonies open only to adult men … Although many paintings of this type were sold and now exist in public and private collections, they can no longer be exhibited or published without offending Central Australian Aborigines.[104]

Christopher Anderson of the South Australian Museum and Francoise Dussart, writing in the catalogue of *Dreamings: The Art of Aboriginal Australia*, set out the sequestration of the early Papunya boards practised by the exhibition's organisers and by the major public collections in Australia in this era as if it were carved in stone. But winds of change were moving through the galleries. The strong market for contemporary

Papunya Tula paintings from the mid-1980s onwards had been led in by the public collecting institutions, several of which had begun establishing collections of Western Desert art, initially with current works direct from the artists' community-based enterprises. By the late 1980s, as a number of galleries looked to hold major exhibitions of their Indigenous art collections in the wake of the 1988 Bicentennial, the hunt was on for early Papunya boards.

Enterprising curators, like the National Gallery of Victoria's Judith Ryan, obtained works from individuals who had been on the spot in the early 1970s to take their pick of what was available. The Gallery acquired ten works from Pat Hogan's private collection, her personal favourites chosen from over six hundred works delivered to the Stuart Art Centre in the first two years of the movement, and smaller numbers of works from Graeme Marshall, Papunya Tula's first accountant, and Mrs Margaret Carnegie, the first major private collector of Papunya Tula works, whose collection included a large number originally purchased from the painting men by Geoffrey Bardon in Papunya. A group of these works was included in the National Gallery of Victoria's 1989 *Mythscapes* exhibition. Wally Caruana at the National Gallery of Australia was also acquiring early Papunya works from the Carnegie Collection, from Papunya Tula Artists – several of them originally from Dick Kimber's collection – and a few from private art dealers. Michael O'Ferrall of the Art Gallery of Western Australia also purchased a small group of Papunya boards from early private collectors of Papunya paintings and a couple from tribal art auctions for the Gallery's *Tjukurrpa – Desert Dreamings: Aboriginal Art from Central Australia (1971–1993)* exhibition in the 1993 International Year for the World's Indigenous Peoples.

But the national collections in total still only accounted for somewhere between a third and a half of the painters' estimated output over the seminal period of 1971–72. What had happened to the rest of the early Papunya boards? It was not that no-one wanted them or wanted to display them after paying significant amounts of money to acquire them – significant for the times that is, although not beyond the modest Indigenous art budgets of most public collecting institutions. But where were they?

5

The Midas Touch

No-one predicted the scenes that unfolded on the floor of Sotheby's auction house in the closing years of the 20th century to seal the place of the early Papunya boards in world art history. The auctioneer's hammer fell on one record-breaking sale after another until on 26 June 2000, Johnny Warangkula Tjupurrula's *Water Dreaming at Kalipinypa* 1972, already a national icon for having leapt over the six-figure barrier for Aboriginal art sales in 1997, doubled its market value again to $440 000,[1] setting a new world record resale price for Aboriginal art. Money had spoken, anointing this painting in particular and the early Papunya boards in general as the standard against which Aboriginal art would henceforth be judged. Papunya Tula Artists' painting sales over the entire decade of the 1970s were less than what that single early Papunya board had cost its delighted American buyer. In those more innocent times, the reduction of the priceless first inscriptions of Western Desert culture to mere commodities, however expensive, would have been viewed with horror and disbelief. In 1976, when Tim Leura Tjapaltjarri and his younger brother Clifford Possum Tjapaltjarri painted the first great map painting

Warlugulong, Papunya Tula Artists told a wealthy Australian art collector[2] who saw the painting on television and tried to buy it for her collection that it was a 'national treasure and should belong to the nation'.[3] The painting is now in the collection of the Art Gallery of New South Wales, which purchased it in 1981 for $2500. Who could have imagined that the long-vanished boards from the first years of the art movement would a decade and a half later come out of seclusion at last, drawn by the irresistible lure of prices close to two hundred times that?

Not Robert Bleakley, when he arrived back in Sydney in 1982 to establish Sotheby's Australia after a decade abroad in London and New York. Following a passion for collecting 'tribal art' dating back to his Australian boyhood, Bleakley had abandoned an arts degree at the University of New England in the early 1970s to enrol in Sotheby's art appreciation course in London. He honed his professional skills as an auctioneer in the company's London salerooms. By 1978, at the age of twenty-eight, he had been appointed to head up the firm's newly formed 'Primitive Art' Department and became Sotheby's youngest ever director. The profitability of his section in a rising market for 'fine ethnographic art' – and Bleakley's offer to put up half the money himself – eventually persuaded Sotheby's then Chairman, A Alfred Taubman, to open a branch in Australia, a market the parent body had hitherto regarded as inconsequential. Shortly after Sotheby's Australia opened its doors, Bleakley received a phone call from Geoffrey Bardon. They arranged to meet in a back lane of the inner Sydney suburb of Paddington, where Bardon laid out forty of his personal collection of early Papunya boards for the man from Sotheby's inspection. Apparently Bleakley 'loved them and thought they were marvellous but just didn't think they were high ethnographic art. He thought they were fantastically interesting-looking things but let them go by.'[4]

This anecdote was recounted to me in 2003 by Tim Klingender who, a decade and a half after this portentous meeting, would himself become known to the close world of Australian Aboriginal art as 'the man from Sotheby's' for his starring role in this next chapter of the history of the early Papunya boards. There were other key players of course, not least of them Robert Bleakley, without whose backing his young protégé Klingender's big ideas might have remained just that. Bleakley used the freedom his partial ownership gave him over the affairs of Sotheby's Australia to adopt Klingender's radical experiments with new sales strategies for Aboriginal art that would prove successful beyond their wildest dreams. Following the European and North American market model for 'Tribal' or 'Primitive' art, according to which indigenous art attracts a completely different clientele from 'Contemporary Art', Sotheby's Australia had for some time been selling Aboriginal art and 'artefacts' at low-profile Tribal Art auctions organised from its Melbourne headquarters. Klingender's suggestion was to break with this 'separate market' model and encourage contemporary art buyers to explore Sotheby's Aboriginal catalogue – and pay contemporary art prices for their purchases – by combining Contemporary and Aboriginal Art in the one auction.[5]

At this time Australia was in the middle of the long boom in sales of contemporary Aboriginal art foretold by James Mollison, Director of the National Gallery of Australia, on Australia Day 1984 when he appeared in the national media posed in front of a large, recently acquired canvas by Johnny Warangkula Tjupurrula, declaring the work of the Papunya Tula artists to be the 'finest abstract art ever produced in this country'.[6] After a long lead time, the primary market for desert art exploded in the early 1990s. And it was only a matter of time before someone recognised the undeveloped potential for a secondary (that is, resale) market in Aboriginal art. A couple of enterprising dealers[7] had tested the waters with some success, but Sotheby's was the first to tailor its venture to Aboriginal art's unique status in Australia, for which Western Desert art was the prototype and primary exemplar of contemporary art which was *also* firmly located within an Indigenous tradition. It also had the resources of Sotheby's to run with the idea as far as it would take them.

Sotheby's discovers 'Aboriginal Art'[9]

And what better to spearhead Sotheby's development of the secondary market in Aboriginal art than the early Papunya boards? These seminal works of the contemporary Aboriginal art movement were a strictly limited set. Somewhere around a thousand had been produced in 1971–72, and no-one yet knew how many of them had survived the intervening decades. Their unsuspecting owners had originally paid a handful of dollars for them. The young Bruce Chatwin,[8] protégé of Taubman's predecessor Peter Wilson, had originally perfected the 'little old lady with the Ming vase which had always been used as an umbrella stand' type storylines that had served Sotheby's so well in the early years of Wilson's chairmanship in encouraging a wider public to experience the art auction as a spectacle. An antipodean version of this 'rags to riches' scenario (for the lucky owners who had bought them as souvenirs of a visit to Papunya or Alice Springs in the early 1970s, not the creators of these works) was about to be played out. True, at the time no-one knew what had happened to most of the early Papunya boards. Some fine examples occasionally turned up in the Tribal Art auctions but in nothing like the numbers required for a major promotional exercise. But Bleakley knew from his experience with the UK firm that the allure of money could be depended upon to draw those diamonds of Western Desert art from their dusty hiding places. And in Tim Klingender he had a young man poised to keep a date with destiny.

The first auction I worked on for Sotheby's was a Tribal Art auction in Melbourne in 1990, put together by Leigh Purcell[10] and Robert Bleakley. I was just assisting them as a casual. In that auction, there were two really major boards. They were fabulous: large scale, very complex, teeming with representations of sacred objects. I'm not sure who consigned them, but they were both bought by the Art Gallery of Western Australia. It was a collapsed art market – they had estimates of around \$8000–\$10000 and they sold for about \$15000 each. A Freddy West[11] and a Ronnie Tjampitjinpa.[12] Both spectacular. They were the first ones that came to my attention.

After that – 1991, 1992, 1993 – I worked part-time for Sotheby's about six months of the year managing the auctions – cars, furniture, paintings, whatever. The one-a-year Tribal Art auctions, we used to have a disparate group of stuff, mainly Melanesian and Oceanic and Aboriginal artefacts with the occasional Papunya work or a number of bark paintings.[13] Basically I was still painting full-time in a studio in Melbourne and if there was an auction in Perth or Canberra or Sydney I would go up and organise the casuals, hang the show, do all that sort of stuff for them. Then in 1993 there was an awful lot of corporate art being dumped on the market – what with the excesses of the eighties, those giant corporate canvases that were so popular during that period, all the corporations were buying them, then all of a sudden they were going broke and sending all this stuff down to Sotheby's. And Sotheby's didn't have the expertise, there was no-one on staff who was a specialist in contemporary Australian art. Whereas that was purely my area. I grew up in the Melbourne art scene in the 1980s. Half the artists were my friends, so I certainly knew about their work. So at the end of 1993 Sotheby's asked me to set up a Contemporary Art Department for them.

I scheduled the first Contemporary Australian Art auction the same week as the Melbourne Art Fair of 1994. And I asked if I could incorporate Indigenous art into that, which was contrary to our practice at the time. It seems to have been reversed now, but at that stage it was taboo. We had unearthed a particularly good collection of Papunya boards from Queensland owned by a guy called Geoffrey Cornish and his wife. There were a half-dozen of them and they were pre- the Stuart Art Centre consignments. Geoff Bardon had taken them into town to show a Rotary meeting in Alice Springs in 1971 and this guy, who was a visiting Rotarian, asked Geoff afterwards if he could buy the lot. Later he lived in Queensland and in 1989 or 1990 he organised an exhibition at Bond University and brought Mick Namarari and Maxie Tjampitjinpa across for it. So he also had three or four paintings by Maxie that were painted down there at the time and one by Mick Namarari that was the big standout. They were probably the highlights of that auction – but I also incorporated a big Howard Arkley block of flats on the cover. There were a lot of Papunya Tula canvases and barks and various other bits and pieces too. And basically those early Papunya boards, in a very depressed art market at the time, sold for very high prices – ranging from $8000 up to $20000 each, and the Namarari canvas, which was only four years old, sold for about $17000, a huge price at the time. And the other things did very well as well.

It became very clear to me at that particular time that nobody specialised in the secondary market in Aboriginal art – not seriously. And interestingly enough, to this point, still don't – which amazes me beyond belief. So I said to Sotheby's, 'Can I go out looking for Aboriginal artworks specifically?

Can I go to Alice Springs and Darwin?' I had an interest in the whole area anyway. I had a long friendship with Wayne Eager and Marina Strocchi[14] and we were all interested from the 1980s and exposed to the exhibitions at the Roar Studios and Gabrielle Pizzi's gallery. I liked the stuff. But when I said to Sotheby's, 'Can I incorporate the Indigenous art into the Contemporary Art?', they said, 'Well you can try, but it won't work'. Because from their experience, never having done it right, it had always failed. Also a number of those works that sold in the 1994 sale were bought by international buyers, so that meant there would be international interest too.

So in late 1994 I went to visit Alice Springs. I just advertised in the *Northern Territory Times* and the *Centralian Advocate.* I also did an interview on local ABC radio saying we were looking for early work. And I found some fantastic things. This Shorty Lungkata on the wall of a caravan in town. Someone had just arrived in Alice Springs and bought it at the Stuart Art Centre, and they'd lived in this caravan and had it on the wall for twenty years. That was quite cathartic basically, and crucial to the way the whole thing developed. Not long after that, in February 1995, I was in Perth doing a similar thing and I turned up that fantastic Clifford Possum *Love Story* and that magnificent Water Dreaming by Mick Namarari which is now in the Queensland Art Gallery. We put the Clifford Possum on the cover of that auction [catalogue]. These people had loaned it to the Art Gallery of Western Australia – just brought it in there one day. They'd owned it for years. And the Namarari – they'd had it in their beach house, unlocked, for twenty years.[15]

Contemporary and Aboriginal art

The stage was set. In the media build-up that preceded Sotheby's first Contemporary and Aboriginal Art auction in June 1995, Tim Klingender was featured holding up a painting which he proclaimed a 'jewel in the crown' of Aboriginal art: Clifford Possum Tjapaltjarri's *Love Story* 1972. He could not have chosen a more appropriate painter or a more appropriate painting for his purpose. Clifford Possum was one of the best known names in contemporary Aboriginal art long before this painting served to kick off Sotheby's upward price spiral for the early Papunya boards. He was the first to break free from the collective identity of Papunya Tula Artists and make his own way in the art world.

Love Story 1972 was one of the very first paintings he did for Geoffrey Bardon in the painting room at Papunya at the beginning of the Western Desert art movement.[16] It was also his first rendering of what had emerged in his independent practice as his key 'signature motif': a striking, non-traditional symbol of a traditional spindle for weaving hair-string which evoked his personal interpretation of his Dreaming story.[17] The painting had been hanging in the Art Gallery of Western Australia almost unnoticed for the previous six years, although its profile had been raised by its publication at the beginning of 1994 in my scholarly monograph on Clifford Possum, the first in-depth study of an individual artist of the Papunya movement. Like the successful copyright actions brought by Aboriginal artists in the early 1990s in defence of their copyright, the monograph's publication was evidence of a growing perception of tradition-based Aboriginal artists as contemporary art practitioners, with the same rights and respect as their non-Indigenous contemporaries.

So why not the same prices? Tim Klingender confidently predicted that Clifford Possum's *Love Story* would break the record of $22 000 set in 1989 (by another Clifford Possum work) when it was auctioned, along with some four hundred items of 'the nation's most important Aboriginal art'. The outcome far exceeded these expectations. On auction night, *Love Story* went under the hammer at $57 500, prompting the first of a string of exultant 'World auction record for Aboriginal art' announcements by Sotheby's. The Art Gallery of Western Australia, which had already displayed its enthusiasm at Sotheby's 1990 Tribal Art auction for adding early Papunya boards to its expanding collection of Western Desert art, must have been kicking itself for not having acquired this masterpiece when it was within its grasp. The successful bidder was Hank Ebes, a Melbourne-based Aboriginal art dealer, whose eagle eye also spotted the artist's late 1970s masterpiece *Warlugulong* 1977 at Joel's 1996 Australian and European Paintings auction and snapped it up at the bargain price of $40 000. Both paintings were to adorn the upstairs room of his gallery,[18] adding lustre to examples of the artist's recent work acquired by direct commission from Clifford Possum.

News of the record-breaking sale soon reached Clifford Possum himself. The artist's response to the reporter from the *Sunday Territorian* who arrived at his Alice Springs camp site to invite his reaction to this development may be compared with painter Robert Rauschenberg's more famous fury[19] when he heard of US collector Robert Skull's huge profit margin on the sale of one of his early works: he demanded a share in the profits of the sale. Recalling that he had originally sold *Love Story*[20] to a 'sheep farmer' for $60, Clifford Possum observed:

> 'They should give me the painting back or pay me half. They should have told me they were selling it. I'm still working now and sometimes I can get $1000, sometimes $2000, for a painting. It is my work and they should pay me properly.'[21]

Clifford Possum's ideas on droit de suite[22] did not penetrate the local cloud of ignorance.[23] Even his 50–50 profit share suggestion is not outside the claims of 'natural justice', just unduly hopeful of their sway: the 'leveller' principle that everyone should share equally in such good fortune is little understood or at least applied outside Aboriginal culture.[24]

Clifford Possum's sense of being ripped off by the art market received no more satisfaction than had his American counterpart's. As Sotheby's in particular and the auction trade in general never tire of pointing out, these transactions provide confirmation of huge resale profit margins on an artist's work, which indirectly helps their primary market. Hank Ebes' response to a journalist who quizzed him as the high-profile new owner of *Love Story* was to point out that 'It is because of people like myself that Clifford can earn as much as $1000 a day'[25] and to insist that his purchase was 'not a money-making exercise and ... motivated by keeping an important work of art in the country', adding, 'Unless people like myself buy pieces like this, important parts of our heritage will be lost'.[26] Within a week the *Alice Springs News* had run a feature article headlined 'Possum art: Sotherby's [*sic*] to bottle shop', whose portrayal of the artist working in a camp full of drunks can hardly have improved his primary sales prospects. The rest of the article focused on the large sums that an Alice Springs art dealer claimed to be paying Clifford Possum for his work. The dealer in question also offered illustrations of the artist's indifference to material possessions which would have ended most readers' sympathy for his plight,[27] concluding with the reassuring notion that:

> 'Money to them really doesn't mean anything. It's survival from morning to evening. The next day they start again.'[28]

That struggle for the cash sufficient to each passing day is precisely what places Aboriginal artists like Clifford Possum at the mercy of the business end of town. But though a $50 million price tag – or even a quarter of a million – might be sufficient to inspire such thoughts, a mere $50 000 clearly was not, and the story died once its novelty value wore off.

A couple of weeks later, the *Centralian Advocate* announced the impending arrival in Alice Springs of Sotheby's Aboriginal art specialist Tim Klingender, who was pictured with Clifford Possum's *Love Story* alongside a prominent headline: 'Hunt is on for Centre artworks'.[29] It was reported that Klingender had 'spent eight months researching and travelling Australia' to locate the works for the 1995 auction. It was also reported that in addition to the Clifford Possum, record prices had been set at the previous month's auction by another early Papunya painter, Mick Namarari Tjapaltjarri – and by Emily Kngwarrey, the woman whose rapturous reception since she started painting in 1989 had been the original catalyst of the surge in Aboriginal art sales to contemporary art collectors which Sotheby's was now riding. Three days later, the *Centralian Advocate* ran a Sotheby's advertisement announcing the dates of Tim Klingender's visit to 'to inspect fine examples of Australian Aboriginal art for inclusion in forthcoming auctions'. 'Free Appraisals' were offered above the same photograph of *Love Story*, this time captioned 'Tim Klingender with Clifford Possum Tjapaltjarri's *Love Story* 1972, sold by Sotheby's in June for $50 000'.

I guess these things tend to perpetuate themselves, when something makes national headlines it pricks up people's ears around the country. Generally the people who owned them didn't know their value. They'd been travellers through Central Australia at that period when there wouldn't have been any sealed roads – nurses, doctors, occasionally a policeman or a superintendent, plumbers, builders – people who were somehow working out there. Generally they were people who particularly liked Indigenous people. They hadn't bought for investment but for love and support. And the paintings too – even though they are always stated as being cheap for the period, actually they weren't, they were pretty expensive. It was a month's wages to buy a painting for $150 – it was lot for a school teacher at that time. And generally they were encouraged by others or made a decision to sell them because by selling them they could put their kid through university or pay off their house or whatever it happened to be. So things started turning up all over the country. Places where they have continued to turn up more than most are Alice Springs, occasionally Darwin, the Northern Territory, Western Australia because when people retire from remote areas they tend to retire to Western Australia rather than the big smoke, and Adelaide because it's the gateway to the Territory and also because of Pat Hogan's exhibitions there in 1972, 1973, 1974 – and the wine district.[30]

The results of Klingender's initiatives, previously unheard of in the staid world of Australian art auctioneering or in Aboriginal art circles, went on display at Sotheby's preview of its next auction, to be held at the company's Melbourne headquarters on the night of Monday 17 June 1996. The shifting emphasis was subtly signalled by the reversed order of its title: Fine Aboriginal and Contemporary Art. Two finely worked paintings by Clifford Possum Tjapaltjarri from 1976 were the first lots, one purchased on the night by the Art Gallery of New South Wales, the other on behalf of an anonymous New York collector. Both fetched more than double the upper limit of Sotheby's catalogue estimate. Klingender's efforts had unearthed a small cache of works from the 1971–72 period at Papunya, most notably Anatjari Tjakamarra's *A Cave Dreaming*

1972, which the vendor had purchased in 1974 from Graeme Marshall, who had bought it while working as Papunya Tula Artists' accountant.[31] It was in Darwin that Klingender found this 'standout' piece of the 1996 auction. The vendor had moved to Darwin where, according to Klingender, the painting 'actually went through Cyclone Tracy. His place was destroyed in the cyclone and afterwards he found it in the wreckage. That's why it's got that little corner missing.' The painting was bought by the Art Gallery of Western Australia for a record-breaking $74 570 – almost three times Sotheby's upper estimate of its market value and well over the record set the previous year by Clifford Possum's *Love Story*.

Although inside the circle of Papunya Tula enthusiasts, Anatjari was recognised as the most meticulous of all the early Papunya painters, excepting only the master painter Kaapa Tjampitjinpa, he was not widely known beyond this circle and $75 000 was generally considered an outlandish price for a public gallery to pay for the work of a relatively unknown artist.[32] According to Klingender, 'the Gallery were almost too embarrassed to admit they had paid that much'.[33] The behind-the-scenes story was a foretaste of things to come. Two of the three paintings the Gallery had earmarked for possible acquisition had already been snapped up at prices over the Gallery's limit, so the Director and Michael O'Ferrall, its Senior Curator of Indigenous Art, decided to put their entire budget on this last item on their shopping list and in doing so managed to knock out the other bidders. In Klingender's view, 'it was a truly spectacular painting and so totally deserved its massive, massive price. It looked fairly expensive, but look what happened a year after it.'[34] The price a painting fetches at auction is rarely a simple reflection of its artistic value, as the bidding process underlying the Art Gallery of

Western Australia's acquisition of *A Cave Dreaming* demonstrates. Sales records require determined bidders with deep pockets, bolstered in the case of private buyers by an unshakeable conviction that the object of their desire will retain its investment value.

Some speculated that the Gallery – or perhaps its determined competition which drove the bidding so high – was inspired more by aesthetics than by the artist's reputation or the esoteric significance of the work (which features two finely decorated sacred objects). The density of the white background dotting with its trademark fluidity increases as the eyes move inwards through a sequence of concentric squares towards a central concentric circle within a final square whose diagonal quadrants are hatched with fine, dead-straight, hand-drawn white lines. The visual effect is like a vortex, drawing the viewer inwards. As Tim Klingender noted in a media report announcing the record sale, it combines 'power and softness'.[35] The same report noted that:

> Other early Papunya works fetched high prices, including a 1972 Mick Namarari Tjapaltjarri at $40 250 and a Johnny Warangkula and a Shorty Lungkarda Tjungarrayi, both $36 800.[36]

The report could also have added to its list of impressive sales performers an untitled work by Mick Wallankarri Tjakamarra, which fetched $48 300 from a presale estimate of $10 000–$15 000. Like the small 1971 work by Johnny Warangkula which likewise trebled Sotheby's presale estimate of $7000–$10 000, it was a simple design on a black background partially dotted in white, whose attraction did not appear to lie in its cutting-edge aesthetics. Perhaps Sotheby's provenance, identifying them both as among the earliest

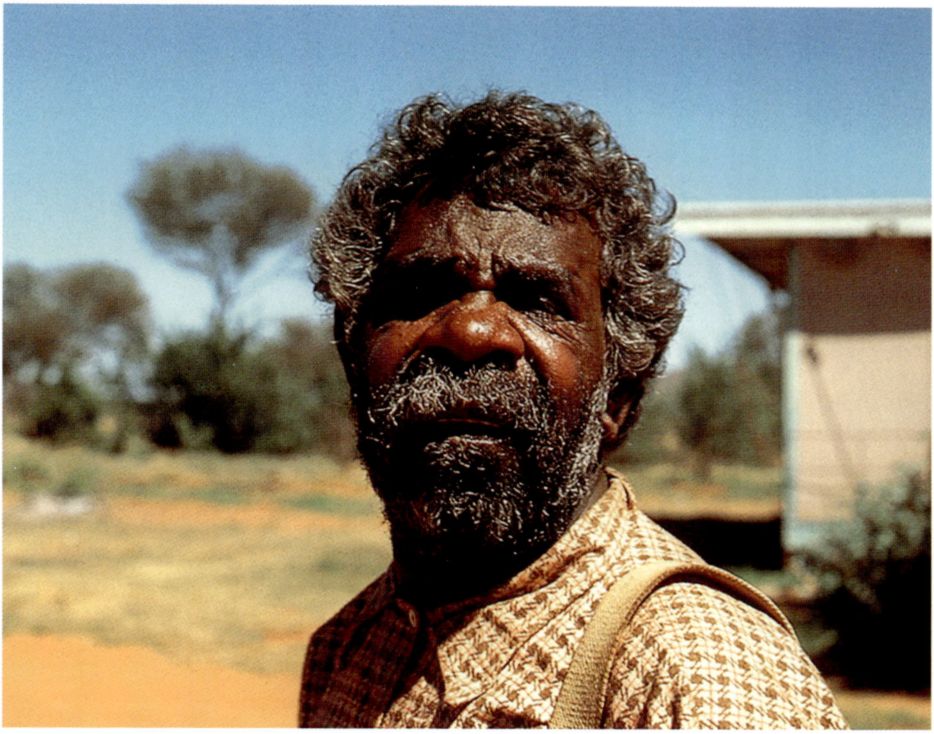

Tim Johnson

Kaapa Mbitjana Tjampitjinpa, Papunya, 1980

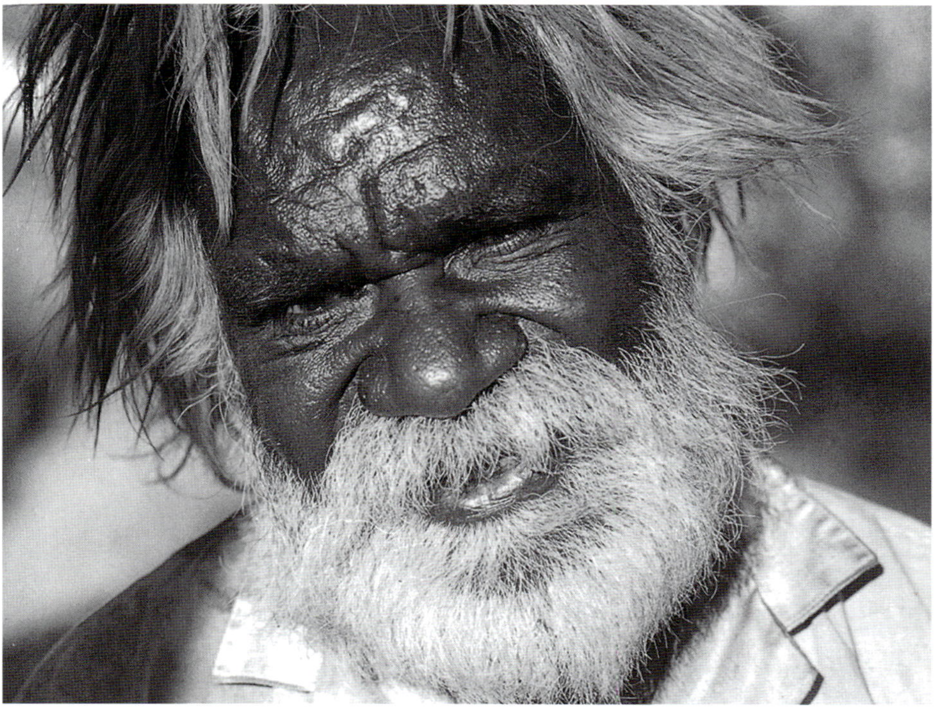

John Corker

Billy Stockman Tjapaltjarri, Alice Springs, c. 1986

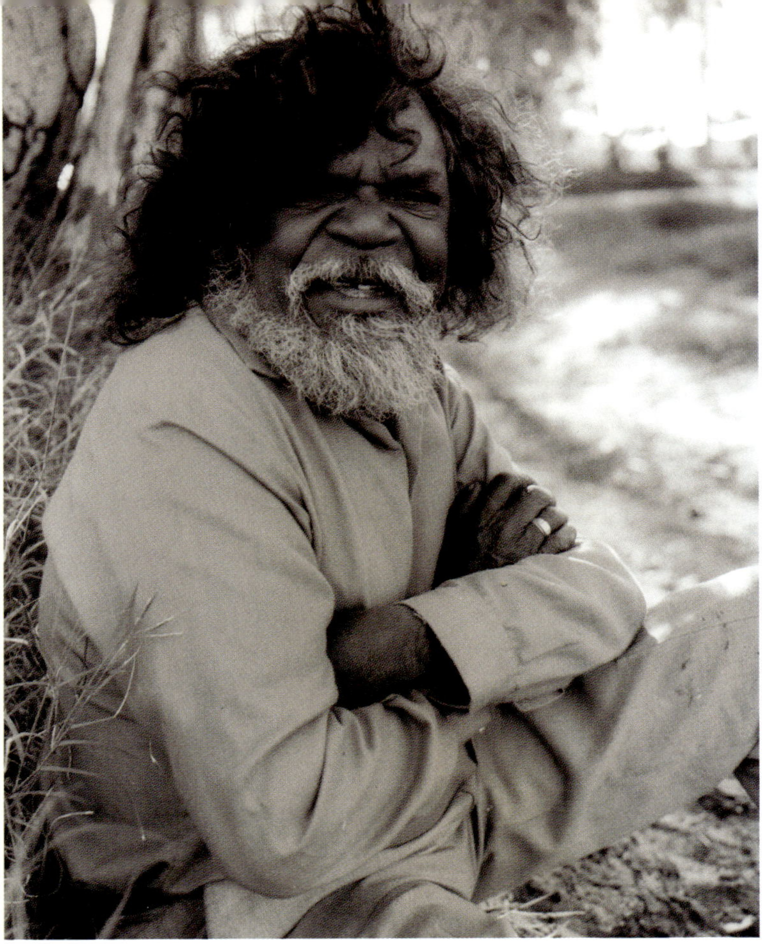

Carmel Sears

Clifford Possum Tjapaltjarri, Alice Springs, 1997

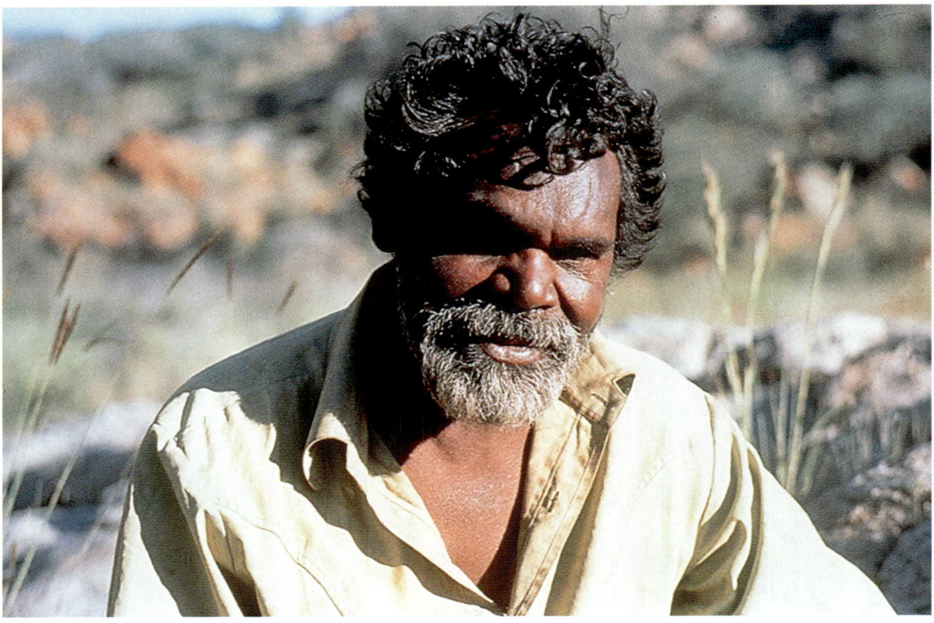

WL Jackson

Tim Leura Tjapaltjarri, Papunya, early 1970s

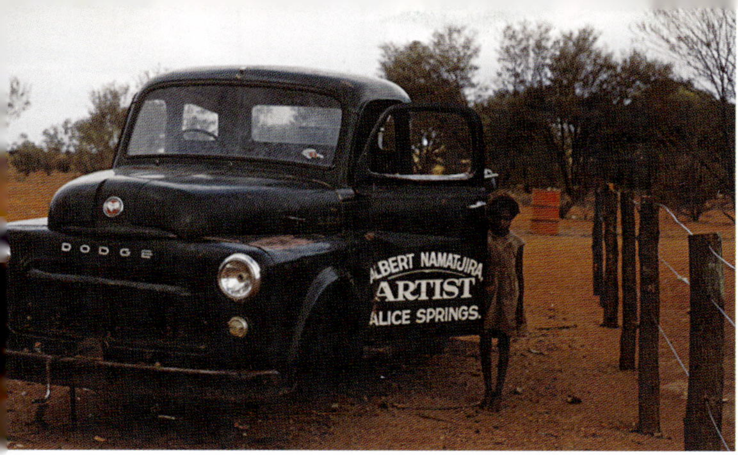

Albert Namatjira's truck, Papunya, early 1960s

Johnny Warangkula Tjupurrula, Papunya, late 1970s

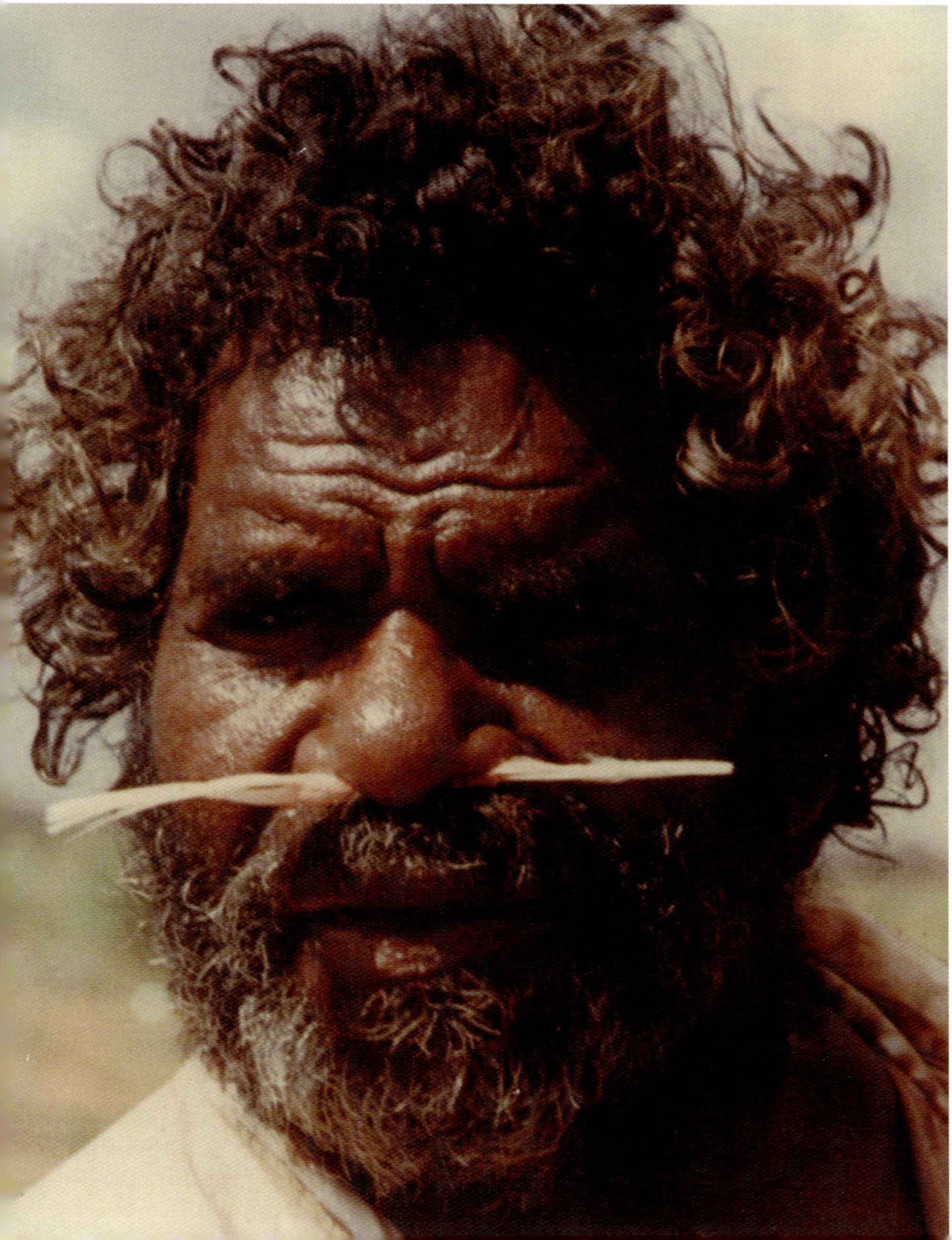

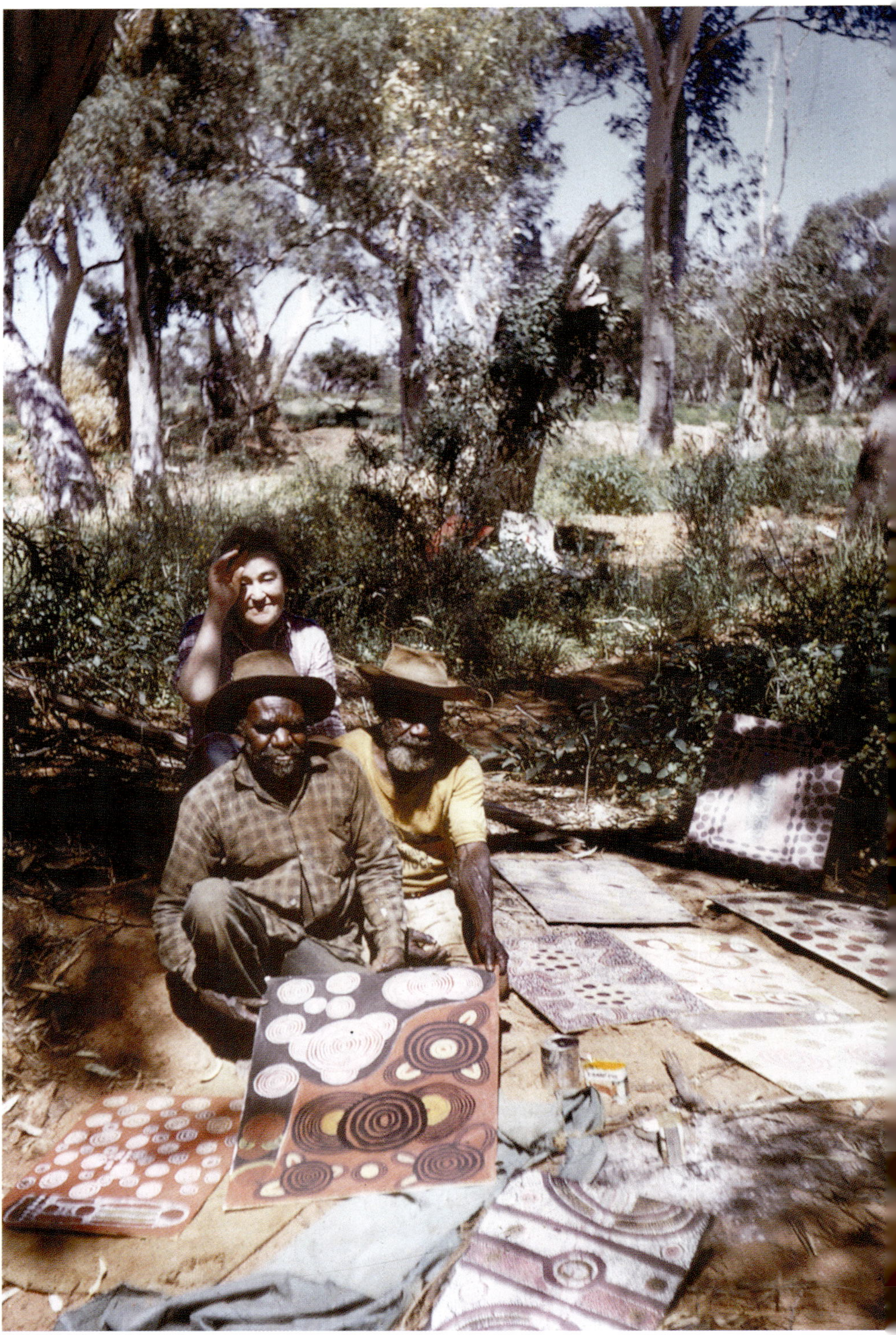

Pat Hogan of the Stuart Art Centre with painters L–R Uta Uta –Tjangala and Shorty Lungkata Tjungurrayi Yai Yai, c. 1973

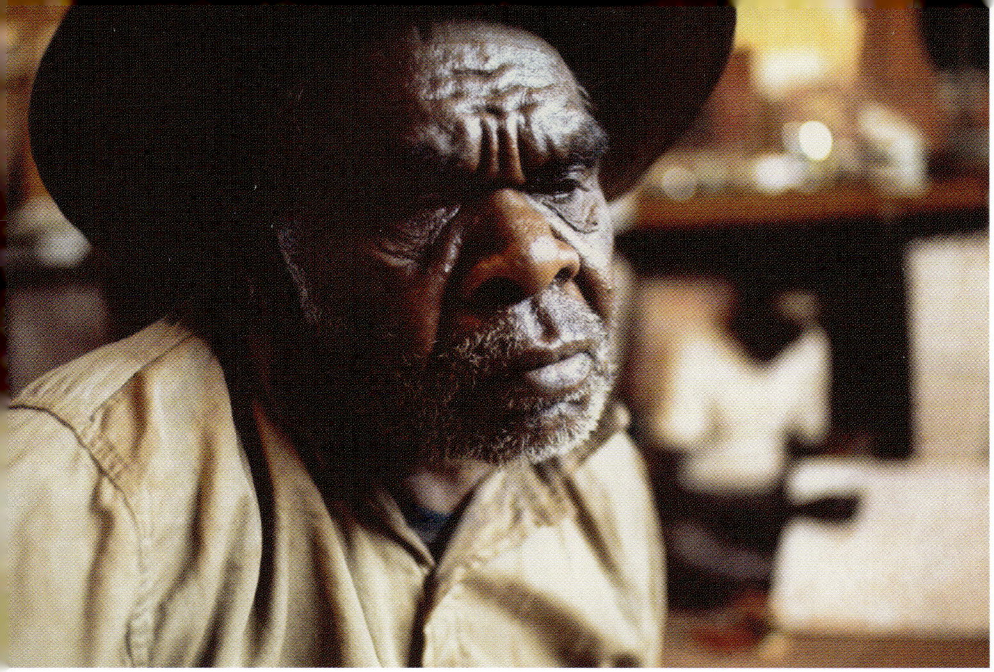

alter Tjampitjinpa, Papunya, 1972

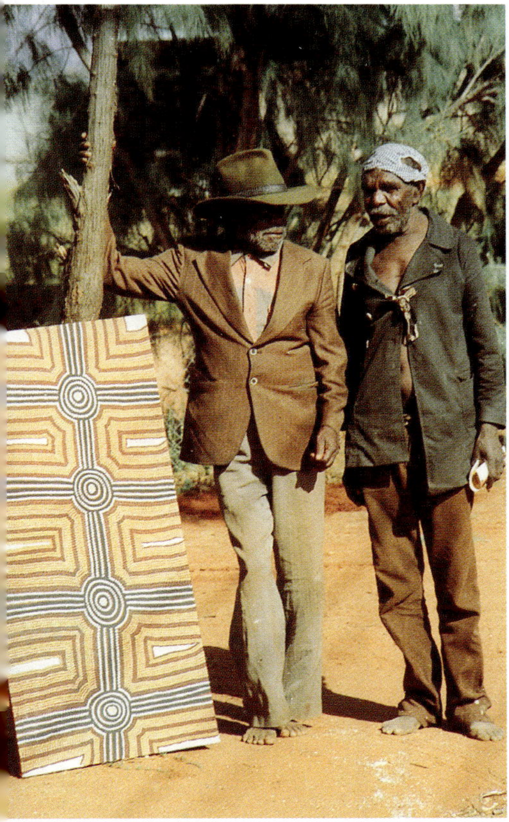

ick Namarari Tjapaltjarri (with painting) and
ıarlie Tarawa Tjungurrayi, Papunya, 1980

Grenville Turner

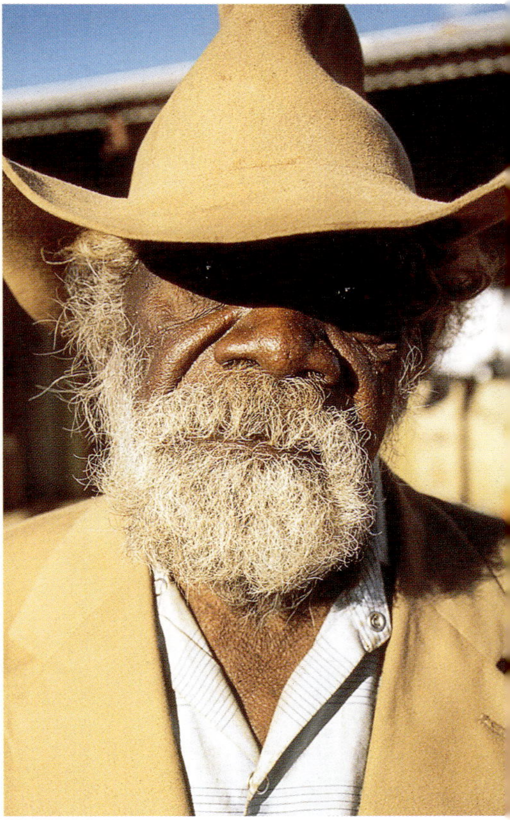

Old Mick Wallankarri Tjakamarra

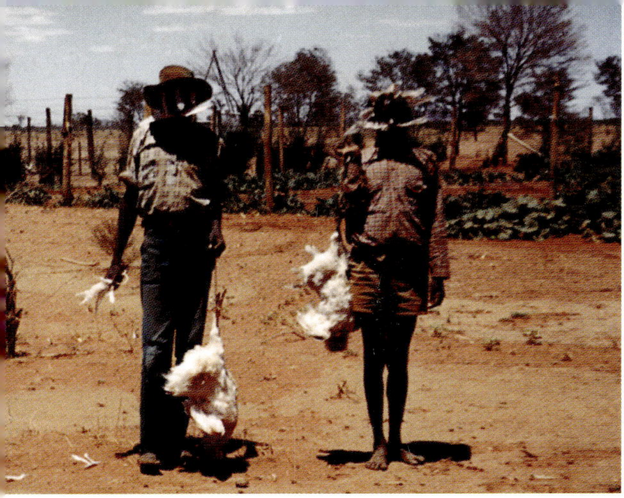

Two friends, possibly Johnny Warangkula and Mick Namarari, clowning with bush turkey feathers in Pastor Petering's 'mission garden', Papunya, early 1960s

Arnold Probin

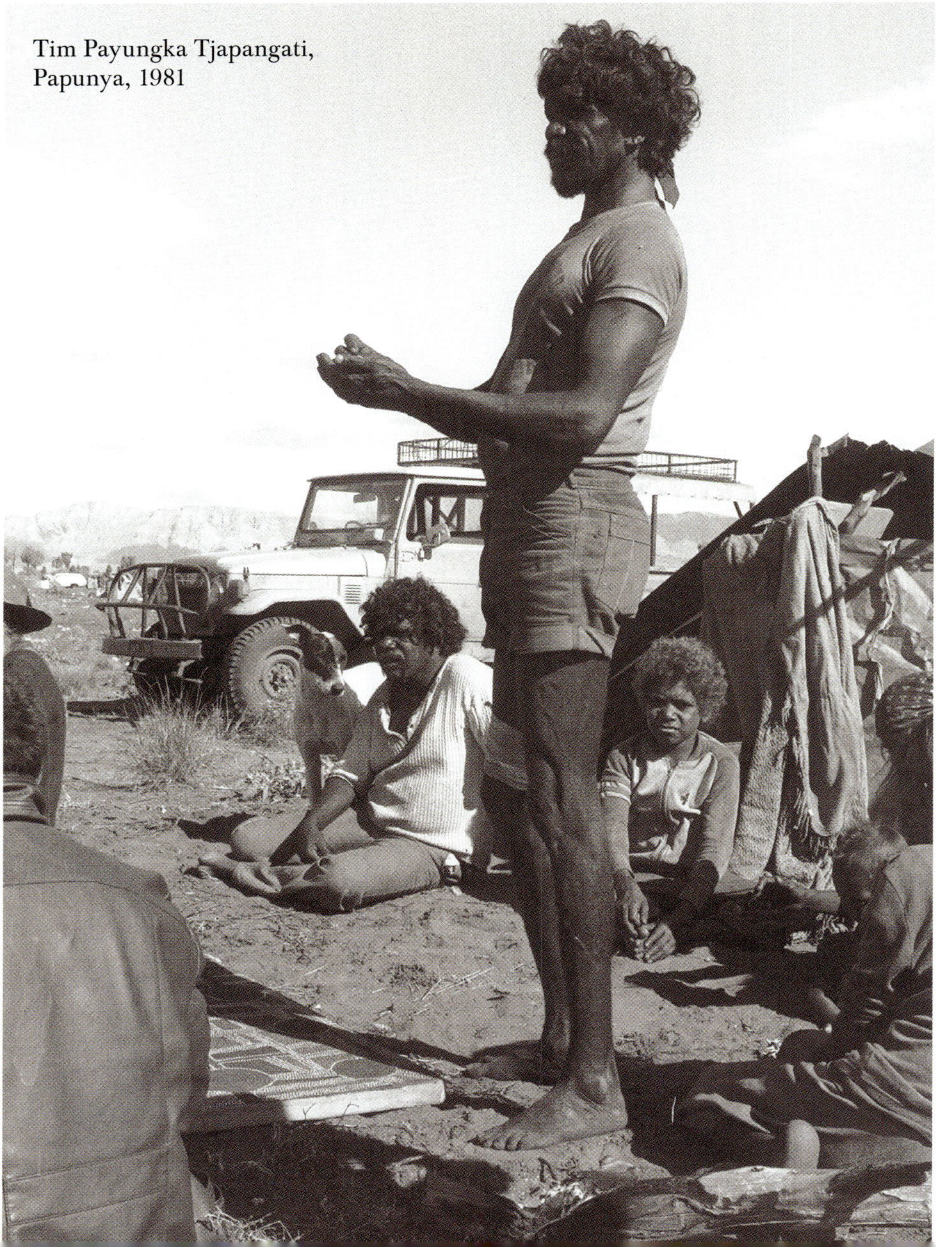

Tim Payungka Tjapangati, Papunya, 1981

JVS Megaw/Flinders University Art Museum collection

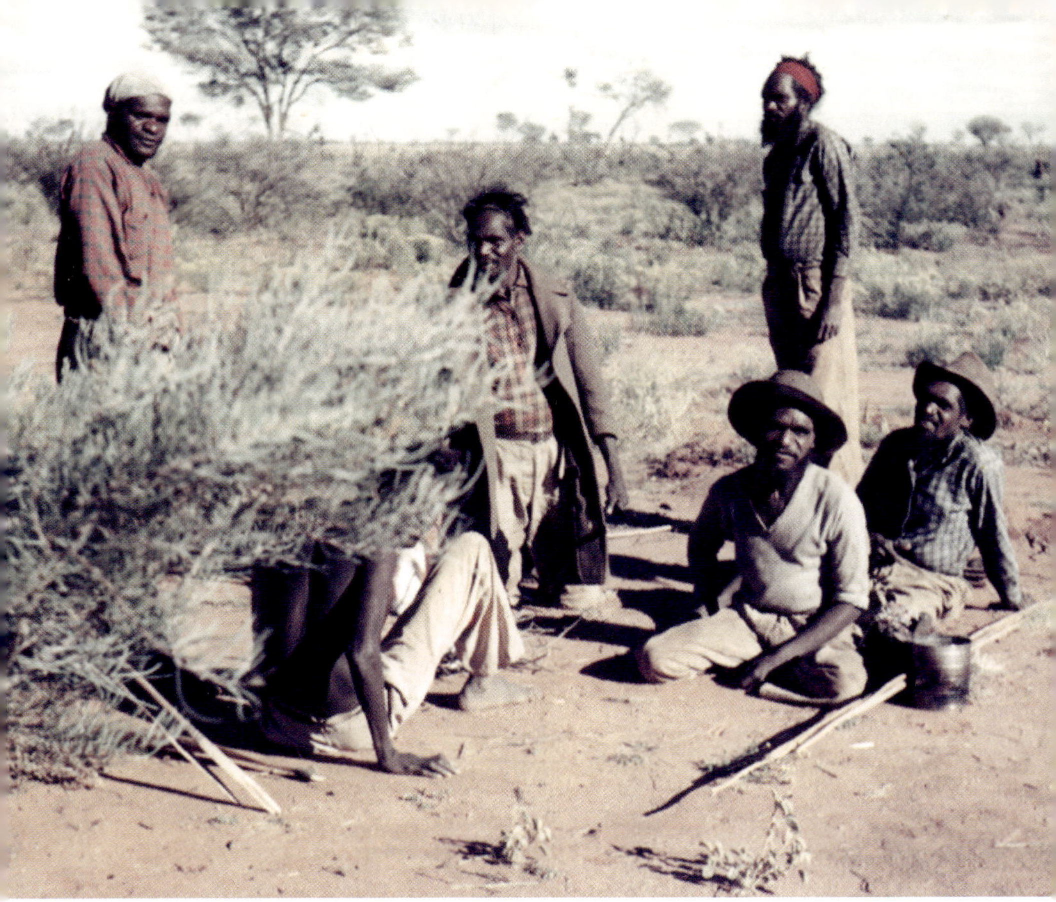

Pintupi farmworkers, Papunya, early 1960s, STANDING L–R Willy Tjapanangka, Timmy Payungka Tjapangati, Tjalyuri Tjapaltjarri, SEATED L–R obscured, John Tjakamarra, unknown

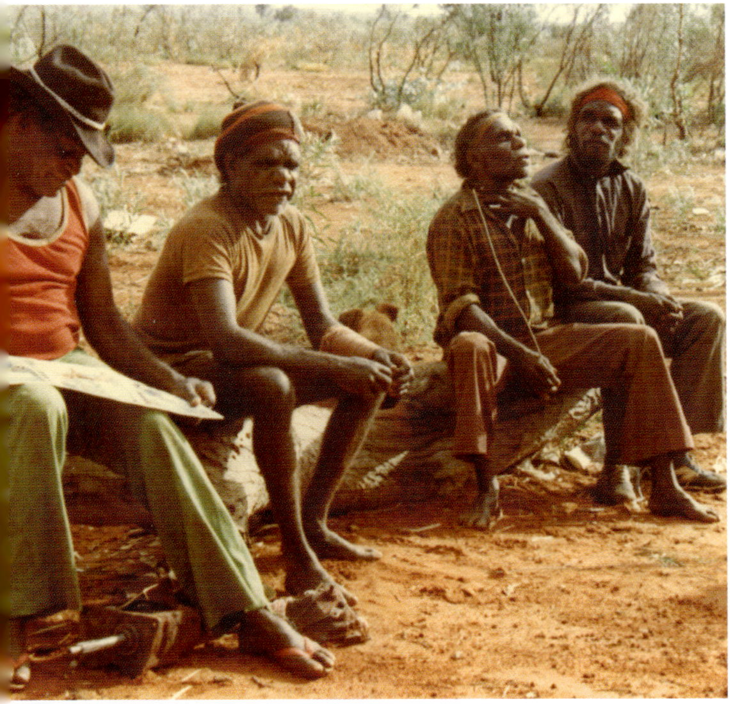

L–R Freddy West Tjakamarra, Anatjari Tjampitjinpa, Willy Tjungurrayi and John Tjakamarra, Papunya, late 1970s

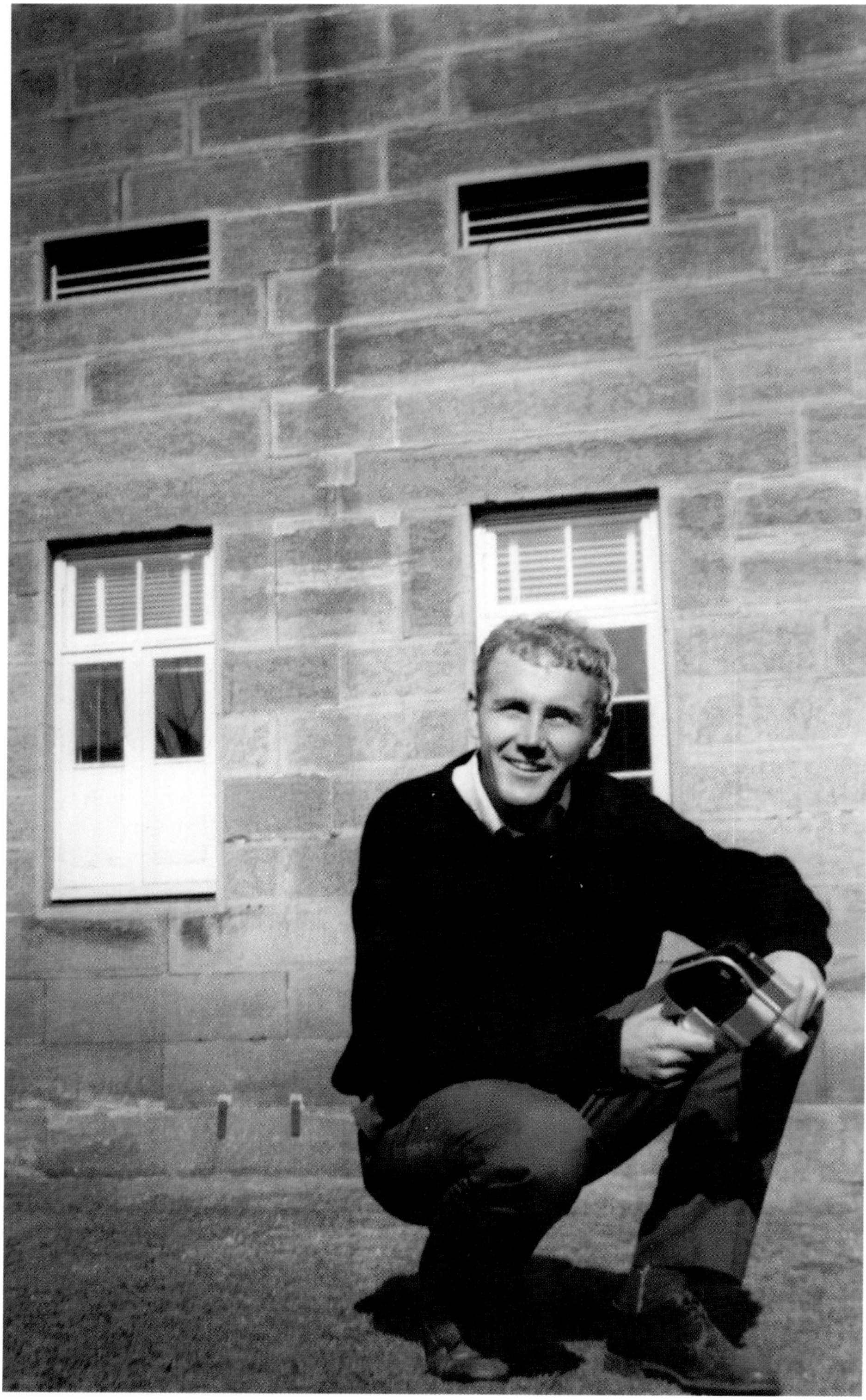
Documentary Educational Resources

Geoffrey Bardon at the National Art School in his student days, early 1960s

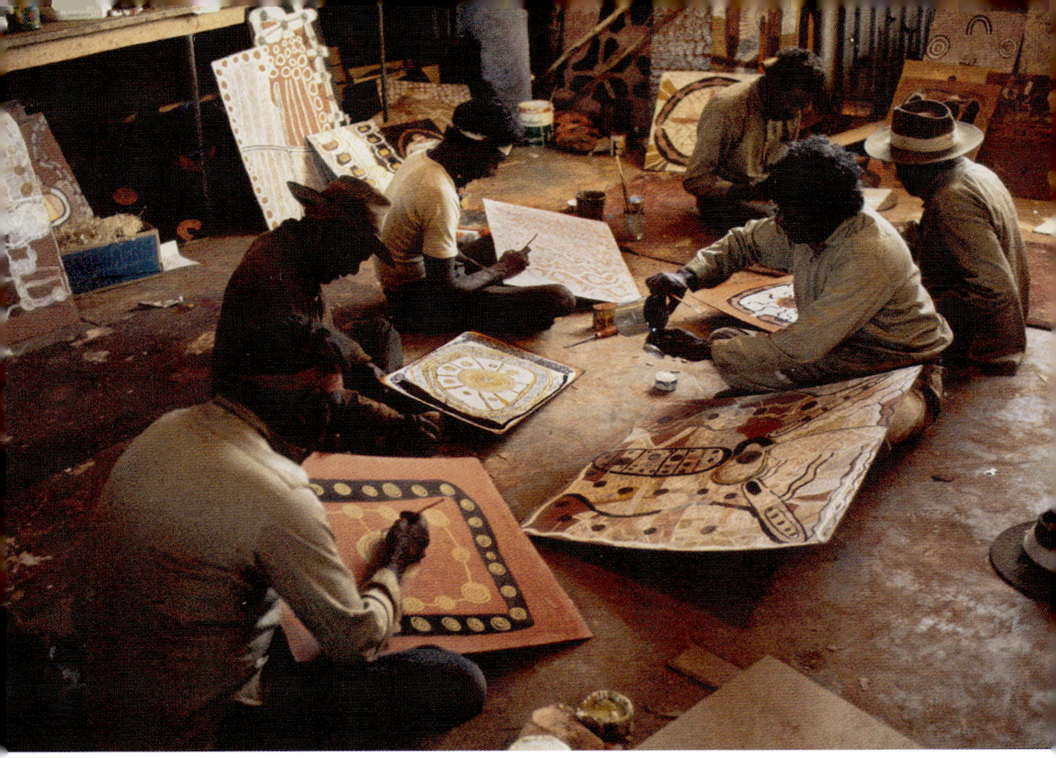

Men's Painting Room, Papunya, August 1972.
L–R Yala Yala Gibbs Tjungurrayi (probably), Shorty Lungkata Tjungurrayi, Tim Payungka Tjapangati, Kaapa Mbitjana Tjampitjinpa, Walter Tjampitjinpa (in hat) and Johnny Warangkula Tjupurrula with unfinished *Water Dreaming at Kalipinypa* 1972

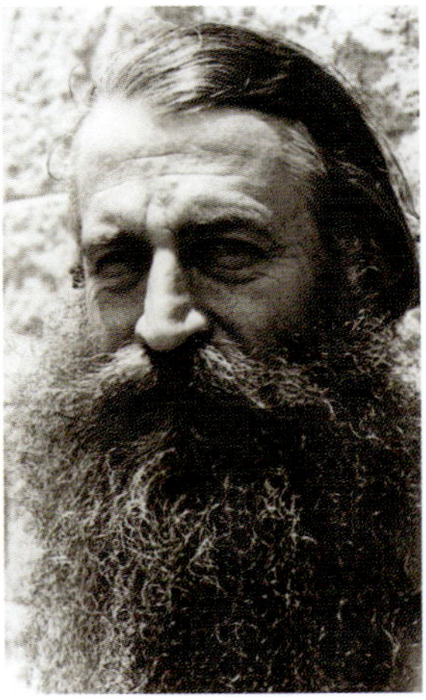

Northern Territory Government Collection PH0107/0376

Dr Colin Jack-Hinton, first Director of the Museums and Art Galleries of the Northern Territory

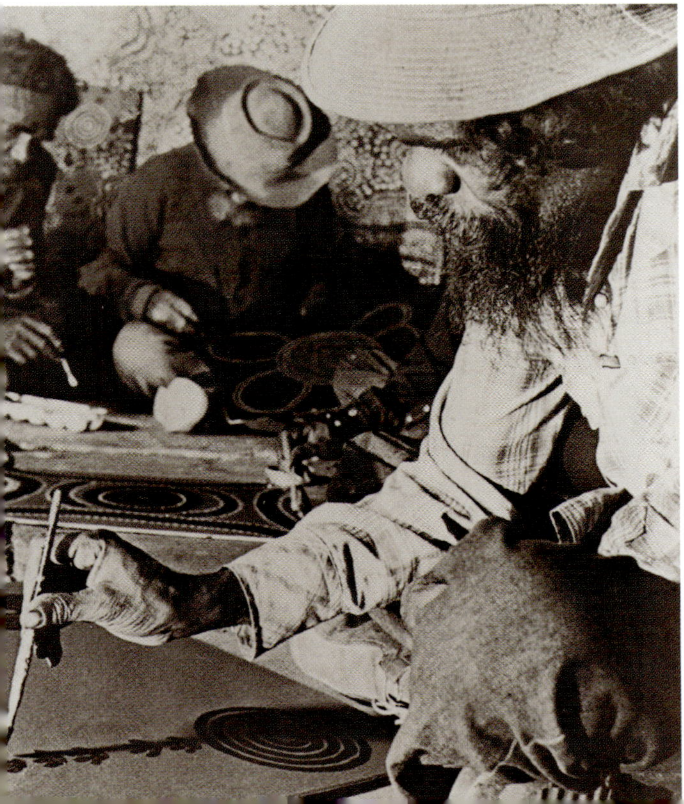

L–R John Tjakamarra, Shorty Lungkata Tjungurrayi and Anatjari Tjakamarra in the Men's Painting Room, Papunya, 1970s

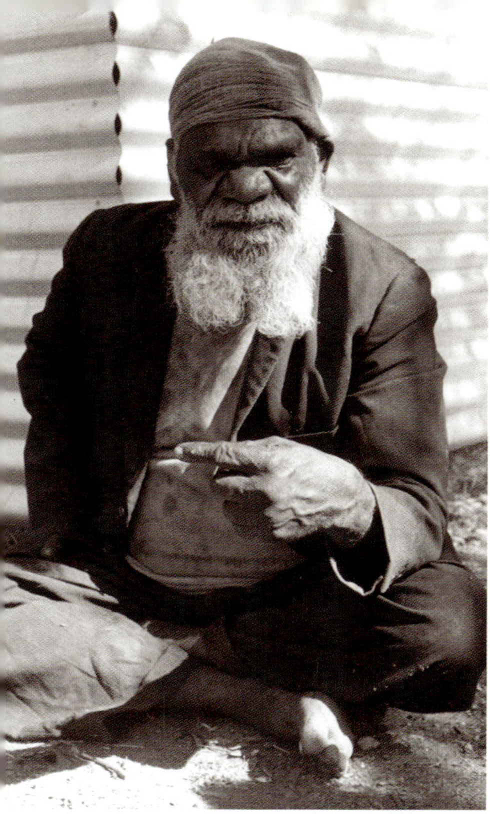

JVS Megaw/Flinders University Art Museum collection

< Nosepeg Tjupurrula, Papunya, 1981

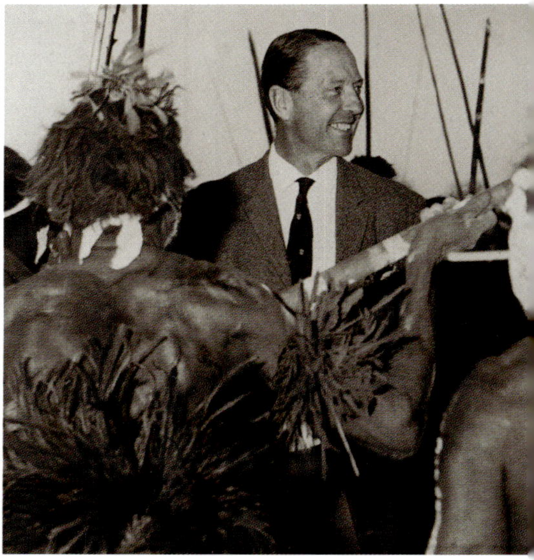

Mr Harry Giese, Director of Welfare in the Northern Territory, at the opening of the Yuendumu Museum, 1972

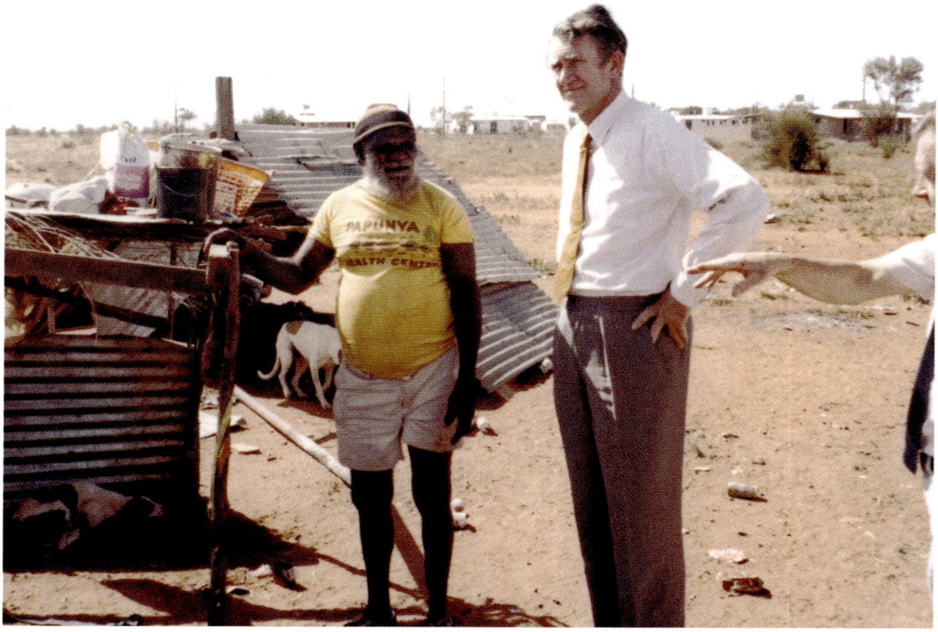

Photographer unknown/University of Melbourne Archives, Malcolm Fraser Collection, UMA/I/6068

Nosepeg Tjupurrula outside his humpy in Papunya, c. 1976, with Prime Minister Malcolm Fraser

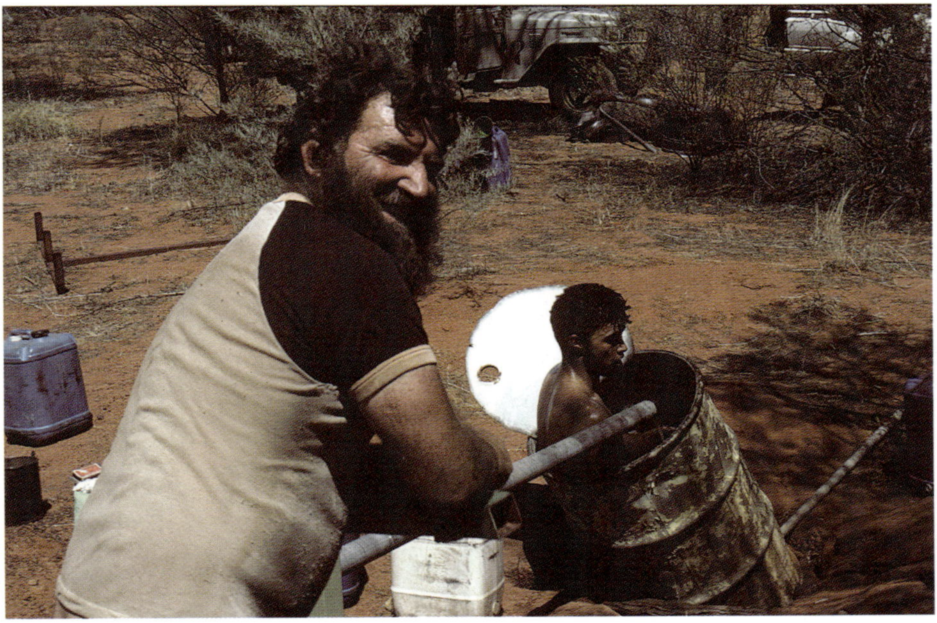

Jeremy Long

RW (Dick) Kimber at Kulkuta Bore, Western Australia, 1987

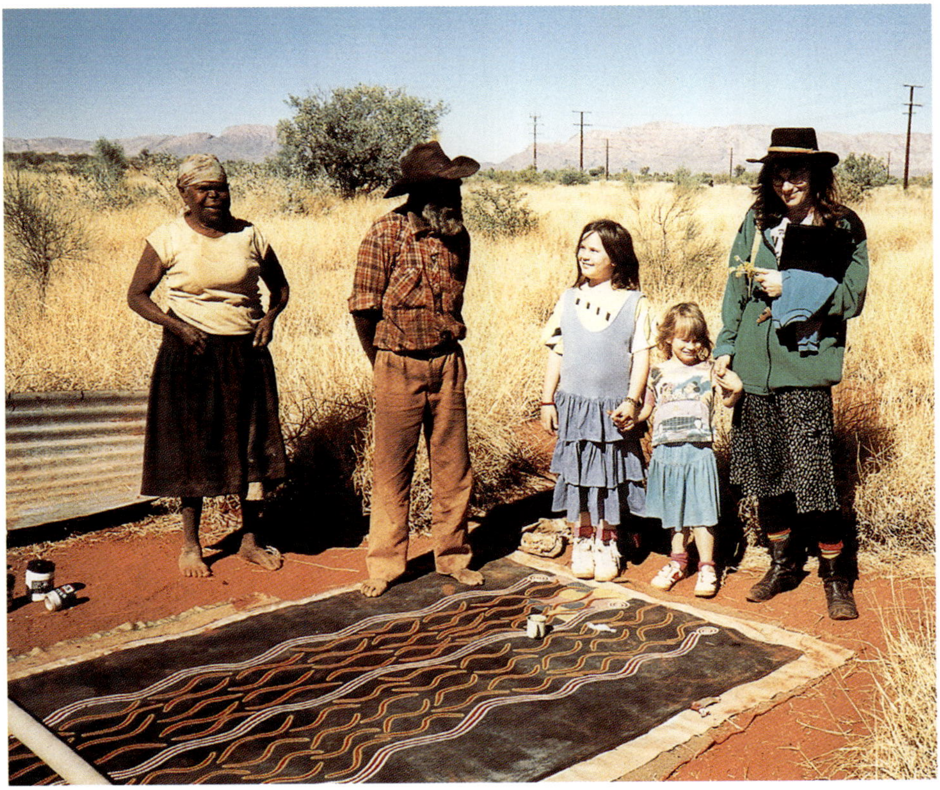

L–R Ruby Nangala, Paddy Carroll Tjungurrayi, Tania Johnson, Ruby Johnson, Vivien Johnson, Papunya, 1989

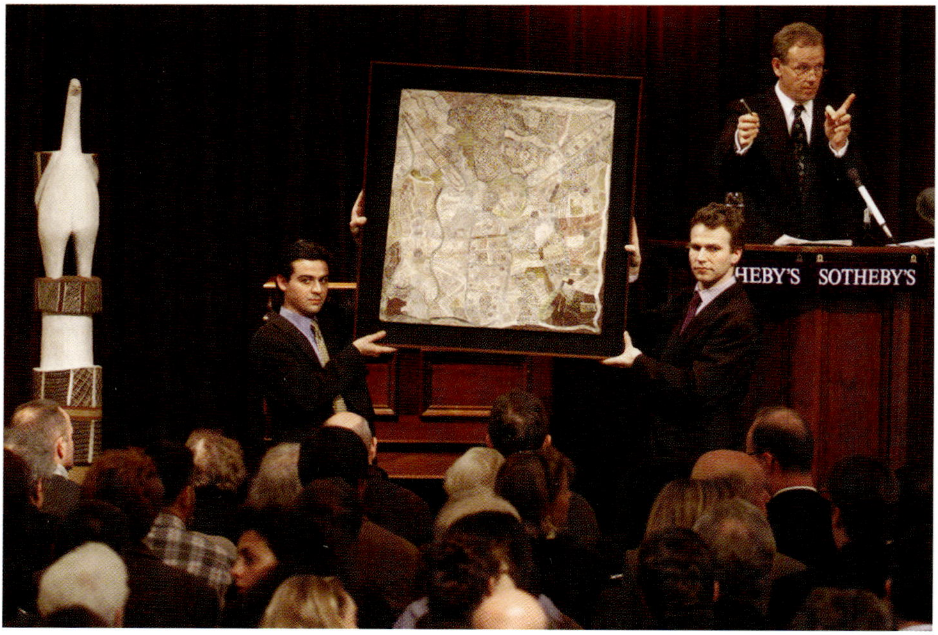

Newspix/Shaney Balcombe

Johnny Warangkula Tjupurrula's *Water Dreaming at Kalipinypa* 1972 is auctioned at Sotheby's Australia, Melbourne, 2000

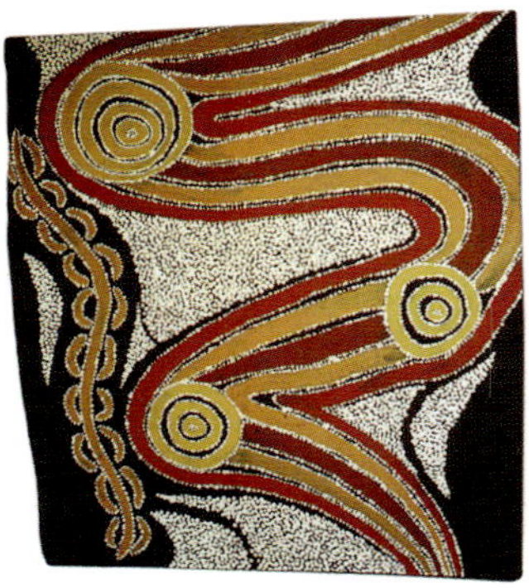

Forgery based on Mick Wallankarri Tjakamarra's Untitled 1971

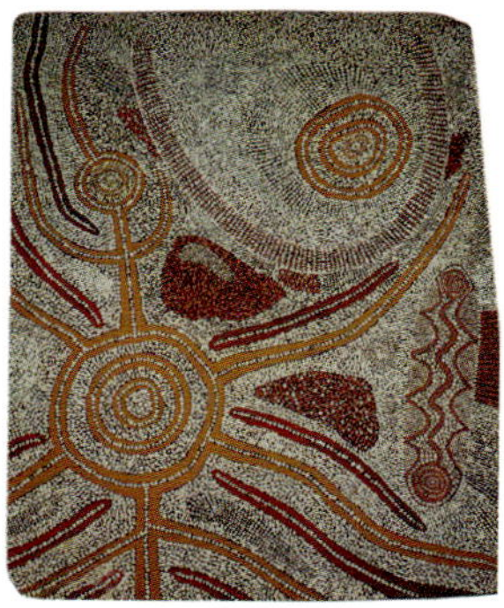

Forgery based on Johnny Warangkula's Untitled 1971

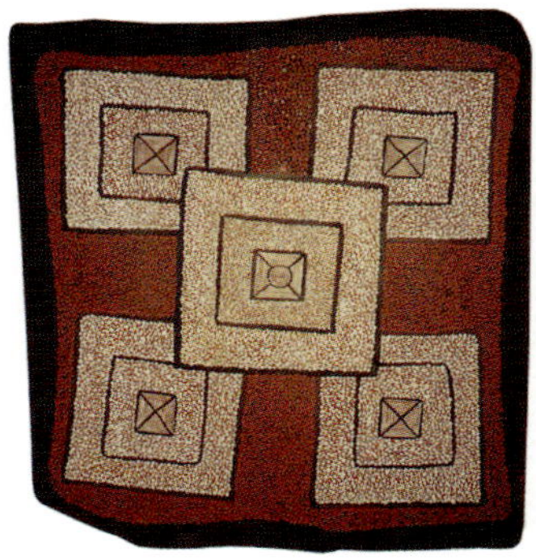

Forgery based on Anatjari Tjakamarra's *A Cave Story* 1972

> Long Jack Phillipus Tjakamarra, standing in front of his painting *Fire Dreaming at Parikulaman* 1975, at 'Papunya Painting: Out of the Desert', National Museum of Australia, Canberra, December 2007 (Note: At Long Jack's instruction, the painting was later re-hung the other way up)

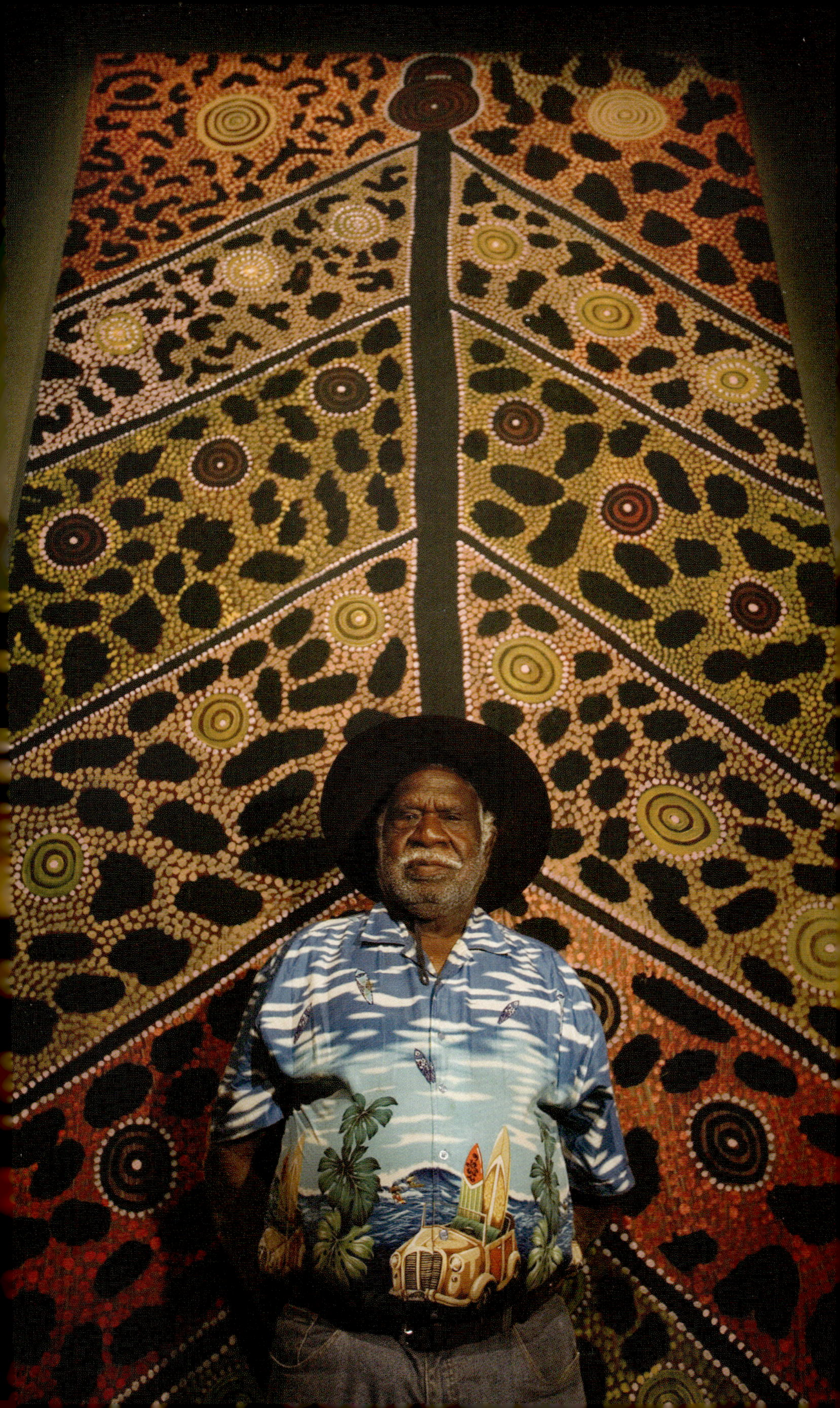

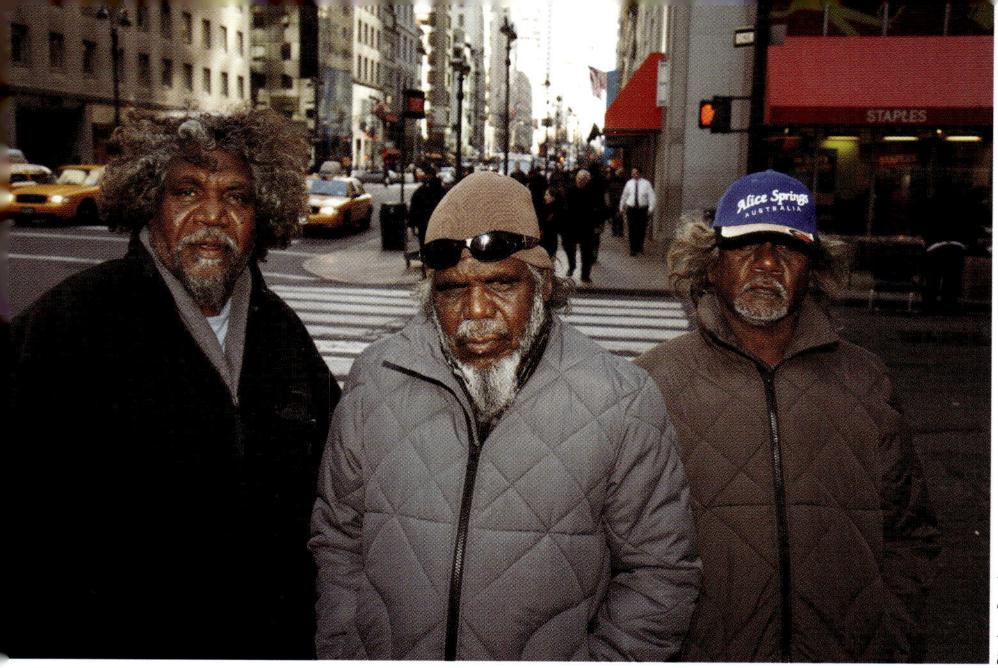

Stephen Oxenbury

L–R Bobby West Tjupurrula, Joseph Jurra Tjapaltjarri and Ray James Tjangala, New York City, February 2009, en route to the opening of 'Icons of the Desert' in Ithaca

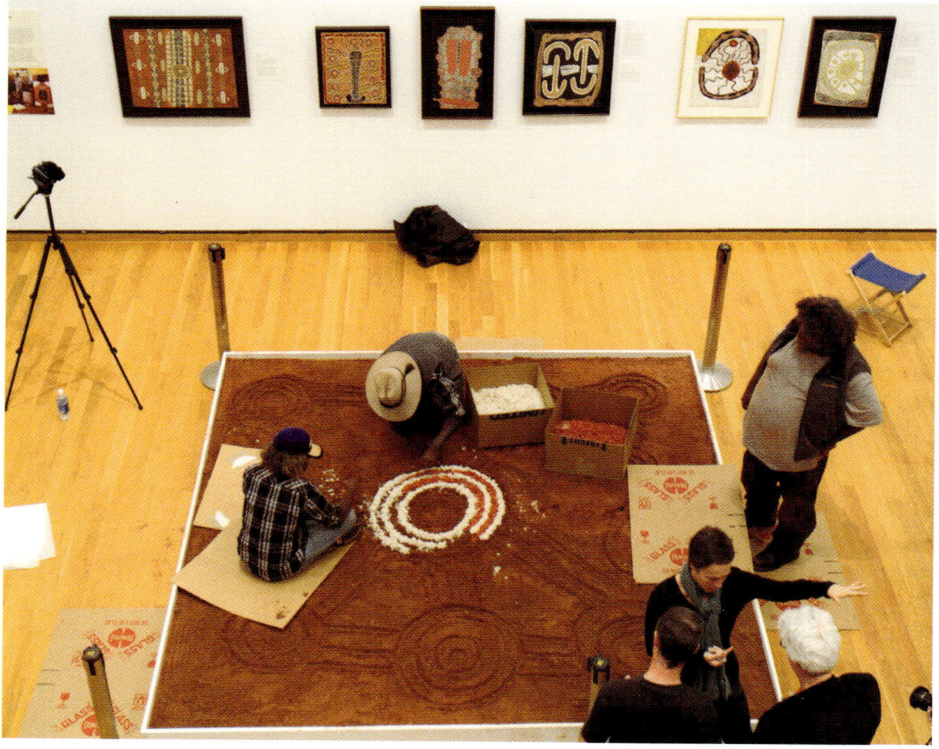

Simon Wheeler/The Ithaca Journal

L–R Ray James Tjangala, Joseph Jurra Tjapaltjarri and Bobby West Tjupurrula at work on the ground painting, Herbert F Johnson Museum of Art at Cornell University, February 2009

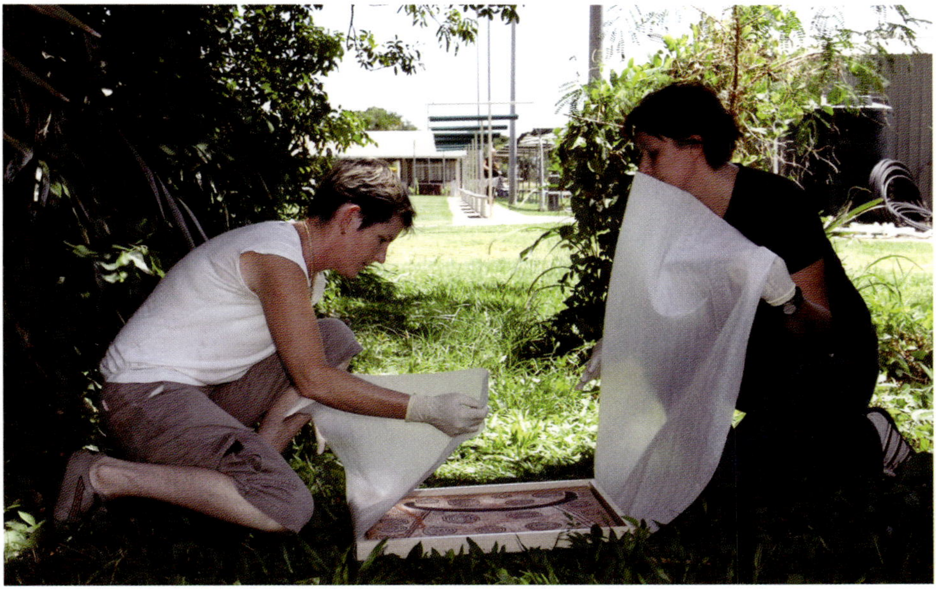

Newspix/Justin Sanson

Staff from the Museum and Art Gallery of the Northern Territory retrieve stolen paintings from behind a Darwin bowling green, April 2008

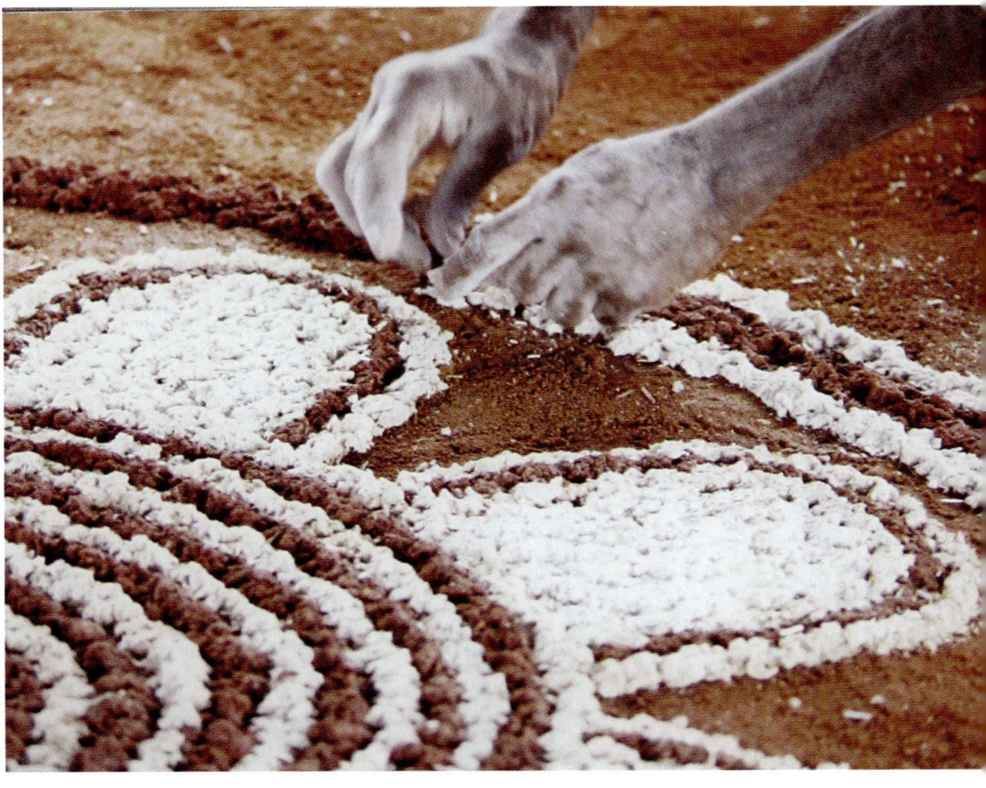

Jennifer Steele

Ground painting by Paddy Carroll Tjungurrayi and Dinny Nolan Tjampitjimpa under construction at SH Ervin Gallery, Sydney, January 1981

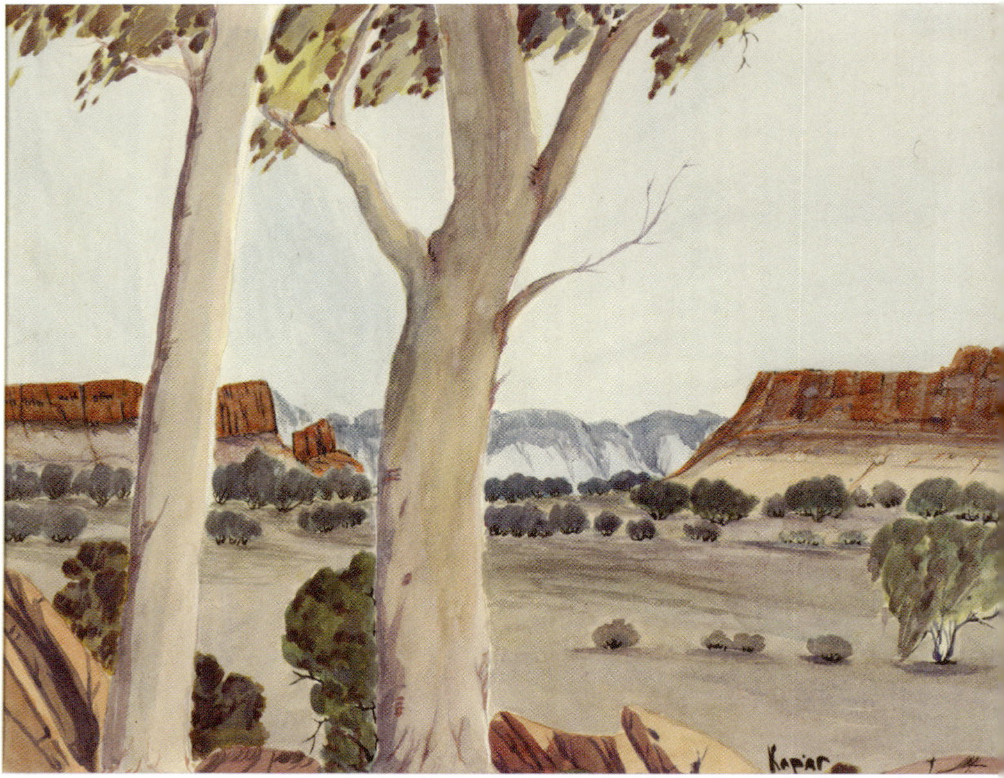

Kaapa Mbitjana Tjampitjinpa
Untitled c. 1970

Watercolour on paper, 27.5 x 36.5 cm
National Museum of Australia Collection

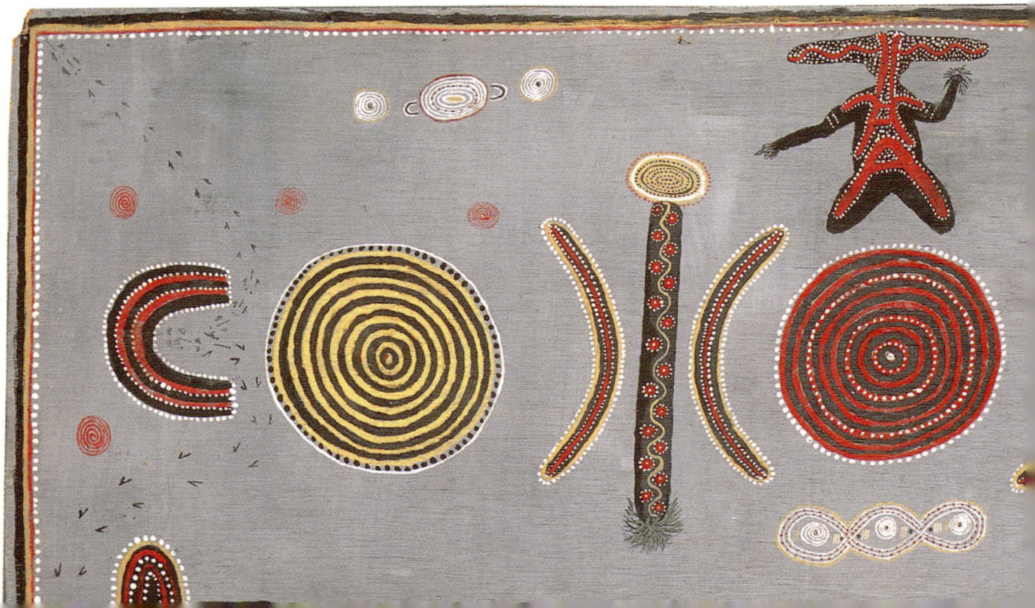

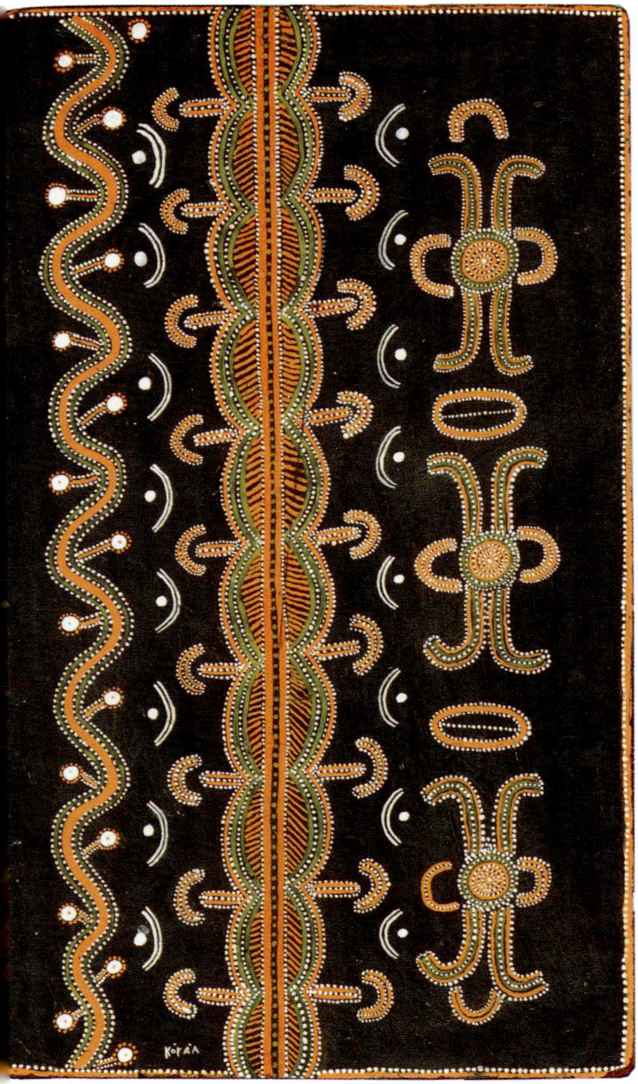

Kaapa Mbitjana Tjampitjinpa
Untitled 1971

Synthetic polymer paint on plywood, 121.6 x 99 cm
Purchased by the Art Gallery of South Australia with a South Australian government grant in 1989

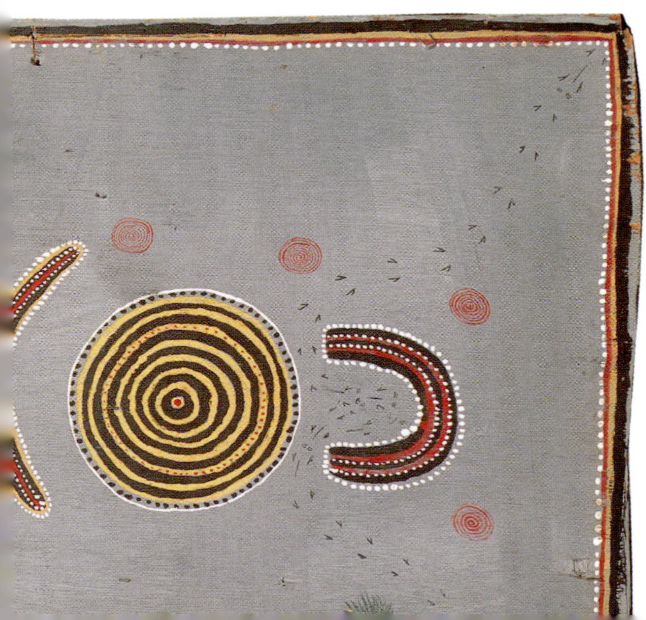

Kaapa Mbitjana Tjampitjinpa
Men's Ceremony for the Kangaroo Gulgardi 1971

Acrylic on hardboard, 61 x 137 cm (irregular), cropped
Araluen Art Centre

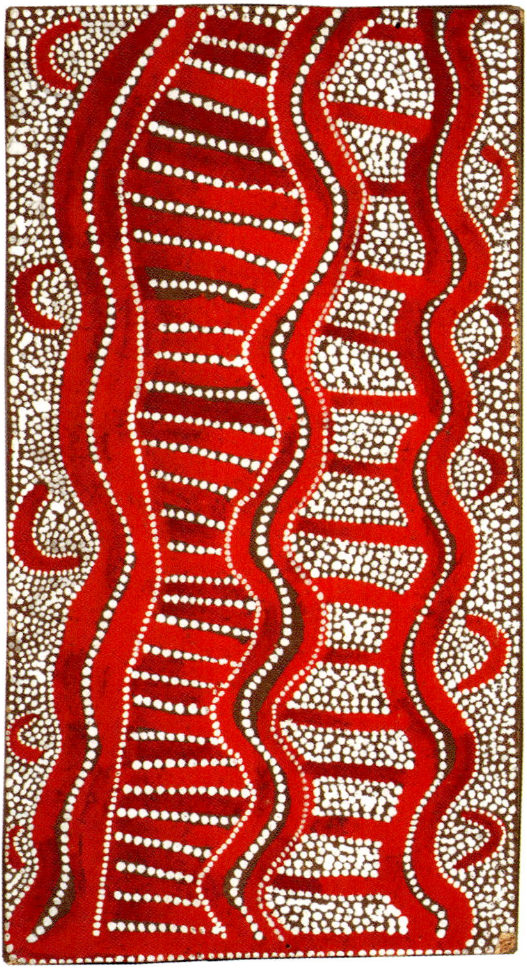

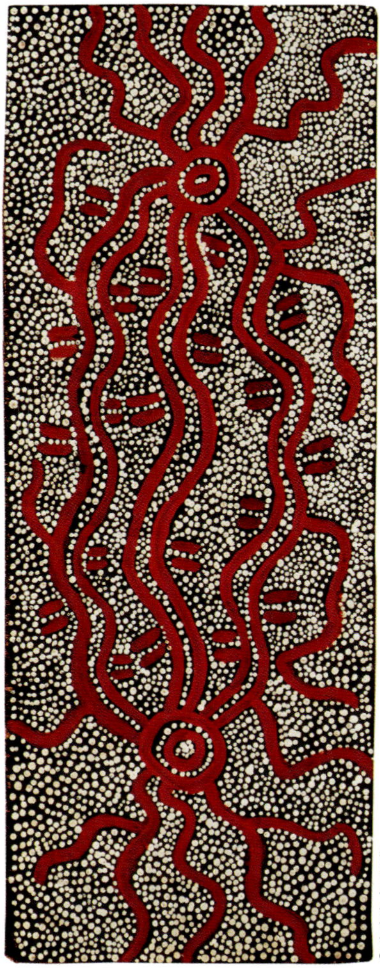

Sotheby's Australia

Mick Namarari Tjapaltjarri
Sandhills and Clouds 1971

Synthetic polymer paint on composition board, 51.2 x 29.3 cm (framed)
Purchased by the Museum and Art Gallery of the Northern Territory in 1971/72
From the 1st consignment to the Stuart Art Centre

Walter Tjampitjinpa
Water Dreaming at Kalipinypa 1971

Synthetic polymer paint on composition board, 91 x 35 cm
From the 1st consignment to the Stuart Art Centre

Kingsley Tjungurrayi
Storm 1971

Synthetic polymer and enamel paint on composition board, 23 x 70.5 cm
John and Barbara Wilkerson Collection
From the 1st consignment to the Stuart Art Centre

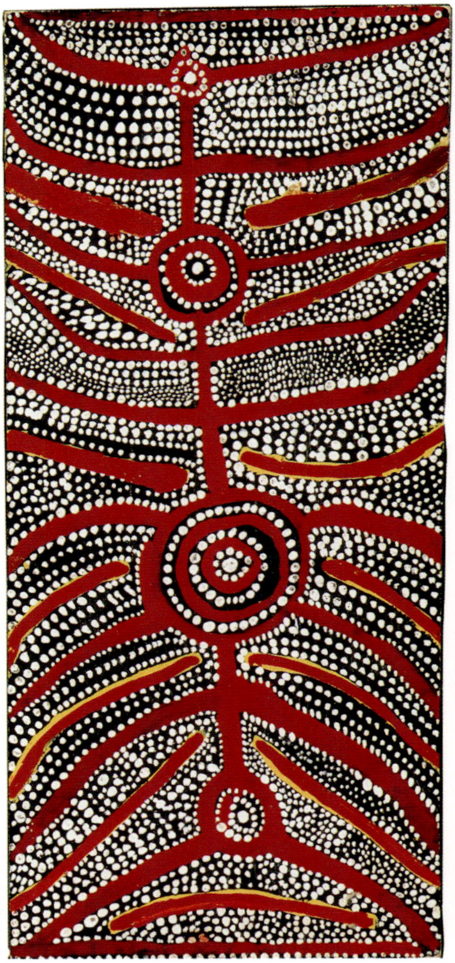

Sotheby's Australia

Johnny Warangkula Tjupurrula
Untitled 1971

Enamel on composition board, 59 x 27.5 cm
From the 1st consignment to the Stuart Art Centre

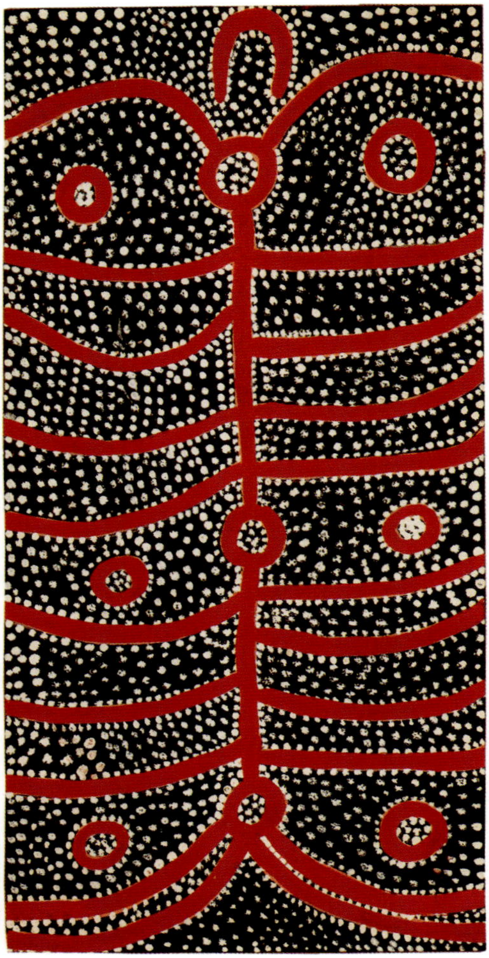

Sotheby's Australia

Long Jack Phillipus Tjakamarra
Water Dreaming 1971

Synthetic polymer paint and enamel paint on composition board, 44 x 22 cm
From the 4th consignment to the Stuart Art Centre

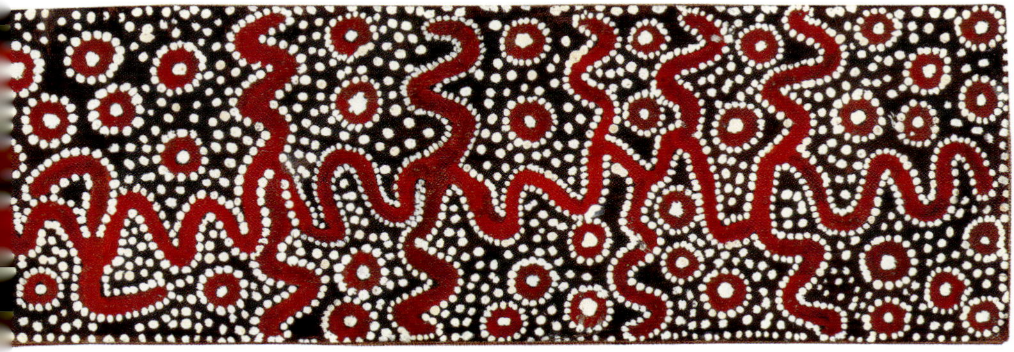

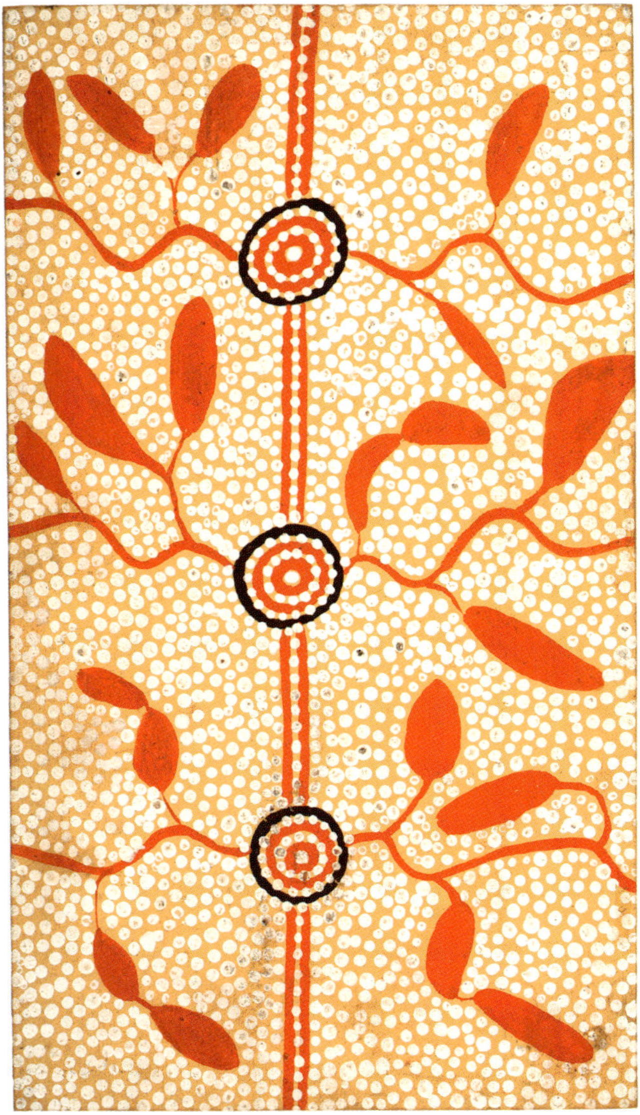

Kaapa Mbitjana Tjampitjinpa
Wild Potato Story 1971

Synthetic polymer paint on composition board, 61.8 x 43.9 cm (framed)
Gift from the Department of Aboriginal Affairs, 1975, to the Museum and Art Gallery of the Northern Territory
From the 1st consignment to the Stuart Art Centre

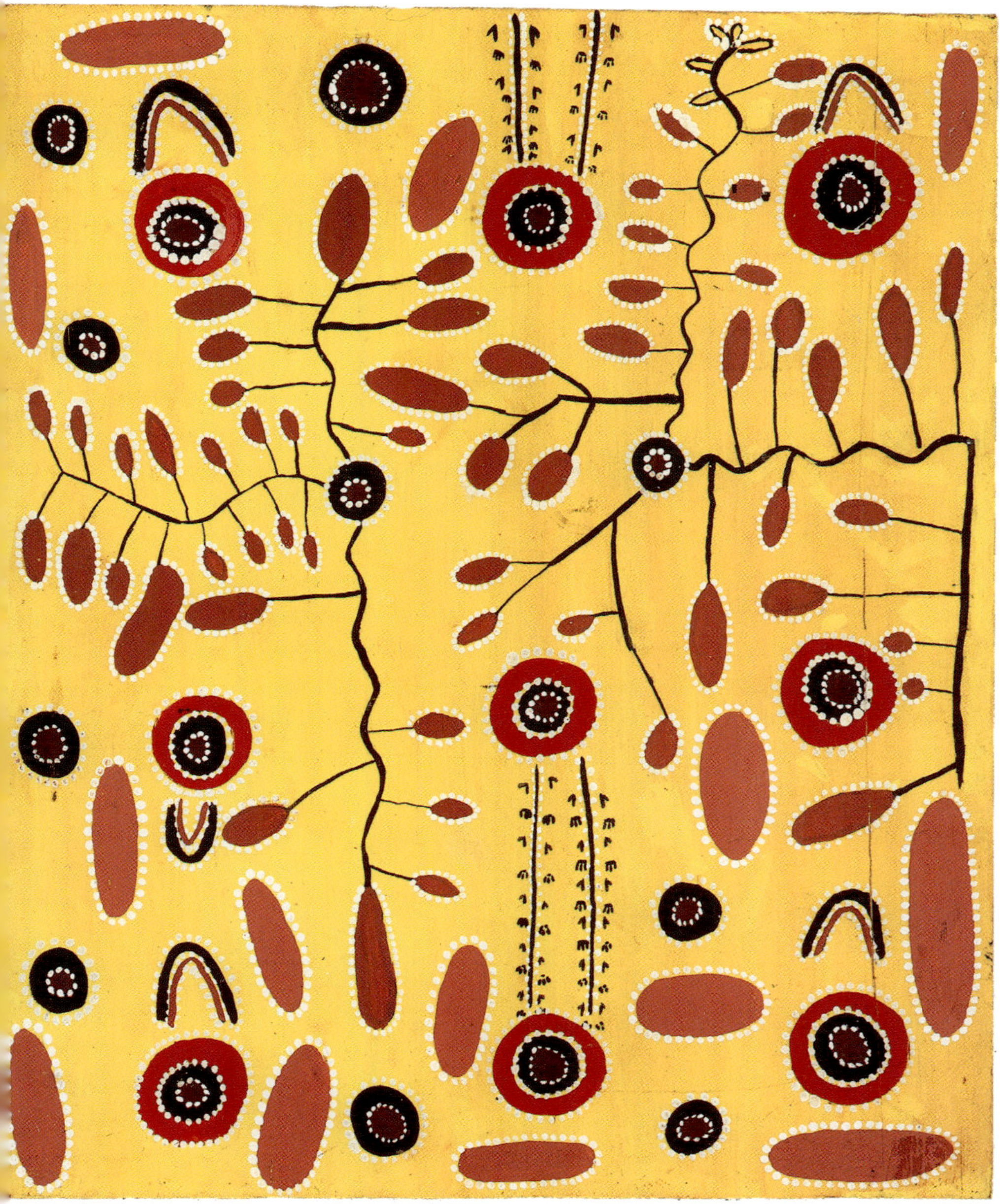

Billy Stockman Tjapaltjarri
Yala (Wild Potato) Dreaming 1971

Powder paint on composition board, 54.5 x 46 cm
From the 2nd consignment to the Stuart Art Centre

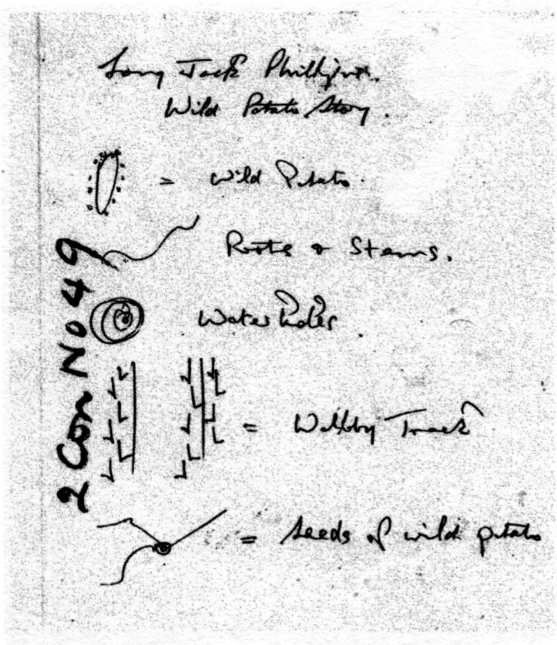

Papunya Tula Artists

Diagram of the 49th painting of the 2nd consignment to the Stuart Art Centre – *Yala (Wild Potato) Dreaming* 1971, showing attribution to Long Jack Phillipus in Geoffrey Bardon's hand

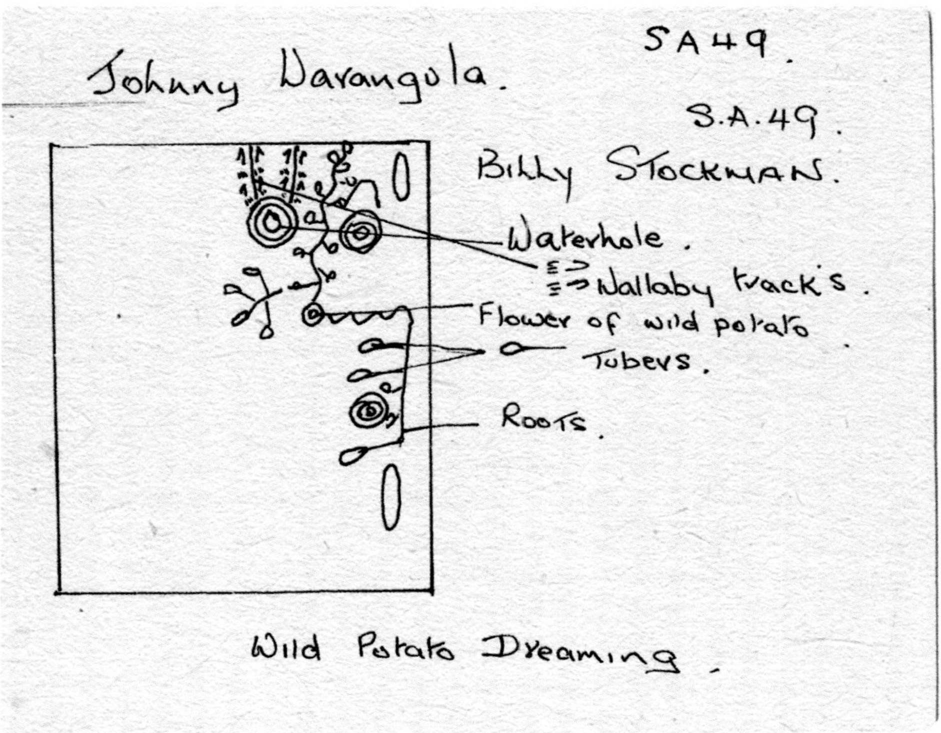

Sotheby's Australia/Papunya Tula Artists

Diagram of *Yala (Wild Potato) Dreaming* 1971, supplied to the original purchaser by the Stuart Art Centre in Pat Hogan's hand, showing attribution to Billy Stockman and Johnny Warangula (*sic*)

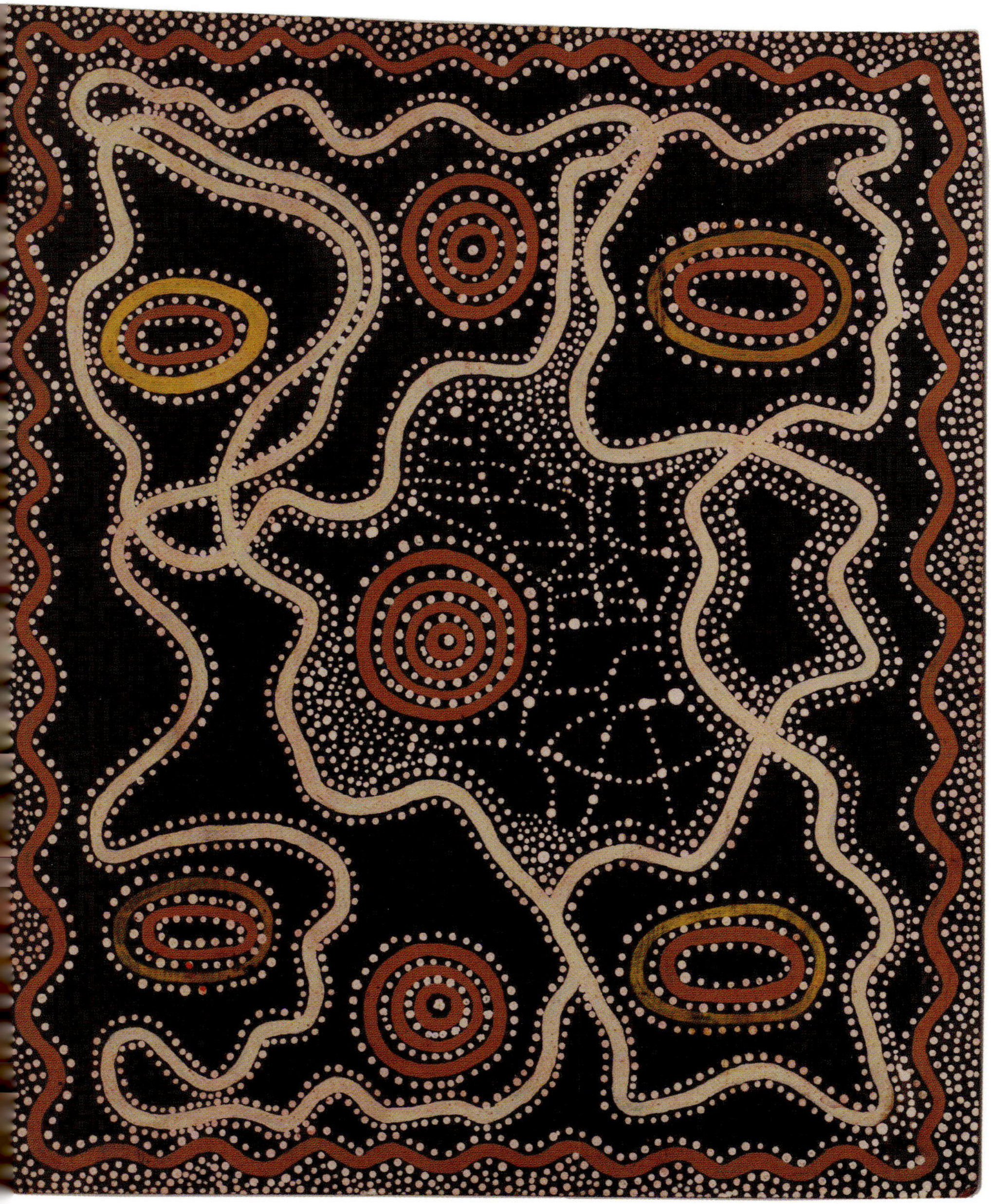

Billy Stockman Tjapaltjarri
Yam Dreaming 1971

Synthetic polymer paint on masonite board, 44 x 36 cm
Wollongong City Gallery Collection, on permanent loan from Orange Regional Gallery
From the 3rd consignment to the Stuart Art Centre

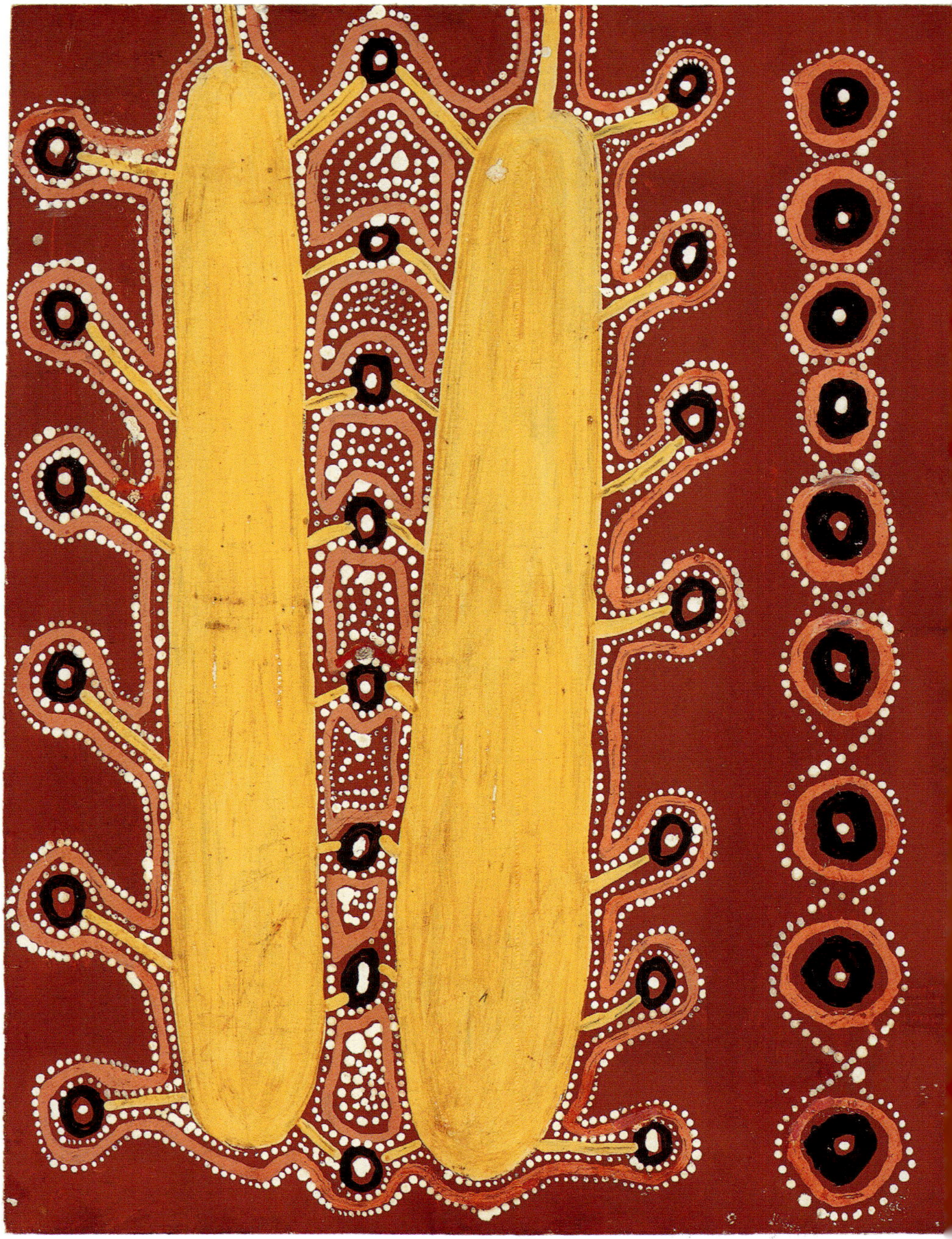

Uta Uta (Wuta Wuta) Tjangala
Medicine Story 1971

Natural earth pigments and synthetic polymer and enamel paint on composition board, 45.7 x 35.5 cm
National Museum of Australia Collection
From the 2nd consignment to the Stuart Art Centre

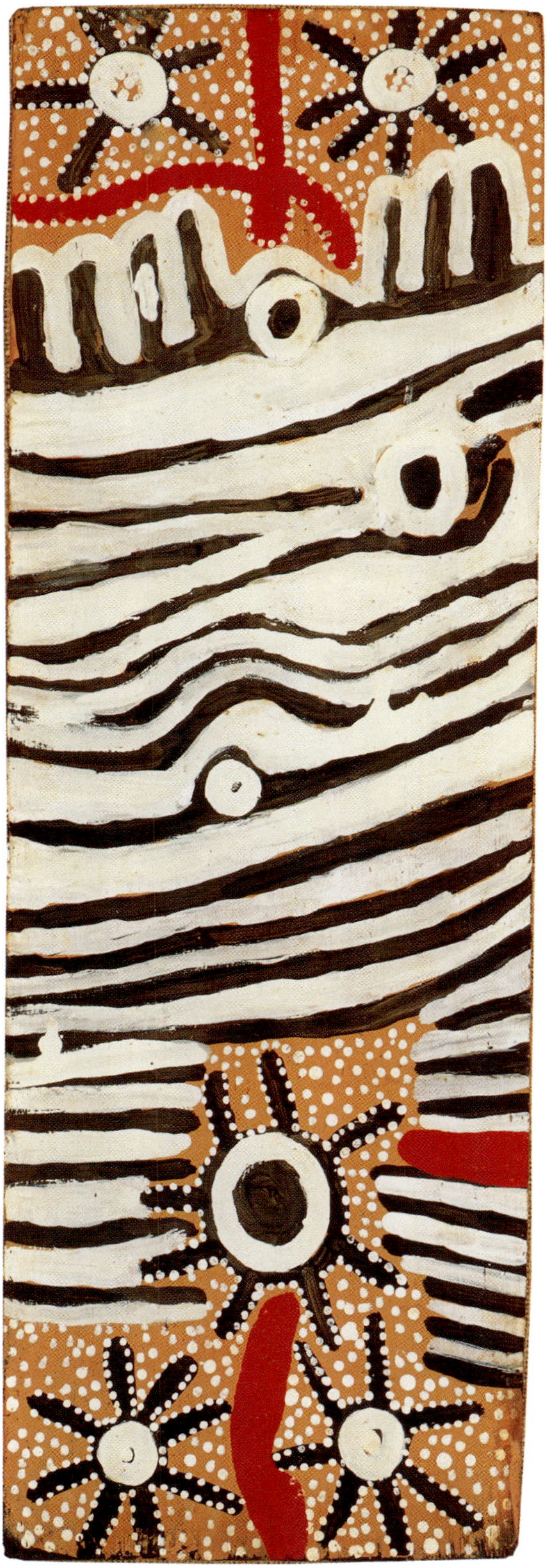

Sotheby's Australia

Charlie Tarawa Tjungurrayi
Fear 1971

Synthetic polymer paint and enamel on plywood, 61 x 20.5 cm
From the 3rd consignment to the Stuart Art Centre

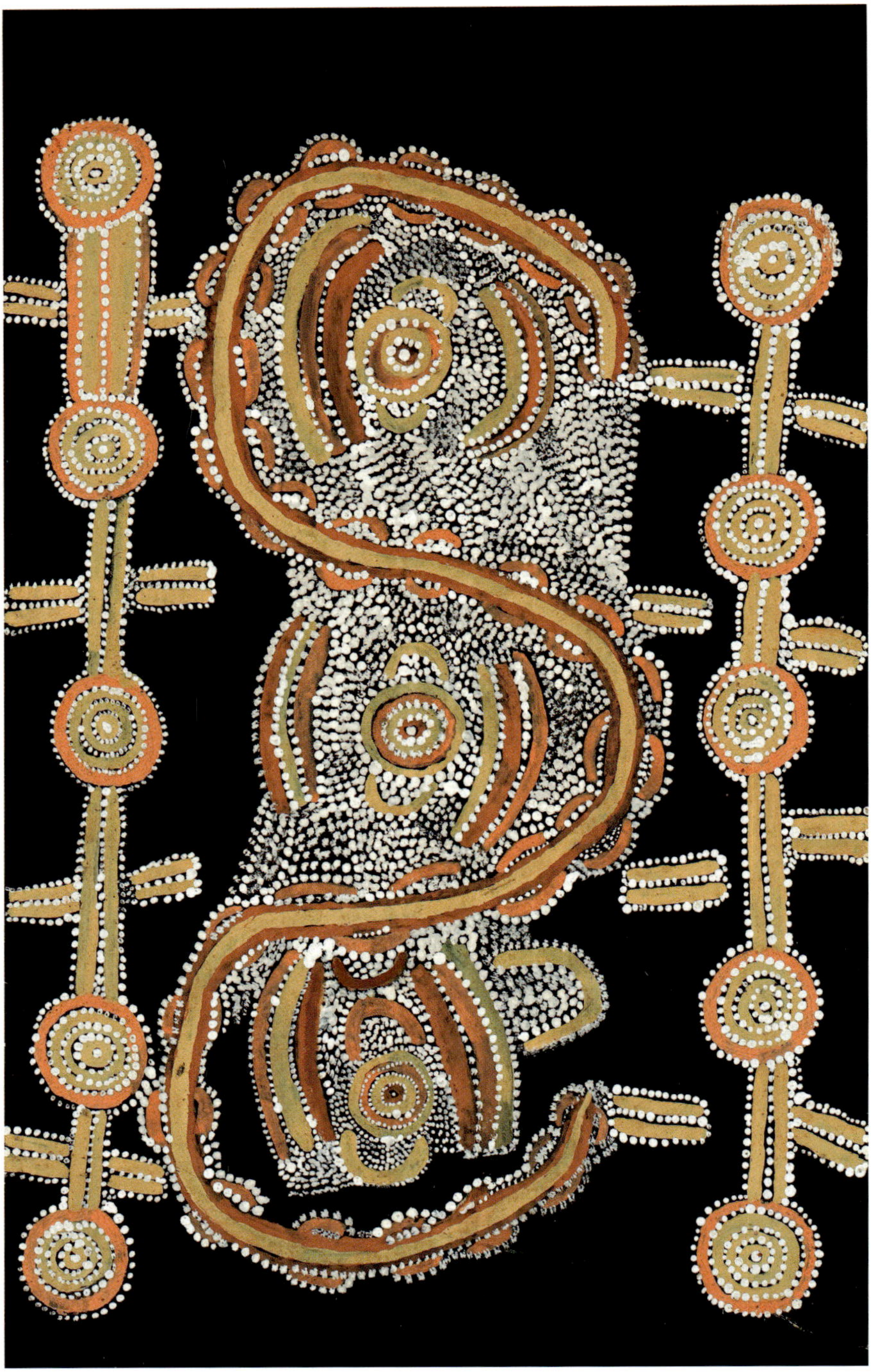

Sotheby's Australia

Mick Wallankarri Tjakamarra
Rain Corroboree 1971/72

Synthetic polymer/powder paint on composition board, 63.5 x 40.5 cm
From the 6th consignment to the Stuart Art Centre

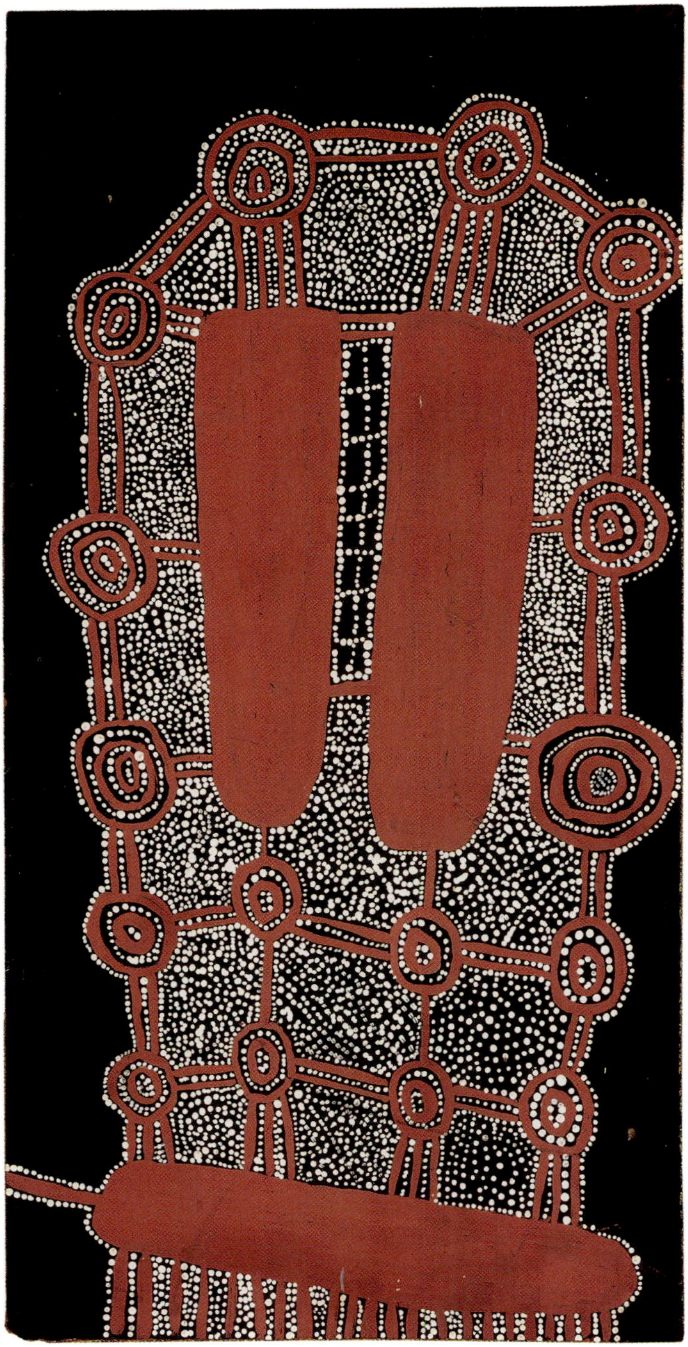

Sotheby's Australia

Uta Uta Tjangala
Medicine Story 1972

Synthetic polymer/powder paint on composition board, 70.17 x 35.24 cm
John and Barbara Wilkerson Collection
From the 7th consignment to the Stuart Art Centre

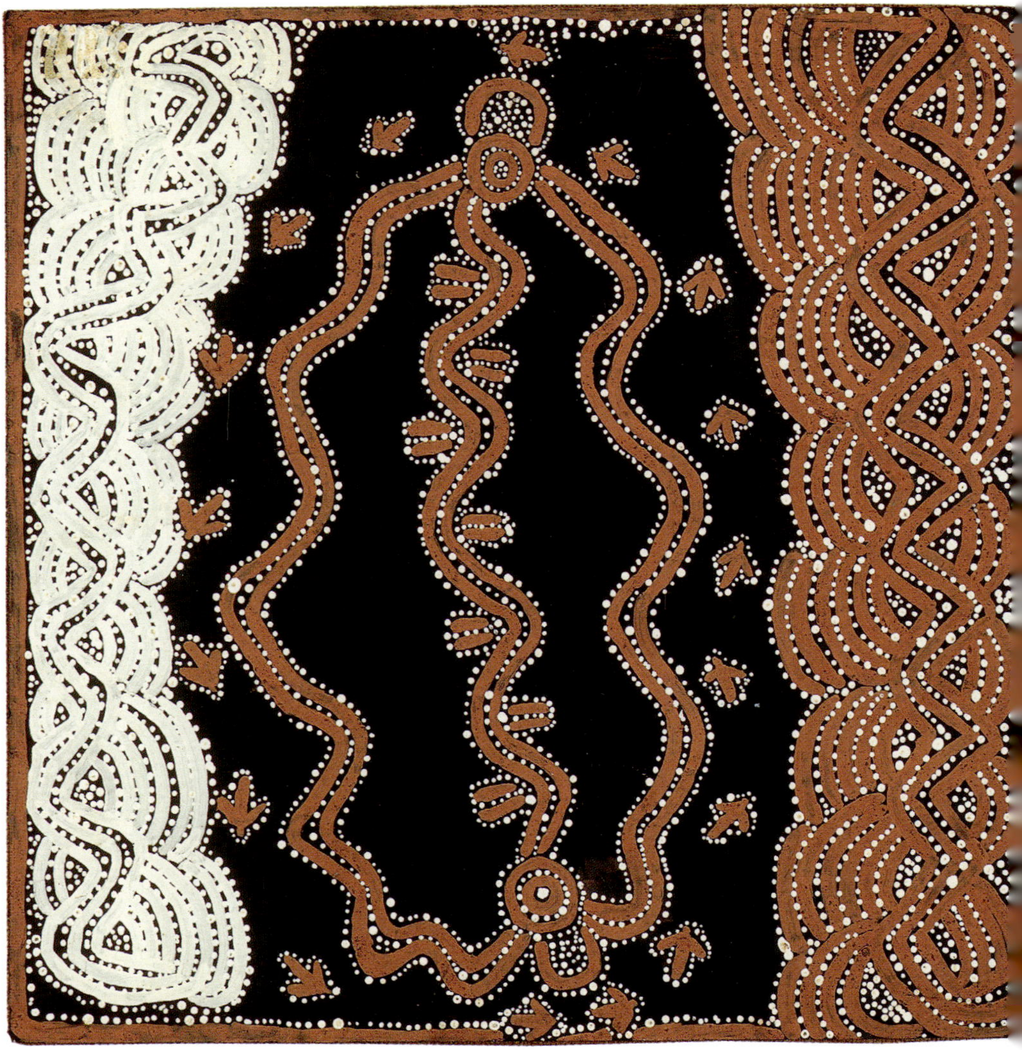

Walter Tjampitjinpa
Water Dreaming at Kalipinypa 1972

Synthetic polymer paint on composition board, 46 x 45 cm
From the 8th consignment to the Stuart Art Centre

>
Tim Payungka Tjapangati
Water Dreaming 1972

Synthetic polymer paint on composition board, 51 x 31 cm
From the 9th consignment to the Stuart Art Centre

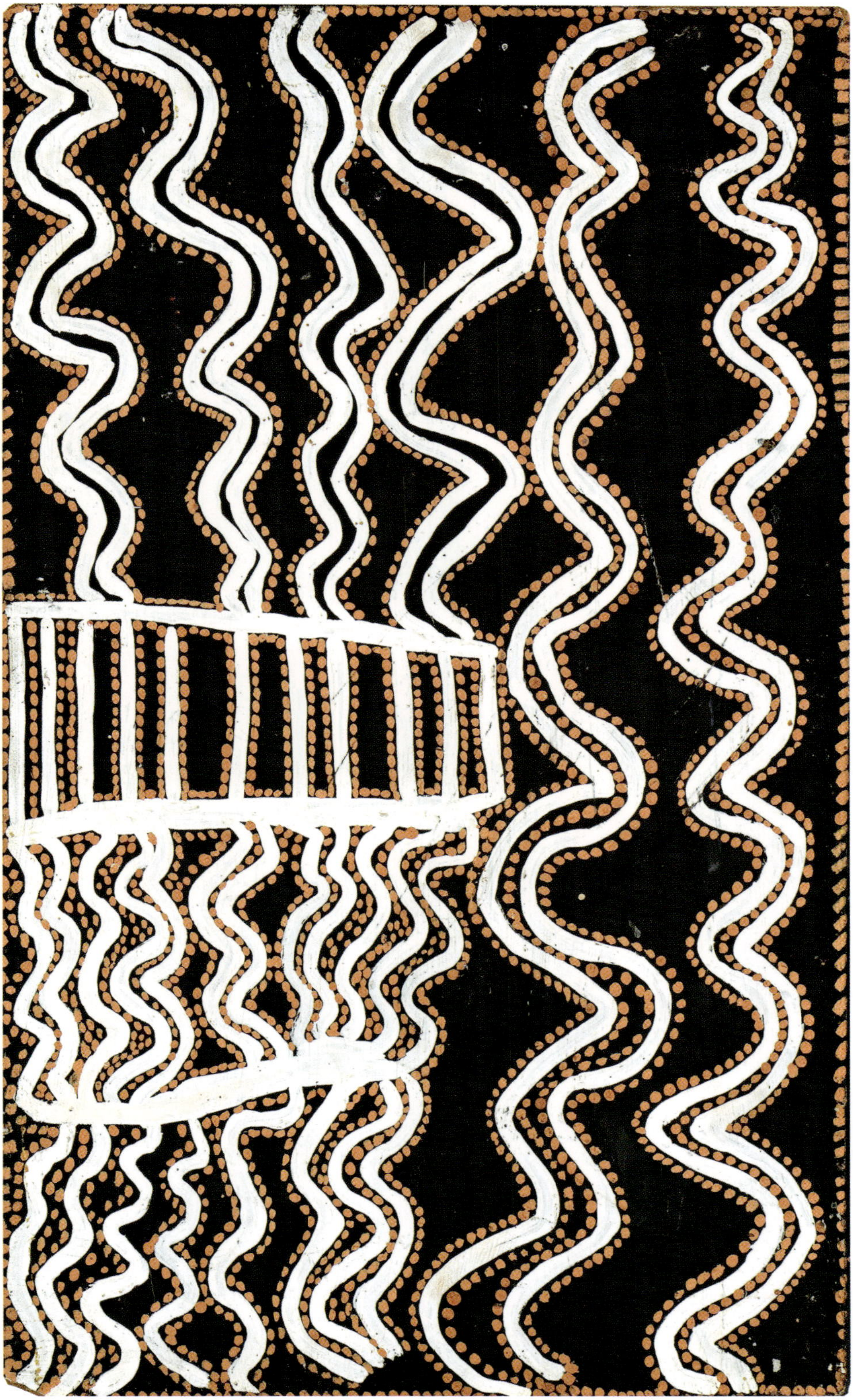

Sotheby's Australia

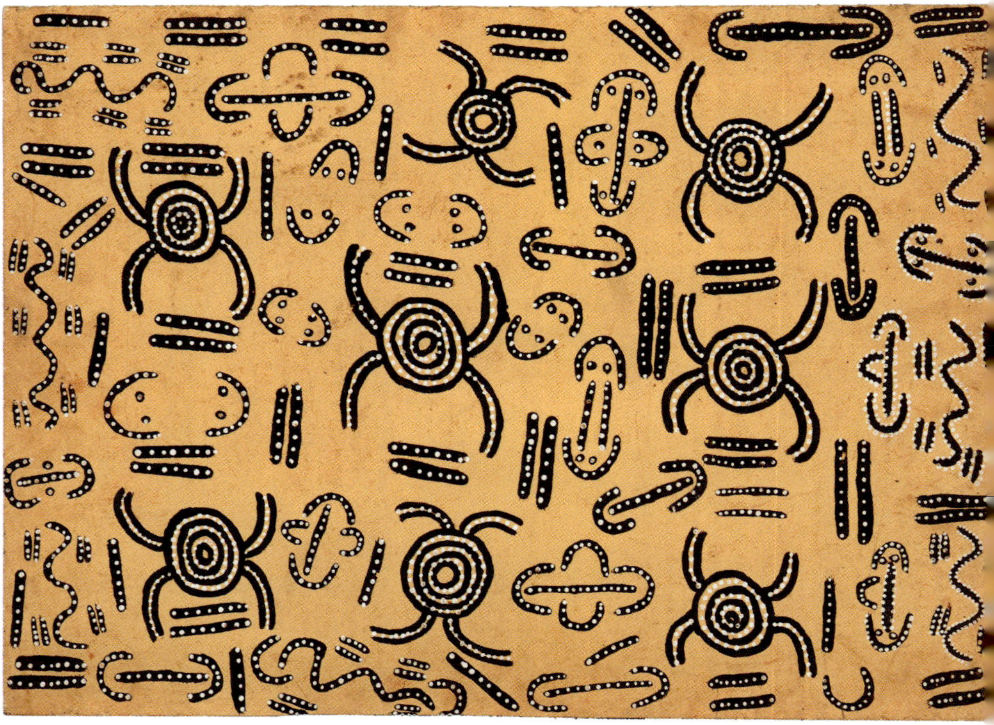

Artist undetermined
Mala Dreaming 1972

Synthetic polymer paints on composition board, 65 cm x 46 cm
Papunya Permanent Collection, Australian Museum
From the 11th consignment to the Stuart Art Centre
NOTE According to the Stuart Art Centre stock number on verso, the painting is by John Tjakamarra

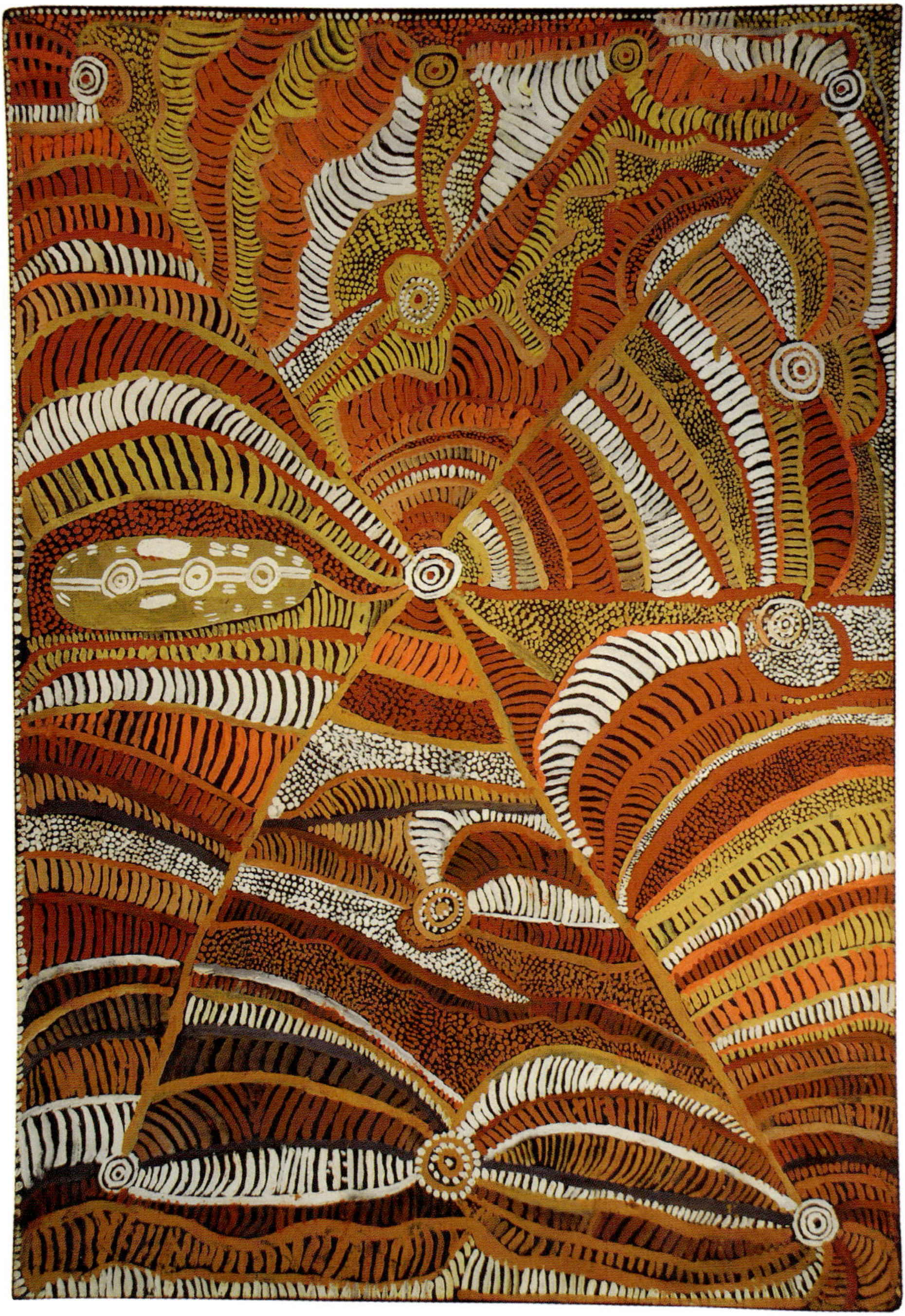

Mick Wallankarri Tjakamarra
Bush Tucker and Water Story 1972

Acrylic on board, 65 x 44.5 cm (irregular)
Araluen Art Centre
From the 12th consignment to the Stuart Art Centre

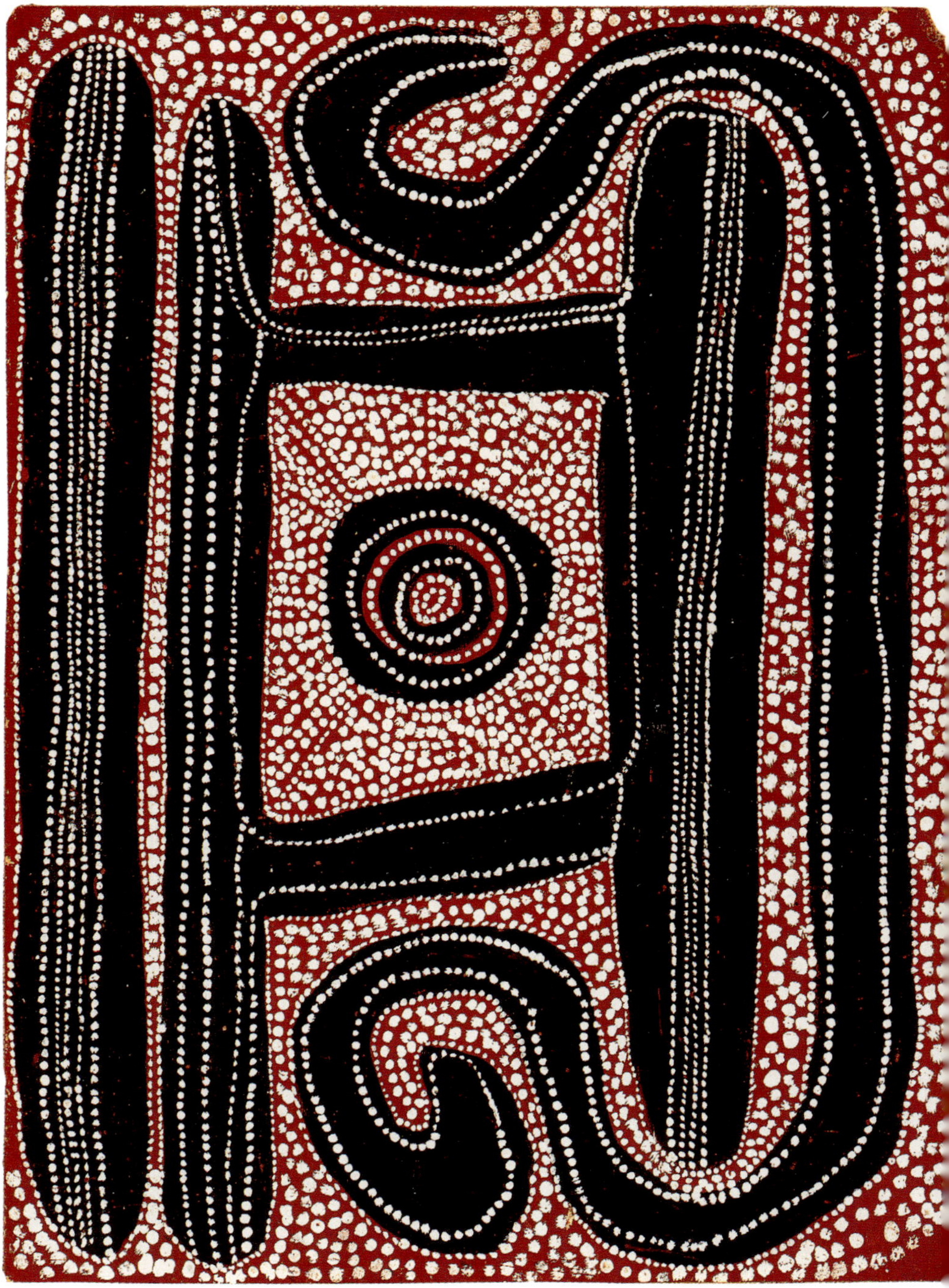

Uta Uta Tjangala
Ground Story 1972

Synthetic polymer powder paint on composition board, 61 x 46 cm
From the 12th consignment to the Stuart Art Centre

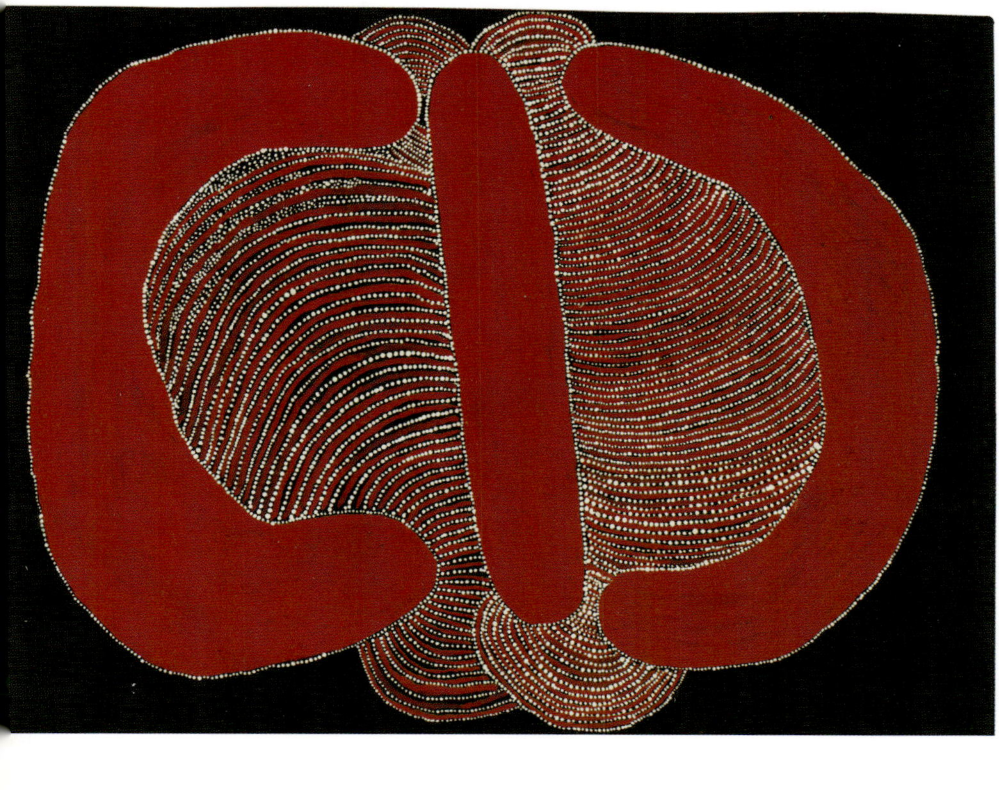

Shorty Lungkata Tjungurrayi
Women's Dreaming (Two Women) 1972

Synthetic polymer powder paint on hardboard, 46 x 64 cm
Purchased by the Art Gallery of New South Wales with funds provided by the Art Gallery Society of New South Wales, 2002
From the 12th consignment to the Stuart Art Centre

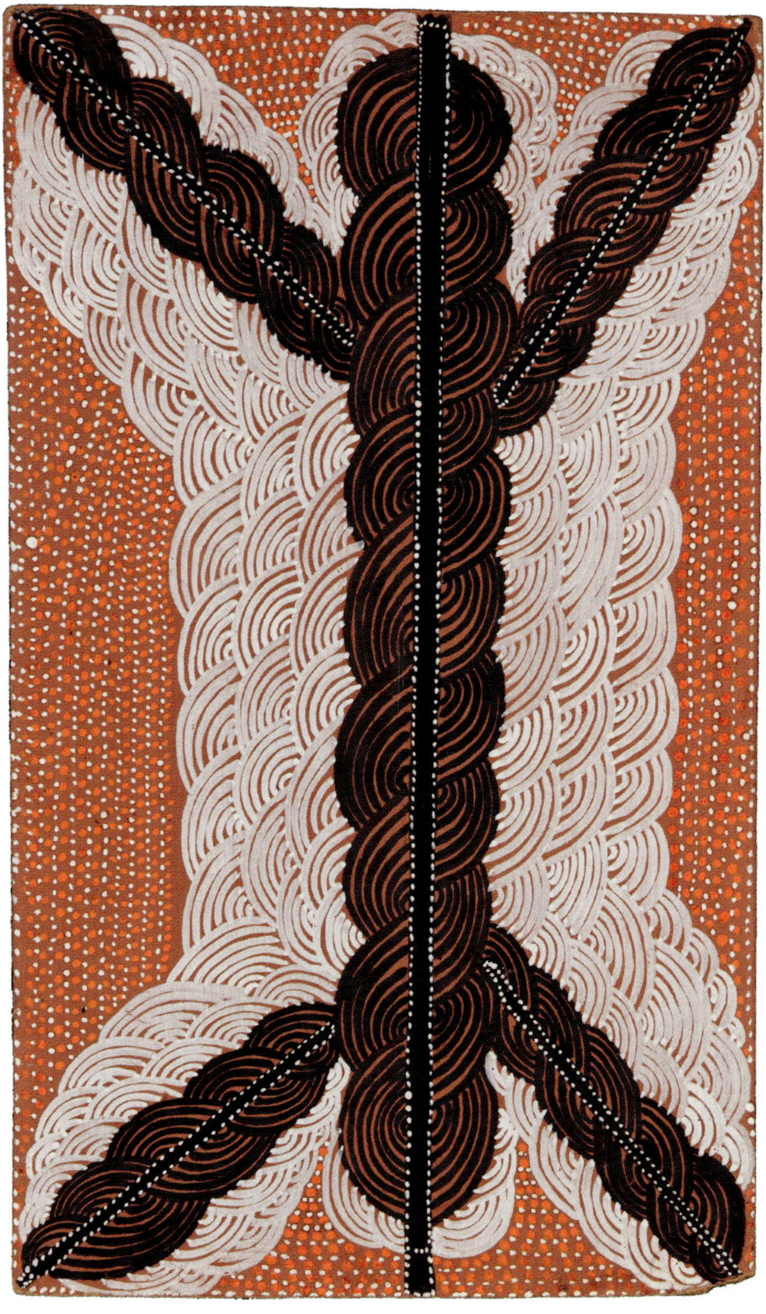

David Corby Tjapaltjarri
Wallaby Story 1972

Synthetic polymer paints on composition board, 47.5 cm x 28 cm
Papunya Permanent Collection, Australian Museum
From the 14th consignment to the Stuart Art Centre
NOTE According to the Stuart Art Centre stock number on verso, this painting is by Shorty 'Jungarai', i.e. Shorty Lungkata Tjungurrayi

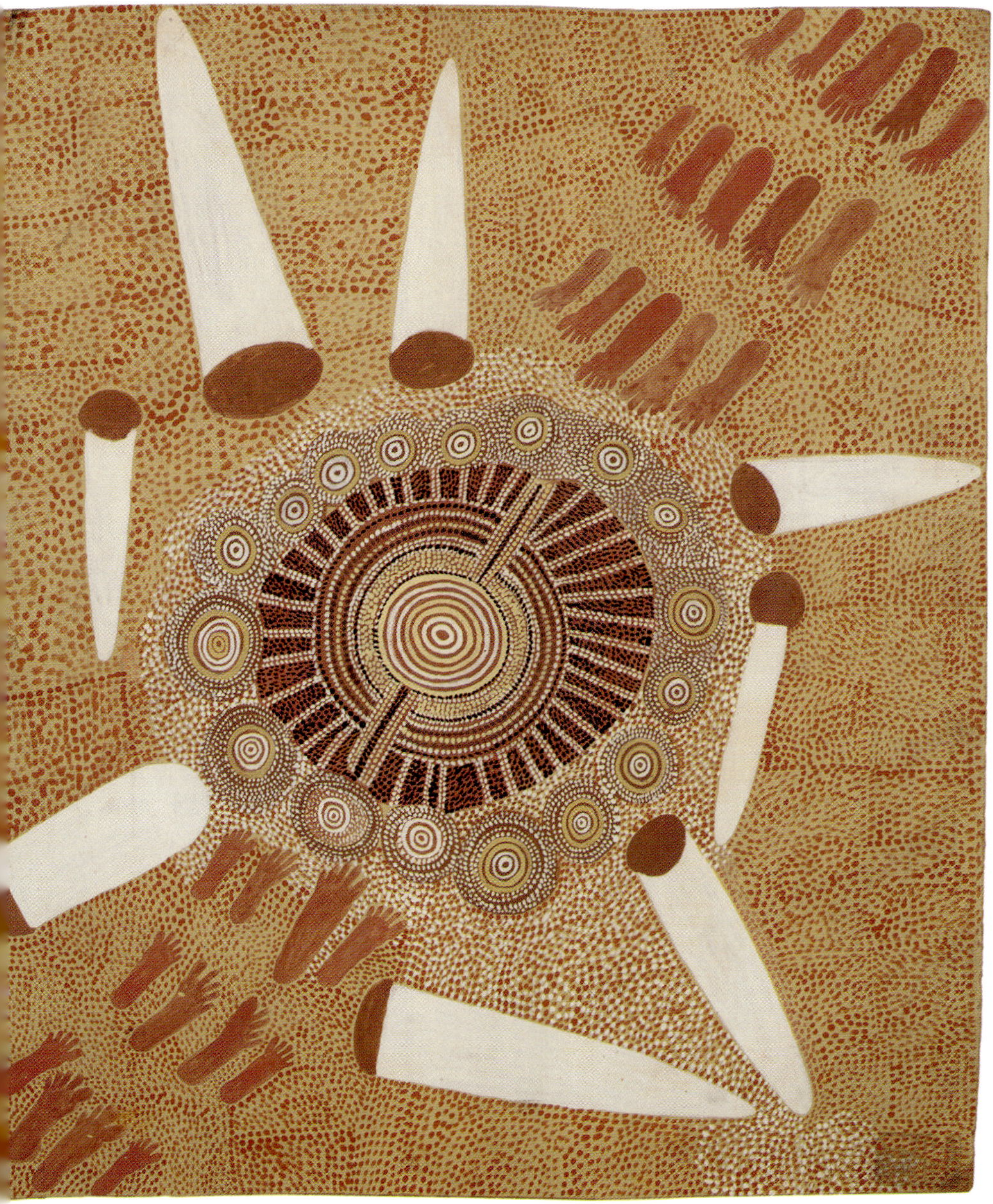

Anatjari Tjakamarra
Big Pintupi Dreaming Ceremony 1972

Ngaatjatjarra/Pintupi, c. 1930–1992
Synthetic polymer paint on composition board, 51.5 x 43.3 cm
Purchased by the National Gallery of Victoria through the Art Foundation of Victoria with the assistance of North Broken Hill Ltd, Fellow, 1987
From the 15th consignment to the Stuart Art Centre

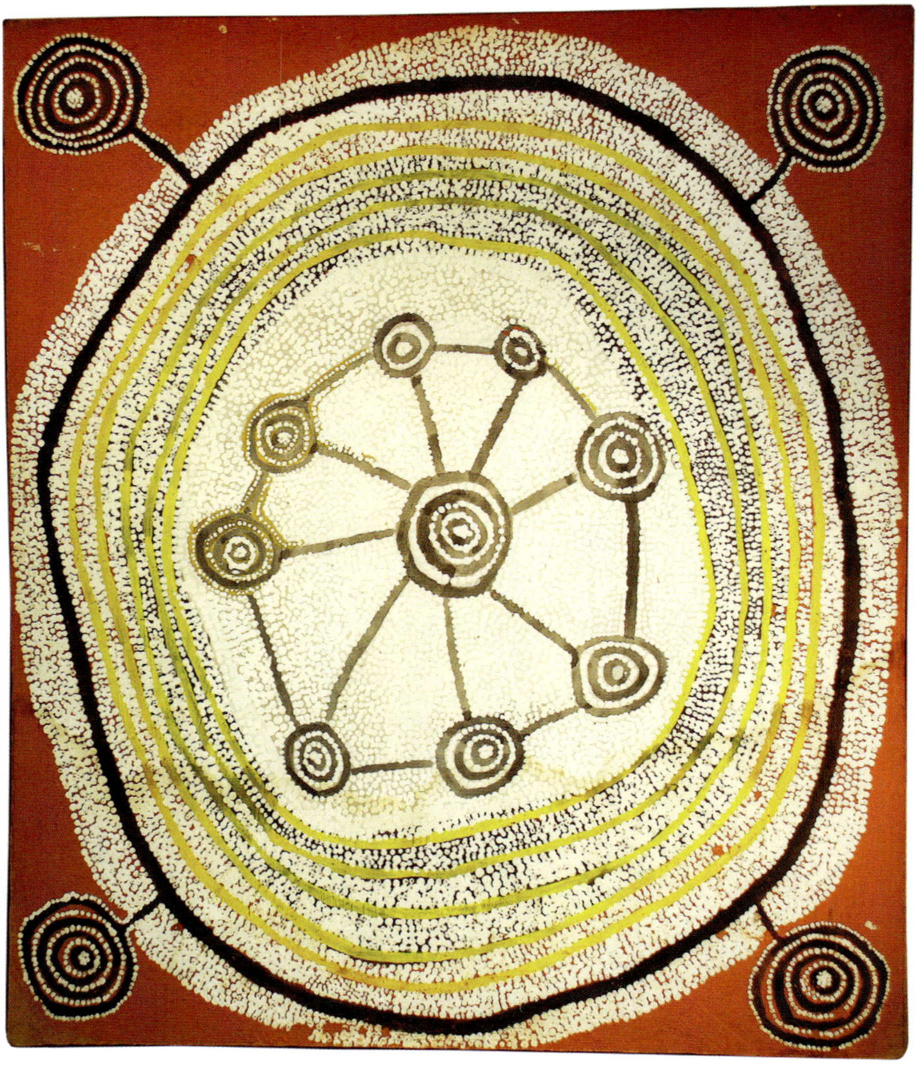

Artist Unknown (Possibly Yala Yala Gibbs Tjungarrayi)
Untitled 1972

Acrylic on hardboard, 64 x 56 cm (irregular)
Araluen Art Collection
From the 17th consignment to the Stuart Art Centre

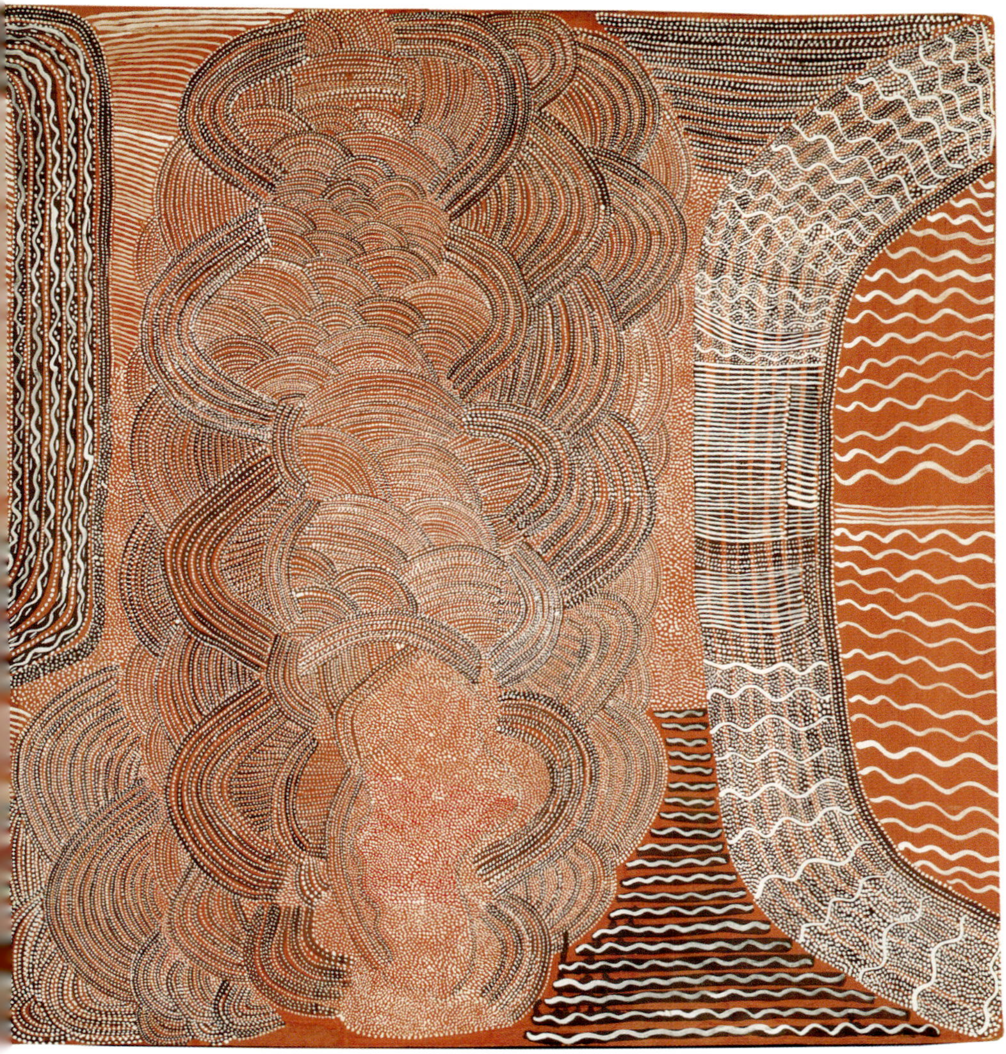

Mick Namarari Tjapaltjarri
Bush Tucker Story 1972

Synthetic polymer paint and natural pigments on composition board, 78 x 76.5 cm
Purchased in 1995 by the Queensland Art Gallery with a special allocation from the Queensland government, celebrating the Queensland Art Gallery's Centenary 1895–1995
From the 17th consignment to the Stuart Art Centre

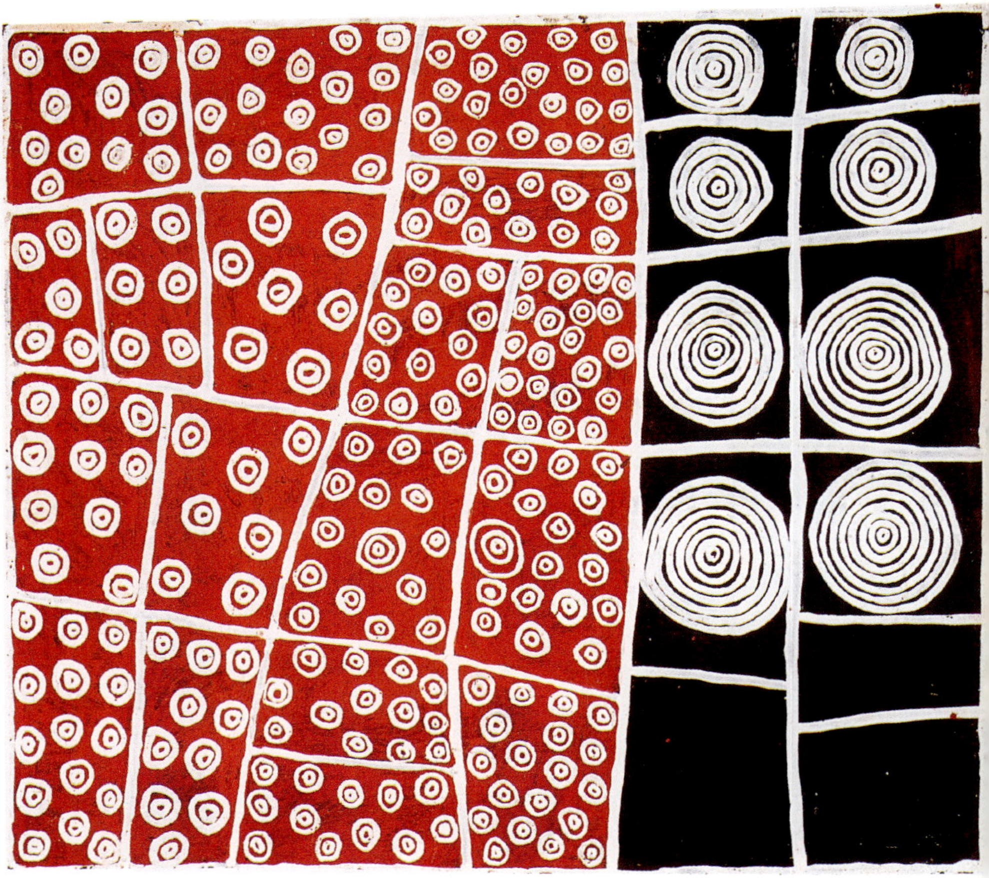

Shorty Lungkata Tjungurrayi
Untitled 1972

Synthetic polymer powder paint on composition board, 46.5 x 53 cm
From the 18th consignment to the Stuart Art Centre

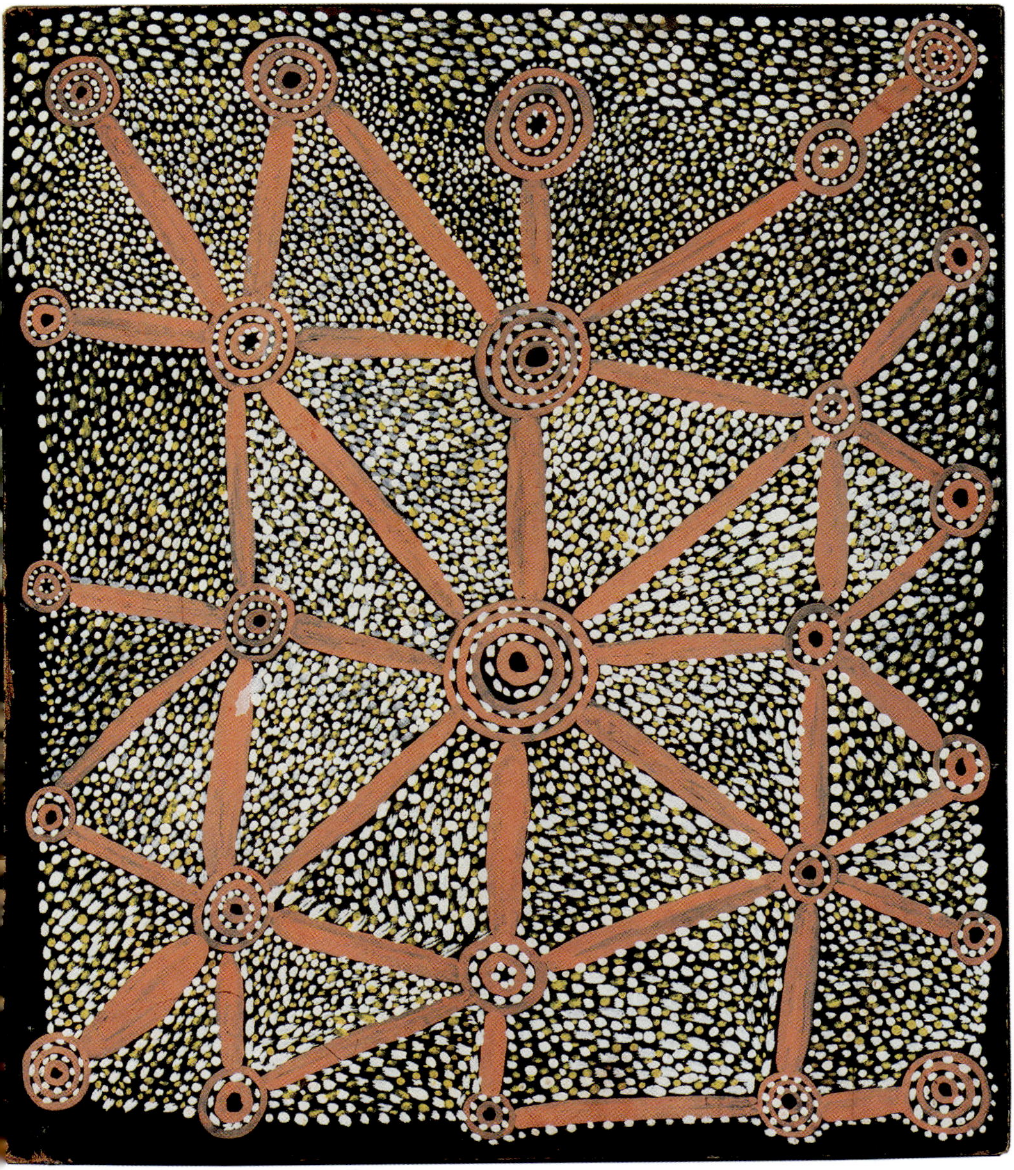

John Tjakamarra
Travels of Tingari Ancestors 1972

Synthetic polymer powder paint on composition board, 40.5 x 35 cm
From the 18th consignment to the Stuart Art Centre

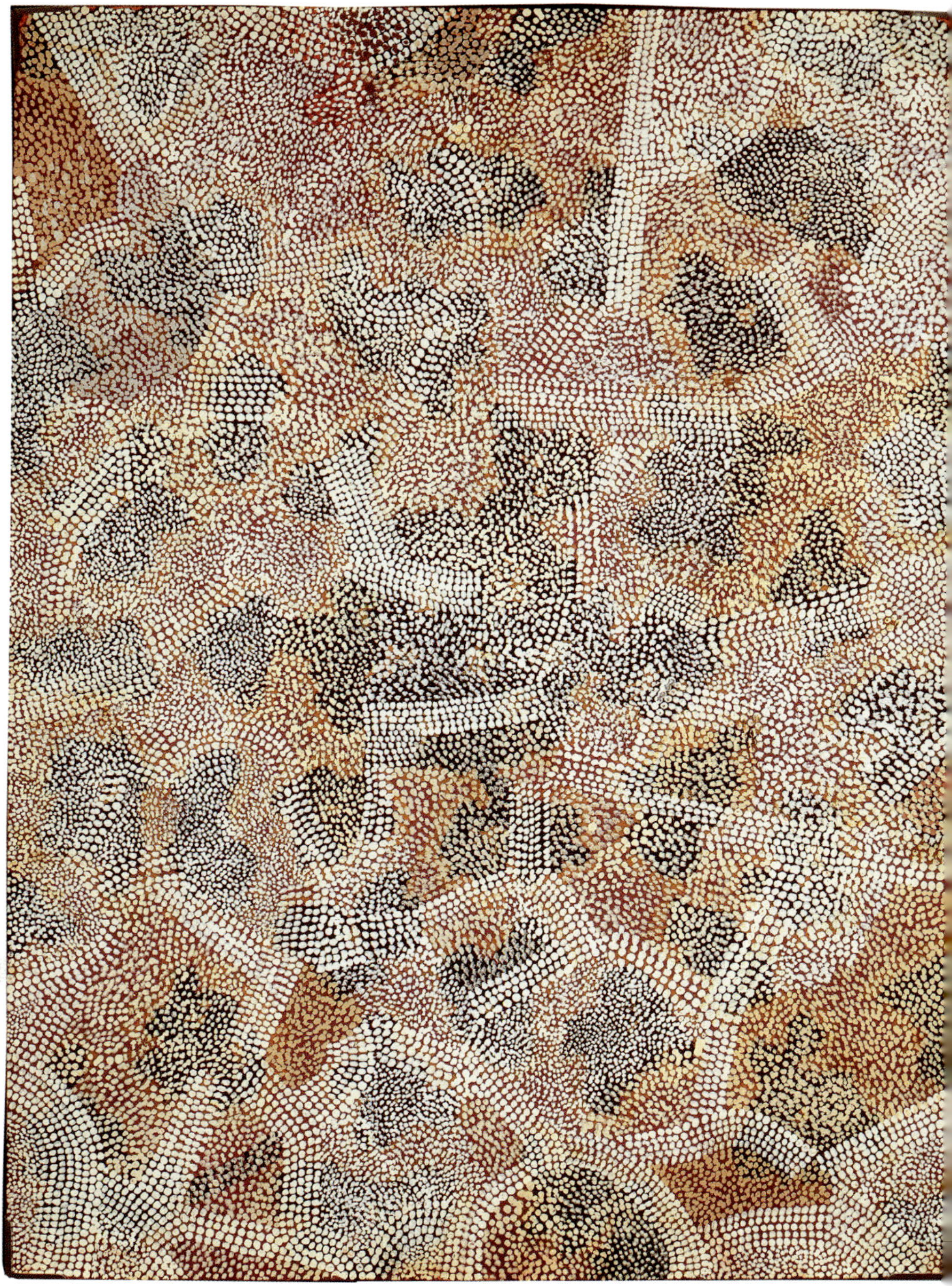

Clifford Possum Tjapaltjarri
Bush Fire I 1972

Synthetic polymer paint on composition board, 62 x 46.2 cm
National Gallery of Australia Collection
From the 19th consignment to the Stuart Art Centre

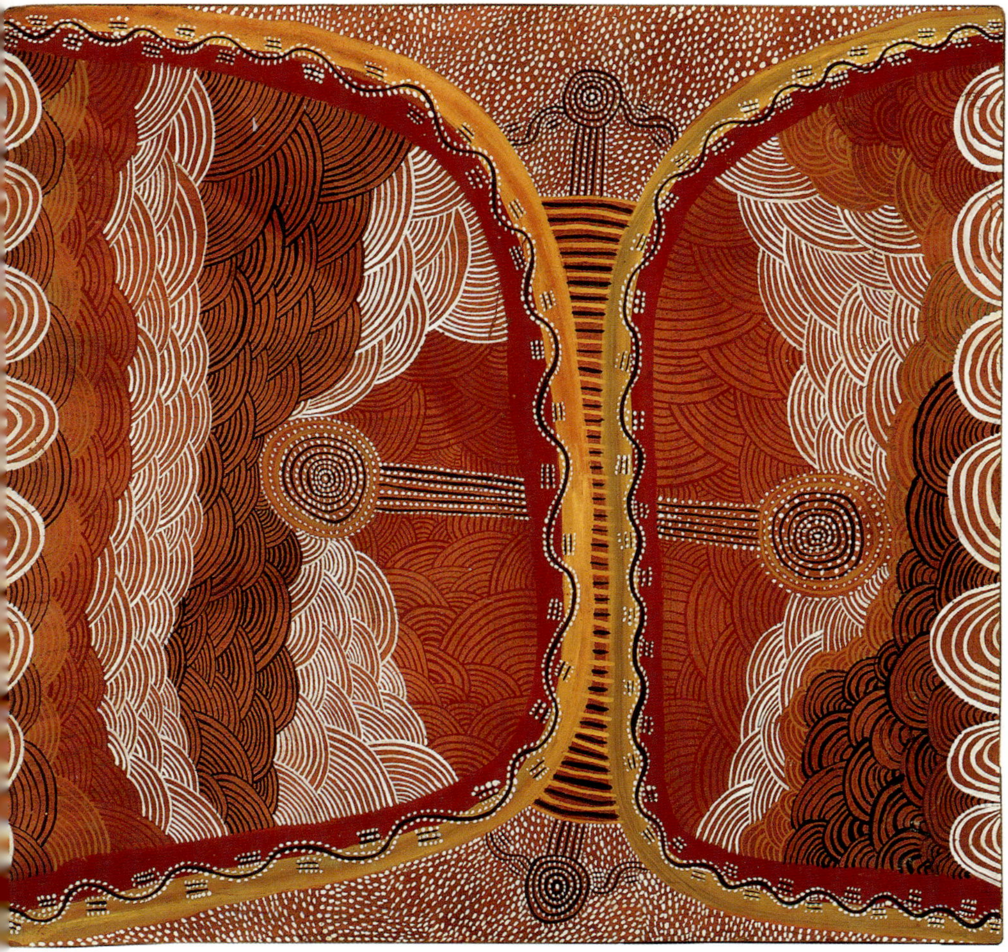

Long Jack Phillipus Tjakamarra
Untitled *(Rainbow and Water Dreaming)* 1972

Natural earth pigments and synthetic polymer powder paint on composition board, 71.5 x 76.5 cm
From the 19th consignment to the Stuart Art Centre

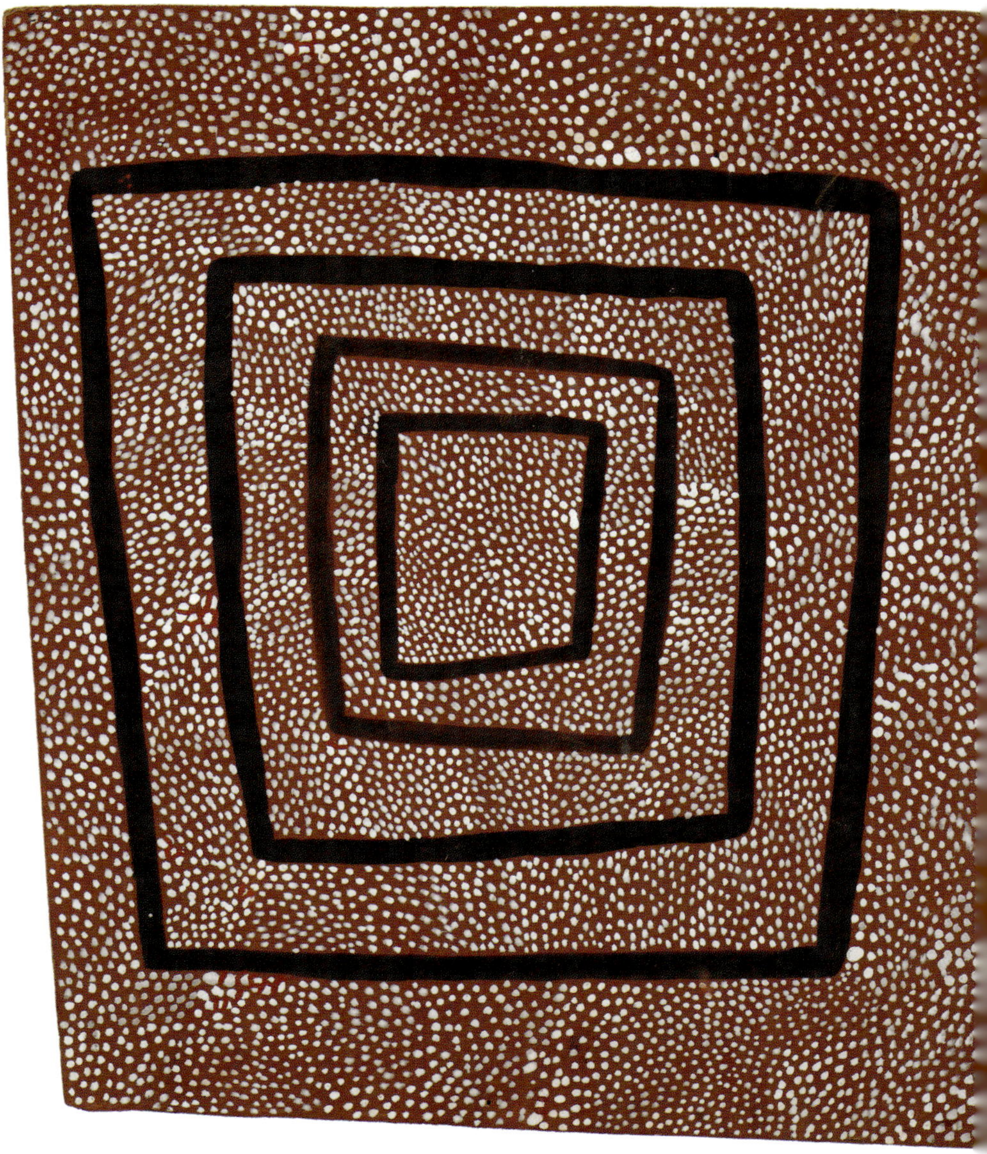

Anatjari Tjakamarra
Untitled 1972

Synthetic polymer paint on composition board,
60.5 x 51 cm (irregular)
From the 19th consignment to the Stuart Art Centre

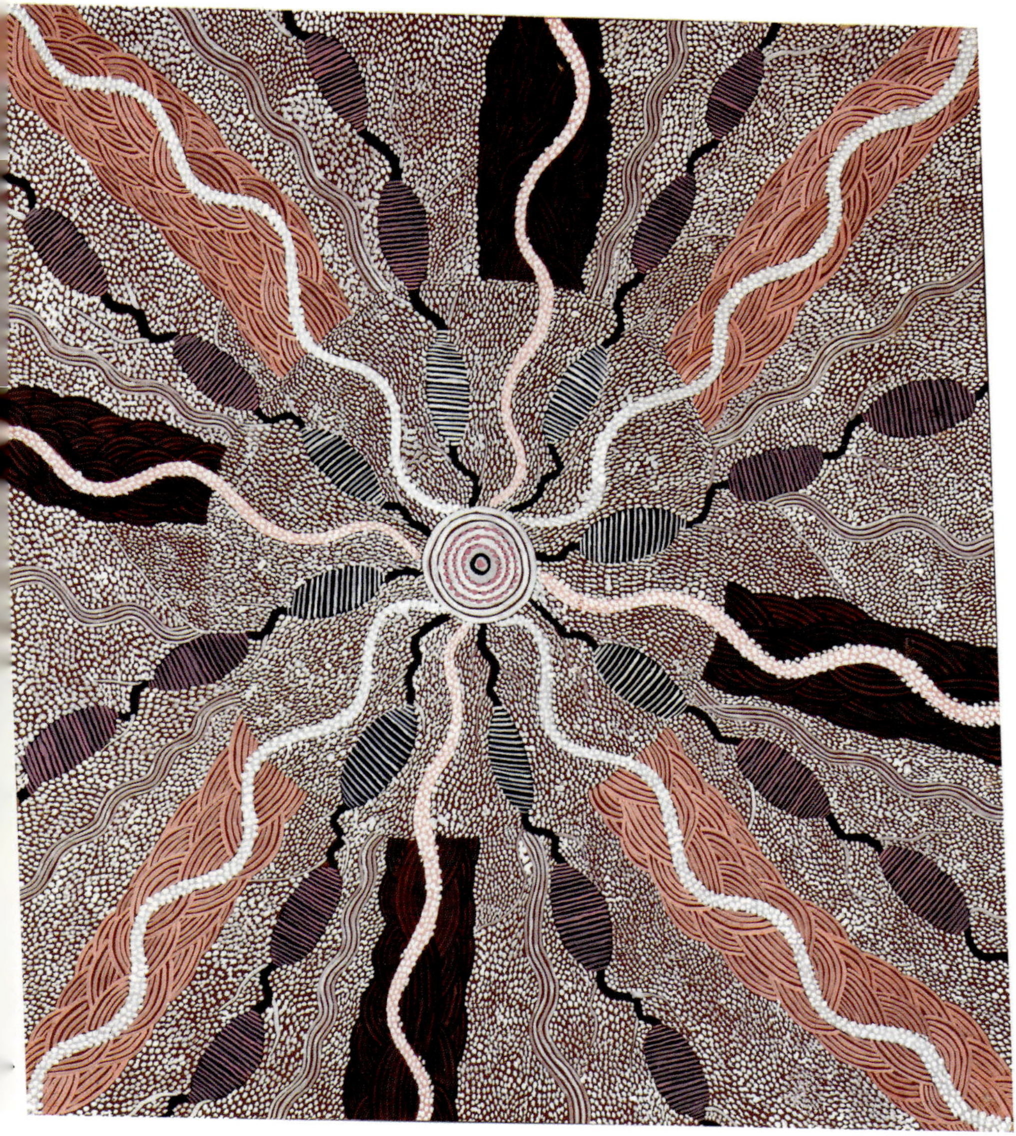

Kaapa Tjampitjinpa
Yala 1972

Synthetic polymer paint on composition board, 57 x 51.5 cm
From the 19th consignment to the Stuart Art Centre

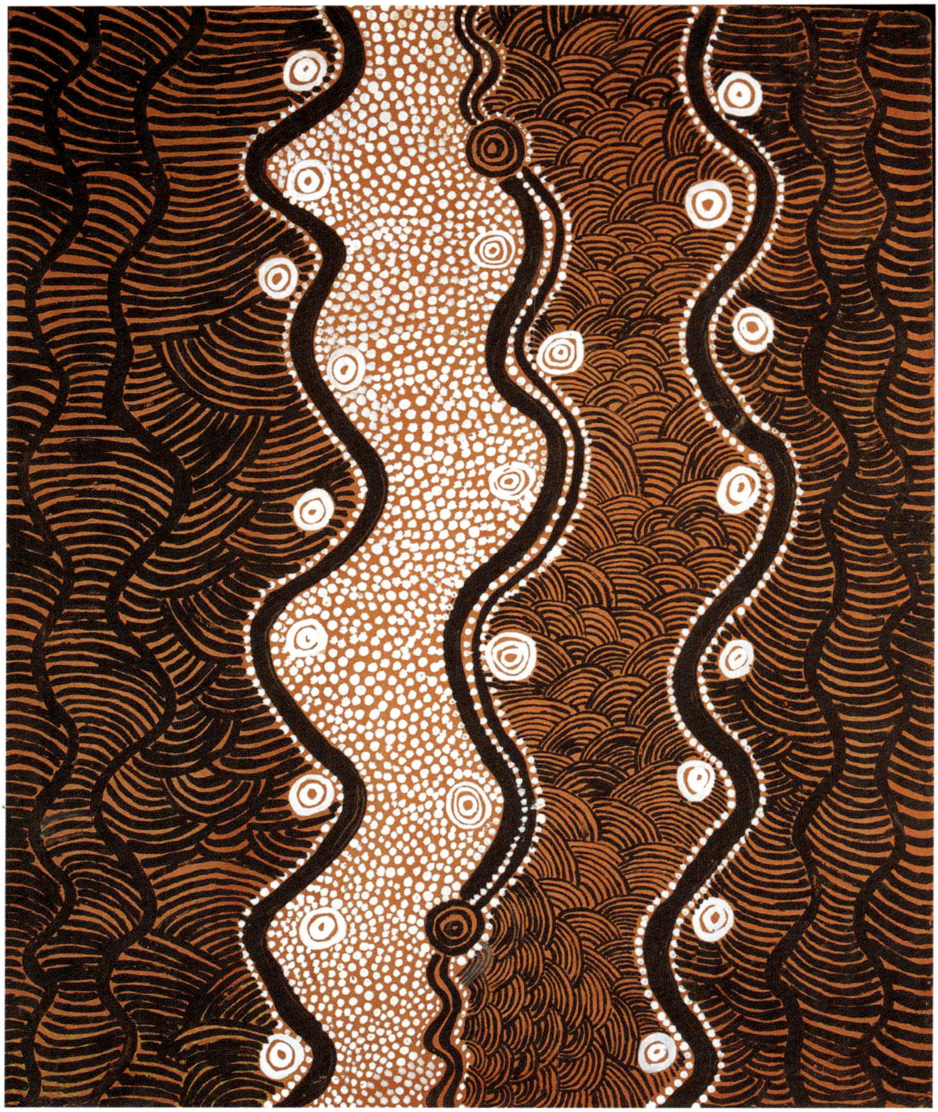

Walter Tjampitjinpa
Water Dreaming 1972

Synthetic polymer paint on composition board, 71.5 x 60 cm
Purchased by the Tasmanian Museum and Art Gallery with assistance from the National Cultural Heritage Committee and the Art Foundation of Tasmania, 2001
Stuart Art Centre catalogue number 1272087

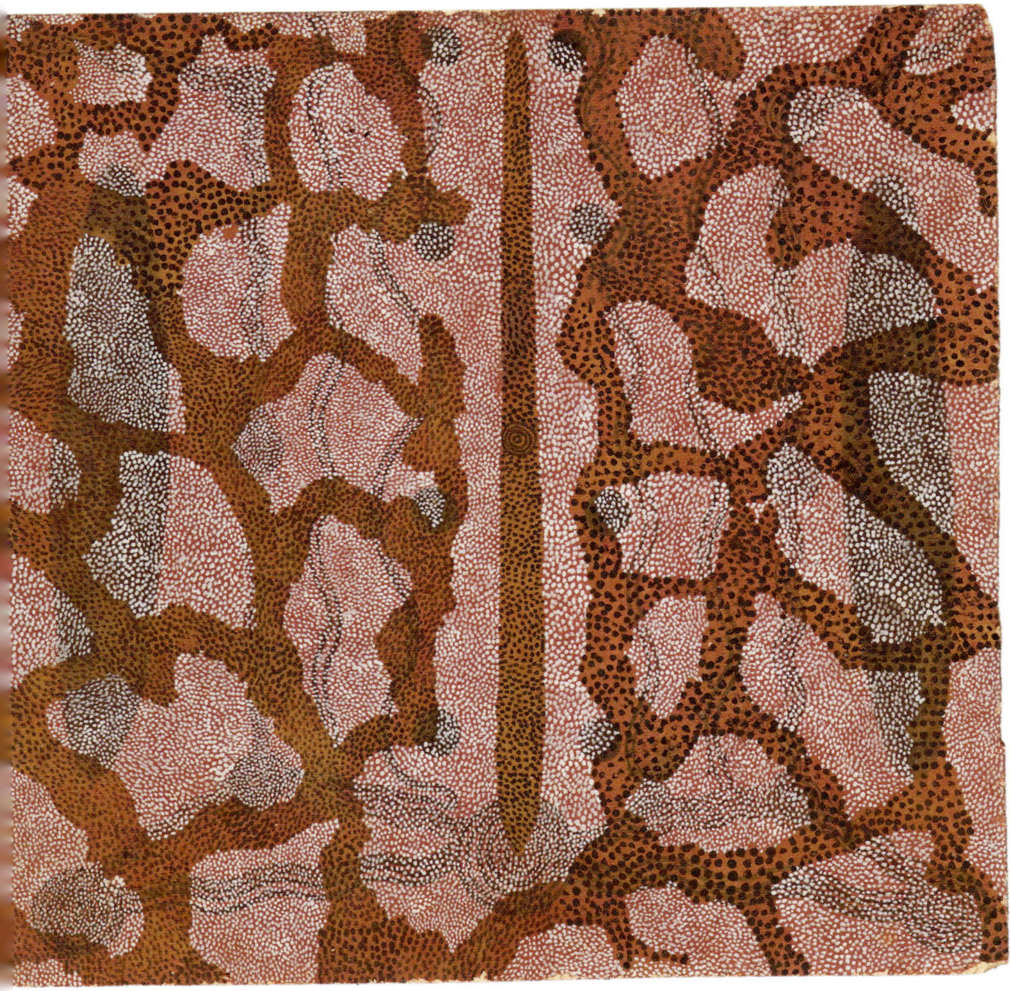

Tim Leura Tjapaltjarri
Honey Ant Dreaming 1972

Synthetic polymer paint on composition board, 62 x 59 cm
Papunya Permanent Collection, Australian Museum
From the 20th consignment to the Stuart Art Centre

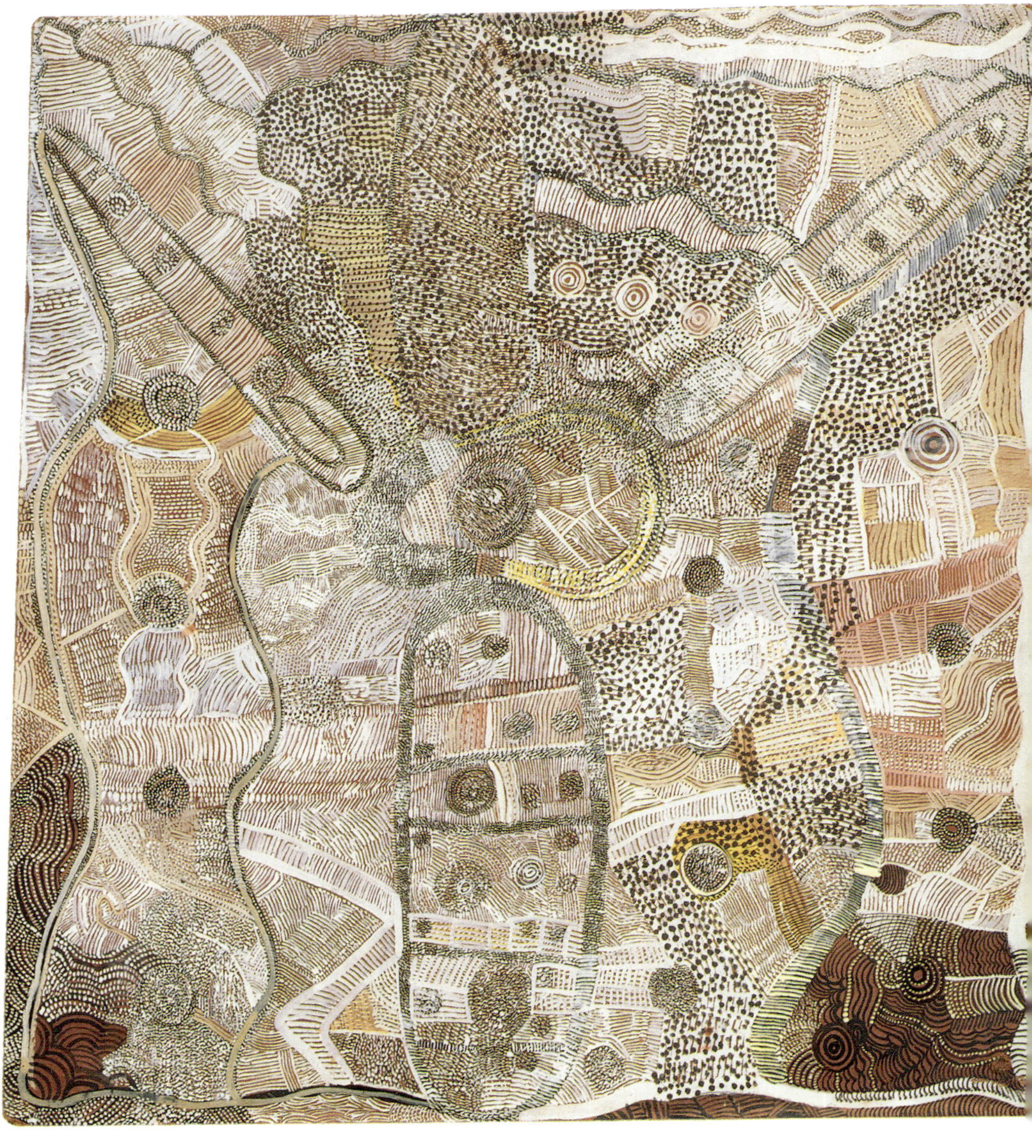

Johnny Warangkula Tjupurrula
Water Dreaming at Kalipinypa 1972

Synthetic polymer powder paint on composition board, 80.65 x 75.57 cm
John and Barbara Wilkerson Collection
Image produced at the time of the 16th consignment to the Stuart Art Centre

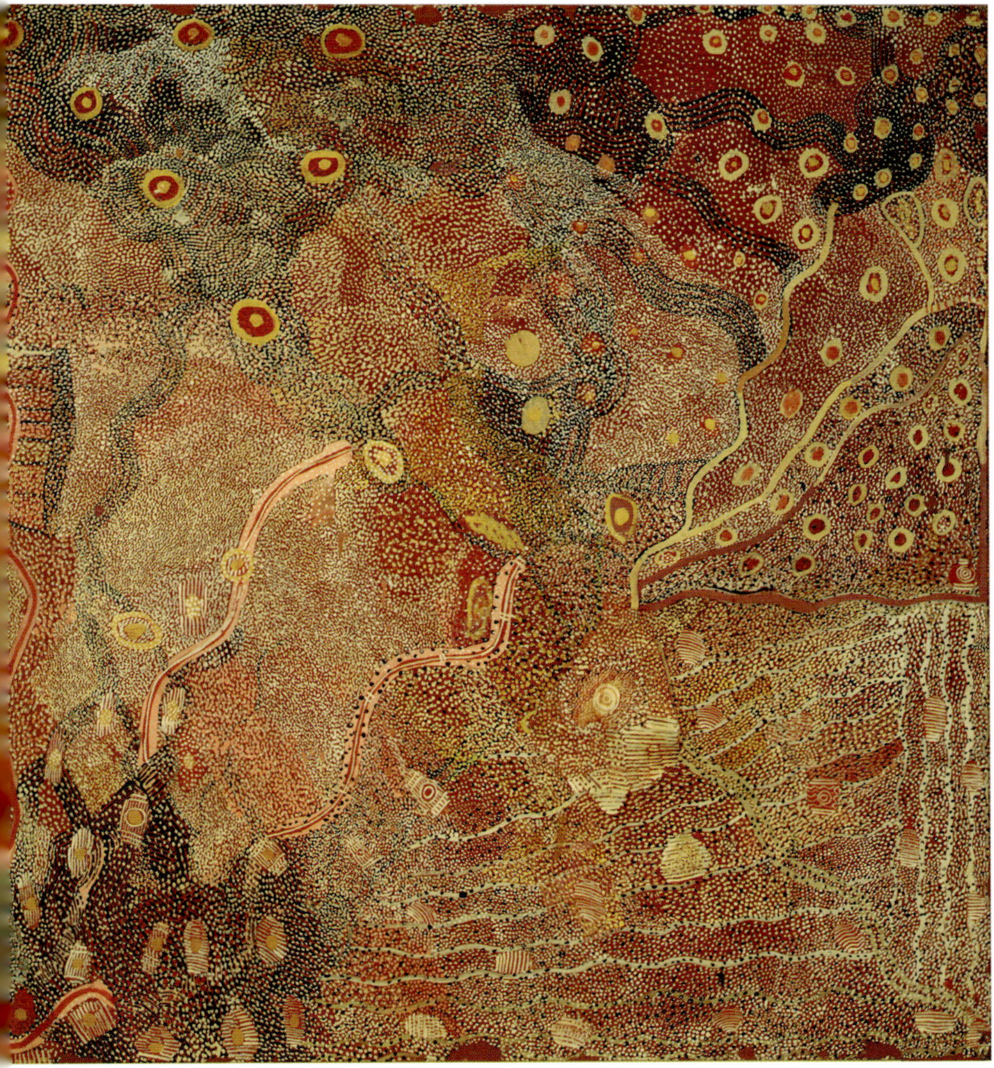

Johnny Warangkula Tjupurrula
Untitled 1973

Synthetic polymer paint on composition board, 118.8 x 112.9 cm (framed)
Purchased in 1978 by the Museum and Art Gallery of the Northern Territory Collection

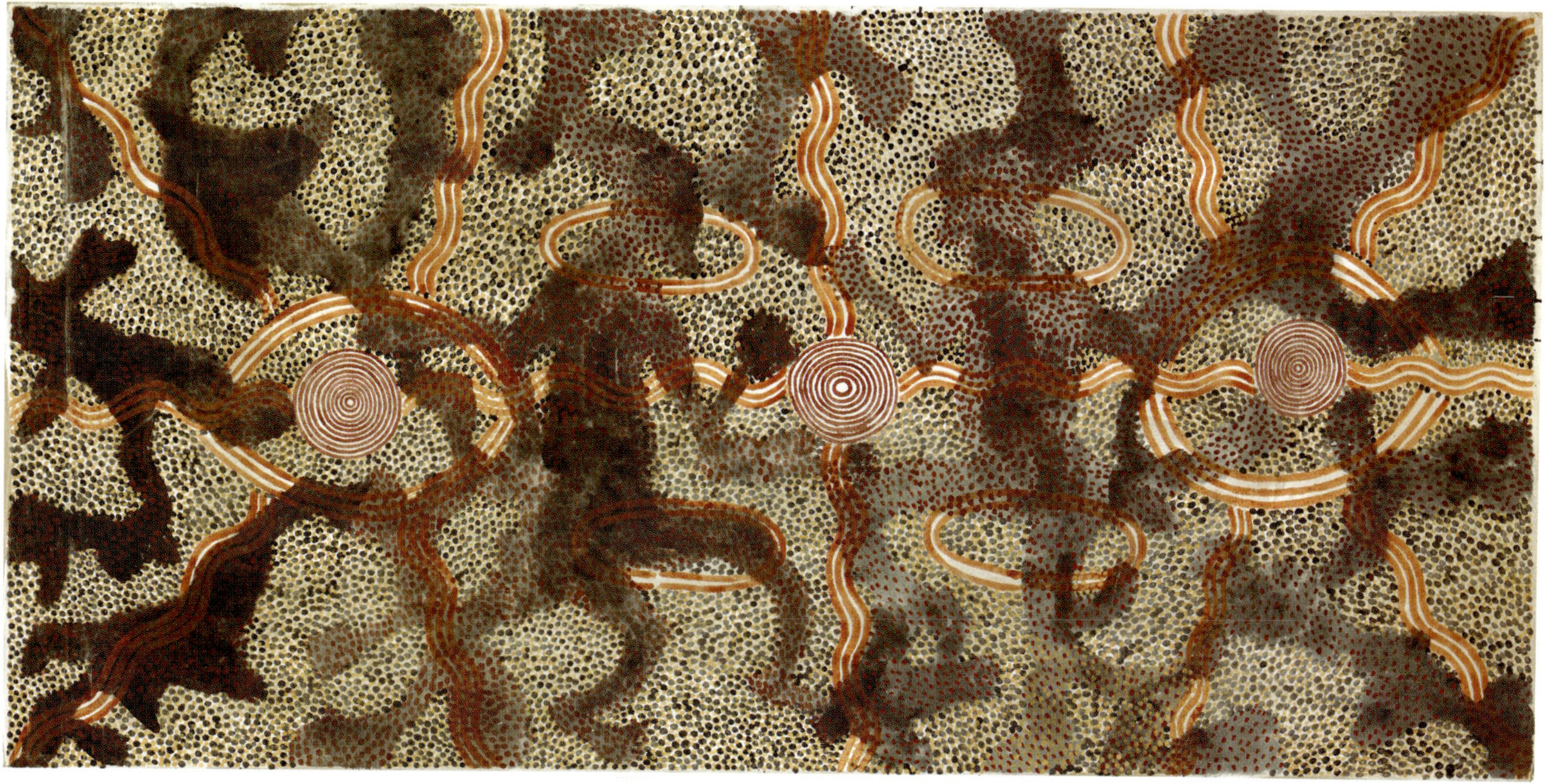

Dean McNicoll

Tim Leura Tjapaltjarri
Trial by Fire 1975

Synthetic polymer paint on canvas, 169.4 x 338.5 cm
National Museum of Australia Collection

paintings to come out of Papunya, had something to do with the outcome. This information could be read off their Stuart Art Centre consignment numbers, which for both works, and most of the other early Papunya boards in the 1996 auction (though not the Anatjari), were cited for the first time in Sotheby's catalogue. This tightening up of provenance reflected a developing understanding of the significance of these stock numbers for placing the paintings in historical sequence – and for purposes of authentication:

> there are such frightful people involved in Aboriginal art that they will invariably use the lack of a number as the basis to produce a fake. There's been a few fakes that people have turned up over the years. Pretty much, they've always been caught out.[37]

Towards the end of 1996, a number of major galleries received a parcel of three photographs from an Adelaide art dealer. His story was that he had acquired the paintings from the home of a house painter who had worked in Papunya at the beginning of the 1970s, and who had bought them directly from the artists as a souvenir of his visit. They had lain in his garage all these years, but he had recently died and the art dealer had bought them from his widow. He was now seeking the assistance of the experts in attributing and authenticating them – and also of course fishing for interest in purchasing them. Many similar stories about where early Papunya paintings had been hidden all those years were already in circulation.

The problem with these paintings was not the story that went with them, but the paintings themselves. Even in photographs they looked decidedly odd, especially one that I shall call the 'faux Anatjari' because of the unlikely coincidence of its pronounced similarity to the record-breaking Anatjari

Tjakamarra from the 1996 Sotheby's auction. It had the same distinctive motif of a concentric circle framed by concentric squares suggestive of an attribution to Anatjari Tjakamarra. But the congealed, unvarying dotting was the antithesis of Anatjari's fluid technique, and the design of four squares with a fifth slightly larger one *overlaid* on the other four was unlike anything seen before in his work – or in Western Desert art. Something was definitely wrong: superficially it might look like an Anatjari, but couldn't possibly be by him. Yet the signature motif is so distinctive of his work, who else could the artist possibly be? I told the dealer as much when he called me in March 1997 and invited himself over to show me his three paintings. Frustrated by the cautious approach of curators at the state galleries whom he had already approached, he was hoping that private expertise would deliver the testimonials needed to transform his 'find' into a major windfall. Tim Klingender was not the only one mindful of the financial advantages of credentialling for the paintings. No artists at all suggested themselves for the other two works, whose odd, asymmetrical designs and floating areas of dotting unrelated to the underlying design were, as I told the dealer, quite unlike the work of any early Papunya painter with which I was familiar.

Presented with the actual works, I was even more mystified: quite apart from the paintings, the pristine condition of the backs of the masonite boards on which they were painted was anomalous in the context of their supposed provenance. I continued in this vein for some time, until the exasperated dealer asked if I had a copy of the 1996 Sotheby's auction catalogue, in which he impatiently pointed out Lots 7 (the Johnny Warangkula) and 233 (the Mick Wallankarri Tjakamarra) as closely resembling the two mysterious paintings. At that moment I think we both knew the game was up. I remarked that the only certainty I had about the three paintings he had brought to show me was that they had all been painted by the same person. At this he finally showed his hand and began making disparaging remarks about how a few lines and dots on an old board could be worth tens of thousands of dollars. In the end he departed, leaving on the table a bottle of Trilogy champagne he had intended to drink with me when I had provided him with letters of attribution.

Oh yeah, the mixed ones. I think before that they came first to us. I thought they were amazing. It was Mark Fraser[38] who said, 'Let's have a look at these. They are too good to be true.' We didn't think that anyone would do something like that. You could tell that the paint was too new and that they were all done by the same hand. When we held up the catalogue we could tell they were a mixture of three different paintings all brought into one and they were all based on the 1996 catalogue. Then we had Judith [Ryan][39] come in. We asked her, 'What do you think?' She agreed, and then we had Vivien Anderson[40] come in and she agreed. So then we notified the fraud squad. Told them the whole story and packaged them up and sent them back to this guy in the crate. We notified the South Australian and Victorian Fraud Squads and said this guy is trying to commit a $100 000 fraud – and they never did anything about it![41]

I heard later that Judith Ryan of the National Gallery of Victoria and Sotheby's had determined that the backgrounds of all three works had been painted with a spray gun. In April 1997 an article in the Adelaide *Advertiser* reported that 'Melbourne and Adelaide fraud squad detectives were investigating the three paintings'[42] and Tim Klingender's comment that it was the first such incident Sotheby's had encountered with Aboriginal art, adding:

'We come across it a fair bit with white art. I guess it is an indication of the value of Aboriginal art, that they are trying to copy it now.'[43]

The article started and finished with 'Mr Tjupurrula', the only one of the three artists copied by the author of these crude fakes who was still alive.[44] In the opening sentence he was 'not flattered' by having his work copied and in the final sentence one of his works was 'expected to better the record at a Sotheby's auction in Melbourne in June'.

Important Aboriginal Art

The day after the 1996 auction, with the papers full of the news of its record-breaking results, Tim Klingender received a phone call.

I got a call from Hugo Guthrie, the son of Tim Guthrie the artist, who had lived in Alice Springs in 1971–72. He says, 'I'm looking at this collection of early stuff of my family that has been left to us and we are considering selling all these early Papunya boards. Can you come and see them?' I went straight down and met Hugo – I'd actually known him for years, went to school and university with him. I went to his house in Richmond, and out the back there was a painting storage where Tim Guthrie had them stored. Now I don't think these things had been unwrapped since he purchased them – at all. They were wrapped in brown paper, none of them framed, all in storage, all with the certificates inside the brown paper like the day Pat [Hogan] packed them up for him.

One by one he brought them out and opened them up and obviously it blew my socks off. Maybe when Hugo was young he had been shown them once or twice but they certainly weren't exhibited in the house. They were so extraordinarily pristine. They had never been framed or anything like that. The way it was according to Tim's family was that they lived there for a couple of years with Tim landscape painting. He would go into the Stuart Art Centre – he loved the boards, and he would go in every time Geoff [Bardon] rocked up with a new consignment or Pat did and there would be fifteen or twenty new paintings and Tim would literally get first pick and chose the ones he loved the most and he had enough money to buy a couple each time they came in.[45] So Pat wouldn't have time to frame them and put them on exhibition. They were all literally bought in that little snap of time.

We unwrapped nineteen of them and then as I was going out the door Hugo was running around the house saying, 'I'm sure there's one more'. He kept going through every room and every closet and could never find it. Then he said, 'I know where it is!' We were in the laundry beside the house and above the washing machine was Johnny Warangkula's *Water Dreaming at Kalipinypa*. It was such a great spot for it to be. I looked at it and thought, 'My God, I've never seen anything like it'. Actually I think I had seen that beautiful complex one at the Museum and Art Gallery of the Northern Territory, but it was still spectacular. They made their decision that they wanted to sell them.

I really wanted to show them internationally. I thought that these things were of such high quality and there was a little bit of world interest that we'd had, and there were too many of them, the Australian public basically wasn't going to be ready for them at all. It's been my theory that great stuff looks after itself and – you know – expose it to the widest possible audience. So I asked Sotheby's two things. Number one: I had this core group of material which was just fantastic. It was the day after the 1996 sale, so there was still a year to go before my next one. So I said, 'Can I form an Aboriginal Art Department just to focus purely on this area?' Number two: I want to take these to New York and show them in May next year in Contemporary Art Week. They said 'Yes' to both. Interestingly enough it was also Tribal/Oceanic Art Week but my real interest at the time was to show it as part of Contemporary Art Week. After a lot of negotiation we finally got the go-ahead. It was not easy, because if you know the Contemporary/Postmodern Art scene, they are not particularly fond of ethnographic material. So there was a lot of toing-and-froing and arguing to actually get it.

In the end, after getting there, we found we actually didn't have any space. The only space they'd give us was this area around the entrance to the main Contemporary Art gallery there, which was filled with million-dollar Rothkos and Warhols and Basquiats and that sort of stuff. So it was actually incredible exposure, these twenty early Papunya boards in pristine condition, sort of surrounding the entrance. They just looked spectacular. It was a really interesting time. People walked in and were immediately taken by them and they'd come up and pan down and look at the sign and see that it wasn't part of the Contemporary Art thing and just walk straight away and turn their nose up. But the odd person would go, 'Wow, what's this?' So we started to raise interest, starting up a lot of talk there and got some interest from some incredible people there who are still collectors nowadays.

Among those who attended the New York preview were John and Barbara Wilkerson, already major collectors of American folk art[46] whose special interest in Johnny Warangkula's *Water Dreaming at Kalipinypa* 1972 imparts particular significance to them among the overseas players who enter the boards' story at this point. They – via their covert representative in the saleroom – had been among the international bidders at the 1996 Sotheby's auction, picking up the 1976 Clifford Possum *Fire Dreaming Associated with the Site of Warlugulong* and Mick Namarari's *Bush Tucker Story* 1971–72, ahead of the Anatjari Tjakamarra sales record, and Turkey Tolson's Untitled 1973,

Ronnie Tjampitjinpa's Untitled 1972 and *Mystery Sand Mosaic* 1974 by Shorty Lungkata Tjungurrayi in its afterglow.

The Wilkersons' enthusiasm for the early Papunya boards had actually begun in Australia a few years previously – with the very Johnny Warangkula painting in the collection of the Museum and Art Gallery of the Northern Territory in Darwin of which the *Water Dreaming at Kalipinypa* from the Tim Guthrie Collection had reminded Tim Klingender. For twenty years this painting was the only work in this Museum's remarkable collection of over two hundred early Papunya boards that it had on public display.[47] Though untitled, it also could very well have been given the title *Water Dreaming at Kalipinypa*. According to its annotation, provided by Pat Hogan at the time of its purchase by the Museum in 1980, it depicts the prolific growth of locally occurring plants before and after a successful ceremony brings rain to the artist's country – and does indeed bear a striking resemblance to its namesake in the Tim Guthrie Collection portraying the same subject. As John Wilkerson tells it,[48] this was the painting that ignited his and his wife's passion for the early Papunya boards. They both fell 'wildly and madly in love' with it when they saw it in Darwin while visiting their son, who was living in Australia in the early 1990s. John Wilkerson wrote down the artist's name in an '89 cent spiral notebook' he was carrying – and still keeps alongside his bed: 'Johnny Warangkula – learn about him'. There and then, in the Wilkersons' desire to replicate the rapture they felt at that moment – which drives all obsessive collectors – a sequence of events was set in train which would end up making the Tim Guthrie Collection's *Water Dreaming at Kalipinypa* one of the most famous – and expensive – Aboriginal artworks in the world.

Another significant encounter in the Wilkersons' strand of

this story took place in one of the sixty rooms of the Gramercy Park Hotel on Lexington Avenue, New York City, during the second Gramercy Park International Art Fair in 1995. The previous year, a consortium of New York art dealers, determined to challenge the hegemony of the Art Show, had rented three floors of this historic lower Manhattan establishment. For US$50 a room, selected dealers could display their merchandise among the twin beds and bathroom fittings. Over ten thousand people visited the thirty-two dealers who took up the opportunity in the first year, and the following year newcomer Melbourne gallerist Irene Sutton threw her hat into the ring. When the Wilkersons met Irene Sutton in that Gramercy Park Hotel room in 1995 a partnership was formed that would make the Wilkersons' dream of 'doing the early boards' a reality and drive the emerging auction market in Aboriginal art to heights of which no-one yet dreamed. The Wilkersons recruited Sutton to study Sotheby's auction catalogues and other sources and advise them on the very finest examples available and affordable.

The catalogue for Sotheby's first auction devoted entirely to Aboriginal art, to be held on 30 June 1997 in the Melbourne saleroom, was titled *Important Aboriginal Art* – a logical choice, given Tim Klingender's insistence since the beginning of his Aboriginal art sales drive back in 1995 that the works he had succeeded in placing on the market were part of 'the nation's most important Aboriginal art'. Building on the more lavish Contemporary Art influence evident in the preceding two years' sales catalogues, the *Important Aboriginal Art* catalogue was larger, glossier and more image-packed than any previous auction house publications in this area. The layout left no doubt where the big money was expected. Almost all the early Papunya boards received full-page spreads, copious documentation and detailed provenancing and Johnny Warangkula's *Water Dreaming at Kalipinypa* 1972 had a double-page spread and a full-page reproduction. Estimates reflecting Sotheby's reassuring optimism about the sale's outcomes accompanied each lot in the catalogue. Although they were expressed in Australian dollars (not till its June 2000 sale did Sotheby's give estimates in Australian *and* US dollars – and that year also in euros), 1997 was to be the year the overseas collectors really came into the picture.

The strategy of attracting vendors by publicising the huge profit margins to be made from auction resales had reaped rich rewards. Out of the woodwork had come some of the long-lost treasures that those who knew the history of the Papunya painting movement had been waiting so long to see. Hung two deep the entire length of Sotheby's Sydney showroom a week before the 1997 auction, brought together for that one time in all their glory, that wall of forty early Papunya boards was indeed a wondrous sight. The centrepiece was *Water Dreaming at Kalipinypa.* It gave off that irreproducible 'shimmer' so many writers now have pointed to as the mark of spiritual power in the so-called 'classical' forms of Aboriginal art, which in this painting is the Water Dreaming itself as the water-soaked land dances in the light after the rainstorm. Clustered around it on the showroom wall were the other nineteen pieces from the Tim Guthrie Collection of early Western Desert paintings – perfectly preserved works from 1972 by many of the leading artists of the early years, lovingly selected with an artist's 'eye', whose appearance in the Sotheby's previews was their first public showing. Sotheby's had enlisted the expertise of Geoffrey Bardon, Dick Kimber and Fred Myers, Professor of Anthropology at New York University, in documenting the paintings. The private collection of Mr Colin Jack-Hinton also warranted special distinction in the catalogue as a group of very early 1971 works from the first three consignments to the Stuart Art Centre. Jack-Hinton had bought these at the same time as his historic purchase of early Papunya boards for the collection of the Museums and Art Galleries of the Northern Territory.

The tactic of encouraging Australian contemporary art buyers to purchase Aboriginal art by auctioning it with Australian Contemporary Art had been hugely successful. Historical value had reinforced aesthetic appeal in this first phase. Sotheby's follow-up strategy of developing the overseas market could have neatly dovetailed with its ambitions for the domestic market. The international stamp of approval is the key to major success locally – as anyone familiar with the Australian Contemporary Art world could tell you. However, over the same period the early boards were driven by Sotheby's energetic promotion into an upward price spiral, the Australian dollar was moving downwards, hitting US50 cents to A$1 by 1999. The Aboriginal art auction scene was about to be invaded by cashed-up overseas buyers taking advantage of the parlous state of the Australian dollar and sidelining the Tribal Art dealers, local collectors and connoisseurs whose exclusive province it had been so recently – along with the curators of public art collections, some of whom had initially shown strong interest. Tim Klingender acknowledged they were entering uncharted territory:

> There are a lot of serious buyers from North America, England, Holland, France and Switzerland. At least one buyer will fly out from the US, but most will bid by phone or use agents in Australia. Historically of the best stuff around 20 to 30 per cent goes overseas. It's hard to know whether there will be more this time.[49]

There were institutional and private bidders from London and New York, phone bids from North America, Europe and Asia. Australian collectors, institutional and private, found it difficult to compete – despite an overwhelming feeling that there would never be so many early Papunya boards of such high quality coming together again in the one auction. Just as the presale media build-up had hinted, on auction night Johnny Warangkula's *Water Dreaming at Kalipinypa* was declared the most radiant of all. Jaws must have been dropping all round the room as the bidding soared and the hammer finally fell at $206 000.

Irene Sutton had been among the bidders driving *Water Dreaming at Kalipinypa*'s price to those dizzy heights, but in the end she was unable to secure it for the Wilkersons at its first resale. She was forced to drop out when the bidding continued above the limit the Wilkersons had agreed upon before the auction. But perhaps, in a reverse-case scenario of the Art Gallery of Western Australia's 1996 impasse, this enabled her to buy more of the rest of the Wilkersons' shopping list: in all, eight early boards, including Shorty Lungkata Tjungurrayi's *Water Dreaming* 1972 from the Guthrie Collection, which also broke the six-figure mark at $103 700. It was an unprecedented outcome. Ordinarily at art auctions one or two 'standout' pieces impressively outstrip their presale estimates, thereby reinforcing both vendors' and buyers' assumptions of the profitability of engaging with the process. At the 1997 Important Aboriginal Art auction the entire category of early boards put on such a standout performance. Not a single 1971–72 Papunya painting in the 1997 auction sold for less than Sotheby's presale estimate, and many far exceeded their upper estimates. Shorty Lungkata Tjungurrayi's Untitled 1972, reproduced on the cover of the sales catalogue and Tim

Klingender's second tip for the night's sales record, came in at $123 500. Even an odd, unfinished-looking piece by little-known painter Tommy Tjapaltjarri was sold that night for over $10 000 – also to the Wilkersons' agent.

Save your pity

The morning after the sale, the news that an Aboriginal artist's painting had been auctioned at Sotheby's for $206 000 was in papers and news reports worldwide: 'Black Art breaks sales records!' was the gist of the Australian headlines. The Aboriginal art world was still reeling a week later when a reporter from *The Australian* sought out Johnny W to ask him what he thought about it – especially as none of the money looked like coming his way. He was found sitting cross-legged on a bleak concrete slab outside his current residence in one of the ill-famed town camps around Alice Springs. His living conditions were probably not dissimilar to those at Papunya when the painting which had just sold at Sotheby's was originally created and sold for something less than the $150 which Tim Guthrie had paid for it in 1972 from the Stuart Art Centre. Barefoot and dishevelled, he was the perfect media image of the starving artist, who had sold his masterpiece for a pittance and now stood to gain nothing from the fabulous sums by which his work was enriching others. Overnight it seemed resale royalties, which had never before been a serious issue in Australian art, were on the political agenda. Totally unmoved by any of this, Johnny Warangkula demonstrated the same spirit that glows from his painting in his response to the reporter's probing of the obvious irony of his situation. Declining the mantle of victim she was preparing to place on his shoulders, he announced:

'I am number one. I am the winner. I am the Boss of my country and I do the best paintings.'[50]

What struck me powerfully about Johnny Warangkula's resurfacing in the media after that first record-making sale was its resonance with the notorious case in the 1960s when a bark painting by David Malangi was reproduced without his prior knowledge or consent on the back of the new Australian dollar note. Malangi too was 'forgotten before he was remembered'[51] – and he too reappeared like the ghost at the banquet in the midst of a mindless celebration of money.

It was Clifford Possum Tjapaltjarri who gently explained to the excited old man that in the white man's world none of this fabulous amount of money was his by right. On this good advice, Johnny Warangkula tempered his rage and his demands to this touching plea:

'If anything comes out of this what I really want is to get a Toyota and go to Kalipinypa – the place of my Dreaming in the painting.'[52]

The Australian's report revealed that before the auction night the National Indigenous Arts Advocacy Association had sent a confidential letter to Sotheby's and the Guthrie estate. The letter had outlined Johnny Warangkula's circumstances and appealed for a donation from the proceeds similar to the 4 per cent accorded artists under the French droit de suite legislation. The request was rejected, though Johnny Warangkula's wish was granted. But not by those who profited from the sale of his painting. Two weeks after *The Australian* ran its story, the *Centralian Advocate* reported that a good Samaritan from Melbourne had been so moved that he went straight down to the bank and took out $2000, which he sent to the artist so that he could buy himself a car and drive to Kalipinypa. An Alice Springs car dealer then sold Johnny a $5000 car for his money and threw in a free tank of petrol and, with a $100 food voucher from a local Aboriginal organisation, Johnny Warangkula set off for Papunya and places beyond with his family.[53] The next news that came through about Johnny Warangkula was that he had taken up his brush again after years of being considered by most people around Alice Springs too old and blind to paint any more.[54] For a while he could earn $1000 a day from the opportunistic private dealers who soon beat a path to his door. From Johnny's point of view at least, life was a lot easier than it had been before the June auction.

Over fifty more early Papunya boards were included in the even weightier sales catalogue for Sotheby's 29 June 1998 auction and its packed Melbourne saleroom witnessed another glittering array of Important Aboriginal Art go under the hammer. This time Sotheby's had also previewed the work in Los Angeles, where the response was described as 'incredible'. In the presale publicity Tim Klingender had predicted that 'many many works will sell for more than $100 000'[55] – and he was proved right yet again. The bonanza of 1997 was repeated, with several early Papunya boards attracting five- and six-figure sums. The biggest shock of the night came from Lot 25, *Wild Potato (Yala) Dreaming* 1971, attributed to Billy Stockman,[56] which sold for $200 500, only just below the record set the previous year by the Johnny Warangkula. But the post-auction publicity for Important Aboriginal Art 1998 did not match the previous year's. Almost equalling a record is evidently not newsworthy, even if it was for a seminal work executed the year before the record-holding work by Johnny Warangkula. The bright yellow little painting combined the historic appeal of the very earliest Papunya works with an uncanny resonance with the work of Miro and other early European Modernists. But though Billy Stockman's stocks rose slightly with the backyard dealers and fast-buck merchants of Alice Springs, he was left to his own devices by the media.

In the lead-up to the 1999 Sotheby's auction, messages of encouragement to bring out those long-forgotten Aboriginal paintings acquired on visits to the Centre in years gone by and dust them off for Tim Klingender's inspection were broadcast into the remotest corners of the country. This one, for instance, appeared in the *Hobart Mercury* under the headline 'A nice little earner in that souvenir':

> If you visited Alice Springs in 1972–73, check the back of the cupboard for that $10 piece of Aboriginal art you might have picked up there. It could be worth 20000 times that amount today. Sotheby's Australia has just reported its highest yearly turnover – and the surge in prices of Aboriginal art has helped it along.
>
> Sotheby's managing director Justin Miller said original pieces from the Papunya Tula School at its outset around 1972–73 had sky-rocketed in value. 'There was only a small number painted in that era but people have them,' he said. 'They might have bought them on their honeymoon for $10 or $15 and now those are getting enormous sums of money – up to $200000.'[57]

Without these kinds of stories in the local press, and without the six-figure sales records produced by fierce competition between wealthy overseas bidders, many of these works might never have seen the light of day. Sotheby's Chairman Justin Miller acknowledged that the result was partly attributable to the weaker Australian dollar and a corresponding increase in international buyers, 'particularly in the fields of antiques, decorative arts, and Aboriginal arts'.[58] More than half the top lots in the June 1998 Important Aboriginal Art auction went to overseas buyers. The 'clamour for Indigenous art'[59] resulted in a record $5.44 million turnover in the Aboriginal Art Department, up $1.27 million on the previous year – albeit helped along by the $1.2 million purchase of the Peter Fannin Collection of Early Western Desert Paintings, consisting of more than seventy late 1972 Papunya paintings, by the National Gallery of Australia, the only local collecting institution with the resources to collect early Papunya boards at their going prices.

In the last days of the 1998–99 financial year, Melbourne was again abuzz as Sotheby's prepared to auction another 321 works of Important Aboriginal Art, including another fifty early Papunya boards. In Tim Klingender's publicity appearances leading up to the sale, his metamorphosis from shy painter to the new kingmaker of Australian Aboriginal art seemed complete. As John Kasmir once wrote of Bruce Chatwin's Sotheby's persona: 'He had the right manner, a mixture of bluff, a good eye and an ability to deal with the rich'.[60] Sotheby's presale media build-up had singled out Lot 102, an extraordinary untitled 1972 work by Mick Namarari Tjapaltjarri. The work came with impeccable provenance[61] and an annotated diagram by Geoffrey Bardon with interpretative notes in which he identified the dominant elongated ovoid form as a tjurunga or sacred board and the two arc shapes as caves within which these boards were stored. The painting sold for $162 000, more than $40 000 above Sotheby's upper estimate. An unusual collaborative work by Kaapa Tjamptijinpa and his cousin Tim Leura Tjapaltjarri fetched $145 000. Both were sold to the Wilkersons' agent. Klingender reported that overseas bidders had taken 'eight out of ten' of the top lots 'including the most expensive'.[62]

The star turn of Sotheby's Aboriginal Art 2000 auction was once again Johnny Warangkula's *Water Dreaming at Kalipinypa* 1972. The painting irradiated the main wall of Sotheby's Sydney showroom at the June preview of the imminent auction. The painting had returned to Australian shores to be auctioned just three years after its purchase for the world record price of $206 000 for an Aboriginal artwork. To the Wilkerson camp, it must have seemed like a minor miracle that its mysterious American owner was preparing to part with it – and an opportunity not to be missed again – for any price. But it was not the only early Papunya board in Sotheby's auction coming up for the second time. There were at least a dozen,[63] giving rise to speculation that the supply might be 'drying up' – and that the owners of these works must have purchased them purely for speculative investment purposes. Why else would they be disposing of them so soon after buying them? Since 1997, the Aboriginal art rumour mill had been churning away at the question of who had bought *Water Dreaming at Kalipinypa* for such an extraordinary sum that year. Some said the buyer was a Californian property developer, but no-one seemed to know who – or if they did, they were not saying.

For the first time in five years of observing from the sidelines, I decided I must attend the 2000 auction and observe this spectacle for myself. I arrived mid-afternoon on the day of the sale, hoping to view the remaining works from the auction which had not been displayed in the Sydney preview. By the time I reached Sotheby's headquarters in the fashionable inner Melbourne suburb of Armadale, the saleroom was already set up for the auction, which was by then only a few hours away.

Empty, it reminded me of a church, with its high vaulted ceiling, dark polished parquetry floor and rows of seats arranged on either side of a wide central aisle leading up to the raised auctioneer's podium – which looked for all the world like a pulpit. Above it, attached to a lush, dark red velvet curtain covering the entire back wall, a blue sign announced in large, old-fashioned white lettering that we were in the presence of 'Sotheby's Established 1744'. Beside the podium, a majestic, white, carved wooden sculpture of a sea bird stood high on a pedestal next to the small antique desk where the recording clerk sits during the auction taking down the prices and winning bidder numbers for each lot. Carvings of gaunt human figures stood close together on a tall plinth. A collection of pukumani or burial poles and log coffins was arranged on a low dais on the other side and in front of that a carved and painted sculpture of a kangaroo. Everything was spotlit against the restrained opulence of the room. One side wall was hung with large canvases from the auction. The smaller works would be brought out by white-gloved and aproned Sotheby's staff and held up as their lot numbers were called during the auction.

The side aisle and the space behind the chairs were packed with people by the time the auctioneer got down to business about 6.30 pm. The atmosphere was tense, despite the free alcohol that had been on offer downstairs in the lobby. During the auction I looked around the room and saw most of the audience with their heads bowed over their sales catalogues – as if in prayer. And when the hammer fell on Johnny Warangkula's *Water Dreaming at Kalipinypa* at $440 000, most of the congregation rose to its feet and applauded wildly – like a revivalist meeting at the performance of the miracle of art and money they had come along to witness or to watch the auctioneer–magician pull out of his hat. The phone bids table, which ran down the other side of the room, headed up by an intense and preoccupied Tim Klingender, dominated the action that night, though it was from the auction floor that the record-breaking bid which secured the Johnny Warangkula came. There was an audible gasp around the room as the hammer fell and the destiny of the painting was sealed in the hands of another wealthy American. The Wilkersons at last had their prize – and in return for having painted it, Johnny Warangkula had one more moment of exultation.

Several papers the next morning reported that 'Mr Tjupurrula is semi-blind and has only two fingers on one hand' and one or two mentioned that he would get nothing from the sale which, with Sotheby's commission[64] added in, came to $486 500. Johnny Warangkula meanwhile had moved to the Hettie Perkins Nursing Home in Alice Springs. The staff reported his delight at the news:

> 'I'm very famous. I'm very famous,' he shouted to the nursing staff. 'I'm number one, number one big-time artist.'

In attendance in his room were his niece Pansy Napangati and her daughter Brenda Nangala, who observed that:

> 'He's very excited. He deserves it. He's worked really hard all his life to support his family.'

The nursing sister added:

> 'He feels he's been recognised for who he is and what he does.'[65]

Johnny W no longer appeared to care about the money issue

– or if he did, he refused to let it get in the way of the joy he had in knowing that he had been right all along in the enthusiastic claims he had always made for his work. But his moment of triumph was short-lived. He went back to live with his family in Papunya, where his grandchildren led him around by the hand. He died in February 2001. I was told that not a single one of the private dealers, who would not leave him alone while he could still paint for them, cared enough to attend his lonely funeral in Papunya. For years afterwards, his relatives used to ask helpful strangers who visited Papunya to help them put a headstone on his grave in the local cemetery. So far as I know, it still lacks one.

The 'Black Art Scandals'

To this point I have described the process by which the early Papunya boards were elevated to their current iconic status in contemporary Australian Indigenous art as if it occurred in a bubble. Inside the circle of Sotheby's seductive influence, swept up and along by the momentum of sales records and extraordinary works of art appearing out of the woodwork, it almost seemed so. The Wilkersons, self-described 'obsessives' driven by their desire to make that one very special painting the centrepiece of their collection and acting through a local operative, were insulated from the 'Sotheby's effect' on the Indigenous art industry in general and on the 'old masters' of desert painting in particular.

But the repercussions, intended and not, of Sotheby's inspired marketing campaign around the early boards are as much part of this chapter of their history as the canonisation of *Water Dreaming at Kalipinypa*. Something must be said about the savage sideshow known as the 'black art scandals' that accompanied Sotheby's stellar performance on the main stage.

Well before Tim Klingender began working for Sotheby's or conceived his winning strategy for developing the secondary market, surging sales of desert art were attracting increasing numbers of private entrepreneurs to Central Australia to cash in on the boom times in the primary market. The focus of their attention was not Papunya Tula Artists, but the Utopia community, east of Alice Springs, home to Emily Kngwarrey, the eighty-year-old woman who blazed a brilliant trail through the Australian art world in the early 1990s and at the time of her death in 1996 was the most acclaimed and successful artist in the entire country. She single-handedly revolutionised the position of women in Aboriginal art, but her brief career was a battleground of warring private dealers, many of whom knew little about any kind of art, let alone Aboriginal art, except that you could turn an easy profit in the capital cities for a canvas picked up for a pile of cash in small denominations from a 'name' artist. For their part, the 'name' artists were drawn to the instant financial rewards which this new private sector, unburdened by the community obligations of the government-subsidised 'art centres' on the remote settlements, was able to offer them, and many gravitated to Alice Springs to reap its rewards for themselves and their sprawling entourages of relatives and hangers-on. When the secondary market, spearheaded by Sotheby's sales drive around the early Papunya boards, began to emerge, the auction house clientele reinforced the private entrepreneurs' preoccupation with 'name' artists: they were looking for investment value, blue-chip stocks, autograph works.

The year 1997 was a crucial one for the fate of desert art. It started with the strange confession of Western Australian painter Elizabeth Durack, scion of one of the oldest pastoral dynasties in the Kimberley, to having successfully impersonated for over a year 'Eddie Burrup', supposedly an old Aboriginal stockman from the Pilbara turned artist, but in fact a figment of her octogenarian imagination. She had entered Eddie's works in the National Aboriginal and Torres Strait Islander Art Award, the country's leading Indigenous art prize and, at curator Doreen Mellor's invitation, in *Native Titled Now*, an exhibition presenting Indigenous artistic responses to the High Court's historic 1992 decision in the Mabo case. Durack's revelations excited a flurry of media interest in what might be construed as a continuation of a fine old Australian tradition of artistic larrikinism – had it not been so pointedly directed by her own actions and by the media at the role Aboriginal art was playing in the emergent discourse of Indigenous sovereignty in the wake of the Mabo and later the Wik[66] decisions. The whole country was caught up in the turmoil. Even Tim Klingender, in the midst of the media build-up to the watershed 1997 auction, was moved to acknowledge what he called the 'issue of the moment':

> 'It's Wik, it's stolen children,[67] it's reconciliation, and I think people are also waking up to how special this art is. The thing about these paintings is they're all about land and people's relationship to land, so they're really just part of the broader land rights movement … Initially people are drawn to it for the beauty and the aesthetics but it has a deeper spiritual meaning and a historical leaning as well.'[68]

While most of the outcry in Aboriginal art circles about the media's scandal-mongering would focus on its potentially damaging impact on the market in Aboriginal art, of yet more profound concern was its potential to weaken the capacity of this art to convey important messages about the significance of art and land for Indigenous people – or even to be seen as an expression of Aboriginal culture.

For a few months after the sensational outcome of the 1997 auction, the only Aboriginal art that had made the front pages of the newspapers was the vast and magnificent Ngurrara Canvas. Painted by senior traditional owners of the Great Sandy Desert for presentation to the National Native Title Tribunal, it was danced upon by ceremonially painted Aboriginal plaintiffs pleading with the politicians for their land. Then the very week the controversial amendments to the *Native Title Act* were introduced for the crucial Senate debate, *The Australian* ran the first of Susan McCulloch-Uehlin's 'Black Art Scandals' series. Under a page 1 banner headline, it reported the claims of a Welsh immigrant named Ray Beamish to primary authorship of certain works by well-known Utopia artist Kathleen Petyarre, including the work which had won her (not Eddie Burrup) the 1996 National Aboriginal and Torres Strait Islander Art Award. The Aboriginal art world sprang to Petyarre's defence, claiming that that such collaborative practices as Beamish alleged were an intrinsic part of art-making in the ceremonial context and in no way impugned the legitimacy of the ritually senior artist's claims to authorship of her work from an Indigenous perspective. The Museums and Art Galleries of the Northern Territory, which sponsors the Art Award, concurred after a lengthy inquiry into the affair. Their report concluded that authorship of collaborative works could legitimately be assigned to the senior artist or Dreaming custodian, irrespective of whose hand had held the brush. But for the collectors, obsessed with the 'hand of the master painter', this was still the burning question.

Clifford Possum, meanwhile, was basking in the fading

afterglow of the 1995 sales record for his *Love Story* 1972, having to this point experienced the Sotheby's effect primarily as a run of requests from the private dealers who frequented his Alice Springs camp site for 'Love Story' paintings. When it suited him he painted for the 'backyarders', the new wave of art entrepreneurs who flourished in the wake of the six-figure sales records, 'picking up' Johnny Warangkula and any other surviving founders of Papunya Tula Artists they could find to work for them exclusively, behind the high fences and locked gates of their painting workshops on the outskirts of town. Clifford Possum was perfectly capable of finding his own buyers, and too much his own man to be indentured by the lure of unlimited 'tucker money' (some said 'alcohol drip') on offer at such places. All his life he loved to paint 'more better than anything' and if he engaged assistants, they were usually members of his entourage, whom he had trained to dot in a style intentionally indistinguishable from his own, working alongside him on the backgrounds of larger canvases. But if they or others to whom he had social and cultural obligations painted their shared Dreamings in a style that could pass to the uneducated eye as an 'Alice Springs' Clifford Possum, why should he criticise them? For flouting the conventions of the whitefella trade in his work, which his Sotheby's experience had taught him gave nothing back to the artist?

After the Petyarre–Beamish controversy, no-one in the Aboriginal art world was prepared to condemn such 'collaborative practices' either. The situation in the primary market was ripe for exploitation by unscrupulous individuals whose business contacts with the artist at his camp made them aware of these practices. Precisely when the 'School of Clifford Possum' genre began to develop into something quite outside the artist's culture and knowledge may never be fully known. But the moment Clifford Possum decided enough was enough and initiated a police investigation in a determined effort to 'clear my name' can be precisely identified. In February 1999, under the headline 'Dealers capitalize on Aboriginal art resurgence', the *Australian* arts writer Ben Genocchio described a visit to the Mascot warehouse of one such dealer, London-based Patrick Corbally-Stourton, to view works from his upcoming Clifford Possum exhibition. Though billed as a retrospective, most works had been painted in the last three years and of these, Genocchio ruefully acknowledged, 'few, in truth, match the detail and intensity of his earlier works'.[69] A fortnight later, the next 'Aboriginal art scandal' hit the front page of *The Australian* when Clifford Possum Tjapaltjarri himself visited Corbally-Stourton's warehouse and in the presence of members of the NSW commercial fraud squad, pronounced this fateful judgment over most of the paintings: 'Not mine'.[70]

The burden of guilt quickly shifted from Corbally-Stourton, the hapless middleman, onto a shadowy group of wholesale dealers in the artist's work – and perhaps even Clifford Possum himself, although his role as the whistleblower and his co-operation with the police investigation should have suggested otherwise. Just when it seemed things could not possibly get any worse for the Aboriginal art market, the Review section of *The Weekend Australian* came out with a cover on which the word 'Fake' had been spelt out and outlined in dots like an Aboriginal painting.[71] Inside was the next in McCulloch-Uehlin's 'Black Art Scandals' series: one of the dealers who had sponsored Clifford Possum's visit to Sydney to denounce the contents of Corbally-Stourton's exhibition was himself denounced by another of the old Papunya masters, Turkey Tolson Tjupurrula – for misattributing to him paintings which he knew to be the work of other members of his family. And there was more. The next day *The Australian* ran a follow-up story, based on another statutory declaration from Turkey Tolson, explaining that he had not understood very well the Luritja into which the first statutory declaration had been translated for him to sign and that the dealer he had denounced in it was a fine fellow who had done much to assist himself and his family. One had to smile at the level of high farce towards which events were rapidly escalating. Two documentary exposés of fraud, forgery and rank commercialism in the Centralian Aboriginal art industry – Jeremy Eccles' *Art from the Heart?*[72] and an ABC *Four Corners* program on the Clifford Possum forgeries affair called 'Dot for Dollar',[73] were screened in the aftermath of these events, spreading the message of *The Weekend Australian* magazine's 'Fake' cover far and wide.

In late November 1999, after nine months of dogged investigation, the detectives assigned to the Clifford Possum forgery case arrested and charged John Douglas O'Loughlin, the Adelaide art dealer who had been the principal supplier to Corbally-Stourton of the fakes identified by the artist, on twenty-two counts of 'obtaining benefit by deception'. In July 2000, just a few weeks after the second record-breaking sale of *Water Dreaming at Kalipinypa*, O'Loughlin's committal hearing commenced in the NSW District Court. O'Loughlin finally entered a guilty plea and went up for sentencing in January 2001. In the end, he walked away with a good behaviour bond. O'Loughlin's defence counsel made a last-minute appeal to the sentencing judge's sophistication in the ways of Aboriginal culture that appears to have carried the day for his client: 'While the conservative art world may be outraged by other artists contributing to an individual's work, it was common practice in Aboriginal circles for family members or trusted friends to help artists finish their work'.[74] Works that the artist himself had declared to be forgeries were declared by the court to be works of artistic collaboration – and the bewildered artist retreated from his attempt to seek redress through the Australian legal system for the damage to his honour as a responsible custodian of his Dreamings. Many people were left with the very impression which Clifford Possum had hoped the police inquiry would dispel: that he was somehow implicated in a crime against himself.

The case took a heavy toll on Clifford Possum's once-robust health. His response to what he experienced as public 'shaming' was to retreat from the world which had for the best part of the past decade been his stage. He rarely travelled outside Alice Springs and seemed to have turned his back on the white art world. He made a brief appearance at the Art Gallery of New South Wales on the day before the grand opening of the *Papunya Tula: Genesis and Genius* retrospective. He was shown over the exhibition, which contained five of his paintings, and shared a cup of coffee with the three Pintupi artists whom Papunya Tula had flown down from Alice Springs for the occasion. The timing of his visit, intentionally or not, was a statement about his connection to the company, which had been an important part of Papunya Tula's history and his own. There seemed little residue of the role he and other members of the School of Kaapa had played in the first two decades of the art movement. He was the outsider, turning up unannounced, with the inevitable roll of canvas under his arm. His marginality to the worlds within which Papunya Tula was now moving was all too plain.

Sotheby's catalogue had stipulated that *Water Dreaming at Kalipinypa* was 'to be sold with the provision that it be included in the forthcoming exhibition *Papunya Tula: Genesis and Genius* to be held at the Art Gallery of New South Wales, Sydney, August–November 2000'.[75] So before returning to its new home in America, the painting joined another thirty-six early Papunya boards in the exhibition, most of which were on display in a major public gallery for the first time since they had been created nearly thirty years before. More than half of them were on loan from private collections – in Australia as well as overseas: a higher proportion than for any other period of the movement except the most recent. The pivotal importance attached by the exhibition's curator Hetti Perkins to the early Papunya boards was evident in her selection of twenty-eight works from 1972 and nine from 1971 – far more from those two years than from any other equivalent period of Papunya Tula's history, and as many as she chose to represent the entire twenty years from 1974 to 1995. Along with *Water Dreaming at Kalipinypa*, the other most frequently reproduced painting in the show's promotional material was the second highest priced early Papunya board to that point: the Billy Stockman-attributed *Yala Dreaming.* Its graphic qualities and attunement to western aesthetic sensibilities made it an ideal icon for the retrospective's take on the Papunya Tula movement as 'a distillation or amplification of quintessential … motifs'.[76]

To express her concern for the artists as well as their art, the curator staged a charity dinner and auction for the Western Desert Dialysis Unit Appeal on the closing night of the retrospective. A group of about thirty paintings had been donated to the auction in support of the Appeal, including the four vast 12' x 8' canvases in which the exhibition hang had culminated. Donated to the appeal by Papunya Tula Artists, all were collaborative works par excellence, involving all the men or women painters who had been present in the communities of Kintore and Kiwirrkura at the time they were painted. Sotheby's had been generous with its resources and expertise in helping organise and then orchestrating the auction, in which its finely honed skills of art salesmanship were put to work for the benefit of the artists and their communities. Close to $1 million was raised on the night. Patrons paid $250 a head for the privilege of being present, though it was an Australian phone bidder who took out the highest priced item of the evening, the resplendent Kiwirrkura men's painting, for $300 000. As Tim Klingender breathlessly revealed over post-auction drinks, it was the highest price ever paid at auction for a brand new work by an Indigenous artist – let alone a collaborative effort by relative unknowns.

But in desert art of the 21st century such works are rare indeed. These days, desert artists work under the surveillance not of their own cultural 'managers' or 'policemen' ('kutungulu') but of art dealers and even art centres. Their aim is ensure that what goes out under an artist's name is all his or her own work, lest they be accused of fraudulent practices in a still fiercely competitive environment. Many private dealers lock out the artists' families for the same reason – and also so that the artists will not be humbugged by them. The pity of these measures for the art movement is that they jeopardise the collaborative painting practices that have ensured the continuation of the art movement through three generations. The senior painters whose work is in high demand in the marketplace have evolved new, less labour-intensive methods to enable them to maintain the massive output required to meet the demands of the trade, and the collective genius of Western Desert visual culture, from which the art movement sprang in the first place, continues to find expression in their increasingly minimalist masterpieces. But how will the next generation of desert artists be trained to take their place? And how will what they produce be more than 'pretty pictures' if the paintings' role in intergenerational cultural transmission is not maintained?

Through all of this, the Sotheby's show had rolled on regardless – its appeal actually enhanced by the cloud of uncertainty now hanging over the primary market. The more uncertain conditions appeared in the primary market, the more buyers looked to the Sotheby's name for reassurance and secure provenance. The side benefits of the authentication scandals for the secondary market were confirmed by other auction houses entering the trade over precisely this period – and profiting hugely by it. The pundits and the media predicted that the Sotheby's auction and the inaugural Deutscher-Menzies Aboriginal art sale would provide a 'litmus test'[77] for the market after the tumultuous events of the first half of 1999 and the ongoing sense of crisis in the Aboriginal art industry. Both houses offered purchasers a money-back guarantee if they could prove beyond dispute within four years (Deutscher-Menzies) and five years (Sotheby's) that the work they had bought was a forgery. The *Sydney Morning Herald* offered its readers a 'hot tip' evidently inspired by the scandals:

> If someone paints their Dreaming, they may be helped by a number of other people in their family. The helpers do not paint the design, they simply help fill it in, just as artisans helped Michelangelo with his larger works.[78]

'If sober, also undismayed'[79] was the assessment of the night's bidding. The *Australian Financial Review* concluded that the international art market appeared 'completely unfazed by the controversies over authorship which have gripped the Aboriginal art market over the past six months'.[80]

When Sotheby's first came on the scene the private dealers were in the process of taking over from the community art centres as the driving forces in the primary market for Aboriginal art. The dealers' disarray created a vacuum into which Sotheby's could step. At the same time there was a resurgence of the art centres, especially Papunya Tula Artists, as wary buyers sought out trustworthy sources of paintings, no longer impressed by the dealers' boast of 'dealing direct' with the artists. They preferred to deal instead with commercial galleries who could claim to have sourced their work through art centres. However, the focus on individual artists produced by media and auction house promotion of their record-breaking prices permanently shifted the buyers' focus away from community-based art collectives to individual 'art stars'. Sotheby's simply tightened its criteria, accepting works by Papunya Tula artists only if the vendor had documentation proving they had been acquired from Papunya Tula – and by Clifford Possum only if they pre-dated his mid-1980s move to Alice Springs and exposure to the machinations of the private dealers.

Auction 2001

The first Sotheby's auction of the 21st century was remarkable as the moment when the early Papunya boards' importance to Sotheby's Aboriginal art marketing apparatus was suddenly and apparently quite unexpectedly eclipsed. The Australian National Gallery purchased a 1991 painting by Rover Thomas entitled *All that Big Rain Coming from Top Side* for a record $786 000 – more than five hundred times what the artist had been paid for it only ten years earlier, more than seven times the top price for a work by this artist recorded at a Sotheby's auction in 1998, and more than double the Sotheby's upper estimate of its current market value. In defence of the price it had paid, the National Gallery claimed that *All that Big Rain Coming from Top Side*, painted in 1991 on commission for Perth Aboriginal art dealer Mary Macha, was 'the last outstanding Rover Thomas in private hands' and that such a significant and beautiful painting should remain in Australia to enrich the nation's cultural heritage.[81] The only public gallery in Australia with sufficient funding at its disposal to do so had finally overcome the apparent reluctance of public collecting institutions to enter the bidding. The acquisition before the auction of the radiant Lot 47, Clifford Possum Tjapaltjarri's *Honey Ant Ceremony* 1972, by the Art Gallery of South Australia for $141 000 and William Barak's *Untitled (Ceremony)* 1900 by the National Gallery of Victoria for $80 000 from its Contemporary Australian Art funds suggested that other public galleries in Australia might also be prepared to adopt extraordinary measures to secure particularly rare and exceptional pieces.

There was something else different about that night from the preceding four years' specialist Aboriginal art auctions. This was the presence in the room of one of the artists, a man who had probably more claim than anyone else alive to be hailed as a founder of the contemporary Aboriginal art movement, of which such luminaries as Emily Kame Kngwarrey and Rover Thomas were later flowerings. Clifford Possum Tjapaltjarri was painting in Papunya before Geoffrey Bardon appeared, and had only just joined the pioneering group of artists when he produced the immaculate, heraldic image of *Honey Ant Ceremony* 1972. There were probably many in the room who hoped that its price would enhance the value of their stockpiles of Clifford Possum's controversial 1990s and current work. The artist himself was above any such considerations; he knew full well that the auction meant no money for him, no matter how much his painting had sold for.

Clifford Possum might have been thinking about this when he was filmed at Sotheby's preview the day before the auction, gazing up at his work, resplendent on the closely hung front panel of the display. He had no defiant words for the newshounds or punters to equal Johnny Warangkula's inspired advice of four years before to a passing journalist to 'Save your pity for those who have no Dreaming'. No words at all. He was wearing the stockman's hat which someone told me later he had not worn since his wife Emily died in 1990, pulled down low. I hope he did not hear a fashionably dressed woman across the other side of the room remark 'Fancy wearing a hat in here!' – or realise if he did that the comment must have been directed at him. The woman was sitting near me, and I saw her join in the round of polite applause at the auctioneer's announcement when Lot 47 came up that we were honoured that night by the presence of the artist, Clifford Possum Tjapaltjarri, whose painting had been sold before the auction to the Art Gallery of South Australia. I wondered whether the audience's enthusiasm was at all tempered by embarrassment that the proceedings were being witnessed by such a man. Outside the bubble, the auction triumphs look more like a sacrifice of his people's art to the god of money, with no returns to the artists. The glittering spectacle had once again brought hundreds of us along like a bunch of ghouls to watch the dividing up of another culture's treasures. The phrase 'culture vultures' takes on a whole new meaning in this context. When Clifford Possum's presence was announced, the sense of all this seemed to hover in the air for a moment, and then was gone, swept away in the tumultuous response to the record-breaking Rover Thomas sale. These were the moments of rising tension and excitement that everyone had been waiting for. No wonder Clifford Possum kept his hat on – the badge of his sorrow. In the world of the art auctions, works of art are just very high-priced commodities to be bought and sold, items in investment portfolios, or pretty pictures to dangle on a wall, not pieces of someone's soul, parts of their culture lovingly inscribed. My impression during the applause that no-one really registered who he was or what his presence meant was confirmed by another fashionably dressed woman at the end of the evening who said to Clifford Possum as he painfully negotiated the stairs back out onto the street: 'Long Tom! I love your work'.

6

The Object of Protection

A fortnight before the 1990 Tribal Art auction[1] that gave Tim Klingender his start at Sotheby's Australia, an article by journalist Bob Evans had appeared in the weekend edition of the *Sydney Morning Herald.* Entitled somewhat prophetically 'Tribal art becomes our Elgin Marbles',[2] its subject was the impact that laws for the protection of cultural heritage could have on the marketing of Aboriginal art. Klingender would return often to this theme in his later role as Sotheby's Australia's Aboriginal art specialist, but this time he was on the sidelines, observing how the auction house used the media to bolster its attempt to put back on the market thirty Aboriginal weapons and artefacts which it had been forced to withdraw from its November 1989 Aboriginal, Melanesian and Tribal Art sale eight months earlier. Managing Director Robert Bleakley acknowledged that Sotheby's Australia had 'erred' in failing to apply for permits to sell the objects. However, he insisted that it had acted in 'good faith' on the advice of the Museum of Victoria that the items were not 'relics' and hence not subject to the newly introduced provisions of the *Aboriginal and Torres Strait Islander Heritage Protection Amendment Act*

1987,[3] designed to protect the Aboriginal cultural heritage of Victoria. Sotheby's Australia would not, he said, have dealt with them if it had thought the items did come under the Act. The firm was not in the business of dealing with protected objects, even though it was offered them from time to time. But the Department of Planning and the Environment, at that time responsible for administering the Act, had 'judged otherwise and pounced'.[4]

The article drew comparisons with an incident in Adelaide a fortnight after the confiscation of the items from Sotheby's, in which officers of the South Australian Wildlife Protection Branch had 'staged a similar raid' on a South Australian auction house and 'to the amazement of the assembled buyers and sellers seized thirty-seven weapons and artefacts a mere half-an-hour before they were due to be auctioned'. In this case the officers were acting under a South Australian law requiring that items potentially significant to any Aboriginal tribe within the state's boundaries be submitted to expert examiners before being put up to auction. In the melee, certain objects from the Northern Territory, which were outside the scope of the South Australian legislation, had also been seized, giving weight to Evans' conclusion that the various acts of Parliament were a 'well-intentioned, if confused' attempt to protect Indigenous cultural heritage, while simultaneously recognising 'the proprietorial rights of non-Aboriginal collectors', but that in the end the legislation was 'the problem, not the solution'.[5]

The Victorian Koori Heritage Trust suggested as a solution that it be given first option to buy works of cultural significance to Victorian Aborigines. 'If we don't match the market price', they could then be placed on the open market. As Evans commented, this might work for 'pieces that belong in the public domain' but:

What about material of a sacred secret nature that ought to be returned to tribal communities or respectfully preserved in public institutions? Are we as a nation prepared to do what is necessary, open up the process and pay a fair price for their preservation?[6]

In the wake of the national awakening to Indigenous dispossession of the 1988 Bicentennial Year, the answer just might have been 'Yes', at least in principle, at least at 1990s prices for 'tribal artefacts'. But over the next two decades as these issues arose around the early Papunya boards, whose prices thanks to Sotheby's energetic promotion were soaring way above their 1990 levels, another scenario would be played out, one that speaks volumes for where Australia sits on Indigenous issues when serious money is involved.

Leigh Purcell, Sotheby's Tribal Art specialist in 1990, served as Evans' mouthpiece in the article for the auction houses' perennial critique of restrictive export laws for cultural heritage: that unless the path is left clear for them to deal legitimately in these items, a black market will develop. But as *their* critics point out just as often: 'the salesrooms act as a magnet for this traffic, *creating* a market'.[7] It is an argument with considerable force in the case of the early Papunya boards – but in this instance it cuts both ways. Before 1995, few people outside a small circle of experts and museum and gallery personnel knew much about the early Papunya boards, and no-one who was not there at the time they were created had seen anything like the exceptional examples turned up by Sotheby's efficient PR machine. Scattered to the four winds almost as soon as they were painted, a great many of the early Papunya boards had moved out from Papunya in every direction to destinations of seemingly impenetrable obscurity. It was the lure of money – the hope of a mortgage repaid or a child put through university – that drew them out. Without Sotheby's 'masterpiece behind the washing machine' stories, and without the six-figure sales records produced by competition with and between wealthy overseas bidders, many of these works might have stayed on their owners' walls as treasured mementos of their times in the desert – or under beds, behind cupboards, in storerooms and garages where they had languished, unregarded, for twenty-five years. And maybe the artists would have preferred it that way …

'A vast and unnecessary nuisance'[8]

The 1970 UNESCO Convention on the Means of Prohibiting and Preventing the Illicit Import, Export and Transfer of Ownership of Cultural Property urges every country to protect its unique cultural property:

> cultural property [constituting] one of the basic elements of civilisation and national culture … it is incumbent upon every state to protect the cultural property existing within its territory.[9]

Australia is one of eighty-five countries around the world (not including the United States of America) that have ratified the Convention. The Protection of Movable Cultural Heritage Act was passed in 1986 as the necessary implementing legislation prior to Australia's accession to the Convention on 30 January 1990. The Cultural Heritage Commission in Canberra has responsibility for the administration of the Act. Behind its closed doors, moves had been afoot for some time to find a way of amending the Act to allow 'significant early works from the Papunya school which did not currently fall under the Act'[10] to qualify for inclusion on the National Heritage

Control List as 'Australian Protected Objects'. This would mean that export permits would be required for them to leave the country, even temporarily, and they could be refused if the National Cultural Heritage Committee, acting on the advice of expert examiners, deemed the works of such exceptional 'cultural significance' that particularly their permanent export would result in 'cultural loss' to the nation – or part thereof.

The Act's main purpose was to ensure the retention in Australia of an 'irreducible minimum' of movable cultural heritage. The wording of the Act, in tune with the multicultural consciousness of the day, referred to the importance of an object to 'Australia *or to a particular part of Australia*'. This had attracted some early criticism as a diffusion of the UNESCO Convention's concept of national cultural heritage:

> Is the Act to apply only to national treasures, or also, for example to the treasures of Sydney, of Murray Bridge, of Australians of Greek ancestry, of Tongan ancestry, of Australian followers of the Shinto religion, or of Australian matchbox collectors?[11]

But the wording 'or part thereof' remained, permitting the concept of cultural significance to encompass the cultural treasures of Indigenous Australians, including those of the Western Desert peoples, whose heritage is arguably significant not only to them but to all Australians – and also to the world.

Noting that 'protection of Indigenous cultural heritage including art has always been a major feature of the Act and was at the heart of international efforts to control illegal export and international trade', the National Cultural Heritage Committee had instigated another review of the regulations in November 1995. It was concerned that 'with the boom in Aboriginal art in recent years ... the current 30 year age threshold does not provide protection for important art from the early 1970s – *particularly the early Papunya period which is regarded as a seminal period in the development of Aboriginal art*' (author emphasis).[12] As the regulations then stood, only Indigenous artworks more than thirty years old and worth more than $5000 were eligible for consideration as Class B protected objects. The Committee accepted the Review's recommendation that:

> Indigenous artworks over 20 years old [currently 30 years] will be protected in order to include works from the 1970s, *including the seminal Papunya period* [author emphasis].[13]

The Committee had used Sotheby's June 1998 Important Aboriginal Art sale to determine that the change would result in an increase from 4 per cent to 30 per cent of artworks potentially caught up in the Act – assuming they were all sold for export. The Committee had no reliable information on that point, only exultant media hype from the auction houses. The consultants engaged by the Committee also recommended that the monetary threshold for Indigenous Fine and Decorative Art be lifted to $15 000–$20 000. The Indigenous representatives on the Committee wanted it kept at $5000, to catch objects which might not necessarily sell for high prices but were nevertheless culturally significant enough to be withheld from export. Eventually a compromise of $10 000 was agreed upon.

For Sotheby's these amendments, to become effective from 1 May 1999, posed a direct threat not to its established market in relatively inexpensive tribal artefacts but to its high-profile operation to develop an overseas market in top-of-the-range

Aboriginal art, spearheaded by the early Papunya boards. When the changes were first publicly mooted mid-1998, *The Australian* ran a story on its Arts pages that the proposed changes to the law had been described as 'ludicrous' and 'potentially damaging to overseas art sales'.[14] The source of these comments was Tim Klingender, who also raised the issue of the 'mountains of paperwork' that broadening the provisions would create for everyone involved. And though the Act provided for 'exemption certificates' to allow works owned offshore to be brought into Australia temporarily to be sold, exhibited, and so on, he claimed that the new provisions would 'very likely put a full stop to them coming back to Australia at all. It could also destroy the confidence of overseas buyers, who won't want to face the red tape involved'.[15] A spokeswoman for the Cultural Heritage branch of the Department of Communications and the Arts pointed out that, in the decade since the Act had been introduced, permits had been refused for only twelve of the 550–600 items which had been submitted for export. The changes, she said, were designed merely to 'provide a screening process for the cream of culturally and artistically significant works'.[16] Klingender's scornful response was that such works would – thanks to his efforts – now be selling for at least $50 000 to $100 000, so that the $10 000 threshold was 'simply ridiculous'.

Sotheby's third annual Important Aboriginal Art auction, the first whose items would be subject to the new provisions of the Protection of Movable Cultural Heritage Act was set down for 28 June 1999 in Melbourne. Sotheby's was pressing on with its international sales pitch. To its New York and LA previews, which had proved such a resounding success in encouraging US interest for the 1997 and 1998 Important Aboriginal Art auctions, it now added European showings.

And as soon as the amended regulations came into force, it submitted over twenty applications under the Act to export permanently works coming up in the 1999 auction – almost all of them early Papunya boards. Sotheby's wanted the export permit applications on these works to be resolved *before* the auction 'to ensure that overseas buyers have confidence to bid'. But government agencies hasten slowly in the face of changes likely to prove politically sensitive and things did not move with the alacrity required for the process to be completed by the end of June. The expert examiners from whom the Committee had requested reports had no previous experience of the process and preferred to err on the side of caution and recommend against export. Due process then required two more expert examiner reports on each 'contentious' item. Auction night arrived and all the export permit applications remained unresolved.[17]

In the weeks after the auction, the Cultural Heritage Committee sent out requests for expert examiners' reports on the works falling within the new age and price thresholds which had been sold to overseas buyers but not been included in Sotheby's still-pending presale bulk applications and also on works which had been considered 'contentious' by their original expert examiners. Neither the National Cultural Heritage Committee nor the Minister with whom the final decision rested were obliged to accept the majority expert examiner advice on these items. Nor was the Minister obliged to take the advice of the Committee. Every stage in the process required a fresh round of decision-making. Sotheby's chafed at the delay, but the announcement, when it finally came in December 1999, nine months after Sotheby's had submitted its initial applications, showed that the procrastination had in the end worked in its favour. How could the overseas buyers be denied, after having been made to wait so long? The government was in no mood to pursue an Aboriginal heritage agenda that involved denying 'ordinary Australians' a financial windfall – or a welcome injection of US dollars into the Australian economy.

In the end, only two works had been refused export permits: Lot 69, *Budgerigar Dreaming* 1972 by Kaapa Mbitjana Tjampitjinpa, and Lot 192, *Water Dreaming* 1972 by 'Old' Walter Tjampitjinpa. There was a powerful case for denying a permit to the Kaapa: the authoritative voice of Geoffrey Bardon had virtually declared it to be Kaapa's masterpiece: it was 'the culmination of a brilliant series of paintings when Kaapa's magnificent talent was fully resolved'.[18] But Tim Klingender was not the only one mystified by the decision on the other painting:

> The Old Walter painting banned ... was a simple generic work devoid of any secret or sacred information and which attracted no interest from any institution or Australian private collector. It sold to the only bidder, who happened to live overseas, for well below the estimate. Yet it has been banned.[19]

In explaining why the Walter Tjampitjinpa painting had been denied a permit, the *Annual Report 1999–2000 on the Operation of the Protection of Movable Cultural Heritage Act 1986* claimed that 'the work depicts a map or blueprint for the construction of ceremonial grounds which would only have been seen by initiated men'.[20] But there seems no way the Committee or the expert examiner could have known this, since no consultation had taken place with the contemporary custodians of Kalipinypa's Water Dreaming. The documentation prepared by the Stuart Art Centre to accompany the painting indicated that its subject matter was perfectly innocuous (a salt lake with running water and 'bush tucker' representing the site of Kalipinypa). The Report also claimed it was 'a rare work in the context of the artist's body of work'. However, while the painting does depart from Walter Tjampitjinpa's favourite Kalipinypa motif of two concentric circles joined by three wavy lines, he painted many far more impressive and unusual works which demonstrate the breadth of his artistic talent, several of which are held in Australian public collections.[21] To an outside observer, it might appear that the decision was driven by the need to ban *something* in order to give the impression that the new regulations had teeth, but also by the desire to make the decision as uncontroversial as possible by holding back two works against whose banning no-one was likely to argue. In the case of the Kaapa Tjampitjinpa, opposing the ban would require going against Bardon's influential evaluation, which Sotheby's itself had endorsed by quoting it in its sales catalogue. In the case of the Walter Tjampitjinpa, no-one would care except the lone bidder.

The strangest aspect of the Walter Tjampitjinpa painting being denied a permit was that permits *were* granted to so many others to which the grounds given for refusal in its case appeared much more applicable. Like Lot 102, an untitled 1972 painting by Mick Namarari Tjapaltjarri, a magnificent work which on the evidence available at the time (also cited in Sotheby's catalogue) 'probably depicts imagery of a highly secret/sacred nature that is possibly sexual'.[22] A member of the National Cultural Heritage Committee later admitted there had been some agonising over this work:

> There was very serious discussion about that painting. It was remarkably important, but in the end we couldn't justify holding it back. I must say it's

a bit difficult, after that, to see what kind of painting we would hold back. But you know there's just not this sense that Australian institutions are around queuing up to buy these things.[23]

This comment seems to indicate that underpinning the Committee's recommendations and the Minister's final decisions in the first tortuous round of applications was the apparent lack of interest of Australian public collecting institutions in acquiring *any* of the items for which export permits had been sought. The Committee may have felt they would be creating an impasse for the vendors – and themselves – if they refused to allow the works to be exported and then could not find an institutional buyer for them. Perhaps this was the real reason the Walter Tjampitjinpa was given the nod – it was the least expensive, and thus more likely to find a home in an Australian public collection, which the Committee's Secretariat busied itself trying to find for both paintings refused permits in the months following the Minister's decision. The Walter Tjampitjinpa painting was eventually purchased, with assistance from the National Cultural Heritage Fund,[24] by the Tasmanian Museum and Art Gallery, becoming the first early Papunya work to enter its collection. But the Secretariat was unable to produce an offer from a public institution of more than one-quarter of the $80 000 which was the lower end of Sotheby's sales estimate on the Kaapa Tjampitjinpa masterpiece. The vendor eventually withdrew it from sale and returned it to its former place above his mantelpiece.

On 23 June 2000, three days before Sotheby's next Aboriginal Art auction, the *Sydney Morning Herald* ran a piece headed 'Curators seek bans to halt exodus of Aboriginal art' in which the 1999 changes to the Act were attributed to the alarm of curators and other critics at the number of early Aboriginal paintings being sold to overseas collectors. Sotheby's were on the offensive to defend the claims of their foreign market, which according to the article had picked up more than half the lots in the 1999 auction. Tim Klingender was quoted complaining that of the 'forty or so' early Papunya boards for which permit applications had been submitted, 'almost all' had been deemed contentious by the expert examiners. He criticised the inordinate delay in reaching a final decision:

> It's hell. It's very complex and bureaucratic and virtually unworkable and it takes up so much time. Last year we sought permits three months before the sale, but did not get notification of the decisions till December. It shouldn't take nearly a year for the process to be completed.[25]

On the very day this complaint was published, the Minister finalised his decision on just over half the thirty-five presale applications which Sotheby's had submitted in mid-May 2000 for items in its upcoming June 2000 Aboriginal art auction. Seventeen export permits were granted prior to the sale, including ten early Papunya boards[26] – a considerable improvement on the preceding year's effort. But only fourteen of the thirty-five works in the original bulk application from Sotheby's were actually sold to overseas buyers on the night.[27] If the Secretariat and the Minister *had* completed the processing of all Sotheby's applications before the auction, on twenty-one of the applications their efforts would have been wasted. A further thirteen applications from Sotheby's were processed after the sale, plus an overlooked application for a painting from the previous year's auction which had sold for $11 000 and required a permit to join its by now absolutely furious new owner in Los Angeles. This permit was granted, and so in the end were twelve of the other thirteen. The post-auction decisions, apart from one 'contentious' work we shall come to in a moment, were all finalised within three months of the auction.

Reviewing these statistics, it seems that Sotheby's did not have all *that* much to complain about. The amount of work involved in filling out an application form for an export permit is minimal. Applicants are not required to give reasons why a protected object should be permitted to leave the country. They don't have to argue the case, except negatively in rebutting the arguments the expert examiners put up for refusing an application. The Secretariat, the expert examiners, the Committee and the Minister had coped with being overloaded with so many applications before the auction, close to two-thirds of which turned out to be unnecessary because they were sold to local buyers or did not reach the required monetary threshold. *They* were the ones doing all the work, but the auction houses, with little more to do than supply the generic description 'early Papunya board' in the first instance, were doing all the complaining. Vivien Anderson, Aboriginal art specialist at Deutscher-Menzies auction house in Melbourne, called the legislation a 'knee-jerk' response to the 'paranoid notion' that the 'corporate and private collectors of the world are poised ready to rip the best of the early Papunya movement out of our arms'.[28] One might ask where this impression had come from, if not from the auction houses' own energetic promotion of an overseas market 'clamouring' for Aboriginal art. Anderson had no reason to complain: export permits for seven of the thirteen works for which Deutscher-Menzies had applied were granted before the auction.[29] None of the remaining six, which had been held over as 'contentious' before the auction, were denied permits when the Minister announced his decisions in September 2000.

Most of the journalists covering what were referred to as the 'export bans' angle of the early boards story cut straight to the bottom line and allowed the auction houses' threats of frightening off overseas business to set the agenda of their articles. Only one, an expatriate recently returned to live in Australia, saw any deeper issues at stake than a stoush between a couple of high-powered prestige auction houses and a federal government generally unpopular with the arts community and the intelligentsia:

> Monday's auction offers a rare spectacle; a nation's cultural guardians permitting the dismemberment on the open market of its choicest artistic jewels. No one is predicting a last minute intervention by the Federal Government to keep *Water Dreaming at Kalipinypa* and the other jewels of Papunya from their commercial destiny.[30]

Meeting at Ali Baba's

On 29 June 2000, three days after *Water Dreaming at Kalipinypa* had met its date with destiny, I had a lunch appointment with two officers from the Cultural Heritage Division of the Department of Communication and the Arts. Like most people I knew in the Aboriginal art world, I was in shock at the outcome on the Johnny Warangkula painting and my summons to this meeting almost seemed like a sign.

The subject of our talk was to be the early Papunya boards. The restaurant was Ali Baba's in Manuka, and I got the reference to the cave of treasure whose contents had been released by Sotheby's 'open sesame' promotional exercise. (This was pre-9/11, and the second Iraq War had not yet shifted the meaning of 'ali baba' to a term for looting bandits.) Over vegetarian plates and glasses of wine, I was ready to begin my career as a government adviser.

I'd made notes in the plane on some of the points I wanted to make. '1. Enforce the provisions of the Act as written.' To me and many others looking on from the sidelines at the first application of the amended provisions of the *Protection of Movable Cultural Heritage Act 1986*, the measures put in place the previous year had had no impact on the flood of newly rediscovered early Papunya paintings leaving the country. They were supposed to stop the most 'culturally significant' of the 'seminal Papunya works' from being sold off to overseas collectors, but what good were they if a painting like Mick Namarari's extraordinary Untitled 1972 could be allowed to go?

'2. Re-examine exclusion from Class A status of objects produced for commercial purposes.' The existing regulations disallowed anything produced for sale, including all the early Papunya boards, from being considered in the category of 'Aboriginal sacred and secret ritual objects', even though according to the Sotheby's sales catalogue the Mick Namarari (for instance) 'probably depicts imagery of a highly secret/sacred nature that is possibly sexual'.[31] What was known at that time about the early history of Western Desert art indicated that there might be large numbers of paintings answering this description, yet such factors seemed to be ruled out of consideration. As far as the Act was concerned, they were 'objects of fine and decorative art in the indigenous tradition' – whatever that meant – *not* Aboriginal and Torres Strait Islander heritage objects. Apparently they couldn't be both.

'3. Importance of effective consultation with *cultural* authorities in Western Desert society.' If paintings with this sort of content were coming up for export permit applications, then matters of Indigenous law were at stake over which the relevant authorities must obviously be consulted. Finally, I wanted to propose a 'moratorium' on granting export permits to allow more research on the early boards – including mine – to proceed so that informed decisions on their fate could eventually be made. I thought I had it all worked out, but the bureaucrats blew me right out of the water with their opening remark:

> 'The people out there now don't know about these boards – what their significance is or what should happen with them.'

They had already consulted 'experts' – nameless and faceless of course. I responded with surprise and indignation: 'How do they know this? Who have they asked?' Experts who adopt the position that the contemporary cultural custodians don't know what their predecessors knew might think they are being realistic about cultural loss. But they also have a vested interest in shoring up their own position as authorities on someone else's culture. The *real* authorities according to desert culture, now and in the past, are those who inherit the right and responsibility to speak for their culture. It was in those anonymous experts' interests to undermine the authority of the 'people out there now' – to prevent them from undercutting *their* authority to speak on behalf of desert culture. I continued:

> 'If people don't have much to say nowadays about the boards to outsiders that doesn't necessarily mean they don't know anything. Maybe they've decided to keep quiet. Having disclosed so much before and getting no recognition of what they saw as the value of it, they may not be so forthcoming now. It doesn't mean they don't know.'

The bureaucrats must have been sighing inwardly. The usual verbal sparring. Experts trying to cut down other experts. They had more. They had also consulted with those in 'day-to-day dealings with the contemporary group of artists and their communities' (by which I guessed they meant Papunya Tula) and *their* response was not so easily dismissed.

> 'They don't want the hassle of being plagued by constant requests from artists and their relatives for a share of the money that is changing hands over these boards.'

I knew this was true. I had been asked by Papunya Tula's management to black out Sotheby's price estimates when I wanted to take one of their sales catalogues out to Kintore to ask a contemporary painter about one of his father's paintings that was reproduced in it. In the end I decided not to take it (because I didn't want to have to explain why I had censored the information), but I was still asked by artists and their families if Papunya Tula was getting the money for those old paintings that were selling for huge amounts in the auctions. They had heard about the sales records on TV and in the local papers and like everyone else they assumed that all the paintings in the auctions were selling for those kinds of prices, not just the record-breaking ones. I explained as best I could that only the auction house and the person who owns the painting get that money, not Papunya Tula, and I think I was believed.

But would Papunya Tula have been believed if they were doing the explaining? Why should they have to take responsibility for a situation not of their making? If they were believed, if the artists and their families accepted that Papunya Tula derived no direct financial benefit from auction sales, the artists might still suspect Papunya Tula Artists of not paying them *now* what their work was really worth. What if they started to demand that kind of money for their new work for Papunya Tula? It's not only early Papunya boards in those catalogues, there are plenty of more recent works by living artists whose resale values at auction are *supposed* to be significantly higher than they sold for on the primary market. The illusion of investment value: that's how the system works. But how was Papunya Tula supposed to explain the art market to their artists? So, not only were the bureaucrats' experts telling them there was no point in consulting 'the people out there'. Papunya Tula, the obvious agency through which consultations might take place, didn't want to stir up these other issues. And who could blame them?

'But surely the artists and their descendants are entitled to know? Someone just needs to explain to them that it's not about the money. It's about keeping these objects for future generations of Western Desert people and Australians in general.'

They were ready for me on that question too. They said that their experts' opinions on whether the paintings should be allowed to be exported fell into three groups. One group was of the view that all the boards should be allowed to go. Another group believed that none of them should be allowed to go. And a third group thought that specific works should be kept and the rest allowed to go. The Minister tended to ignore more extreme views, so the National Cultural Heritage Committee was going for the third, the middle way.

'But they seem to have fallen down even there. Like letting that Mick Namarari go and insisting the Old Walter stayed. It makes no sense.'

Apparently some members of the Committee had agreed, but now felt that their future decisions must be consistent with their past ones, even if they were mistaken.

'Why not just say sorry, we made a mistake. Next time we'll enforce strictly the provisions of the Act?'

They smiled – at my political naivety I thought then, but in retrospect perhaps also at the idea that if ever they needed a fall guy they had found the perfect candidate. I had a lot to learn about apparatchiks – and myself. There the conversation ended, but in writing this account, I have been struck by how much those three points I intended to make to the bureaucrats that day continued to define my own agenda – even though I should have known from the outset that none of those issues were or would ever be on theirs.

Consulting Bobby West

The only work ultimately denied a permit in the 2000 round was Sotheby's Lot 173, an untitled 1972 work by Ronnie Tjampitjinpa. I was one of two additional expert examiners whose views were sought after the first examiner had declared it 'contentious'. Ronnie Tjampitjinpa himself was on private painting business and not available for comment. However, I took the opportunity during a visit in September 2000 to Kiwirrkura, 450 kilometres west of Papunya across the Western Australian border, of showing an image of the work to Bobby West Tjupurrula, at the time Chairman of Papunya Tula Artists, former Chairman of Kiwirrkura Community Council and the eldest son of Freddy West Tjakamarra, one of the original artists painting at Papunya in the early

1970s. Bobby himself had already raised the issue of the early Papunya boards with me. He wanted to know if Papunya Tula was receiving the money from their resale at auction.

VJ: You asked me before if Papunya Tula got money for these paintings when they are resold in the auction and I explained that they don't – only the auction house and the person who owns the painting.
BW: Not right. Artist or his family should get money behind[32] for this.
VJ: In Europe they have a law so the artist or their descendants get some money when the painting is resold for a profit.
BW: Not every time, but if sold for lots of money, artist or family should get something. Don't need to have the paintings back, but artist should get something for this.

This conversation bore out what the bureaucrats had told me about their advice from the front lines of the industry: Papunya Tula Artists were reluctant to complicate an already complex cross-cultural relationship with artists by showing them a Sotheby's sales catalogue. Bobby West is a sophisticated bicultural negotiator and still his first impulse was to point the finger of blame at Papunya Tula Artists. We continued with discussion of the painting.

VJ: Bobby, can I ask you what do you think should happen with these paintings? For instance, what should the government do about applications for export permits for them to be sent overseas? Who should give permission? Who *can* give permission in your view?
BW: The person who painted that canvas. That's the person they should ask permission. They shouldn't be frightened. They should come out here and consult us.
VJ: In some cases it might not be right for a painting to be seen by people outside the culture. Might be secret.

BW: Some of them might be secret.

VJ: Like this one maybe?

BW: That one not secret. But sacred.

VJ: What makes it sacred?

BW: It is sacred because those things are sacred [pointing to representations of tjurungas in the painting]. Sacred because it's about sacred things. Not all of them. Like this one [pointing to another painting], this really easy one, you know. Really simple one. But that other one [that is, the Ronnie Tjampitjinpa] is … questionable.

VJ: What do you think should happen to those paintings – the sacred ones, the questionable ones?

BW: Maybe an art gallery or a museum. So they can look after them. And people can see.

VJ: What about some private person buying it to hang on their living room wall?

BW: No, this is not right.[33]

I included this interview transcript in my report. The work was ultimately refused a permit on 18 January 2001. The 2000–01 Annual Report on the operation of the Act gave the following reasons for the Minister's decision:

This is an important work by the artist, highlighting his personal development and demonstrating the religious knowledge of a young man under the instruction of Pintubi [*sic*] elders. Very few works were produced by the artist during the early Papunya art movement of 1971 and 1972 and of these, only two of comparable significance are held in public collections in Australia. The export of this work would be a significant loss to Australia's Aboriginal heritage, given the rarity and religious sensitivities associated with the imagery in this particular painting.[34]

Reviewing the 1999 and 2000 outcomes of the permits process, it seems that 'religious sensitivities' *did* rank high with the Minister and the Committee as grounds for refusing export permits, notwithstanding the 1995 amendments which disallowed consideration of Indigenous artworks as 'objects of Aboriginal and Torres Strait Islander heritage' if they are being considered as 'objects of Aboriginal or Torres Strait Islander fine and decorative art'.[35] For both the Ronnie Tjampitjinpa and the Walter Tjampitjinpa, 'religious sensitivities' were the reasons given in the Annual Report for the works being held back – alongside considerations of the rarity of the painting in the artist's oeuvre. These justifications were also applied to the Kaapa, alongside the weight of Bardon's testimonial:

> The artist is now regarded as the first Master Artist of the Papunya Tula group. The work contains anthropological and cultural information evidencing ritual knowledge and intellectual property about the religious beliefs practised in Central Australia.[36]

National Conference on Papunya Tula Art

Between submitting my report on the Ronnie Tjampitjinpa and the news of this outcome, I received an invitation to attend a National Conference on Papunya Tula Art convened in Canberra by the National Cultural Heritage Committee. The conference, held on 1 December 2000, was attended by members of the Committee and Secretariat and a group of eight 'Papunya Tula experts', comprising mostly curators of Indigenous art from major Australian public galleries and museums, and Tim Klingender, now elevated to Director of African and Oceanic Art, Sotheby's Australia. Apart from

Brenda L Croft, then Senior Curator of Indigenous Art at the Art Gallery of Western Australia and a member of the National Cultural Heritage Committee, the only Indigenous faces around the table were Ron O'Brien, Executive Director of Desart, and Avril Quaill, Senior Assistant Curator from the National Gallery of Australia. Professor Marcia Langton and Hetti Perkins had been invited but could not attend. So had the management of Papunya Tula Artists, as well as Geoffrey Bardon and Dick Kimber, who both provided written submissions. But none of the artists, no community leader or contemporary cultural custodian of the knowledge encoded in the paintings had been invited. From this gathering the Committee and Secretariat hoped to make some headway on the vexed question of what to do about export permits for the early Papunya boards.

No-one at the meeting was happy with the operation of the Act so far. Sotheby's was angry with the Committee and their expert advisers for making life difficult for them with 'ludicrous' amounts of paperwork and 'outrageous' processing delays. Tim Klingender claimed the process was discouraging their overseas clientele from bidding and stopping works from going overseas. He was also angry with the curators of the public galleries, not only for their role in the expert examination process, but also for complaining about so many early Papunya boards being sold off overseas, yet making no attempt to acquire them for public collections – at least not at the prices Sotheby's could get for them on the open market. The curators were angry too. For the first two years that the new regulations had been in operation, the Act appeared to give no meaningful protection if it could allow works like Mick Namarari's Untitled 1972 and others whose export they had recommended against as expert examiners to be granted permits and sold off overseas. They were angry with Sotheby's for what they saw as a calculated marketing exercise around the early Papunya boards whose net result was to inflate prices beyond the reach of their budgets – and then chastise the galleries publicly for not buying from them. Tim Klingender was unrepentant. He was incensed with the unreasonableness and parochialism of anyone denying the right of the rest of the world to own a piece of 'the nation's most important Aboriginal art' or supporting any impediment to Sotheby's economic interests, which were, he claimed, also to the benefit of Aboriginal artists.

The beneficial effects of Sotheby's promotion on Papunya Tula Artists' market position are undeniable, although arguably plenty of other factors have contributed to the prolongation of its sales boom into the 21st century.[37] But the reason the prices of early Papunya boards in particular had risen so high was not due solely to the assiduous marketing of the auction houses. The explicit provision for them in the Act's recently revised provisions had provided official acknowledgment of their significance – perhaps with unintended consequences. As *Australian Financial Review* journalist Terry Ingram provocatively suggested in the wake of the 1999 auction results:

> the tightening up of the rules on earlier Aboriginal art might have had the opposite effect to what was intended. It may have increased the attractiveness of Aboriginal art to overseas buyers because some of it is considered part of the national estate.[38]

In a world where art prices were a reflection rather than a fabrication of cultural and historical significance, the group of paintings produced at Papunya in the early 1970s might even justify the prices they fetch. Why shouldn't a painting like

Water Dreaming at Kalipinypa fetch the same kind of price as the best of non-Indigenous Australian art? Because that makes it too expensive for the public galleries to buy? Sotheby's was not to blame for the continually falling value of the Australian dollar against the US dollar and other overseas currencies over this period, which in the late 1990s had made the early boards such easy pickings for American collectors with an eye for 'the most sophisticated aesthetic Australia produces today'.[39] But what was to be done?

The bureaucrats' answer, predictably enough, was not to call in the cultural custodians of the communities from which these paintings come and engage in a long, messy, drawn-out and probably highly controversial exercise of consultation on the critical issue of their cultural significance in the here and now. Instead, a new procedure for streamlining the expert examiner process was devised in the hope that it would silence the complaints from Sotheby's and the other auction houses by enabling the next presale bulk applications to be completed *before* the auction. Time to bring on the fall guys.

The Papunya Tula Reference Group

Early in 2001 I was one of three people[40] with close associations with Papunya Tula and no obvious commercial interests to inspire conflict of interest claims[41] who received invitations from the Cultural Heritage Secretariat to form a panel of expert examiners to be known as the Papunya Tula Reference Group.[42] We would be responsible for processing export permit applications for early Papunya boards. Instead of the applications being sent out to a single expert examiner and if he or she recommended against export another expert examiner being consulted and if these two disagreed a third, the Reference Group was to discuss and, if possible, agree among ourselves on a single expert examiner report and recommendation to go forward to the Committee. If consensus could not be reached, minority reports were allowed, but disagreements rarely arose that could not be resolved by discussion. We all accepted the invitation. At the time, I think we saw it as an opportunity to work together using our knowledge of Papunya Tula art in the public and national interest. We set about our task with due diligence.

Sotheby's had twice put back the date of its 2001 Aboriginal Art auction to allow time for its applications to be processed before the sale. By the night of the auction, all except one had been resolved. The understaffed Cultural Heritage Secretariat of the Department of Communications, Information Technology and the Arts had been working for six weeks since the day the applications were submitted to achieve this outcome for Sotheby's. So had the Papunya Tula Reference Group, whipped along by the bureaucrats, who appeared determined to make this trial of the new procedure a success. In the pre-auction media build-up, Tim Klingender had kept the pressure on with more complaints about the length of time that applications took to process and the 'massive problems' which the Cultural Heritage Act was causing the company. He claimed that 'restrictions were damaging the booming overseas trade in Aboriginal art'[43] (though apparently 'almost all the highest priced paintings' at Sotheby's 2000 auction – conducted under the shadow of the Act's offending new provisions – had been sold to foreign bidders). Despite this build-up, the Minister's decisions were not announced at the auction – though presumably Sotheby's made them known to their overseas clientele.

Export permits for six of the twelve early Papunya boards which had been sought before the auction were refused by the Minister and a seventh was still under consideration when the work was sold at the auction to an Australian buyer and the application was withdrawn. All our recommendations on export permits had been accepted by the Committee and the Minister. For the Papunya Tula Reference Group, it was a moment of satisfaction in an otherwise rather unsatisfactory process. At the beginning of it all, we had been flown to Canberra for a face-to-face meeting at which our consideration of the works under application from the 2001 Sotheby's auction was preceded by an hour's discussion during which we aired our criticisms of the process as it then stood. (Only much later did we learn that this discussion had not been minuted, much less acted upon.) In the course of preparing our reports, many of these same issues kept coming up, but the Cultural Heritage bureaucrats shepherding us through the process repeatedly set our objections aside, telling us we had to work within the Act (just as I had told the bureaucrats at Ali Baba's) and that issues of process had no place in individual reports and would not be considered by the Committee if they were raised in this context.

So where could they be raised? In our frustration, we put together a long letter in our best bureaucratese and sent it in with our reports to the National Cultural Heritage Committee. Our first recommendation was for the establishment of a 'process of consultation with the artists where possible,[44] or the appropriate persons at Papunya and other Western Desert communities, particularly about those of the early Papunya boards which are "Restricted"'. It so happened that one of the works under application, to which a permit was ultimately denied, was Lot 113, Anatjari Tjakamarra's *Porcupine Danger.*

Men Only 1973. The Reference Group's report argued that the inscription 'Danger. Men Only' which Peter Fannin had written on the back of the painting (presumably on advice from Anatjari at the time it was painted) unambiguously identified it as one of that group of early Papunya works which – in 1973 at least – presented particular problems with respect to reproduction and public display *because of their weighty 'cultural significance'*.

Though we had recommended in our report that it be refused a permit without further consultation with the artist or representatives of his culture, in our letter we argued that the absence of explicit depictions of sacred boards and other ritual paraphernalia generally thought to identify works in the 'Restricted' category actually underlined the need for consultation. In making our point, we drew on the 'continuing relevance' of inaugural Aboriginal Arts Board Chairman Wandjuk Marika's eloquent 1975 assertion that '*only we know if a particular painting is of special sacred significance, to be seen only by certain members of a tribe, and only we can give permission*' (author emphasis).[45]

Sotheby's had acknowledged the issue of 'restrictedness' in an inconspicuous 'Important Notice' at the beginning of its 2001 sales catalogue, warning that 'Some imagery in the … early Western Desert paintings in this catalogue may be of a secret/sacred nature'. It also suggested that 'art coordinators on Aboriginal communities show the catalogue to community elders for approval before distributing the catalogues for general viewing' and that they 'mask illustrations … deemed unsuitable for the viewing of women, children or uninitiated men'. We have already considered some of the reasons for Papunya Tula Artists' reluctance to show auction catalogues to its artists. The idea that, on top of all those other hassles, such an action might also reignite these ancient disputes was yet another reason they would *not* do any such thing.

Helping to drive the Reference Group's sense of urgency on this subject were some things Bobby West had said to me about other works I had shown him after our conversation concerning the Ronnie Tjampitjinpa painting six months earlier. I hadn't included these comments in my report to the National Cultural Heritage Committee because they weren't about the painting under assessment. Bobby had stressed that I would need to ask Anmatyerr and Warlpiri people about some School of Kaapa paintings I had shown him – that he could only speak from a Pintupi perspective. From this perspective, he said, it would be better if the 'secret' paintings were as far away as possible from the artists and their communities.

But his concern was not with women and children seeing these things. It was about safeguarding the artists who had painted them from the harm that might come to *them* if others saw these things and took revenge or exacted punishment for it. They might be sung, he said, and they might sicken and die like the many older artists who had already done just that. Better to send those paintings off overseas – but even then, they should be handled with great care. Maybe better to keep them in drawers out of sight, like the ones he had seen at the Australian Museum[46] in 2000 when he came down for the opening of *Papunya Tula: Genesis and Genius.* He gave the example of a New Guinea mask or an African object he might buy and hang up on the wall, not knowing what it was. Harm might come to those who looked at it – they might accidentally activate it. Bobby couldn't explain why the old artists had created such dangerous things, except that they might not have understood what would become of them – though again he stressed that it was for Anmatyerr people to say if Kaapa's work was okay – not him.

The Reference Group's letter also accused Sotheby's of 'assuming there was no problem about display of these works outside Western Desert communities'. Two years later when I interviewed Tim Klingender, he insisted that Sotheby's had consulted with the management of Papunya Tula on this point:

> When I turned up that early collection of boards and no-one was showing them anywhere, I went to Alice Springs and produced a folio of the early Papunya boards. I said to Daphne [Williams, former Manager of Papunya Tula Artists] and whoever else it was at the time, I can't remember, it was years before Paul [Sweeney, current Manager of Papunya Tula Artists and former senior field officer], it might have been Bryce or somebody like that, I said, 'Can we take these out and show them to various people? Is it okay to show them?' Which they did, and they said it was fine. That's why we went ahead and did it. Then for the next few years, every time we had any early boards, I sent up a folder months and months before it went to press and sent it to Papunya Tula to say 'Can we show them?' And the answer was always 'Yes you can'.
>
> But there was some concern about the images being seen out there. That's why I always sent the images to the art co-ordinators. If they don't want anybody to see it they should mask them in the catalogue or chop out those pages before they go out there. Nevertheless, there never seemed to be any problem. I've seen my catalogues handed around out there. A couple of them have a 'Restricted' thing on the back of them but what I have always experienced with Aboriginal people when they see something they shouldn't – it doesn't result in murder or anything like that. That overt political correctness of the late 1980s and 1990s – probably erring very heavily on the side of caution I would think.[47]

Our letter's second recommendation was that early Papunya boards 'be appraised as both Aboriginal and Torres Strait Islander Heritage Objects (Part 1) *and* fine and decorative art in the indigenous tradition (Part 5)'. We had prepared our 2001 Reference Group reports on this basis since in our view the claims to the Act's protection of seminal works from Papunya should be recognised under both these headings. Technically the regulations did not allow them to be both, but those advising us on the interpretation of the Act had agreed to this for the 2001 round because of the uncertainty as to whether works created in late 1971 were quite thirty years old and hence in which of the two categories they properly belonged. After 2001, no such leeway would be permitted. The 1999 amendments to the regulations stipulated that objects recognised as works of fine and decorative art 'in the indigenous tradition' could *not* also be treated as objects of 'Aboriginal and Torres Strait Islander Heritage'. *But*, the Reference Group's letter argued, *the early Papunya boards are quite obviously both of these things*. The difficulty went back to the 1991 Ley Review of the *Protection of Movable Cultural Heritage Act*, which had attempted to 'clarify' the definition of objects relating to Aboriginal heritage by 'clearly excluding all objects which have been made solely for the purpose of sale and not for traditional use'.[48]

This helps to explain why Tim Klingender's criticisms of the Minister's decisions in the 2001 round did not address the rights and wrongs of particular works being held back but the fundamental principle that the early Papunya boards were legitimate objects of protection under Australian cultural heritage legislation in the first place:

The works they are targeted at protecting – the first works painted at Papunya at the start of the acrylic desert painting movement in the early 1970s – were all painted for sale and to introduce the complexities and depth of Aboriginal culture to a non-indigenous audience.[49]

Why the Papunya painters produced the early boards, but particularly the 'Restricted' works, is one of the great mysteries of this story. With respect to these restricted works, the two explanations proposed by Klingender seem among the least plausible that have been offered. One of the explanations offered for their creation by knowledgeable observers at the time it will be remembered,[50] was precisely that these works were *not* made for sale, but for the personal instruction of Geoffrey Bardon – and to show *one another* what they knew.

The requirement that objects of Aboriginal and Torres Strait Islander heritage must not have been 'created specifically for sale' rules out not only all Indigenous art that *was* made for sale but also everything else Aboriginal and Torres Strait Islander people have made which has been bought and sold, including objects like weapons and tools. Nowhere else in the legislation or Control List is having been created for sale considered a reason to exclude objects from having the status of cultural heritage (for example, tractors and vintage cars). Why should Aboriginal and Torres Strait Islander heritage objects be subjected to this requirement?

It seems a hangover from earlier times, when anthropologists dictated that the only 'authentic' Aboriginal and Torres Strait Islander 'artefacts' were those made for daily or ceremonial use within the culture. Anything produced for external sale was automatically considered 'inauthentic'. Colonised peoples everywhere in the world engage in commodity production based on their traditional skills and cultural knowledge in order to subsist in their changed social and economic circumstances. The difference in Australia is that Indigenous cultural commodity production has moved beyond the production of ethnographic artefacts for the museum trade and 'folk art' for the tourist trade into the category of fine or decorative art. This migration has been facilitated by the fact that these same objects also have cultural significance for Aboriginal and Torres Strait Islander peoples, as embodiments of cultural knowledge and as cultural achievements.

Furthermore, outside the context of Indigenous art, to suggest that an artist is creating their art 'specifically for sale' would be considered an insult, insinuating that they did not make art for its own sake but for purely commercial purposes. Indigenous artists are not usually so precious about these matters, but this does not disentitle them to the same respect as other artists are accorded. Some of the early Papunya boards are extraordinary artistic achievements by the individual artists concerned, several of whom are now regarded as major figures in the history of Australian art and culture in their own right.

In 2001, early Papunya works dated 1971 could for the first time qualify as Aboriginal and Torres Strait Islander Heritage protected objects (that is, under Part 1 of the National Cultural Heritage Control List) – *but only if it could be established that they were not 'created specifically for sale'* (1.2 (b)). They satisfied all the other necessary requirements: they were made by Aboriginal people and were culturally significant to them (1.2 (a) (i) & (ii)); they were (or could be) 'at least thirty years old' (1.2 (c) (i)); as the earliest works by the founding fathers of Western Desert art they related to 'important Aborigines or to persons significant in Aboriginal history' (1.4 (a)); they were also 'made on reserves' (1.4 (b)) – Papunya was on reserve land until the Haasts Bluff Reserve was returned to Aboriginal ownership by the *Northern Territory Land Rights Act 1976*; and they relate to 'the development of Aboriginal … self-help movements' (1.4 (c)) – Papunya Tula Artists remains *the* most successful Indigenous art enterprise, and has been independent of government subsidies since the early 1980s. As Aboriginal and Torres Strait Islander heritage objects, the boards' representation in 'Aboriginal and Torres Strait Islander community collections, or public collections in Australia' (1.2 (c) (ii)) would have to be taken into account, whereas this is not explicitly required for objects of 'fine and decorative arts in the indigenous tradition'.[51] However, in every other respect, the classification of early Papunya boards as Aboriginal heritage objects significantly raised the stakes in the export permits process, because their significance to the peoples of the Western Desert as 'a part of Australia' would have to be taken into consideration – including presumably consulting them on this issue.

As objects of Aboriginal and Torres Strait Islander heritage, they would also fall under the protection of the separate *Aboriginal and Torres Strait Islander Heritage Protection Act*, which protects objects as well as sites, if they have sufficient importance to Aboriginal people. In particular, it protects them from 'desecration' as well as physical injury, where desecration is defined as 'use in a manner inconsistent with Aboriginal custom' – a principle which could conceivably be applied to the display of Papunya boards which Western Desert cultural authorities deem unfit for public exposure.

Our letter's third recommendation, that the applications process occur *after* not before the auction, was the only one that was immediately accepted and put into practice. Our foolish boast that 'a month would suffice for this task' undoubtedly helped our case. We also argued that the timing change would remove the possibility that information provided by the expert examiners could be 'misused to add value to the works at auction' and 'in the case of Restricted works would prevent the dissemination of culturally sensitive information beyond the decision-making process'. Perhaps the acquiescence by Sotheby's in this change, despite their insistence on the necessity of their overseas clients having the 'confidence to bid', arose from the reflection that the auction houses had actually fared much better in 1999 and 2000 when the decisions on export permits were taken after the auction than they had in 2001. They might inadvertently have disadvantaged themselves by being so vociferous in their demands for pre-auction clearances. Decisions made before an auction do not have the complicating factor of the work already having been purchased by an overseas buyer, a consideration which may have helped to sway the Minister's mind in previous years.

Our questioning of the wisdom of the 'right of rebuttal' giving applicants access to examiners' reports before any decision had been made fell on deaf ears, as did our alternative plea that the 'natural justice' which justified its inclusion in the process should be extended to the cultural custodians. The letter's final recommendation alluded to the fact that two members of the Reference Group were from public collecting institutions and were keenly aware of the problem that these institutions could not afford early Papunya paintings at their current prices. As a way out of the dilemma that works would be held back but no institution would be able to buy them, we proposed that 'the Government of Australia take a proactive role with regard to ensuring that there is a broad representation of high quality Papunya Tula paintings from the general period of 1971–73 in the distributed national collection'. Our suggestions were to increase the amount available in the National Cultural Heritage Fund and to create special tax incentives for individuals and corporations who donated works to public or Aboriginal and Torres Strait Islander collections which had been identified in this process as being of such significance that their export would result in cultural loss to Australia. These suggestions have not been acted upon, let alone what, in a spirit of compromise, we did not dare suggest: that as happens in other countries with protective cultural heritage laws, the government should step in and acquire all such works for the nation and for those to whom they are of such significance that their permanent export would constitute a 'cultural loss'.

7

Give Those Men a Real Voice

For five years nothing happened about any of the procedural recommendations contained in the Papunya Tula Reference Group's letter. Perhaps we should have resigned in protest, but we were repeatedly assured there would be a response on the consultation issue and, apart from this increasingly vexed question, the Reference Group was having a significant impact on the export applications process – or so it appeared from our perspective. For the first two years after the amendments were put in place to bring the early Papunya boards into the process, only three paintings had been held back in spite of the recommendations of expert examiners that ten times that number should have been. Between 2001 and the end of 2008, every painting to which the Reference Group recommended refusing a permit was refused one – eventually. When you look at the numbers of boards refused permits, this may not sound like much: only thirteen early Papunya paintings[1] were held back between 2001 and 2008 – which averaged over the period comes to about the same rate as in the first two years. But not nearly so many early boards were coming up for assessment as in previous years. The reason for this was not the collapse in the overseas market predicted by Sotheby's as a result of the 'export bans'. The main problem was supply, not demand. There just weren't large numbers of early Papunya works coming onto the market over this period and most of them weren't of interest to choosy overseas collectors. Some of the best works that did come up for auction, like Clifford Possum Tjapaltjarri's *Emu Corroboree Man* 1972, were already owned overseas and thus not subject to the legislation. Looking back, it seems the 1999 amendments and then the establishment of the Reference Group were a case of shutting the stable door after the horse had bolted; the biggest years for early Papunya boards for the auction houses were 1996, 1997, 1998, 1999 and 2000. Since 2001, there have been steadily dwindling numbers of boards coming up for auction and sales records have largely shifted to more recent works.

The underlying problem for the Reference Group was that no-one, apart from ourselves, dealing with the export permit process for the early Papunya boards really seemed to care. At the time of our appointment there did seem to be genuine interest on the part of some of the officials we were dealing with in the Cultural Heritage Secretariat. Call me a cynic, but I now think the prospect of a media stoush between auction house impresarios keen to make their names by selling the boards to their cashed-up overseas clients and a Minister keen to make political capital out of thwarting their ambitions by refusing to let the boards leave the country was mainly what got their attention. The early Papunya boards episode was the first time the operation of the Act had attracted any sustained media coverage. Fossils, postage stamps and combine harvesters excite little interest from most people. Money and art, especially Aboriginal art, make front-page news.

The way the Cultural Heritage Secretariat kept getting moved around was symptomatic of the general lack of interest. When the Reference Group was formed, the unit was in the Department of the Arts and Communication. Later this became the Department of Communications, Information Technology and the Arts (DCITA) – and there were plenty of resources for lavish DCITA functions for Information Technology, but Cultural Heritage continued to struggle along on a wing and a prayer. From DCITA the Cultural Heritage Secretariat was moved to the Department of the Environment and Heritage which later became Environment, Water and Heritage and the Arts – very much in that order. There was a succession of Ministers in the various portfolios responsible for Cultural Heritage and a succession of officers assigned to the unit itself. It was hard to keep up with all the changes and impossible to keep track of the number of times we had the same arguments over which Part of the Control List the early Papunya boards belonged in. Every year or two there would be another name on the end of the emails and another voice on the phone to insist we must work with the Act and the Control List as it stood and submit our suggestions for changes to the upcoming Review of the Act. As we did – but the Act has so far remained unchanged.

How things were actually working is revealed by consideration of the reasons provided for the Minister's decisions on the fourteen early Papunya boards held back since the Reference Group's formation in 2001 (including here the untitled 1972 Ronnie Tjampitjinpa finally refused a permit in 2001). The reference to 'religious sensitivities' in the Ministerial rationale for the Ronnie Tjampitjinpa was noted in the previous chapter. This was the painting about which I consulted Bobby West on my own initiative as the second examiner of a work declared 'contentious' by the first examiner, before the Reference Group arrangements were in place, although the decision was not announced until after they were. Between 2001 and 2008, for eleven of the thirteen early Papunya boards refused permits, in every case something along the lines of 'religious sensitivities' was cited or at least hinted at in the Ministerial rationale.[2] The other two early boards refused permits were both by Kaapa Tjampitjinpa and both exceptional paintings. Ironically in the case of Papunya board Untitled 1972, its *suitability* for public display (on the presumption that much of Kaapa's work may not be) was cited in support of the Minister's decision. For *Budgerigar Story* 1972, the artistic excellence of the work – 'his ultimate achievement' – and, given Kaapa's importance as the 'first artist', his inadequate representation in Australian national collections, was the Ministerial rationale, although there seems little doubt that this work *is* 'Restricted'.

Many of the other twelve boards refused permits were also said to be 'fine' or 'rare' examples of the artists' work, and in every case the Reference Group had supported its recommendation against export on grounds of the work's importance as a work of art to the adequate representation in the national collections of this key episode in the history of Indigenous and Australian art *as well as* its weighty cultural significance (usually accompanied by calls for consultation to verify this point). In other words, a de facto process had developed in which the Reference Group assessed the early Papunya works as *both* fine art in the Indigenous tradition *and* objects of Aboriginal and Torres Strait Islander heritage, notwithstanding the regulations to the contrary – and the Ministers justified their decisions on the same basis.

This did not happen as smoothly as that concurrence might make it sound: in fact, the Reference Group had to fight the cultural heritage bureaucrats for the inclusion of 'cultural' grounds every step of the way. But except for the two Kaapas just mentioned, these grounds were explicitly crucial to the permits being refused. In fact, except for the Kaapas, the Reference Group hadn't recommended against export *unless* the work contained these sorts of elements because in our view most of the works coming through didn't justify being withheld purely on aesthetic grounds. Over time, Sotheby's seemed to accept that works with potentially 'Restricted' imagery would probably be held back. It may not have worried them unduly since their international customers were usually interested in the more abstract-looking early boards – or in other works entirely.

But if we were winning these minor battles over particular paintings, we were losing the war on the consultation issue. Whenever paintings came up with imagery that looked like tjurungas and other sacred objects, the Reference Group would draw attention to these factors, or to the work's similarity to some other work that had been already identified as 'Restricted', and ask that there be consultation with the relevant authorities on its cultural significance. The bureaucrats would get back to us and say that cultural considerations were irrelevant since the work had to be assessed as a work of fine art in the Indigenous tradition and not as an Aboriginal heritage object since the regulations didn't allow that it could be both – even though we were in many cases effectively assessing these works as both. We felt like a scratched record stuck in a groove replaying the same thing over and over, never moving forward.

Just once, when we had dug our heels in and were refusing to proceed without consultation, the bureaucrats approached Paul Sweeney, the Manager of Papunya Tula, for assistance.

He showed Long Jack Phillipus the painting in contention, a Honey Ant Dreaming by the Anmatyerr artist Tim Leura Tjapaltjarri and was told: 'That is a dangerous one and ... women shouldn't view it'. Sweeney had added to this the sensible observation that since Tim Leura was Anmatyerr and Long Jack was not, they might not necessarily share the same views on this question. He had also asked Dick Kimber's opinion and been told that the work was 'immediately sensitive because of the bullroarers in each corner', but also that Tim Leura had been 'very open about his representation of sacred objects and considered his painting his business, and that if he chose to depict sensitive images then it was his choice and no-one else's'. Yet Geoffrey Bardon's account singles out Tim Leura as the one person who did voice objections to the inclusion of restricted material in the paintings – specifically to one of the Pintupi painters including a ceremonial hat in what was supposed to be a 'children's painting'[3] – unless this was Tim Leura 'rattling spears', as Jennifer Isaacs suggested. Paul Sweeney sent back this information with the comment that it was not uncommon for people to be 'reserved' about the early paintings and that it had been difficult to find anyone else appropriate for comment. The Cultural Heritage Secretariat forwarded this email to the Reference Group with the observation: 'Hence the above feedback is as much as we can hope to gain from this process'. In the end, the painting didn't sell, so the issues remained unresolved.

The first official consultation

Early in February 2006, the news came through that the Cultural Heritage Secretariat was prepared to sponsor a trip to Central Australia 'to develop a consultation process with the

Indigenous cultural custodians of the early Papunya boards in relation to the operation of the Protection of Movable Cultural Heritage legislation'. If public servants can be acknowledged for their individual contributions to history, it must be said that the person responsible for this remarkable development and therefore the hero of this section of the early boards story is Alison Reid. She was the one who championed the Papunya Tula Reference Group's calls for a community consultation process and badgered her bosses until it happened. From her Blundstone boots and ankle-length black skirts to her outlandish spectacles, bicycle chain necklace and waist-length black hair flecked with grey, Alison looked more like a Gothic Edna Everage than any senior Canberra official I ever met. She would have looked more at home on the streets of Newtown than in Todd Mall, let alone Papunya or Kiwirrkura. But her eccentric appearance and brusque manner did help differentiate her from the steady stream of fawning dealers and eager curators and collectors, anthropologists and art students to whom the artists were accustomed. Everyone I later talked to about our visit referred to her as the 'government lady'. If the letters on Australian government letterhead sent beforehand to arrange our meetings with senior initiated men in Papunya, Kintore and Kiwirrkura were not enough, her authoritative demeanour established beyond doubt that this was an official consultation with the Australian government's representative.

I put my hand up as the accompanying expert examiner. Because of my work over the previous five years on my book *Lives of the Papunya Tula Artists*, I was the Reference Group member with the strongest network of current contacts in all the relevant communities; besides, none of the other members was able or willing to go. Despite having taken five years to get to this point, the bureaucrats were only prepared to allow five days for the process of consulting relevant stakeholders about whether there should be a consultative process for the export permit applications for early Papunya boards and, if so, what form it should take. Such a tight timeframe meant that inevitably many people we might wish to talk to would be unavailable. The discussions began in Sydney with Bob Edwards, one of the key early supporters of Geoffrey Bardon and the painters at Papunya in the early 1970s, and Jeremy Long, who had meticulously maintained detailed genealogies of the people he knew at Haasts Bluff and Papunya in the 1950s and 1960s, many of whom had later 'turned into' artists. We were very concerned at that stage with locating the most appropriate people to consult about a particular artist's work, and Jeremy was willing to make his information available – and if necessary to accompany us to Alice Springs to assist with the consultations. But after concerted application of Alison's persuasive powers, Dick Kimber agreed to assist us. Dick's involvement as Papunya Tula's Manager in the mid-1970s in the difficult round of meetings and negotiations required to mend the Papunya painters' relationships with their offended neighbours[4] made him perfect for the role.

Alison had expected that Papunya Tula Artists would assist with our travel to the communities. She might not have looked like a Canberra bureaucrat, but she had enough of the official mindset to be shocked when Paul Sweeney told us bluntly that his focus as Manager was on what the artists and the company shareholders wanted and expected of him: to maintain and increase their income from sales of their current paintings. 'Let history take care of itself,' he said, when we dropped by the gallery on our first morning in Alice Springs, echoing Tim Klingender's sentiments on the fate of the early boards. Alison's carefully laid plans of sealing a formal agreement with Papunya Tula to act on behalf of the Cultural Heritage Secretariat in organising an annual meeting at its premises with relevant cultural custodians to discuss early Papunya works up for assessment that year had just gone up in smoke. She'd persuaded her boss to fund the exercise on the basis of some such concrete outcome being achieved.

Despite this setback, Alison stuck to her broader objective of moving forward on the consultation issue, indifferent to the reactions of the locals. I thought Bobby West Tjupurrula, incumbent Chairman of Papunya Tula Artists, looked a bit startled when he met us at the Outback Steakhouse on our first night in Alice Springs. We had intended to see him in Kiwirrkura, but he was on his way to Kalgoorlie for a meeting about mining royalties in his other capacity as Chairman of the Kiwirrkura Council and had agreed to discuss the consultation issue over a meal at a venue of his choice. He seemed to be a regular customer – the manager came over to greet him personally when we arrived – 'Good evening Mr West'. Bobby had brought along his brother-in-law Matthew Tjapanangka from Balgo.

The first thing Bobby said after the introductions was 'Where's Dick Kimber?' and it soon became clear that it was Dick's absence he was worried about, rather than Alison's appearance. Bobby had expected Dick to be there – the letter he had received out in Kiwirrkura from Alison about our impending visit had said that Dick would be with us. Dick Kimber famously has neither mobile nor landline and can only be contacted by snail mail or his wife's work phone, so there was no way I knew of reaching him in a hurry. This might also explain why he was not present in the first place – Alison had been unable to contact him at short notice once she realised we would have to meet Bobby that night or not at all because he was leaving for Kalgoorlie in the morning. Alison had earlier shown me a letter delivered to her motel room when she arrived and addressed to us both in which Dick announced his intention of pulling out of the visits to remote communities, seeing no justification for the expense of his being involved at all other than in Alice Springs, where some of the key contact people were now living permanently. However, that would leave us to conduct a delicate operation for two women on our own. What happened next at the Steakhouse showed just how delicate.

Bobby at first agreed to proceed without Dick and after some preliminary general conversation I started talking to him about my database of early Papunya boards. Another thing Alison was hoping might come out of the consultation was that the men we were consulting would look through the database and indicate the kinds of things in paintings that made them 'Restricted'. If we knew this, then we might not have to come on an expedition like this every time an early Papunya board came up for export. I had put my computer on the table while I was talking and opened up the database. The first painting is Mick Namarari's 'easy' *Sandhills and Clouds* 1971 from the first consignment and Bobby was looking over at it with interest. Then I did a search on Bobby's father Freddy West who was an occasional painter in 1971–72, being responsible for about half-a-dozen early boards. The first Freddy West entry that came up was *Old Man's Ceremony*, the large board later included in the *Icons of the Desert* exhibition. It was only a thumbnail – I had not even clicked on it to bring up the larger image, but Bobby saw it all right – and visibly flinched. He asked me not just to move off that image but to close down the computer. Then he explained to me and Alison that he *did* want to talk about these issues, but not with us. He asked Alison very pointedly: 'Don't you have any men in your department?', then lapsed into loaded silence.[5]

What followed was one of the more uncomfortable meals of my life – sitting across the table from Bobby and the still-silent Matthew Tjapanangka, trying to make casual conversation after the purpose of our meeting had been very firmly taken off the agenda even before our main courses arrived. The only moment of genuine camaraderie I recall was when Alison and Bobby made their selections from the dessert mobile. In the course of that conversation, Bobby revealed that there had been a number of paintings in the *Papunya Tula: Genesis and Genius* catalogue that should not have been reproduced. They had let it go at the time, he said, because they did not want to make trouble when they were the Gallery's invited guests for the opening. 'That's okay but don't do it again,' was what he said. Another thing I remember him saying was: 'We thought nobody cared' – meaning that nobody cared what he and other Indigenous men with traditional responsibilities thought about these matters. I would not have dared tell him what the bureaucrats at Ali Baba's had said about the 'people out there'. As he was leaving us he made even plainer his view that the paintings were 'men's business' and could not be discussed with women of any cultural background whatsoever, including us. He said straight out that that he only wanted to speak on this subject to older men – men with grey hair and beards and preferably who knew something about the culture – in short, men like Dick Kimber.

Dick met us at Papunya Tula Artists gallery in Todd Mall first thing the next morning as previously arranged. Over coffee, Dick described the settlements as 'war zones'. He said he hadn't been there in a long time and had no desire to go. I was reminded of the words of the manager of the ANZ bank in Alice Springs where I'd first seen the early boards who had warned us that Papunya was like a 'concentration camp', all high wire fences and desolation and a 'murder a week'. But Dick is a good, old-fashioned bloke, who wouldn't leave a couple of helpless women in distress. He had a funeral to attend in Alice Springs in a couple of days, so it was agreed that he would drive back to Alice Springs in the late afternoon in his own vehicle after we'd spoken to people in Papunya, leaving us to go on alone to Kintore (the Kiwirrkura leg had earlier been called off because of the arrangement to meet Bobby West in town). So we set off in convoy – me eating dust in the hired Nissan Pajero that would take us to Kintore the next day, while Dick and Alison travelled together in his lead vehicle. Before we got away I managed to back the hire car into a barbecue at Alison's motel and caused a bit of damage to both barbecue and vehicle. An ominous sign, or at least one calculated to upset Alison, who had worked so hard to get $10 000 out of her boss to fund the entire exercise – with no scope for such extra expenses.

We arrived in Papunya after a few hours and got settled into the Health Department flat we had been assigned. It was palatial by the standards I was used to – no-one had ever offered me such accommodation in all the years I'd been coming to Papunya: a fridge, a phone, TV, even a yard and food left in the refrigerator still fresh from the previous occupancy. Clearly our being on federal government business made a difference to *someone.* Michael Nelson, one of the senior law men we hoped to consult, was expected back later that day, but Long Jack Phillipus came over and had lunch with us before the consultation began. After what Bobby had told us, Alison and I just sat and listened. For the first half-hour or so, Dick and Long Jack talked about wild camels, Dick saying they were ruining the country and Long Jack defending them on the grounds that they had helped Aboriginal people in the past. Alison, who wasn't familiar with the protocol that you don't just launch into a serious subject like the early boards without opening up the lines of communication with this type of casual conversation, was looking more and more irritated. Long Jack was being paid $200 an hour. Eventually the camel conversation died away and Long Jack turned to what had brought him there, the subject of the early boards.

These are my notes on this part of the consultation, his exact words in italics. *'Only law men. No-one else can see.'* Then, underlined to indicate strong emphasis: *'Put them away.'* Then *'Long way – can't see – or might get in trouble.'* A long pause, then *'Before people understood what happened, before motor car* [that is, car ownership]*.' 'Too much drinking – we didn't think. Other men pass away because drinking too much.'* (Both Long Jack and Dick Kimber are teetotallers.) Then *'Others have rights in these stories* [need to consult with other men who also have rights]*.'* Then Long Jack said, using the same words as Bobby, '*We thought no-one cared'*. And again, I thought of the expert advice about the 'people out there'. At this point I handed Long Jack a brown paper envelope with A4 photocopies of images of five early Papunya paintings that were currently under application for permits. Then Alison and I withdrew outside and out of earshot, while Dick and Long Jack continued the consultation. As we left the room I heard Dick asking Long Jack whether the paintings should be allowed to go overseas. I can distinctly remember Long Jack's reply: that they should be sent to *'Africa – or New Zealand'*.

Less than half-an-hour later, Long Jack was paid for his trouble and went on his way. After discussing with us (some of) what Long Jack had said to him, Dick headed back to town.

On the Papunya road, he met Michael Nelson coming back to meet with us and took the opportunity of showing him the contents of the brown paper envelope. Michael's response was identical to Long Jack's: all but one of the images contained sacred and secret information and were extremely problematic. Both men thought the Johnny Warangkula painting among them could be viewed by any person at all, even though it too had images of a possibly sacred nature. But they were so 'covered up' by overlays of dotting that the ceremonial objects underneath were considered invisible. The other four images were all considered 'dangerous' and unsuitable for publication or exhibition in Australia. Like Long Jack, Michael Nelson was at pains to point out that other men had rights in these images and should be consulted about them. He could not speak on their behalf. And also like Long Jack, while stressing that only senior law men should see these images, he also allowed that they could be bought and exported overseas.

By this he may simply have meant that he understood what was happening to them – as Long Jack's reference to the paintings being sent to Africa and New Zealand might also be interpreted as a memory of the inclusion of early Papunya paintings in Aboriginal Arts Board exhibitions to New Zealand in 1976 and Nigeria in 1977. On the other hand, they may both have been giving in principle agreement to export along the lines of the 'safe distance' solution that had worked for the painters back in the early 1970s for a quarter of a century: sending them away as far as possible, so no-one would know. But these are different times. Long Jack and Michael Nelson and their contemporaries in Papunya cannot be expected to be computer literate enough to know it, but being exported is no guarantee of the images not being seen again in Australia – perhaps even in the computer-equipped classrooms of Papunya School. Though on the other hand – there are parts of Africa where you *could* send them and be pretty sure you would never see them again …

The next morning Alison and I woke early, Papunya Tula having told us that there would be a funeral at Kintore that afternoon. We were initially reluctant to disturb such an event, but Papunya Tula management assured Alison that the morning would be a good time to consult because people had come together for the sorry business and would be dispersing once the funeral was over. The field workers had assembled a group of senior men for us to talk to and we were planning to try out the brown paper envelope technique we had used successfully with Long Jack. It was just getting light behind us about half-an-hour along the road west from Papunya when I asked Alison to look out her window on the passenger side and see if the tyre was okay, as the car wasn't handling well. Not only was the tyre not okay – it wasn't there. We climbed out into the freezing wind to discover it had ripped into shreds and wrapped itself around the rear axle behind the wheel bearing. Alison sat down on a rock and announced 'I'm never going bush with you again!' She chose that moment to tell me she had arthritis in her hands and couldn't change a tyre to save her life. I wasn't sure I could either – not this one.

For the first half-hour, between bouts of hysterical laughter, we got no further than gathering together the tyre-changing kit from where it was stowed in different parts of the Nissan Pajero, and trying to decipher the instructions in the manual. There were no instructions on how to get a tractor-sized, steel belt radial off the axle. Aboriginal cars passed us in the semi-darkness, loud, dust-covered Ford Falcons and Holdens, sitting low to the ground with their full complement of passengers and more. No-one gave any sign of sympathy with our plight, let alone any inclination to leave the warmth of the blankets in which they were wrapped and come and help. Some didn't even slow down, others simply said 'Funeral. Kintore,' and moved away. It was too far to walk back to Papunya – 50 kilometres at least – and the only food we had with us was an apple. I had brought a small fruit knife to cut the apple into segments to share, and I realised that our only possible salvation was to jack up the car and, against everything I knew or it said in the manual, lie under the car and cut the tyre away from the axle so I could reposition the jack to change the tyre. I hoped the car wouldn't fall on my head and kill me – it would be an ignominious ending. It was still freezing out there in the pre-dawn light, but at least my desperate exertions warmed me up a bit. It took nearly two hours to get the tyre off. When I finally pulled it free I made Alison take a photograph of me at my moment of triumph. It was short-lived.

Alison immediately announced that we would abandon the trip to Kintore that day and go back to Papunya and try to get another spare. She wasn't prepared to risk being totally stranded out there with another flat and no spare – and neither was I. So slowly and carefully we drove back to Papunya, where the heap of shredded rubber in the back of the Pajero was greeted with unfeigned astonishment by the locals. 'What happened!' they exclaimed. Lance McDonald, President of the local Papunya Council, said he had never seen a worse flat. Of course the store didn't stock Nissan spares – only Toyota. Alison's next decision was that time and her funds had run out and she wasn't going anywhere except back to Alice Springs the next morning. While she holed up in the Health Department flat, I busied myself distributing the boxes of canvases and paints I had brought from Sydney for the people who had signed up to be founding members of the new Papunya Tjupi

Art Centre. We used Michael Nelson's car because I didn't want to risk the Nissan getting another flat driving around the camps and stranding us in Papunya for Easter. Michael's daughter Julie helped with the 'hand-out', the first Papunya artists had had in two years.

It was more of a relief than usual to reach the bitumen the next morning after an hour-and-a-half on the dirt from Papunya. With all the bad signs, I was feeling more and more conflicted about my role in the consultation process and for that matter the Reference Group. What purpose did my involvement serve if I wasn't supposed to look at the 'Restricted' works? We'd been saying for years that there might be problems about the revelations of some of the early boards, but until that moment across the table when I saw the look in Bobby's eyes, I'd never really thought through just how problematic it might be. Like a lot of people, I'd been lulled into a sense of security by years of seeing these paintings hung up in auction house previews and reproduced in sales catalogues as if they presented no problems. Now there were problems everywhere I looked.

Like the catalogue essay I was supposed to be writing for an exhibition of early Papunya boards called *Icons of the Desert* which was scheduled to tour a couple of venues in Australia including the Art Gallery of New South Wales after its debut in the US in a year's time. I had deferred this task to make the trip to Alice Springs with Alison, but I knew exactly what was in the show: Freddy West's *Old Man's Ceremony* and a lot more like it. What were the implications if they turned out to be 'problematic' – as I suspected they would? I had the images of the works in the exhibition I had been sent by the *Icons* curator with me on my computer, so I asked Dick Kimber if he would mind having a look at them to see if they presented similar problems to the ones Michael and Long Jack had declared 'dangerous'. He agreed and in the secluded back corner of an Alice Springs coffee shop he confirmed my own misgivings that about half of them looked to contain 'Restricted' imagery. The report for the National Cultural Heritage Committee which Alison and I were beginning to map out on the consultation process wouldn't be the only bombshell dropped in the aftermath of our expedition, although at the time it seemed the most significant.

The problem about *Icons*

The first person I contacted when I got back to Sydney was Fred Myers, whose personal and research interests in the Papunya Tula movement went back further than mine, to 1973–4 when he'd lived at Yai Yai with the Pintupi as a graduate student for a year and a half. He was now Professor of Anthropology at New York University and we'd spent a lot of time together in 1999 when I was in New York, attached to his department as a Senior Fulbright Fellow. We'd kept in touch over the years. A lot of my recent contact with him had involved requests for background on paintings the Reference Group was assessing. I'd let him know about the consultation trip to Alice Springs as soon as we knew of it, asking him for his thoughts on the most appropriate people to consult and the most appropriate way to ask the questions. He'd written back his congratulations (that we'd managed to make some progress on the issue at last) and suggested we ask our Pintupi consultants 'palya yutintjaku?' meaning 'Good or okay to see?'. He also offered his 1974 genealogies with the cautionary note that he had not updated or corrected them, and that though close relatives might be a good place to start it wouldn't be an absolute or certain guide as to who had the rights to speak for particular Dreamings. Fred too was writing an essay for the *Icons* catalogue and had helped negotiate the Grey Art Gallery at New York University as the last venue of the exhibition's US tour. I was contemplating pulling out of writing the catalogue essay and I wanted to confer with him before I called *Icons* curator Roger Benjamin to tell him this – and why.

As soon as I got back, I emailed Fred to say that I had returned from the Community Consultation for Export Permits trip 'with more questions than answers – which in a way counts as a success'. One of those questions, I said, was whether any of the paintings in the *Icons* exhibition seemed likely to him to be *not* 'palya yutintjaku'. I told him about Bobby's reaction to the thumbnail of his father's work and Dick Kimber's preliminary assessment of the *Icons* paintings, which both suggested the answer to that question might be 'quite a few'. As I had hoped, Fred's response was scholarly but pragmatic. 'This is a big question,' was his first line. He raised the issue of what was acceptable practice now in Australia and overseas (since it might be very difficult to impose standards that have not been observed elsewhere) and whether the *Icons* paintings or ones like them had already been exhibited (quite a few were included in *Papunya Tula: Genesis and Genius* – although after what Bobby had said, this might not mean they were 'acceptable' now). His final line was 'We need to sort this out right away'.

I also called Hetti Perkins. We'd been working together on the Reference Group since 2001 and I knew that the hardline attitudes revealed by the men we had consulted would be far more problematic for her as an Arrente woman than for me. I also knew that another reprint of the *Papunya Tula: Genesis and Genius* catalogue was in the pipeline and I thought she should know first about Bobby's comment that some of the paintings should not have been reproduced in it, that it was 'Okay, but don't do it again'. I knew she would see to it that there was appropriate community consultation on the reprint, and her influence could be critical in giving the lead to other cultural institutions in reviewing their display practices on early Papunya boards. The Art Gallery of New South Wales was also one of the venues booked in for *Icons*' Australian tour.

With the Easter break behind me, I rang Roger's mobile. A relaxed-sounding voice answered, with the cries of seagulls and children playing in the background. Roger told me cheerfully that he was walking on Hyams Beach with his kids. I said I'd ring back. I didn't want to break into his family holiday, but I guess he was curious why I'd rung unexpectedly and he said it was okay to go on. I told him where I had just been and what the men had said. I didn't know whether I could still write for the catalogue and I did not see how I could be involved at all if the show went ahead in Australia after hearing first-hand from the men how they feel about 'dangerous' works being displayed and reproduced. Roger took it remarkably well. I remember his jagged, slightly disembodied laugh. It reminded me somehow of Alison and me on the Kintore road looking at where the Nissan's tyre had been. Out of nowhere you're in the middle of a situation you don't know how to deal with but know that you must. I might have tried to soften the blow by saying I didn't know how much of the concern Alison and I had encountered in our dealings with the senior men we consulted had to do with us being women raising topics that were 'men only' – but then hadn't Dick Kimber got similar responses? I also pointed out that my own project – a systematic investigation of the early Papunya boards – had also gone down in flames.

The problem about *Icons* – as Fred had observed – was that the show was already organised, booked into five venues in the US and Australia. Authors had been given an April 2006 deadline for catalogue submission, one year out from the first opening at Cornell University. In May 2006 Fred happened to be coming to Australia for a short trip and Roger met with us both to try to find a way forward. One thing was obvious – if Fred (and possibly I) were to continue our involvement – there would have to be a consultation process with the community over the *Icons* images. If the reaction to a substantial number of the paintings was the same as we had received in the Reference Group consultation process, then the Australian leg of the tour would have to be indefinitely postponed. It would stretch even Roger's formidable diplomatic skills to negotiate this impasse with the Wilkersons as a positive development for the exhibition. But at least it would involve a trip to the Papunya Tula outposts of Kintore and Kiwirrkura at the earliest opportunity, this time with the full support of its management, who no doubt would grasp the potential of the *Icons* exercise for developing their US market for contemporary Papunya Tula works.

Reporting the first consultation

But what was the way forward for the Reference Group? Alison and I had started work on a report to the National Cultural Heritage Committee on the consultation process while we waited in Alice Springs for our flights home and we continued working on it for many weeks afterwards. What the men had told us was going to be a bolt from the blue in these quarters too and our conclusions would need to be carefully worded to have a chance of being accepted and acted upon.

I was concerned that *something* happen as a result, after raising expectations in those who had confided in us that it would – by the very fact of our visit. A draft was written with Alison's assistance, then referred to the rest of the Reference Group, under whose name it would go forward to the Committee. I was in Melbourne on other business and discussed the draft with John Kean, who wanted more acknowledgment of the need to investigate further the position of non-Pintupi, 'Eastern end' artists like Kaapa, Tim Leura and Clifford Possum, who were raised at a time in Anmatyerr society when the boundaries of men's knowledge were becoming more permeable. John acknowledged that a consultation process would seek the views of the contemporary custodians of ceremonial knowledge associated with their works, but his personal relationships with these men during his time at Papunya Tula in the 1970s and beyond made him want to see their point of view represented in the discussion too. He was also wary of the role of a gatekeeper implied in the report's recommendation that the Committee might now need to consider what was being *imported into* Australia for public display as well as what was being exported from Australia, temporarily or permanently.

Our report stressed that the Reference Group was not proposing handing over its responsibility for export permit recommendations to the contemporary cultural custodians, but that our decisions must be informed by the views they had expressed. Some of the bureaucrats might have preferred that we did hand over to the cultural custodians, since we begged to differ from their 'safe distance' solution of allowing 'dangerous' works to be exported as far away as possible for as long as possible. We pointed out that export of the physical object could provide no guarantee that the image would not be seen in Australia, for example on the Internet. What the men had told us meant that even a simple public information measure like putting up images on the Protection of Movable Cultural Heritage website of early Papunya boards that had been refused export permits (as had been proposed) was now problematic, especially if depictions of secret/sacred material (that is, 'religious sensitivities') were among the grounds for their refusal. The report also raised the possibility that inappropriate public display of 'Restricted' early Papunya boards might constitute 'desecration' within the meaning of the *Aboriginal and Torres Strait Islander Heritage Protection Act* – which in retrospect may have been a critical strategic error. However, our main recommendations were that our initial scoping exercise be followed up by a two-pronged research effort. One: to identify appropriate cultural consultants from among the painters' descendants and other ritual authorities for each artist's work. Two: to alert the public collecting institutions that the display of early Papunya boards is still problematic. We proposed that the galleries and museums be asked to assist in the development of a visual register of works in public collections to support the work of the Reference Group in determining whether particular artists were adequately represented in the national collections, given that some of their holdings of artists' work might be unsuitable for public display.

At the 71st meeting of the National Cultural Heritage Committee in February 2007 our report was tabled, and rather to my astonishment all the recommendations we eventually made were agreed to. The National Cultural Heritage Committee agreed to undertake an audit of the national collection of Papunya boards in public collecting institutions; to establish 'thresholds of national significance' for early Papunya boards and how secret/sacred content fits within these thresholds; to review the Certificate of Exemption process (covering the importation of works into Australia for exhibition and sale); and to liaise with those currently conducting a review of the *Aboriginal and Torres Strait Islander Heritage Protection Act*. One of the Indigenous representatives on the Committee had further proposed that the Committee write to public collecting institutions to inform them of the issue of 'Restricted' content of early Papunya boards and recommend that they continue to liaise with communities on these issues.

This recommendation was also accepted, and in retrospect provided the only tangible outcome. Three months later in May 2007, just over a year after our trip to Central Australia to consult on a process of consultation, a letter from the Committee's chairman was sent to the chairs of the councils of national cultural institutions. The letter alerted them to concerns of 'relevant Indigenous people' regarding the display and publication of Papunya Tula art that had been revealed to the Papunya Tula Reference Group and reported to the Committee. 'Specifically concerns were expressed regarding the prohibitions surrounding sacred and secret depictions in early paintings.' The Committee 'would like to inform' them of these concerns and 'reiterate the importance of managing appropriately cultural issues when planning exhibitions'. It was so carefully worded to avoid accusations that the Committee had overstepped the bounds of its brief that it is unsurprising it seems to have had negligible impact – apart from informing every public collecting institution in Australia of the identity of the members of the Reference Group and its 'mission' of locking away what they were just beginning – or about – to recognise as some of the jewels of their collections.

The Canberra consultancy

The highlight of the Sotheby's Important Aboriginal Art auction on 24 July 2007 was the record-breaking sum of $2.4 million fetched by Clifford Possum Tjapaltjarri's brooding masterpiece *Warlugulong* 1977. It is the second of five paintings in Tjapaltjarri's great map painting series of the late 1970s, whose assemblage had been the highlight of the 2003 Clifford Possum retrospective I curated for the Art Gallery of South Australia. It was spectacular enough to convert the Gallery's then Director Ron Radford (now the Director of the National Gallery of Australia), who had recognised Tjapaltjarri's genius early on, from his previous preference for the artist's post-1980 work. In mid-June the Reference Group was asked for a report on the painting, following a last-minute application from Sotheby's for a permanent export permit. Other permit applications from the 2007 auction were processed *after* the sale. But the restoration of 'Important' to the Sotheby's sale title (after being merely 'Aboriginal Art' since 2000) was partly in recognition of the importance of this particular painting. It was featured on the cover of the Sotheby's catalogue and in the media build-up to the auction not even Tim Klingender seemed to think it would – or should – be given an export permit.

When the news broke the day after the auction that the National Gallery of Australia had been the successful bidder, I wondered for a second if the rivalry between the two institutions could be overcome to allow the painting's inclusion in an exhibition of large and very large canvases from the first decade of the Papunya painting movement that I was curating for the National Museum of Australia at the time. But *Papunya Painting: Out of the Desert* was opening in less than three months and the object list and exhibition design were long since set in stone. The focus of the exhibition was the Museum's large collection of 1970s and early 1980s Papunya Tula works, acquired in 1991 from the Aboriginal Arts Board, supplemented by four large canvases originally from the same source and now in the collection of Te Papa Tongarewa (Museum of New Zealand) – and one early Papunya board.[6] In late October the Museum flew the Chairman of Papunya Tula Artists, Bobby West Tjupurrula, and Long Jack Phillipus Tjakamarra and Charlie Tjapangati whose canvases from that era were featured in the exhibition, from Alice Springs to attend the opening. Pansy Napangati also drove up from Adelaide where she had been staying with family to be present at the opening when she learnt that the pair of dancing boards she had swapped for her first canvas and paint from Papunya Tula at the beginning of the 1980s were included in the exhibition to signify the entry of women as painters in their own right at this point in the painting company's history.

John Kean, whose stretch with Papunya Tula Artists in the late 1970s – beginning with the documentation of *Warlugulong* 1977 – was commemorated as 'John Kean Time' in the *Papunya Painting* exhibition,[7] was also in town holidaying with his family and turned up unexpectedly at the Museum at lunchtime on the first day of the men's visit. I had last seen John in Sydney in September at a rare face-to-face meeting of the Reference Group whose main purpose was to distribute the next round of export permit assessments. Most of the paintings to be assessed were from the mid-1970s to the mid-1980s. After Kaapa Tjampitjinpa's 1971 *Goanna Corroboree at Mirkantji* was acquired by the National Museum of Australia, the only painting from the so-called 'seminal Papunya period' we were being asked to examine was Long Jack Phillipus' fine exemplar of the School of Kaapa, *Hunting* 1971. The painting depicts a ceremony in meticulous detail and is dominated by two large tjurungas at the top and bottom of the painting with detailed inscriptions and was pretty obviously 'Restricted'. As the Reference Group member assigned to draft an expert examiner report based on my School of Kaapa research for the approval of the other members, I made a note on the application form at the meeting – 'Refer for consultation LJP: Can it be seen? Is it an important story?' But how was this consultation supposed to occur? Perhaps I had been thinking about the opening of *Papunya Painting* in Canberra: I knew Long Jack's name was on the guest list and when I had last seen him in Papunya in late July, he had said that he 'might come', giving me his sweetest Santa Claus smile. But I was still unsure how the brown paper envelope technique would go without Dick Kimber.

A new federal Labor government had been swept into power the day before the artists arrived and Canberra was buzzing with excitement. I remember Bobby's jubilant throat-slitting gesture at the news that Mal Brough, the man responsible for the Intervention in the Northern Territory, had lost his seat. The atmosphere at the Museum was particularly upbeat at the prospect of new political masters after so many years of conservative rule, often trenchant in its criticisms of the Museum's engagement with Indigenous issues.[8] Catching the mood, John and I decided to 'seize the day', not only to consult Long Jack about *Hunting* 1971 but to continue what Alison and I had started the previous year to advance the stalled community consultation agenda on the early Papunya boards. I let Alison Reid know what was happening and she agreed that the presence of the three senior artists was too good an opportunity to miss. She also welcomed John's involvement. He was an ideal candidate to conduct the consultation in accordance with the advice we had received from Bobby West: male, grey-haired and knowledgeable. He was also – at that point – not committed one way or the other on the issues he set out to investigate. He was certainly not committed to the views that the men had expressed in the first consultation. If anything, he was personally inclined to wish the boards *could* be shown and had often raised with me in previous discussions what the now-deceased artists' views might have been about their work being accessible only to senior initiated men. In our email correspondence on the restrictedness issue he had expressed the view that 'Like the atomic bomb, it's out there and its dangers have to be lived with'.

But how to raise the subject? Dick Kimber's long preamble on camel culling that Alison found so infuriating had been an attempt to warm up his connection with Long Jack before moving on to topics that it would be highly inappropriate to launch into cold – not if you want people to be forthcoming about them. With the early boards it is particularly difficult, because you are dragging up matters from decades ago that were troublesome then – and might be still. Usually when Papunya Tula artists travel to exhibition openings, shopping is their first priority. Their role as law men with the authority and experience to handle secret/sacred men's business is the last thing on their minds. But on the first afternoon of their stay, Peter Thorley, one of the Museum staff previously acquainted with Bobby and Charlie from his time as a linguist in Kintore, and Thorley's colleague Ian Coates invited the artists to visit the collection of sacred objects from Central Australia that the Museum had also inherited from the Aboriginal Arts Board. They were stored in the Museum's off-site warehouse. John Kean was invited to join this expedition; Pansy Napangati and I were pointedly not invited. Nor did I inquire what transpired, but it served our other purpose well in bringing up the subject of secret/sacred men's business in a way that made it easier for John to ask the men if they would be prepared to look at some of the images of the early paintings and comment on them as law men for the information of the federal government – popularly known as 'Canberra' where the painters come from. They readily agreed that John should come over the next morning to the apartment where they were staying to conduct the consultation.

While the men were examining the Museum's tjurunga repository, I spent the afternoon printing out a selection of twenty-four images from my early Papunya boards database for John to show them. Unlike the approach taken with the export permit process, where the Minister had made it clear that paintings must be considered individually on a case by case basis, we were looking to obtain from the consultation some general insights into what makes a board 'Restricted'. The paintings I selected were mostly from state and national gallery collections. I guess I was hoping that if we could produce some information about early Papunya boards in the public collections from the consultation it might help jump-start responses to the dormant National Cultural Heritage Committee letter about 'vetting' their early board collections. Most of the works I chose had been identified at some stage in their time with the collecting institution as containing 'Restricted' content that related to aspects of men's ceremonial life. Though it was sometimes not at all apparent why they should have been: about a third of them did not contain explicit representations of sacred objects, but they too had at some point in the past been identified as 'Restricted' and this information noted in the catalogue. I hoped the inclusion of such works in the consultation would signal to the men involved that their comments were sought on a broad spectrum of works, from most explicit and detailed through to more abstracted representations. If the men now declared some of these works were suitable for public display, we could also argue that the vetting process might release works for exhibition that had previously been thought to be 'Restricted'. I also included Long Jack's *Hunting* and a couple of early Kaapa images in this style, including Dick Kimber's *Mikanji* 1971 and three works with whorled arcs in the background from the Peter Fannin Collection of Western Desert Art at the National Gallery, to check Long Jack's assertion to Dick Kimber in Papunya that it was not just sacred objects but also certain patterning that could be 'dangerous'.

Previous consultations had placed the issue of whether those consulted wanted the paintings exported at the forefront of the discussion. This was the first question I had heard Dick Kimber ask Long Jack as Alison and I left the room. We had decided that this consultation would focus on the men's responses to the boards first, and only later would the issue of export be raised. John also tried to make sure that his questions were 'open-ended'. So often when Aboriginal people are placed in situations like these, they try to give the interrogating whitefella the answers he's looking for – in legal circles where the phenomenon is particularly pronounced it's sometimes called 'gratuitous compliance'. So often in permission discussions the men consulted are led, if not in the specific questions they are asked, then by the context in which they are asked and who asks them. Thus if the Manager of Papunya Tula Artists asks one of the company's artists, 'Is it okay for people to see this one?', he is more likely to get a 'Yes' answer because why would he be asking unless someone wanted people to see the painting? Maybe the person who wants to put that painting in their exhibition or a picture of it in their book or catalogue is standing right there, with the Papunya Tula worker brokering the exchange for her or him. People are also very conscious of their entitlement to the payment of 'copyright' if a painting is reproduced and this would provide a further inducement if these questions were asked in the context of an exhibition or some other use to which the painting or its image is being put. The artists also know that the current management of Papunya Tula would not be troubling to ask them these questions unless there *was* some such purpose in mind.

During the consultation John Kean transcribed what the men said of a general nature about the paintings, sometimes translating from Pintupi as he did so. The men's comments are italicised; John's are in square brackets.

Should not have made them, it was too early.

As is often said in explanation of the 'Restricted' content of the early boards, at first the painters did not understand the implications of the paintings moving beyond the painting room, in which only initiated Aboriginal men and their 'novice' Geoffrey Bardon were present.

People might see these paintings and realise that we use these objects [in secret men's ceremonies].

[The reason they did not want the paintings seen is the same reason they did not want the objects themselves seen: because these objects are used in the ceremonies and under Aboriginal law women and men without ritual experience are forbidden to see them.]

That is dangerous (pointing to a graphic depiction of a large ceremonial pole bisecting one of the paintings).

[Ceremonial poles, like tjurungas, belong to the secret men's realm and knowledge about the details of markings on them puts uninitiated witnesses into a compromised position; in earlier times the witness's life may have been placed under threat by the accidental revelation of such objects.]
They can't see this.
[Depictions of bullroarers where the attached string was evident and the details of the designs incised on the surface of the wood were explicit were also declared] *Private* and *Dangerous. No good. Too dangerous. Can't see 'em. People can't see that.*

Rather to John's surprise – and mine when he reported it to me – the men were just as strongly opposed to the display of works in which unmarked tjurungas were shown as when they were decorated in such explicit detail as would enable their use to identify the originals. In three cases where there were simply tjurunga shapes with no markings, in combination with other silhouettes of objects without decoration, they too were identified as 'Restricted'. John commented: 'In my experience and talking to other men previously, such works have not caused concern'. But Dick Kimber once told me that such unfinished works may have been left in this state because others had objected and the painter had decided not to complete the work. String crosses were also problematic, as was the depiction of kangaroos, an important animal sacred to men, rendered ancestral kangaroos by their body decorations. '*Malu, no good,*' they said.

Every now and again the men would say *'They can see that one, it's good for all people to see it'* or *'Easy one, they can see it'.*
[Only three of the twenty-four images shown them were regarded by the men as okay to exhibit publicly.]

In apparent contradiction of what Long Jack had told Dick Kimber in the Papunya consultation, none of the men in the Canberra consultation, including Long Jack, appeared to find any of the patterning – especially the whorled backgrounds on some of the paintings by David Corby and Anatjari Tjakamarra and Walter Tjampitjinpa which at some point I had been told had been stopped because they were too similar to the markings on sacred objects – caused the men any concern at all.

[The men were also comfortable with the idea of initiated 'countrymen' seeing the paintings under similar conditions, that is, in a secure environment, where there is no possibility of intrusion and with only initiated men present, even if they are not the owners of that particular Dreaming.]
Other Aboriginal men can come and look, just like we are looking at these pictures.

The most startling outcome of the consultation was the suggestion that future Pintupi artists could draw on the detailed information about the visual traditions of their culture contained in these early 'dangerous' paintings to create new 'versions' of them that would be open to public display. This suggestion was made without any prompting from John and quite early in the conversation, before the question of whether the boards could or should be exported had been raised:

That one has got to go back so that the grandsons [that is, of the artists] can see it. After we die, they have got to come back so all the family [that is, male custodians] can see it.
The grandsons can come and have a look and they can learn from that one, and after they can make a new style [that is, which avoids explicit depictions of ceremonial detail]. .

Now is a new generation, new ideas. We should put good ones [that is, paintings without explicitly depicted secret content]. From that mistake [that is, the production of works which reveal restricted aspects of ceremony] we won't be putting it any more.

The idea that these paintings might be both a cultural and an artistic resource for the coming generations of Pintupi artists, and that their availability for these educational purposes within the artists' culture could provide a basis for the 'future vitality and creative dynamism of the painting movement' came from the men – it was not suggested to them by the direction of John's questions. The idea of the paintings' usefulness to future generations may have been suggested to the men by their experience the previous day looking at the tjurungas stored in the museum. I had half-expected them to dismiss the contentiousness of the boards after their exposure the day before to the 'real thing', but for them it seemed the boards were, if not the 'real thing', then so closely related to them that they constituted an invaluable resource from which they did not want their culture alienated irrevocably by their permanent export. In John Kean's words: 'They revealed the "real thing" in a visceral way with verisimilitude. It was these qualities the artists believed would provide a great reference for future generations.' Importantly, the paintings which caused most concern because they were 'dangerous' were also those considered of particular value for the information they could provide to future generations. This explains why when the question about export was raised, after a full and open-ended discussion of the paintings, the men were on this occasion completely unequivocal that such 'dangerous' paintings should not be exported because they were *too important to them.*

Direct exposure to the men's reactions to these elements

of the paintings brought about a dramatic change in John himself. From his non-committal position, he became 'radicalised' – to the point of proposing in his report on the consultation 'a blanket ban on the granting of export permits to 1971–72 Papunya paintings which contain explicit depictions of ceremonial poles, "tulku" (tjurunga), bullroarers'. Instead, he suggested, they should be 'acquired into secure collections where the descendants of the original painters and their "countrymen" can view the works and learn from the information that they contain'.[9] He further proposed that a 'self-regulating embargo' be put on the publication and exhibition of paintings produced at Papunya in the period 1971–72 which contain explicit depictions of ceremonial poles, 'tulku' (tjurunga), bullroarers, 'to be reviewed in ten years, in recognition of the capacity of cultures to change perspective over time':

> My position did change on the basis of the Canberra consultations. We [Reference Group] had long called for a consultation process. That having been achieved, I felt obliged to respond in good faith to its findings. I am personally saddened that the boards, as matchless representations of Aboriginal belief, may be suppressed. I remain conflicted that I may have had a role in suppressing such significant images, but I do not resile from my report or my recommendations.[10]

Break-out at the museum: The art thief as connoisseur

At 3.39 am on Tuesday 1 April 2008, the security alarm of the Northern Territory Museum and Art Gallery startled the birds roosting in the rambling thickets of Bullocky Point. Located just 4 kilometres from Darwin CBD, the Museum was built in the wake of Cyclone Tracy to withstand the toughest of storms, but the building is a little light on other kinds of security for the various collections it houses. This oversight became apparent when the police arrived about fifteen minutes later to discover that thieves had gained entry by the simple expedient of smashing a window with a rock. While the alarm rang out, the thief or thieves were captured on the security cameras as they snatched seven Aboriginal paintings from the walls of the Gallery and made a clean getaway.

Six of the seven paintings were 'synthetic polymer paint pieces (commonly known as Papunya boards) by important ceremonial leaders (now deceased)' according to the Museum's subsequent media release. The Museum's collection of over two hundred of these works from the earliest years of the Papunya Tula art movement has been mentioned numerous times already in this story. It is the largest and arguably the most historically significant in the world. The six works taken were fine examples of some of the earliest paintings of founding artists and elder statesmen of the movement: Mick Namarari Tjapaltjarri, Uta Uta Tjangala, Kaapa Tjampitjinpa, Charlie Tjaruru Tjungurrayi, Yala Yala Gibbs Tjungurrayi and Tutuma Tjapangati. The seventh was a watercolour on paper by Hermannsburg artist Walter Ebatarinja, entitled *Ceremonial Man with Tjurunga*, which received scant attention in the media once it was disclosed that the estimated worth of the early Papunya boards taken by the thieves was at least half a million dollars.

From China to Kuwait, India, Europe and North America, the world news media was ablaze with the story when, early afternoon Australian time, the case of the stolen Papunya boards took a sharp turn into bathos. During a search of the grounds, police came upon the stolen artworks lying under the trees in bushland about 500 metres from the Museum's front door. Soon after this, following a tip-off from the public, police arrested an intoxicated, 37-year-old man standing at the bus stop further down the road. The Museum's delighted conservation staff pronounced the works unharmed by their ordeal. Tim Klingender, who happened to be in town on the night of the robbery, was quoted reflecting on the Museum's good fortune considering the season that no rain had fallen in the interim.

Graham Heath, the man arrested at the Parap bus stop, was convicted of the robbery on his own admission of guilt but did not receive a custodial sentence. The *New York Times* story explained his abandonment of the paintings as a 'change of heart', but Heath himself could offer no explanation of his actions to the court other than that he had been 'drunk at the time'. What on earth can he have been thinking? Was he egged on by a second man captured on the security camera footage according to the initial reports? Why did he steal those seven paintings? Did he just grab whatever was closest to the door and easiest to carry? That seems the most likely explanation, but then how did he manage to take the six most valuable paintings from the Museum's display of Papunya boards and leave behind equally portable works by complete unknowns?

The content of the works in his selection is equally fascinating: was it just an accident that all were of such culturally consequential subject matter? Ebatarinja's *Ceremonial Man with Tjurunga* is an obvious case in point, but the six early Papunya boards also contained more or less explicit references to the ceremonial sphere. Was Heath aware of this when he took them? Or might that explain why he dropped them as soon as he got them outside and had a better look at them? Or was that the plan, and someone else bungled the pick-up? If they had known that the Museum would – initially – take the view that they could not publish images of the stolen paintings because they might offend 'cultural sensitivities', might the thieves have gone through with it after all?

I'm very glad they didn't, but the thieves were not the only ones who didn't know what they had until they – almost – didn't have it any more. It's only a slight exaggeration to say that the tribesmen who demonstrated in Alice Springs in 1974 in protest at some of these paintings being on public display are some of the few people in the more than three decades since the Museum acquired its collection of early Papunya boards to treat them with the seriousness they deserve. For thirty years the Museum allowed most of the collection to remain in the acid-emitting hessian frames in which they arrived at the Museum, despite the obvious fragility of works often created from waste materials scrounged by the artists from around the Papunya settlement. Nor until the last decade did they exhibit them – although perhaps in retrospect this may have been the wisest course.

The wonderful thing about what happened at Bullocky Point on April Fools' Day 2008, which in a way does make this 'the most important art theft in Australian history'[11] (as I rashly announced to a journalist covering the story before it became rather the most bizarre and short-lived), is that the thief did that history an enormous service by bestowing on the early Papunya boards – however briefly – the sanctifying aura of world media attention. All of the hundreds of articles on the incident had qualified the monetary value attached to them with an explanation of their importance as the founding works of an internationally renowned Indigenous art movement. And the Museums and Art Galleries of the Northern Territory – or their political masters – finally understood that its collection of Papunya boards is of unique historical significance and, in a word, 'priceless'. However, not only the means, also the *timing* of this realisation could hardly have been worse, for the moment when they might unproblematically have put them on display had passed them by.

Groundhog day

It was late February 2008 when John Kean dispatched his report on the Canberra consultation to the National Cultural Heritage Committee. In the meantime, I had sent in my report on the Long Jack Phillipus painting *Hunting* 1971, citing the results of the Canberra consultation with respect to this particular painting: that it was *'Not to go on display'* but be kept so that descendants of these artists could come and look at it and learn from it – and from that work out how to paint acceptable versions that were suitable for public exposure. The Reference Group's recommendation was that it be denied a permit.

A few weeks after the break-in at the Museum, I received a letter from the new head of the Cultural Heritage Secretariat – renamed 'Maritime and Movable Heritage' – requesting that I reconsider and resubmit my report. Apparently, it did not give sufficient grounds 'under Part 5' to support the recommendation that the painting should not be exported. The letter pointed out that much of my report addressed issues of cultural significance, particularly secret and sacred, but that such considerations only apply to objects of Aboriginal and Torres Strait Islander heritage under Part 1. Since Part 1 'specifically excludes objects which were created for sale, thus Papunya Tula paintings can not be considered under Part 1, only under Part 5 of the Control List.' I could not resist this exasperated response:

Perhaps someone in your Department should be assigned responsibility for informing the contemporary cultural custodians involved in these consultation processes that their grave concerns about early Papunya paintings with explicit secret/sacred depictions are not able to be raised due to the current wording of the National Cultural Heritage Control List. I respectfully remind you that their views, communicated through the reports submitted by the Papunya Tula Reference Group to the National Cultural Heritage Committee and the Secretariat, were sought over several years during consultation processes which had the support of your Department.

There is no need for you to tell any member of the Papunya Tula Reference Group about this problem with the Act. The group has been trying to draw it to the attention of the Protection of Movable Cultural Heritage Secretariat for almost seven years. In our letter of June 25th 2001, following the first meetings of the Reference Group, we recommended that 'Early Papunya Boards be appraised as *both* Aboriginal and Torres Strait Islander Heritage Objects (Part 1) and Fine Art 'in the Indigenous Tradition' (Part 5)'. No written response to this and other concerns raised in this letter has yet been received by the Papunya Tula Reference Group. In my comments for the Review of the *Protection of Movable Cultural Heritage Act 1986*, associated Regulations and Administration (2004) this issue was raised again, again without response.

On the issue of secret/sacred depictions in early Papunya paintings, we have sent two reports on consultations with senior contemporary cultural custodians, whose advice the Department eventually sought at our urging. If the legislation is so framed that their wishes cannot be given consideration perhaps it should be amended so that they can. I fail to understand why something cannot be considered part of Aboriginal and Torres Strait Islander Heritage because it has been produced for sale, when evidently this is no barrier to something being considered part of *Australian* cultural heritage. Surely the circumstances of its production are irrelevant?

With much help from John Kean, who is masterful at elaborating the relationship between form and content in a painting, I duly rewrote my report on the Long Jack to include extensive discussion of its artistic merit and wider cultural significance for Australia:

> Not only is it of exceptional value as an object of fine art, but its significance resides in many of the same features which make it significant for traditional law men such as those we consulted. The ceremony is depicted in meticulous detail commensurate with its importance, but which also shows Long Jack to have been a masterful exponent of the 'pre-Bardon' style. The kneeling figures of the two corroboree men are individualised as to their different expressions, body sizes, skin tones, facial forms and expressions. The size of the larger figure may reflect its representation of the artist himself, whose height (at least 168 cm) is most unusual amongst his countrymen. Only their body paint, most delicately applied to the head, limbs and torso is the same. The two large tjurungas and the smaller bullroarers show cognate designs, again executed with great skill and delicacy. The spearthrowers are likewise decorated with matching motifs with extremely fine brushwork. The painting succeeds brilliantly as a work of art giving graphic form to its underlying themes. Thus the two figures are dwarfed by the scale of the large ceremonial objects in a symbolic representation of the relative insignificance of human actors alongside the forces of the Dreaming invested in these objects. The upper large ceremonial object bears identical markings to the lower one, but in contrasting colours, complementing the variant colours of each ritual participant's shield and bullroarer. There is subtle differentiation in variations of palette and placement within the overall symmetry.

The recommendation was eventually approved and *Hunting* 1971 added to the list of Prohibited Exports. But I think none of us were surprised to be told after the next meeting of the

National Cultural Heritage Committee, whose response to John's report we had been patiently awaiting, that this item had been taken off the agenda. The excuse was that yet another review – this time of the *Aboriginal and Torres Strait Islander Heritage Protection Act* – was underway. The report had been sent to that division where apparently it had not been well received. After all, its findings and recommendations were a direct contradiction of the views of those nameless experts quoted by my lunch companions at Ali Baba's all those years ago. I think the bureaucrats much preferred to believe that the secret/sacred is not important any more to the 'people out there'. It's so much simpler for everybody that way. The issues had been opened up by the Reference Group's dogged insistence that the contemporary cultural custodians must be consulted especially about the 'Restricted' works. But having opened them up, it was beginning to look as though none of our latest recommendations would 'float'. Instead, they would be funnelled into more reviews and forgotten as yet more changes of personnel within the Cultural Heritage section removed the few people who had tried to support community consultation to somewhere else in the bureaucracy.

They 'weren't sure where it's going to go', I was told. But I knew: nowhere. As soon as the men said they wanted the boards to stay, it was all over for the bureaucrats. So long as the men consulted were saying 'Yes' to export, the bureaucrats had been prepared to go along with the idea of developing a consultation process. If it could facilitate the permits process, never mind that the men might be saying this out of a mistaken belief in the efficacy of their already disproven 'safety of distance' solution to the disclosures of the 'Restricted' early boards. Process is what matters in these circles, nothing else, including the concerns of the cultural custodians if they involved more expense, more hassle, and more work for the bureaucracy. It was suggested that the activities of the Papunya Tula Reference Group might themselves be under review. At the end of this conversation, the question hung in the air: What else can be done to give those men a real voice?

8

The *Icons* Precedent

In the end I did write an essay for the catalogue of *Icons of the Desert.* By that time, the Australian leg of the tour had been cancelled. The US tour opened at the Herbert F Johnson Museum of Art at Cornell University in upper New York State in February 2009, two years behind its original schedule. In the interim, the organisers had commissioned their own consultation with senior members of the painters' communities of origin and obtained permission to exhibit all the works in America. To accommodate the cultural custodians' wish that the 'Restricted' paintings not be available in reproduction either in Australia, nine paintings had been removed from the main part of the catalogue and only reproduced in a special insert at the back of the volume, which the publishers had agreed not to include in copies distributed in Australia. In the main catalogue those nine paintings had been replaced by black squares and rectangles in the shape of the missing paintings with a small inscription: 'For reasons of its secret/ sacred imagery, this image is reproduced in the supplement only'. Compared to the endless procrastination and prevarication the Reference Group had experienced in Australia from the cultural heritage bureaucrats, this was an astonishing response. I never imagined that my call to Roger Benjamin's mobile just after Easter 2006, breaking into his South Coast holiday to tell him why I might have to withdraw altogether as a contributor to the *Icons* catalogue, could have unleashed such a sequence of events. Faced just one year out from *Icons*' original opening date with what the contemporary cultural custodians had told me and an officer of the Cultural Heritage Secretariat of the federal government about their views on the publication and display of early Papunya boards containing 'Restricted' imagery, the exhibition's organisers were able to reconceptualise these difficulties as an opportunity for the exhibition to trailblaze. When *Icons* finally did open, they could justifiably claim to be the first to explore with an Indigenous Australian community how to handle the exhibiting of this kind of 'Restricted' material in private hands, thereby giving the lead to public collections in Australia still dragging their heels on the issues raised in the National Cultural Heritage Committee's letter.

As Professor Fred Myers, whose advice and support was integral to achieving this outcome, had immediately grasped when I contacted him about the results of the first official community consultation, the problem with *Icons* was that its organisation was so far advanced when the issue of 'restrictedness' broke. But that was also *Icons*' great strength from the point of view of finding the will to work out a solution acceptable to all stakeholders. By the time the organisers of *Icons* became aware that there was a problem with exhibiting some of the paintings (at least in Australia) and with reproducing them in the catalogue, the project was so far along, so much time and effort and money had already gone into it, that everyone involved was ready to engage with the issues as the only way out. Abandoning the exhibition at such a juncture would have been the very last resort. A solution had to be found – and was negotiated, with the assistance of people who might not have been persuaded to assist had the situation not been so desperate. Like Dick Kimber, who overcame his reluctance to re-involve himself with these thorny issues to procure for the organisers the permission of the artists' relatives and descendants for all the paintings to be exhibited in America.

Kimber's vital contribution to a successful resolution of the problems they faced is gratefully acknowledged by organising curator Andy Weislogel of the Johnson Museum and referred to in Roger Benjamin's essay. No details are provided of the process which resulted in the selection of nine of the paintings as unsuitable for public display in Australia or for reproduction in the Australian edition of the *Icons* catalogue. Instead, there is a brief essay by Kimber titled 'Relatives of the Artists Respond to the Paintings', in which he records his encounters in the town camps of Alice Springs with Kaapa's younger brother Dinny Nolan Tjampitjinpa, Dinny's nephew Keith Kaapa Tjangala and daughter Doreen Nangala, and Emma Nangala, Walter Tjampitjinpa's daughter, and how they responded to the contents of a spring binder containing images of the paintings in the *Icons* exhibition which he asked them to look through for him. Much of this essay describes Kimber's travels with the pioneering group of Papunya artists and the elation of their descendants on being presented with images of their paintings – although the women barely glance at some of them. Doreen Nangala, for example, on seeing the first of Kaapa's paintings after immediately naming Mikantji as the site depicted, 'turned her head away so that she was no longer viewing it'.[1] She observed to Kimber that it showed things 'she had never previously seen' which she believed to be 'men's business' and that therefore 'she should not look at it or any of the others'.[2] Kimber cites Kaapa's firm assurances to him in the past that women, specifically Kaapa's wife, were permitted to view this and other paintings by him.[3] She agrees to view the works to oblige him, but deliberately avoids any close study of them. When Kimber points out elements to her that she believes she is not supposed to look at, she finds a way out of her predicament in deliberately misinterpreting them as something she can see. Thus a ceremonial pole becomes a 'digging stick with white feathers' and bird tracks are emu (which she can see) not budgerigar, because she is not allowed to look at paintings of this subject.

Kimber expounds what he understood from his close association with Kaapa over many years to have been his view on the secrecy question:

> that because no responsible Aboriginal men would ever discuss the nature of certain depictions, other people could 'no more learn 'im' – in other words, the non-initiated could not come to know anything proprietary or harmful about the paintings ... They could only comprehend the surface not the country or songs or ceremonies of association.[4]

According to Kimber, 'many men have taken Kaapa's view'. He mentions Long Jack Phillipus as someone who had always taken a 'much more conservative' view, although he does not elaborate on the details of the conservative position and can only recall Long Jack expressing reservations about his own early paintings or those of his deceased Pintupi-Luritja countrymen, not men of Anmatyerr, Arrente or Alyawarr backgrounds. Kimber also cites the authoritative voice of Pintupi leader Nosepeg Tjupurrula saying that since the uninitiated do not understand what they are looking at, they see only a 'pretty picture'. It sounds as if Kaapa's view was the majority view in previous times, with only arch-conservatives like Long Jack adhering to a stricter position and then only with respect to other Pintupi-Luritja artists.

Dinny Nolan, however, takes a more conservative position in the present. He accepts the presence of Aboriginal women during his initial cursory inspection of the paintings, but they and children are not allowed to be present for his more in-depth discussion of the paintings with Kimber, from which four young men and a middle-aged man are also excluded, although Kaapa's son Keith is allowed to be present. Dinny defers to Keith on the response to Kaapa's *Budgerigar Dreaming (Version 1)*, because it is not his Dreaming. As Kaapa's eldest surviving son, Keith would traditionally have inherited his father's rights in this Dreaming, but though he is almost fifty years old (he was born in 1959) Keith says he is not entitled to talk about the painting either, because he has not been through the appropriate ceremony: 'Before I can do the painting I have to go through the ceremony'.[5] Like the women, he then deliberately misreads the bird footprints as emu tracks, about which he can speak. According to Keith, the only three senior men left who know the Dreaming well are Dinny, Murphy Roberts and Long Jack Phillipus. Keith refers to the last generation that had in-depth knowledge of the Dreaming or 'tjukurrpa', of which these three men are some of the last surviving members, as the 'old people', an expression I hear often nowadays on my visits to remote communities with reference to this generation. Finally Dinny and Keith discuss *Ngalyilpi (A Small Snake)* 1972, Painting 34 in the *Icons* catalogue, which was passed for public display and reproduction by Kimber's informants in the undisclosed consultation process: 'Ngalyilpi. That one dangerous again. Like "business" way,' Keith explains. Dinny adds an unexplained hand gesture which enlightens Kimber to the painting's subject matter being 'Man's Love Magic', forbidden to women, not in this case because of the danger, but in order to protect its efficacy.

The Australian edition of the *Icons* catalogue, from which the US supplement containing the nine 'Restricted' images was omitted, was the first time most of the Indigenous art audience in Australia became aware of any problem with the display and reproduction of early Papunya boards. Twelve years of exposure to early Papunya paintings as high-priced commodities in auction catalogues and sales previews had made people forgetful – if they ever knew – about these issues. More than sixty early Papunya boards had been included in the *Papunya Tula: Genesis and Genius* retrospective at the Art Gallery of New South Wales in 2000, with no discernible repercussions. Those who did know something of the early history of the controversies about the display of the early Papunya boards would probably have assumed that curator Hetti Perkins took precautions about what she included.[6] But the men from Papunya Tula Artists who attended the opening had expressed no disquiet when she asked them about it before the opening, and Bobby West had told Fred Myers that it made him happy to see his father's paintings. If his happiness, like that of the female descendants of George Tjangala and Walter Tjampitjinpa who saw the images of their fathers' paintings in Dick Kimber's spring binder, was accompanied by reservations about the paintings' contents being on display, he did not say so when Hetti gave him the opportunity.

And yet, as we have seen, six years later Bobby West told me and a senior officer of the Cultural Heritage Secretariat that there *were* works in that exhibition and its catalogue that should not have been displayed or reproduced. Why didn't they say something when they had the opportunity in 2000? Had they changed their minds in the meantime? Fred Myers has explored this possibility in a recent paper,[7] and that may indeed be the case. However, there is another possible explanation for their silence on that occasion which makes sense of the apparent inconsistency. It also explains the lack of 'excitement' among the people in Dick Kimber's essay over what they were looking at – which some Australian readers of the *Icons* catalogue had been puzzling over.[8]

What would have happened if Bobby West and his countrymen had pointed out their concerns to Hetti Perkins in 2000? The catalogue of *Genesis and Genius* was already at the printers, the exhibition already hung. The opening of an art exhibition is obviously not a ceremony in Western Desert terms, but it is a non-Indigenous ceremonial occasion at which the artists are present as guests of honour. The exhibition organisers are their hosts. To disrupt such an occasion by raising concerns about some of the paintings being on display would be a serious breach of protocol to men of the painters' cultural background.[9] Apart from distressing their already stressed-out hosts and disrupting the opening ceremony, all that would have been achieved would be to draw everyone's attention to the secret/sacred content of those works. Similarly the lack of 'excitement' of the men and women in Dick Kimber's essay could be designed to deflect attention from the weighty cultural significance of what they are trying so hard not to 'see'. And as a strategy of 'damage control' in situations where the display – and in the case of the *Papunya Tula: Genesis and Genius* catalogue the reproduction – of the works in question is a fait accompli, it was effective.

This is also consistent with Bobby West waiting six years to inform anyone of the impropriety of certain paintings being on display in *Genesis and Genius.* The feeling of powerlessness conveyed by the comment, 'We thought no-one cared', which both Bobby West and Long Jack Phillipus made during the first Reference Group consultation, explains why Bobby West *was* now prepared to provide this information – his assumption that since the 'government lady' was asking the question this time, the government was prepared to do something about it.[10] Apart from such exceptional circumstances, the appropriate protocol is to say nothing if something inappropriate is on display – so that those looking at it will not 'see' what they are looking at.[11] This was presumably also Dick Kimber's own judgment in keeping the tone of his *Icons* catalogue essay low key.

The confusion of Australian readers of the *Icons* catalogue did not end here. Not long after the catalogue became available in Australia, I received a call from a journalist trying to get to the bottom of the mysterious black squares. His first question was: 'But didn't the artists paint all these pictures to teach the world about Aboriginal culture?' This had been Tim Klingender's argument against export restrictions on early Papunya boards,[12] though it was not the argument from any of the original artists or from the Reference Group's consultations with the contemporary cultural custodians, where the only reason for sending the paintings out into the world was to get them as far away from themselves as possible to avoid any repercussions with their neighbours for having painted them. It is true that some of the more articulate spokesmen for Papunya Tula Artists did put forward this view during their travels overseas with exhibitions of their art from the late 1980s onwards, but they were speaking of contemporary works, not the early Papunya boards. *Icons of the Desert* was the first exhibition of paintings from the earliest years of the Papunya movement to tour the United States – or anywhere else – since *Wailbri and Pintubi Art* all those years ago.

'But didn't Kaapa say they were okay?' was the journalist's second question. He is not the only one who has the impression, initially obtained from Geoffrey Bardon's memorable line: 'along with sacredness and secrecy, Kaapa threw his traditions to the winds',[13] that Kaapa was the sole source of the problems with secret/sacred elements in the early Papunya boards. Dick Kimber's essay in *Icons* unintentionally reinforces this impression by talking almost exclusively with Kaapa's relatives about Kaapa's paintings. None of the other artists whose work was declared off-limits by the *Icons* consultation process are mentioned, yet four paintings in the sealed section are the work of Pintupi (or Pintupi-Luritja) artists.[14] Roger Benjamin's essay likewise names only the four works from the School of Kaapa as having 'been recently judged problematic by community elders for viewing by Aboriginal women and uninitiated men from Central Australia'[15] and bases his discussion of 'moves towards protecting the public from potentially dangerous images in the early Papunya boards'[16] on a series of works by 'Kaapa's countryman Tim Leura Tjapaltjarri'. The journalist could be forgiven for thinking that the problem of restrictedness started and ended, if not with Kaapa himself, then with the iconoclastic School of Kaapa. This would be ironic, considering that almost every explanation of the uncensored depictions of items from the secret/sacred men's ceremonial sphere relies upon an innocence of the outside world implicitly attached to the *Pintupi* artists, who were the most numerous group among the painting men, and particularly the recent arrivals from the desert known as the New Pintupi (Freddy West Tjakamarra and Anatjari Tjakamarra being cases in point).

If the School of Kaapa had been the main source of problematic disclosures then wouldn't the argument that Dick Kimber ascribes to Kaapa – that it is okay for anyone to see these problematic paintings if they don't know what they're looking at – imply that there isn't any problem? That everything can be shown – not only in America, but even to Kaapa's own wife? Indeed, if Kaapa's argument is taken to its logical conclusion, wouldn't it apply to Aboriginal women and uninitiated men who don't know about these things either? But why have traditions of visual secrecy at all if this was the majority view? Or did the Anmatyerr not have such traditions, or more liberal traditions in this regard than the groups further west – as Clifford Possum Tjapaltjarri twice told me in relation to *Emu Corroboree Man*, during our discussions in 1993 about the work being reproduced in *The Art of Clifford Possum Tjapaltjarri*[17] and later displayed in his 2003 retrospective?[18]

And do the diagrams reproduced alongside some of the black squares in the *Icons* catalogue which explain the paintings' content risk endangering more diligent visitors to the exhibition who try to decipher a painting like *Budgerigar Dreaming* using this information, whereas if Kaapa's argument was followed to the letter, it would be better to reproduce the painting without explanation?[19] Or were these explanations, and the explanations provided generally by the artists to Geoffrey Bardon, too schematic to present any real danger? Or is there danger to anyone apart from senior Indigenous law men viewing the most 'dangerous' of these paintings, as the Pintupi and Pintupi-Luritja men who took part in the Canberra consultancy had said? They took the 'much more conservative' (but also internally consistent) position that they didn't want anyone seeing the paintings with depictions of ceremonial objects because they didn't want people to know they used these things in the ceremonies.

But it is probably pointless and inappropriate to ask for ideological purity in whatever compromise the organisers of *Icons* reached with the community elders with whom Dick Kimber consulted. Like the men and women who 'saw' emus, knowing the painting's title said budgerigars, what was involved here was a solution that everyone could live with in the circumstances, not an ideal modus operandi for the display – or not – of early Papunya boards with 'Restricted' content. That was the unique significance of the Canberra consultation – that for once there was an opportunity for the cultural custodians to say what they would like to happen *in the best of all possible worlds.* The real world, as they know full well, is not that.

The rapture of New York art lovers at the 'cutting edge aesthetics'[20] of the early Papunya boards they saw in auction previews in the late 1990s puts me in mind of Pat Hogan's exclamation on seeing the first consignment of Papunya paintings delivered by Geoffrey Bardon to her Stuart Art Centre in Alice Springs late in 1971: 'They were so beautiful!'.[21] Such a response to something both visually arresting and utterly unfamiliar is perfectly understandable. However, to persist in seeing these paintings simply as aesthetic objects would be wilfully to ignore not only all the ethnography that has gone on in the name of Western Desert art ever since but also their creators' repeated requests for recognition of their significance to them. Such obdurate disinterest would call for a new version of Duchamp's famous riposte: 'I threw the Urinoir in their faces and now they come and admire it for its beauty'. For the [early Papunya boards] are more than beautiful.

While there can be few works of late twentieth century art to which the spirit of Dada is more alien, the conceptual aspect of the appreciation of art to which Duchamp's gesture drew attention applies equally to these paintings. They too were a defiant and brilliant gesture, not in the face of Art History but from the midst of the historical catastrophe of colonisation to which the painters' society had been subjected. Those twenty or thirty men went on to found the Papunya Tula Artists company, the acrylic painting enterprise which a decade later became the first Aboriginal art ever taken seriously as contemporary art by Australian audiences. Admirers of the sheer beauty of the seminal works of this remarkable art movement must come to terms with the sometimes 'inconvenient truth' that they are also key documents in the history of the painters' culture. Notwithstanding the thrill of the new for outsiders to Western Desert society, they retain for members of that society a paramount importance as the first and most detailed coded memorisations of ceremonial acts repeated by their ancestors over countless millennia.

If I had known at the time what I would learn several years later about the origins of the Wilkerson Collection,[22] I would have understood why John Wilkerson asked that this opening paragraph be removed from my essay for the *Icons of the Desert* catalogue. Though bewildered by this response to what I had thought a clever segue from my original title 'They were so beautiful' to the American context in which I imagined the early Papunya boards were about to be displayed, I nevertheless complied and rewrote the beginning of my paper. At the time, I thought I had been troublesome enough to the beleaguered organisers of *Icons of the Desert* without adding insult, however unintentional, to injury. In his speech in February 2009 at the *Icons* opening at Cornell University (which I attended, courtesy of the organisers), John Wilkerson gave an account of the beginning of his and his wife's magnificent obsession with the early Papunya boards that had nothing to do with the shallowness of hyped-up Sotheby's sales previews. There was something tender and real about his story of falling 'madly and wildly in love' with that marvellous painting of Johnny Warangkula's from the Museums and Art Galleries of the Northern Territory collection which my paragraph had indeed rather brutally defiled. I apologise therefore for repeating the offending paragraph here, but it is no longer to the American readership of the *Icons* catalogue, but to the largely Australian readership I anticipate for this work, that it is now addressed.

The Australian's Nicolas Rothwell, in his characteristically effusive review of *Icons*, compared its 'paradigm changing potential, if on a smaller stage'[23] to the 1939 Picasso retrospective. It was not clear whether he was referring to the effect usually attributed to the 1939 show of opening up a market for 20th-century art in America or championing Roger Benjamin's defence of an autonomous modernist perspective on the paintings in his rapturous discovery of a 'new kind of beauty'[24] in the paintings – perhaps both. But I prefer my Duchampian reference point: it is more resonant. The 1995 Gramercy Park International Art Fair where the Wilkersons first met Irene Sutton was renamed the Armory after it became one of the world's largest art fairs and moved to the premises that once housed the 1913 exhibition. As we have seen,[25] their meeting was the spark that ignited the booming auction market in Aboriginal art in Australia and the beginning of the partnership whose fruits were displayed in *Icons*. The 1913 Armory exhibition also coincided with the recognition of Native American art and its resonances with modernism, summed up in Theodore Roosevelt's famous comparison of Duchamp's *Nude Descending a Staircase* with a Navajo rug on his bathroom floor: 'from the standpoint of decorative simplicity, of sincerity, and of artistic merit, the Navajo rug is infinitely ahead of the picture'.[26] It was also Irene Sutton who proposed Roger Benjamin as the ideal curator to achieve the Wilkersons' aim with the *Icons* exhibition of 'migrat[ing the paintings] from ethnography to art'. Although a surprising vision for the Wilkersons to have had given that, like Roosevelt, they were fans of 'folk' rather than 'fine' art, Benjamin's credentials as a modernist art historian[27] and curator specialising in Matisse and Orientalism certainly make sense of his curatorial appointment to facilitate the reception of the early Papunya boards as art rather than as ethnographic curiosities.

One reason for recycling the rejected opening paragraph of my essay for *Icons* here is precisely that from the point of view of the history spelt out in the previous chapters the most impressive thing about *Icons* was the way its organisers *did* come to terms with the 'inconvenient truth' that [the boards] are also key documents in the history of the painters' culture – even at the price of their primary objective. The Wilkersons are of course not the first to have sought the recognition of Aboriginal art as fine art – nor the first to see their project upset by trailing clouds of ethnographic glory. In one of those ironies with which the history of Papunya painting is replete, it was Andrew Crocker, a man whose mission was also to 'migrate [the paintings] from ethnography to art', who ended up sponsoring the first-ever ground painting to be constructed outside Central Australia, thus ensuring that the emerging art audience's appreciation of Papunya Tula art would be grounded in its original inspiration in the ceremonial ground and body painting traditions of the Western Desert peoples.[28] Crocker prepared this succinct declaration of his position and displayed it at exhibitions he organised during his time as

'Secretary/Art Supervisor' of Papunya Tula Artists (1980–81), including the 1981 *Mr Sandman Bring Me a Dream* exhibition in Los Angeles, one of the earliest touring exhibitions of Papunya paintings in the United States:

> Much could be said of the genesis of the Western Desert School and also of its role in the artists' society. I think that for the purposes of this exhibition the paintings should be allowed to exercise their own aesthetic appeal and that explanations of content and symbolism be best kept to a minimum.

Crocker's indifference to the ethnographic probably explains why during my first visit to Papunya in July 1980, Kaapa Tjampitjinpa and Dinny Nolan took me and my then husband Tim Johnson aside and gave us the mission of finding them a venue in Sydney for this ground painting event. The artists had originally been invited to create a ground painting in Canberra for the opening of the new National Gallery of Australia, but the building was still incomplete. The Gallery's then Director James Mollison had reservations about what the Papunya painters were doing, and the invitation had apparently been withdrawn, but the artists were still keen to do it. In September 1980, we received a telegram from Papunya which I still have somewhere, a reminder of what was expected of us. It said simply: 'Sand painting materials take one month to collect. Love Papunya'.

In the end, and not without some difficulty, we secured a scenic venue on Observatory Hill alongside the National Trust's SH Erwin Gallery during the 1981 Festival of Sydney. Paddy Carroll Tjungurrayi and Dinny Nolan, the two senior men chosen by their fellow countrymen to perform this historic task, approved the red ochre colour of the sand brought in from Matraville in Sydney's eastern suburbs on which to construct the ground painting. They spread out a large circle of the sand on the emerald green lawns behind the Gallery and set to work hardening it with a mixture of sugar and water. Then, in wooden carrying vessels brought with them for the purpose, they dyed the plant down with white pipe clay and a darker red ochre. Then they began. Dinny, who is renowned for his singing voice, deep and rich, sang softly, while Paddy placed the first ball of red down in the centre of the hardened circle of sand, then surrounded it with a ring of white, then one of red, then white. Dinny soon joined him in this activity and both sang as they worked steadily, each ball of down carefully formed between their fingers then stuck down with the sugar mix applied with a paintbrush. I remember thinking there was no mystery about where the dots, which were at that time the hallmark of desert painting, came from: the connection was palpable. By the end of the first day a nest of concentric circles about a metre and a half in diameter was completed. It was a Women's Dreaming, Paddy volunteered. I wondered why they had chosen this but never got an opportunity to ask them because I had to go to hospital to give birth to my first child – a daughter. Before this though, I returned with them the next morning to find a dozen small ant hills pushing up through the dyed down.

The first sand paintings to be constructed in America were the ones Michael Jagamara Nelson and Billy Stockman Tjapaltjarri created for the opening of the *Dreamings: Art of Aboriginal Australia* exhibition at the Asia Society Galleries in New York City in 1988. In what Michael described as a 'big showground building next to the exhibition',[29] each of the men produced a mosaic on the supplied Brooklyn sand. They had brought the materials for the ground painting with them in their suitcases – and little else.[30] Theirs was self-consciously a performance. Painted up on their chests and faces, the men sang for the cameras of the *MacNeil/Lehrer NewsHour* and hundreds of New Yorkers, including a 'big mob' of African American 'brothers' whose interest particularly pleased them: 'They was asking us questions. "That's our way. That's how we dress up for traditional corroboree."' At the end of the performance the men complied with the US organisers' request and performed a dance on the ground paintings to destroy them, much to the amusement of Chris Anderson, then Curator of Anthropology at the South Australian Museum and one of the organisers of *Dreamings*:

> they were really doing acrylic art although in different materials on the ground. It wasn't a ceremony ... They knew exactly what they were doing. It was traditional and it was not traditional. And people were crying – it was such an incredible experience for them, this fantastic thing. And Michael and Bill were just playing it to the hilt.[31]

As Michael Nelson explained their actions to John Kean, who accompanied the men on the US trip, to them the dance was not merely performance art. It was the Snake dance for one of the Dreamings depicted in Michael Nelson's acrylic painting *Five Stories* 1984, which was featured in the *Dreamings* exhibition next door. Asked why they had chosen this dance, Michael Nelson replied: 'Because it's an easy one, you know ... We picked that Snake Dreaming because everyone can look at it. Even in Central Australia the video team comes and they can see it. It's clear.'[32] The ground painting was 'real' enough to have attracted criticism from the 'old people' for having taken it overseas:

> No, it's a real one, this one. We even got a little bit of argument from them old people here for doing it. 'You shouldn't take it overseas. Only in Australia, that's all.' But that was a couple of years back eh? Back then at Yuendumu, specially from my elders – uncles and everything like this, 'You shouldn't do this'. I say 'It's all right, show another world what we do here.' I'm just getting this from Yuendumu, Mt Allan, Mt Liebig, that's all. But nothing – it's okay now, Yuendumu mob go to Paris – even Lajamanu.[33]

As with the strategies discussed earlier for deflecting attention from the seriousness of things disclosed in the early Papunya boards by not 'seeing' them, the philosophical concept of performative contradiction, or some Western Desert variant summed up in Anderson's 'traditional and not traditional', hovers over these ground painting events also.

The idea that there would be a ground painting at the Johnson Museum for the grand opening and first stage of the *Icons* tour was not originally part of the concept of the exhibition. According to *Icons*' Australian project manager Sarah Tutton, who was brought on board to organise the exhibition team's trip in July 2007 to the communities of Kintore and Kiwirrkura serviced by Papunya Tula Artists, it was she who suggested the idea of a ground painting as a way of involving the contemporary group of artists in the exhibition. She was also responsible for the travel arrangements of participating artists Bobby West Tjupurrula, Joseph Jurra Tjapaltjarri and Ray James Tjangala and the rest of the Papunya Tula entourage to Ithaca.

After the obligatory morning's shopping in New York City and a four-hour bus ride through the snow fields of upstate New York which impressed on all our minds the remoteness of the exhibition's location, the men were ready for work the next morning. The buckets of plant down collected outside

Kiwirrkura and shipped Express Post to the Museum were opened and fed into a leaf mulcher to be broken down and then tipped into large bins to be dyed with red 'mortar color' from the local hardware store and white flour. The next day the men started work on the painting itself in a large, deep, square box set in the middle of the first court of the exhibition filled with red sand shipped (I believe) from Central Australia. A first-floor balcony supplied a convenient bird's eye view for the phalanx of photographers, amateur and professional, that soon hovered there. Bobby supervised the proceedings, as he had the construction of the ground painting in the central court of *Papunya Tula: Genesis and Genius.* There the design had mirrored the classical Tingari map or journey design of many concentric circles joined by lines of travel seen in the large 1970s and early 1980s Pintupi paintings hung around the walls of the court. Here the finished ground painting was a simpler design of eleven smaller circles joined by lines of travel forming a border for a larger circle in the centre, to which six of them were also joined. It looked like the sort of classical iconographs found in early Papunya boards, and in this way also mirrored the exhibition space in which it was located.

Joseph carefully drew up the design in the sand with his finger, Bobby overseeing the process to make sure the drawing filled out the space inside the box. As Bobby later explained to the opening night crowd, the painting was a representation of Kiwirrkura itself, where the three men live and where Joseph was born, long before an Aboriginal community was established there. That first time, back at Observatory Hill in 1981, Paddy and Dinny had worked with the plant down straight onto the hardened ground – there was no 'drawing-up' phase. But the design they then produced was simple:

this one more directly echoed the contemporary painting process of most Papunya Tula artists, in which an elaborate drawing-up phase is followed by fast and loose outlining of the design and blocking in of the background. Then the three men followed the contours of the drawing on the sand to map out the design with the dyed plant down and then blocked in the background, applying the down in handfuls, leaving one side unfinished to allow them access to the centre of the box. They worked in absorbed silence, apparently oblivious to the parties of fascinated primary school children who filed in and out of the gallery. Fred Myers brought along a recording of Bobby's father singing the songs for some of his paintings to encourage them to sing, but they declined, preferring not to sing themselves because, they said, the 'old people' weren't there. Bobby West remarked to me over lunch on the first day of this three-day event, that this one was 'for the tourists', although for their audiences, like the audiences of *Dreamings*, the artists were the 'old people' and what they were witnessing was a genuine ritual act. The completed ground painting dominated the exhibition, suffusing it with the ethnographically induced 'aura of meaningfulness'[34] I had feared *Icons*' art historical approach might discourage in its audiences.

I couldn't help wondering what Bobby West and Ray James Tjangala and Joseph Jurra Tjapaltjarri were thinking about the paintings on the walls above where they were working on the ground painting – even about the propriety of me looking at the 'Restricted' works on account of what Bobby and I both knew he had told me on this subject in another context. When I saw the men back in Kiwirrkura a few months later I didn't know if I should raise the subject with them – or even how I could. The closest I got to it was one of the photos from Ithaca I had brought with me to leave at the Papunya Tula art shed for people to look at while they sat around sociably. (My book *Lives of the Papunya Tula Artists* was reduced to a box of whirling papers by people's enthusiasm for photographs of one another – and the 'old people'.) When I took the photos out of my bag I noticed the painting that Bobby had been so concerned about seeing back in 2006 when I opened my database of early Papunya boards and searched on his father's name was showing clearly in the background of one of the shots. All the other paintings visible in the photos I had brought were 'clear' or 'easy ones'. I showed the photographs to Ray James in the art shed at Kiwirrkura one day, making sure he looked at them first, though there were women and children about keen to see. I asked Ray about the photo with the Freddy West in it: 'Is that one okay?' Ray's response was that it would be 'all right'. I pointed silently to the Freddy West painting in the photograph. He repeated that it was okay, but then told me I should take my questions to Joseph Jurra Tjapaltjarri who was 'son-in-law' for that painting. Joseph had come in and was standing on the other side of the art shed by himself. I went over and showed him the photo. He told me I should be asking Bobby West about that painting. Neither he nor Ray could speak for it – only the son of the man who painted it. He told me that he and Ray were obliged to be 'blind' to whatever was there in the photo that certain people should not look at. Otherwise they would be giving away information that wasn't theirs to disclose: the fact that there was 'Restricted' content. They weren't permitted to speak of it or even to reveal its presence to others who should not know of such things. Not long after this, Bobby West himself turned up in a cloud of red dust from Kintore. I went over to his house to give him the copyright cheques for his and his father's paintings in *Lives of the Papunya Tula Artists.* He wanted to see the photos of *Icons* and his wife

Lorna Napanangka was eager to see them too, but she was told not to look at that particular one. Bobby confirmed Joseph's account of the appropriate protocol for seeking information about the display of images of his father's painting. I mention this because it might be useful for those who in the future undertake consultation processes for exhibitions planned in the coming years to celebrate the origins of the movement, or to audit the national collections of early Papunya boards for this generation. If you ask the wrong person, you might get the wrong answer, however 'right' it may be for you.

In his opening speech at Ithaca, John Wilkerson described *Icons of the Desert* as the 'embodiment' of a 'tripod' of goals that he and his wife had for their collection: connoisseurship, scholarship and sharing. The goal of connoisseurship had been well served by the appointment of Irene Sutton as his agent at the auctions and Roger Benjamin to select from her purchases the paintings to be included in the exhibition. Everything about the way *Icons* was organised demonstrated the Wilkersons' generosity of spirit. The goal of scholarship signified by the university venues to which the exhibition toured (Cornell University's Herbert F Johnson Museum of Art, University of California Los Angeles' (UCLA) Fowler Museum and New York University's Grey Art Gallery) was amply realised by the catalogue and by an extensive program of lectures, floor talks, film screenings and symposia of 'experts' at the various venues, which gave audiences a rich context of history, ethnography and aesthetics from which to appreciate the boards' significance. At the UCLA showing, a companion exhibition of paintings from the Kelton

Foundation Collection, *Innovations in Western Desert Painting 1972–1999*, contextualised the works in *Icons* in the rest of Papunya Tula's history and in New York Papunya Tula Artists mounted *Nganana Tjungurringanyi Tjukurrpa Nintintjakitja – We Are Here Sharing Our Dreaming*, a very successful selling exhibition of its artists' current work to coincide with the Grey Art Gallery opening.

The New York showing of *Icons* at New York University's Grey Art Gallery included a 'secluded lower floor' where the nine paintings identified as 'dangerous' by Dick Kimber's informants were hung. A warning sign was incorporated into the introductory signage and also placed at the entrance to the Lower Level Gallery:

> Please Note: Following consultation with the descendants of the artists represented in *Icons of the Desert*, works with restricted imagery are exhibited only in the Lower Level Gallery. Many Aboriginal communities consider these paintings' religious iconography inappropriate for viewing by Indigenous Australian women and children.

The idea was Professor Fred Myers', motivated partly by his concerns that the two women painters from Kiwirrkura featured in *Nganana Tjungurringanyi Tjukurrpa Nintintjakitja* who had travelled to New York with the Papunya Tula staff would not have to encounter the restricted works. He reported that they were 'very relieved to know that the paintings they should not see were out of sight, which meant they could be upstairs without worrying'.[35] So was Hetti Perkins, who was also present for the opening at the Grey with her young daughter. Myers acknowledged in private correspondence that such warnings could 'always raise more questions and fetishize the "dangerous"' but that it had also 'made people think'. Unfortunately some, like the *Wall Street Journal* correspondent for whom 'the asymmetries between the sexes, the guarding of male power with secrecy, the tribally enforced segregation and the like' connoted 'looking back at our species in a more primitive state',[36] were, in Myers' words, 'inclined to be confused'.[37]

The idea of this kind of limited removal of 'Restricted' works was tried out in the inaugural exhibition at the Yiribana Gallery within the Art Gallery of New South Wales in 1994. Two early Papunya boards from the long unseen Papunya Permanent Collection[38] housed at the Australian Museum were placed on display in this 'Special Viewing Room'. Responding to critics who pointed out that the paintings selected contained no obvious secret/sacred imagery, co-curator Margo Neale concluded her catalogue essay with the following statement:

> It is an attempt to address the issue of the proper display of significant objects that are not totally restricted and need not be relegated permanently to the storerooms of institutions. It thereby makes an important point about the place of consultation with the communities from which these objects came. This display publicly recognises the continuing significance of these objects to Aboriginal and Torres Strait Islander communities and is a declaration of a partnership role in which communities retain ownership rights whilst the Gallery performs a guardianship role.[39]

There is also a precedent of kinds for a 'special place for restricted viewing of objects' in *Etant donnés*: 1. *La Chute D'Eau*, 2. *Le Gaz d'Eclairage*,[40] Duchamp's last major work, executed in utter secrecy in New York over the final twenty years of his life, which can be seen by only one viewer at a time through two small holes in an old Spanish door: enigmatic, unreproducible and only exposed to the world after his death.

In addition to Professor Fred Myers' exhaustive canvassing of the issues in his keynote address 'Showing Too Much or Too Little: Predicaments of Painting Indigenous Presence in Central Australia' at the Grey symposium, the Fowler organised a special session for the Friends of the Fowler on 'Exhibiting the Sacred' at which I was invited to speak. Considering the traffic jam occasioned by President Barack Obama's concurrent fundraising dinner for the Democratic National Committee at the Beverly Hills Hilton, it was surprisingly well attended. The session was billed as a 'public conversation' between myself and art historian Dr Zena Pearlstone, whose exhibition *Katsina/Kachina: Tradition, Appropriation, Innovation* at the Fowler in 2003 had featured an empty glass case labelled 'Sacred Spirits: Not on Display' as its centrepiece, wordlessly addressing the issue now again at hand. Dr Pearlstone recounted the shifting history of indigenous recalls and museological responses to the exposure of Native American ceremonial objects, illuminating by contrast and comparison my contributions on the history of the early boards' exposure.

In the early 1970s, she had encountered no prohibitions to her dissertation research on Iroquois masks, including photographing them. Over the same period in Australia, Wandjuk Marika's campaign for the removal of sacred objects and paintings from museums and art galleries[41] was heard and heeded. Meanwhile in Papunya the founding fathers of the desert art movement were creating the boards, with no idea that they might ever end up in such places. In those days Johnny Warangkula's *Water Dreaming at Kalipinypa* cost its original purchaser $150 and Aboriginal art generally was marketed as modestly priced 'tribal art'. A quarter of a century later, in 1995, the Grand Council of Haudenosaunee, the Six Nations Iroquois Confederacy, prohibited public display of the masks, asserting that exhibiting Iroquois masks in violation of their intended purpose was a desecration of sacred images and did not serve to enlighten the public regarding Haudenosaunee culture. The Grand Council's edict coincided with the moment Sotheby's commenced its campaign to market the early Papunya boards, resulting in the five- and six-figure price tags which make their purchasers understandably loathe to 'lock away' their treasures. The value-adding publicity that has attended the *Icons* tour for the past year will surely increase that pressure, but at least the precedent that it must be done with the negotiated consent of the painters' descendants and heirs in the Dreaming has been set.

The final question of the night was from a woman distressed at being unable to obtain from the Fowler bookshop a copy of the *Icons* catalogue with its special US-only supplement containing the restricted images: 'Which are the ones we're not supposed to look at?' she wanted to know. Clearly the painters' society is no longer naive about the 'outside world' in the way it was when the early Papunya boards were created. But perhaps it will never be 'sophisticated' enough to comprehend the western art world's fascination with the breaking of taboos – their own if any are still available, but if need be someone else's.

There was no Grand Council of the Western Desert Nations to speak for the painters, their descendants and communities on the display and reproduction of the early boards when the issue resurfaced in Australia via the convoluted paths traced in this story. But in May 2009 Alison Anderson, the Labor member for MacDonnell in the NT Legislative Assembly, at whose community of Papunya the boards were painted, lashed out at people who exploit sensitive aspects of Aboriginal culture as 'culture vultures':

> Soon we'll just become people without identity and people without law and culture, because everybody else knows about our law and culture. The laws we hold must be followed but kept secret. To those who want to unravel that mystery, that secretness, just for your own gain, I say – leave it alone.[42]

At that time Alison Anderson was the most senior Aboriginal politician in the Northern Territory, and as the Minister for Indigenous Policy, Environment and Heritage, Arts and Museums in the Northern Territory government had the power to translate her words into action. According to *The Australian*'s report, she was 'Responding to growing disquiet in Central Australia, where senior artists from her home community Papunya are angry that secret cultural material contained in paintings is being exhibited internationally'.[43]

The reference was not, it transpired, to *Icons*, but to a proposal put forward in July 2008 by the NT government as part of its re-election platform: that it would fund the conservation, consultation and research needed to stage an international touring exhibition of the Museums and Art Galleries of the Northern Territory's Papunya boards collection. A pre-election media release in May 2008 that read like something dreamed up in the wake of the April Fools' Day break-in, even mapped out an itinerary starting in Alice Springs and ending in Darwin after 'travelling internationally'.[44] In September 2008, after the NT Labor government had been re-elected with the narrowest of margins, Marion Scrymgour, another key Indigenous politician representing the Top End electorate of Arafura, and Minister for Museums and the Arts[45] at the time, had announced funding of $300 000 to enable the Museum to undertake a program of extensive research, documentation and consultation with the artists' families in preparation for a touring exhibition and publication in 2012.

The planned international tour, vowed Anderson, would not go ahead. Accordingly, the announcement just four days later that she *had* given her Ministerial approval to an exhibition of the Museum's collection of Papunya boards in the Northern Territory received wide press coverage. Her concern had reportedly been only that the works must be seen first 'in the country of their birth'.[46] It was also reported that the Minister had ordered a consultation process to 'ensure that paintings deemed too sensitive are not exhibited':

> A government agency will bring senior traditional desert men to Darwin to inspect the works in the next few weeks. They will include Ms Anderson's grandfather Long Jack Phillipus, 77, who is considered one of the grandmasters of the movement.[47]

I had been wondering when I was in Ithaca what Long Jack might have thought about the *Icons* exhibition, particularly as it included one of his *Medicine Story* paintings from the second consignment, cleared for public display and reproduction in the main catalogue by Dick Kimber's community consultation process. I thought about asking him next time I was in Papunya, although by the time I was I had thought better of it, not wanting to arouse his anger by bringing up an exhibition of the early boards – which were after all painted in Papunya – to which no-one from Papunya had been invited. The one-day symposium at the Herbert Johnson Museum was called 'Papunya: Then and Now', although for all that was said – or rather *not* said – on the day it was as if Papunya no longer existed.

Alison Anderson predicted that when the paintings that were too sensitive to be put on display had been identified, the others would form a sensational exhibition that would draw the world's art lovers to the Territory to see it.[48] She would not elaborate on the stories of the paintings nor explain why they were sensitive: 'The men have to do that. Whatever is sacred in those boards needs to be maintained and kept sacred [and] handed down generation to generation'.[49] It sounded like a line out of John Kean's shelved report on the Reference Group's Canberra consultation and I inwardly rejoiced. But suddenly the early boards issue was eclipsed by Anderson's spectacular resignation from the Ministry and the Labor Party over the lack of progress on Indigenous housing, leaving the NT government hanging by a thread. A year later, the conservation and documentation work on the boards is presumably progressing behind the closed doors of the Museums and Art Galleries of the Northern Territory. Whether or not a show is now planned, no-one seems to know. This is not something I lament, although I would one day love to know what they find on the backs of those boards. What remains for me to say has already been said much better by Ludwig Wittgenstein in his 1921 *Tractatus Logico-Philosophicus*, Proposition 7:

> Whereof one cannot speak,
> one must pass over in silence.

Epilogue

Other books that I have published, I wrote because there seemed a need external to myself for them to exist. This book is different, in that the need was also mine. Having written it, I can say that I needed to, though I took so long about it that my publishers weren't the only ones who asked: 'Do you really want to write this book?' I do feel a sense of relief in having put the whole story down, though I also have misgivings about meddling in things that are none of my 'business'. But the 'people out there' whom I asked whether I should write it, told me that I should, that it might help *them* if people knew more about the recent history of the early Papunya boards. I hope so, and that is why I am publishing it, rather than putting it away in a cupboard with a couple of other manuscripts and a 1981 canvas by John Tjakamarra which just vibrates before your eyes. When he saw it in a photograph, Wenten Rubuntja told me: 'That's a real one. You should put that one away in a cupboard.'

Perhaps the enigma, but also the greatness, of the early Papunya boards lies – to borrow a line from the Mabo judgment – in their having been painted 'as against the entire world'. Not even Geoffrey Bardon wanted the artists to paint the 'powerful' stories. But they must have believed in what they were doing, because they did it anyway. This wonderful tale, told to me by Fred Friis, Bardon's supportive Head

Teacher at Papunya Special School in 1971, exemplifies in its own gently humorous way these same human and artistic qualities.

The raking story

The superintendent used to fly the British flag. One of the men's duties was to rake the quadrangle outside his house where the flagpole was with big iron rakes. If someone crossed it, it was their job to rake it again. He was always yelling at the men: Why didn't the same men come each day? Why didn't they rake it in straight lines? One day, the nephews of the previous head teacher climbed the water tower (which wasn't allowed) and understood why – though they didn't understand the significance until much later. It was a traditional sand painting. The men sang under their breath as they raked – the songs of the designs they were raking out in the sand. Nosepeg used to sit on the fence giving instructions, correcting them, as befitted his senior ceremonial position.

Notes

Abbreviations

AAB	Aboriginal Arts Board
AGNSW	Art Gallery of New South Wales
AGSA	Art Gallery of South Australia
AGWA	Art Gallery of Western Australia
MAGNT	Museums and Art Galleries of the Northern Territory
NGA	National Gallery of Australia
NGV	National Gallery of Victoria
NIAAA	National Indigenous Arts Advocacy Association
NMA	National Museum of Australia
QAG	Queensland Art Gallery
RMIT	Royal Melbourne Institute of Technology

Introduction

1 Annotation of paintings by Mick Wallankarri Tjakamarra, from the records of Papunya Tula Artists.
2 Vivien Johnson, *Lives of the Papunya Tula Artists*, IAD Press, Alice Springs, NT, 2008.
3 Geoffrey Bardon, *Papunya Tula: Art of the Western Desert*, McPhee Gribble, Melbourne, 1991, p. 108.

1 School of Kaapa

1 See Geoffrey Bardon, *Papunya Tula: Art of the Western Desert*, McPhee Gribble, Melbourne, 1991, pp. 36–39.
2 A rustler.
3 Arnold Probin, interview with author, Alice Springs, 2002 and John Kean, personal communication, 2005. Aboriginal adults gained the right to drink alcohol in 1964 in the Northern Territory.
4 Peter Fannin, interview with author, Uluru, NT, 2004.
5 Jack Cooke, interview with author, Adelaide, April 2002.
6 She went on to add the name of co-winner Jan Wesley-Smith for her

work *Rain! Emerge Now Australia and Grow.*

7 Jack Cooke, personal communication, March 2002.

8 The Araluen Trust preceded the establishment of the Araluen Arts Centre, which opened in 1984. The art collection it would eventually house was displayed in various locations around Alice Springs.

9 *Centralian Advocate*, 30 August 1971, p. 3.

10 Caddy's actions provided the Papunya painters with much-needed outside encouragement for their enterprise. She not only purchased one of Kaapa's paintings in Alice Springs. She came out to Papunya and was shown the Papunya Special School murals, the school art collection and Geoffrey Bardon's art room by principal Fred Friis, further exciting the men's interest in painting.

11 'Kaapa Tjampitjinpa was painting before I arrived at Papunya. He used scrap wood, fibro cement sheets and school slates, and had been dismissed as school yardman for allegedly stealing brushes' (Bardon, *Papunya Tula*, p. 108). Fred Friis suggested that it might have been Ron Gallagher, his predecessor as Papunya Special School Principal, who relieved Kaapa of his position, though he doubted that the disappearance of paintbrushes was the main reason. Kaapa had a reputation as an 'unenthusiastic' worker.

12 J Maughan & J Zimmer (eds), *Dot and Circle: A Retrospective Survey of the Aboriginal Acrylic Paintings of Central Australia*, Communication Services Unit, RMIT, 1986.

13 Geoffrey Bardon, *Aboriginal Art of the Western Desert*, Rigby, Adelaide, 1979, p. 13–16.

14 Pat Hogan, 'Notes and Inventory for the Early Consignments of Pintupi Paintings', in Maughan & Zimmer (eds), *Dot and Circle*, p. 55.

15 'I took the first group of fifty paintings sold in September 1971 to Alice Springs' (Geoffrey Bardon & James Bardon, *Papunya: A Place Made After the Story*, Miegunyah Press, Melbourne, 2004, p. 37).

16 RG (Dick) Kimber, 'Papunya Tula Art: Some Recollections August 1971 – October 1972', in Maughan & Zimmer (eds), *Dot and Circle*, p. 44.

17 ibid., p. 59.

18 Dick Kimber, personal correspondence with author, 27 February 2002.

19 Dick Kimber, personal communication, May 2002.

20 As we shall see in chapter 2, Pat Hogan's delivery date of July 1971 for the first consignment of paintings to the Stuart Art Centre is also mistaken.

21 Dick Kimber, personal communication, May 2002.

22 See chapter 5, p. 158ff

23 The new title seems to be a new error: Mikanji is a major Water Dreaming site north-west of Yuendumu which Kaapa often depicted in his paintings. The Napperby Lakes district to which the mythological snakes depicted in the painting are considered to belong (see Roger Benjamin & Andrew C Weislogel (eds), *Icons of*

the Desert: Early Aboriginal Paintings from Papunya, Herbert F Johnson Museum of Art, Cornell University, Ithaca, NY, 2009, p. 84) is south-east of Yuendumu.

24 ibid.

25 ibid.

26 Bardon & Bardon, *Papunya*, p. 85.

27 Clifford Possum Tjapaltjarri, Tim Leura Tjapaltjarri, Billy Stockman Tjapaltjarri and Long Jack Phillipus Tjakamarra (among others) also produced paintings in the School of Kaapa style.

28 In recent years the only works in this style that have come to light through the auction process are Kaapa Tjampitjinpa's Untitled 1971, purchased by the QAG; Clifford Possum Tjapaltjarri's *Untitled (Ceremony)* 1971, Sotheby's Aboriginal Art auction, 2004; and a work attributed to Clifford Possum Tjapaltjarri in the 2009 Mossgreen Early Aboriginal and Oceanic Art auction.

29 For example, *Warlugulong* 1976 by Tim Leura Tjapaltjarri and Clifford Possum Tjapaltjarri whose execution was the subject of the 1976 BBC documentary *Desert Dreamers* and *Warlugulong* 1977 by Clifford Possum Tjapaltjarri, which in 2007 sold to the NGA at Sotheby's Aboriginal Art auction for $2.4 million – the highest price ever paid for an Indigenous work of art.

30 Kaapa Tjampitjinpa, interview with John Kean, Papunya, NT, 1987.

31 Paul Hasluck, *Shades of Darkness: Aboriginal Affairs 1925–1965*, Melbourne University Press , 1988, p. 58.

32 F Myers, 'Truth, Beauty and Pintupi Painting', *Visual Anthropology*, vol. 2, 1989, p. 166.

33 Dick Kimber, 'Recollections of Papunya Tula 1971–1980' in Hetti Perkins & Hannah Fink (eds), *Papunya Tula: Genesis and Genius*, AGNSW, Sydney, 2000, p. 210.

34 Laura Ulcoq, personal communication, 2002.

35 The implication of 'they decided to return to their old style of painting', that the School of Kaapa dates from even earlier, lacks supporting evidence, but is noted.

36 Clifford Possum, interview with author, 1992.

37 ibid.

38 Central Australian Aboriginal Media Association.

39 Helene Burns, daughter of Pastor Albrecht, who knew the family well. Interview with author, Adelaide, 1992.

40 'Kaapa Tjampitjinpa had established a mastery of brush method before I came into contact with him' (Bardon, *Aboriginal Art of the Western Desert*, p. 68).

41 Jeremy Long, interview with author, November 2000.

42 Roy Monks, from the Centre for Aboriginal Artists and Craftsmen in Alice Springs, also known among the artists as 'the government gallery' since it was set up and run by the federal government to prevent exploitation of Aboriginal artists, 'A Report on a Trip to Papunya Settlement in March 1975', Graeme Marshall Papers, Adelaide.

43 Kaapa Tjampitjinpa, interview with John Kean, Papunya, 1987.
44 Bardon & Bardon, *Papunya*, p. 82.
45 Bardon, *Papunya Tula*, p. 28.
46 Jack Cooke, personal communication, March 2002.
47 ibid. A 'cleat' is a small wedge-shaped piece of wood; a 'brad' is a small wire nail.
48 Bardon, *Papunya Tula*, p. 22.
49 Iris Harvey, personal communication, March 2002.
50 Bardon, *Aboriginal Art of the Western Desert*, p. 14.
51 Geoffrey Bardon, personal communication, 2001.
52 Jo Caddy's purchase *Goanna Corroboree at Mirkantji* was quietly resold at Lawsons Aboriginal Art auction in Sydney in September 1994 as Lot No. 154. According to the provenance cited in Lawson's sales catalogue, it had been No. 35 in the same exhibition from which the Town Council had purchased the remarkably similar *Corroboree at Waru*. It is now in the collection of the NMA.
53 D Mellor & JVS Megaw, *Twenty-Five Years and Beyond: Papunya Tula Painting*, Flinders University Art Museum, Adelaide, 1999, p. 24.
54 Bardon, *Papunya Tula*, p. 23. Although there is a Kaapa work in the School of Kaapa style in the QAG in which the circles have been drawn in first in pencil – with a compass! The point mark is clearly visible.
55 Hogan's consignment lists from 1971 use yet another superseded spelling: 'Jambatjimba'.
56 All of these paintings have been reproduced elsewhere, including: *Gulgardi* and *Corroboree at Waru* in Bardon & Bardon, *Papunya*, p. 135; *Mikanji* in *Dot and Circle*, p. 58 and *Icons of the Desert*, supplement, p. 3; AGSA works in Vivien Johnson, *Dreamings of the Desert*, AGSA, Adelaide, 1996, p. 19; *Goanna Corroboree at Mirkantji* in P Corbally-Stourton, *Songlines and Dreamings: Contemporary Australian Aboriginal Painting*, Lund Humphries, London, 1996, p. 87 and Sotheby's *Aboriginal Art* catalogue, October 2008, Lot 95, p. 101.
57 Bardon, *Papunya Tula*, 1991, p. 21.
58 Bardon, *Aboriginal Art of the Western Desert*, p. 14.
59 Bardon, *Papunya Tula*, p. 21.
60 See chapter 4, pp. 105–6.
61 Bardon, *Aboriginal Art of the Western Desert*, p. 68.
62 Kaapa Tjampitjinpa, interview with John Kean, 1987.
63 'Nothing wrong with this?' 'No, no. That's all right. That's easy one.' RG Kimber, interview with author, 1992, cited in Vivien Johnson, *The Art of Clifford Possum Tjapaltjarri*, Craftsman House/G+B Arts International, Sydney, 1994, p. 38.
64 Sotheby's *Aboriginal Art*, auction catalogue, 2001, Melbourne, Lot No. 87, p. 986.
65 Bardon, *Aboriginal Art of the Western Desert*, p. 20.
66 Bardon & Bardon, *Papunya*, p. 384. Strangely, in light of his earlier accounts of meeting Clifford Possum in February, Bardon dates this

work (and Clifford Possum's copy of it) to June–July 1972.

67 Bardon & Bardon, *Papunya*, p. 385.

68 ibid.

69 See Vivien Johnson, *Papunya Painting: Out of the Desert 1971–1981*, exhibition catalogue, NMA Press, Canberra, 2007.

70 Clifford Possum, interview with John Kean, cited in Johnson, *The Art of Clifford Possum Tjapaltjarri*, p. 31.

2 'So Beautiful'

1 J Maughan & J Zimmer (eds), *Dot and Circle: A Retrospective Survey of the Aboriginal Acrylic Paintings of Central Australia*, Communication Services Unit, RMIT, 1986, p. 55.

2 ibid.

3 Geoffrey Bardon & James Bardon, *Papunya: A Place Made After the Story*, Miegunyah Press, Melbourne, 2004, p. 37.

4 Laurie Owens, interview with author, Canberra, 2002.

5 Geoffrey Bardon, personal communication, 2001.

6 Geoffrey Bardon, *Aboriginal Art of the Western Desert*, Rigby, Adelaide, 1979, p. 16.

7 The organisation to which Bardon refers (for example in Geoffrey Bardon, *Papunya Tula: Art of the Western Desert*, McPhee Gribble, Melbourne, 1991, p. 96) as the Papunya Artists Co-operative was the forerunner of Papunya Tula Artists. Given the letterhead, its name was presumably the Papunya Art and Craft Council.

8 Bardon, *Papunya Tula*, p. 36. However, see Hetti Perkins & Hannah Fink (eds), *Papunya Tula: Genesis and Genius*, AGNSW, Sydney, 2000, p. 305, which says September; as do D Mellor & JVS Megaw, *Twenty-Five Years and Beyond: Papunya Tula Painting*, Flinders University Art Museum, Adelaide, 1999, p. 20.

9 Perkins & Fink (eds), *Papunya Tula: Genesis & Genius*, p. 305.

10 Bardon, *Papunya Tula*, p. 44.

11 Maughan & Zimmer (eds), *Dot and Circle*, p. 55–57.

12 Stuart Art Centre Archive.

13 Most recently in Roger Benjamin & Andrew C Weislogel (eds), *Icons of the Desert: Early Aboriginal Paintings from Papunya*, Herbert F Johnson Museum of Art, Cornell University, Ithaca, NY, 2009, p. 31, where Roger Benjamin cites 'the introduction of dotting … [to] creat[e] a busy visual environment that distracts from the major objects and players' as an act of self-censorship on the part of School of Kaapa painters (in particular, Tim Leura) designed to '[protect] the public from potentially dangerous images in the early Papunya boards'.

14 This painting and two others from Sotheby's Fine Aboriginal and Contemporary Art auction in June 1996 were the subject of a forgery attempt in 1997. See chapter 5, pp. 153–56.

15 Sotheby's, *Fine Aboriginal and Contemporary Art*, June 1996, Melbourne, p. 11.

16 Long Jack Phillipus, personal communication, Papunya, April 2010. This work was sold at Sotheby's 2002 Aboriginal Art auction as *Water Dreaming* 1971, identified as the first painting of the fourth consignment. The fate of the fourth consignment is discussed in chapter 3.

17 See chapter 5, p. 158ff, for the story of how John and Barbara Wilkerson assembled their renowned collection of early Papunya boards.

18 The NGV's generic 'synthetic polymer paint' at least covers the possibility that it is house paint.

19 Determined by the notation 'Darwin' or 'D' alongside the entry for the painting.

20 Pat Hogan, 'Notes and Inventory for the Early Consignments of Pintupi Paintings', in Maughan & Zimmer (eds), *Dot and Circle*, p. 55.

21 Sotheby's, *Important Aboriginal Art*, Melbourne, 1997, p. 111.

22 Thankfully, the frames are being removed as the paintings finally undergo extensive conservation work (see chapter 8, p. 294), but though the process has been underway for over at year at the time of writing, as yet no information has been made available about what has been disclosed.

23 The often lengthy delays between the making of an institutional purchase and its formal registration as part of the collection could place this acquisition date anything up to six months after the actual date of purchase, so this date is not terribly helpful in determining the arrival dates of the first three consignments at the Stuart Art Centre.

24 The one extra Walter Tjampitjinpa and one extra Long Jack Phillipus may be explained by the fact that one of those four red, black and white enamel Walter Tjampitjinpas and one of the two by Long Jack Phillipus came with 'no data'.

25 There are another half-a-dozen works without annotations in the Darwin 105, mostly by these same artists, in various combinations of red, white, black and yellow enamel paint. In one or two, the artist has used a pink, probably mixed from white and red. Two others have beige backgrounds. Almost all share the same features of simple, uncontentious designs and dotted backgrounds. So the basic palette for these very early works is really red, white, black and yellow.

26 Bardon said almost the opposite in his 1991 account (see Bardon, *Papunya Tula*, p. 28) of the beginnings of the painting movement: 'The most independent men in the community, possibly those who had the most contacts with European lifestyles, were the very last to join the group'. But he was thinking of the Anmatyerr stockmen (like Kaapa Tjampitjinpa and Clifford Possum Tjapaltjarri) who were members of the School of Kaapa, and Johnny Lynch, David

Corby and Charlie Egalie who also had backgrounds in the pastoral industry – though he surmised that Shorty Lungkata Tjungurrayi's reticence derived from other causes connected to his 'special eminence' in the Pintupi group. It is true that, with the exception of Kaapa, these men were for a long time only peripherally involved with Bardon's painting group.

27 Pastor Albrecht, in D Leske (ed.), *Hermannsburg: A Vision and a Mission*, Lutheran Publishing, Adelaide, p. 49.

28 ibid., pp. 53ff.

29 Paintings from the Darwin MAGNT: WAL 22 (LJP); WAL 31, 32, 33 (JW); WAL 44 (OM); WAL 44, 53, 57 (OW).

30 Nowadays 'Luritja', a term originally coined by the local Arrente at Hermannsburg to identify non-Arrente speakers.

31 Jeremy Long, interview with author, November 2000.

32 Kaapa Tjampitjinpa, interview with John Kean, Papunya, 1987, recording held at South Australian Museum.

33 Bardon, *Papunya Tula*, p. 22.

34 RG (Dick) Kimber, *Friendly Country – Friendly People: An Exhibition of Aboriginal Artworks from the Peoples of the Tanami and Great Sandy Deserts*, Araluen Arts Centre, Alice Springs, NT, 1990.

35 It was sold at Sotheby's 1998 Important Aboriginal Art auction for $200 500. Clifford Possum Tjapaltjarri's *Emu Corroboree Man* 1972 is currently the record holder.

36 Tim Klingender, personal communication, May 2010.

37 In her list of artists represented in the second consignment in *Dot and Circle*, Pat Hogan refers to Uta Uta as 'Uta Uta Tjangala No. II', adding that 'After the death of his older brother Uta (spelt in 1971 as 'Oata'), Uta is now Tjangala No. I'. While this seems to suggest that the death of the elder Uta Uta had already occurred, this impression is contradicted by subsequent references in the consignment lists to both Uta Uta No. I and Uta Uta No. II. The Stuart Art Centre stocklist for the second consignment lists four works by 'Oata Jungali' with no indication of whether this is No. I or No. II, and not until the eighth consignment does the name 'Uta Uta' appear. Were there two Uta Utas, one of whom subsequently died? There is a painting in the Darwin Museum dated 1976 which was acquired in one of two large purchases from Pat Hogan's private collection in 1978 and 1980. It carries strict instructions that it is not to be displayed to the public, being a 'sorry painting' produced by a group of men on the occasion of the death of Uta Uta's brother. Uta Uta did have a surviving older brother in 1971 who died in 1976, but his name was Minpuru, not 'Oata', and he was at least twenty years older than Uta Uta, according to Jeremy Long. While there is a family resemblance, it is hard to believe anyone could have mistaken them for the same person – or that Bardon would not have mentioned the existence of a second artist by the name of Uta Uta if there had been one. Since there is no genealogical evidence to support the existence of such a person, and

there is nothing to indicate that early works attributed to Uta Uta are the work of two different people, the mystery of Pat Hogan's two Uta Utas must simply stand for now.

38 Although Tim Payungka Tjapangati's name does not appear on Pat Hogan's list in *Dot and Circle* of artists in the second consignment, there are two paintings by 'Timmy Jabanadi' included on the Stuart Art Centre stocklist for this consignment.

39 Painting from the Darwin MAGNT: WAL 75.

40 Bardon, *Aboriginal Art of the Western Desert*, p. 44.

41 Jeremy Long, 'Leaving the Desert: Actors and Sufferers in the Aboriginal Exodus from the Western Desert', *Aboriginal History*, vol. 13, nos 1–2, p. 24.

42 ibid.

43 Hogan, 'Notes and Inventory', p. 55.

44 Bardon, *Papunya Tula*, p. 108.

45 Billy Stockman Tjapaltjarri, *Kangaroo Dreaming*, MAGNT: WAL 79; Long Jack Phillipus Tjakamarra, Untitled and *Corroboree Body Paint*, MAGNT: WAL 27, 28.

46 From the MAGNT: WAL 49, 50.

47 From the MAGNT: WAL 72.

48 From the MAGNT: WAL 81.

49 Australian Institute of Aboriginal Studies.

50 F Myers with J Long, 'In Recognition: The Gift of Pintupi Painting', in Hetti Perkins & Margie West (eds), *One Sun One Moon: Aboriginal Art in Australia*, AGNSW, Sydney, 2007, p. 173ff.

51 Perkins & Fink (eds), *Papunya Tula: Genesis and Genius*, pp. 164–67. Perhaps he was referring to the ground painting Colin Jack-Hinton saw in 1970 (see chapter 4, pp. 119–20).

52 From the MAGNT: WAL 25.

3 The Pintupi Factor

1 See chapter 2, p. 69.

2 D Tjapaltjarri, quoted in N Amadio & RG Kimber, *Wildbird Dreaming*, Greenhouse Publications, Melbourne, 1988, p. 61, as a personal communication to RG Kimber; see also Barbara Henson, *A Straight-Out Man: F.W. Albrecht and Central Australian Aborigines*, Melbourne University Press, 1992.

3 P Latz, *The Flaming Desert: Arid Australia – A Fire Shaped Landscape*, Peter Latz, Alice Springs, NT, 2007, pp. 138–39.

4 Jeremy Long, interview with author, November 2000.

5 See chapter 2, p. 71.

6 Murdoch flew out to Warburton mission in the wake of sensational claims made in the Western Australian Parliament in late 1956 by MLA William Grayden that Aboriginal people in the country around the mission were starving. Murdoch photographed a few of the mission's Aboriginal residents and a pool of water left

over from the recent wet and dismissed the findings of the Select Committee, headed by Mr Grayden, which had conducted the original investigation. In response, Grayden threatened Murdoch with contempt of Parliament charges, ensuring maximum coverage for the issue. Grayden and other supporters of the Select Committee's report further aroused public controversy with a series of meetings at which Pastor Doug Nicholls told audiences that 'instead of bringing out 10 000 Hungarians we should be looking after our own people' (William Grayden, *Adam and Atoms*, F. Daniels, Perth, 1957, p. 110).

7 One was George Tjapanangka ('Yuendumu George'), who later became a well-known artist for Papunya Tula. He was about nineteen years old at the time.

8 Jeremy Long, 'Leaving the Desert: Actors and Sufferers in the Aboriginal Exodus from the Western Desert', *Aboriginal History*, vol. 13, nos 1–2, 1989, p. 28.

9 See chapter 2, p. 72.

10 Jeremy Long, report to the Welfare Branch on October 1957 patrol.

11 Jeremy Long, report to the Welfare Branch on July 1962 patrol.

12 According to Jeremy Long, during his time as Superintendent at Haasts Bluff (1957–59), an old laundry-type copper was used to boil up a midday stew of beef (or goat) and vegetables from the garden at Haasts Bluff, which was doled out to workers on weekdays. Long expanded this service to improve the diet of pregnant and lactating women. Rations of flour (and baking powder), tea and sugar, supplemented with tins of jam, fruit and butter were issued from the ration store each week, collected mainly by the wives and mothers. The other end of the store was occupied by the mission cash store. Jeremy Long, personal communication, May 2010.

13 ibid.

14 Jeremy Long, interview with author, November 2000.

15 Memorandum from District Welfare Officer to Assistant Director (Southern), 13 July 1964, Welfare Branch, File 63/44.

16 Laurie Owens, interview with author, Canberra, 2002.

17 NT Welfare Branch, *1957–58 Annual Report.*

18 Arnold Probin (Papunya Farm Manager, 1960–62; Settlement Manager, 1962–73). Interview with author, Alice Springs, 2002.

19 Minutes, 6th Meeting of Standing Committee on the Central Aboriginal Reserves, Canberra, 4 May 1964. Quoted in Long, 'Leaving the Desert', p. 34.

20 In E Leske (ed.), *Hermannsburg: A Vision and a Mission*, Lutheran Publishing House, Adelaide, 1977, p. 48.

21 Arnold Probin, interview with author, Alice Springs, 2002.

22 This is the only painting by Anatjari Tjakamarra in the Darwin 105 and the only painting by him in the third consignment marked by Pat Hogan as having been sold to 'D' (Darwin).

23 RG (Dick) Kimber, 'Notes on the Peter Fannin Collection of Early Western Desert Paintings', NGA, Canberra, 1998.

24 ibid.
25 Geoffrey Bardon, *Aboriginal Art of the Western Desert*, Rigby, Adelaide, 1979, p. 60.
26 In 1981, the Pintupi left Papunya and established the homelands community of Kintore (Walungurru) 275 kilometres to the west, just inside the Western Australian border. By 1985 they had pushed a further 175 kilometres further west across the border to establish another community at Kiwirrkura.
27 Hogan mysteriously wrote the letter 'P' alongside one of these entries (not the one sold to MAGNT).
28 From the MAGNT: WAL 59.
29 See Vivien Johnson, *Lives of the Papunya Tula Artists*, IAD Press, Alice Springs, NT, 2008, p. 36.
30 Turkey Tolson Tjupurrula, interview with Paul Sweeney, in Hetti Perkins & Hannah Fink (eds), *Papunya Tula: Genesis and Genius*, AGNSW, Sydney, 2000, p. 167.
31 Turkey Tolson Tjupurrula, personal communication, 1989.
32 Sotheby's Aboriginal Art auction 2001, catalogue notes.
33 Including the late Pinta Pinta Tjapanangka, a pioneer Papunya Tula painter who became the grand old man of Kintore painting in the 1990s. See Perkins & Fink (eds), *Papunya Tula: Genesis and Genius*, pp. 134–35.
34 ibid., p. 257.
35 P Hogan, 'Notes and Inventory for the Early Consignments of Pintupi Paintings', in J Maughan & J Zimmer (eds), *Dot and Circle: A Retrospective Survey of the Aboriginal Acrylic Paintings of Central Australia*, Communication Services Unit, RMIT, 1999, p. 55.
36 ibid.
37 There are also ten more paintings by three of the artists included in the Stuart Art Centre stockbook version of the fifth consignment than are accounted for in the *Dot and Circle* version: six Uta Utas, three Walter Tjampitjinpas and one Charlie Tarawa. These too are presumably from the fourth consignment.
38 Marked E29, Stuart Art Centre Archive.
39 Jack Cooke, personal communication, Adelaide, 2002.
40 From the MAGNT: WAL 108.

4 The Problem of Secrecy

1 From the MAGNT: WAL 106–135.
2 *Warlbiri and Pintubi Art* was the first touring exhibition of Papunya paintings. In July 1972 the MAGNT mounted an exhibition of the 105 works that made up Colin Jack-Hinton's original purchase called *Symbolic Sandpaintings and Drawings by Pintupi and Warlbiri Artists from the Papunya Settlement* in a temporary display premises on Smith Street, Darwin. This was the first exhibition of Papunya paintings under the auspices of a public gallery. Also in July 1972, Pat Hogan

organised an exhibition of Papunya paintings which she called *Wailbri and Pintubi Aboriginal Sand Stories* at the Lidums Art Gallery in Adelaide. This was the first exhibition of Papunya paintings through a commercial art gallery.

3 The other four paintings in *Wailbri and Pintubi Art* were from the sixth consignment (three) and the second (one).

4 The catalogue of *Wailbri and Pintubi Art*, copies of which have survived (for example, in the Stuart Art Centre Archive), provides not only a checklist of all the paintings it included by artists' names, but also annotated thumbnail diagrams, often with a short accompanying text explaining their symbolism. From these diagrams it is possible to identify all of the thirty paintings accessioned by the MAGNT in July 1974. Any possible doubt is removed by the Stuart Art Centre labels on the backs of the frames of several of the paintings from the 1974 gift, which somehow survived both the rigours of the tour and the intervening years of neglect.

5 'It took some time for me to realise the differences and problems over twenty-five men had in expressing themselves to one hurrying European with no anthropology.' Geoffrey Bardon & James Bardon, *Papunya: A Place Made After the Story*, Miegunyah Press, Melbourne, 2004, p. 26.

6 ibid., p. 17. See also 'The Children's Stories', p. 474. Bardon inserts this comment under an image of Version 2 of the Honey Ant Mural, though it was Version 1 that the girls were photographed in front of.

7 ibid., p. 17.

8 ibid., p. 23.

9 ibid.

10 See Fred R Myers, *Painting Culture: The Making of an Aboriginal High Art*, Duke University Press, Durham, 2002, pp. 118–19.

11 Bardon & Bardon, *Papunya*, p. 38.

12 ibid., p. 23.

13 ibid., p. 29.

14 ibid.

15 Jennifer Isaacs, 'Epilogue: Encounters with Geoff Bardon', in Bardon & Bardon, *Papunya*, p. 502.

16 ibid.

17 ibid.

18 ibid., p. 503.

19 Bardon has it as May 1972 – see Bardon & Bardon, *Papunya*, p. 37.

20 RG (Dick) Kimber, 'Politics of the Secret in Contemporary Western Desert Art', in Chris Anderson (ed.), 'Politics of the Secret', *Oceania Monograph* 45, University of Sydney, 1995, p. 128.

21 ibid., p. 132.

22 Bardon & Bardon, *Papunya*, p. 38.

23 ibid., pp. 23–24.

24 Kimber, 'Politics of the Secret', p. 132.

25 Isaacs, 'Epilogue', p. 503.

26 Originally suggested to me by the redoubtable Mrs Daphne Williams, Manager of Papunya Tula Artists, 1981–1993 and 1995–2003, in one of our many conversations on this subject.
27 Bardon & Bardon, *Papunya*, p. 24.
28 ibid.
29 ibid.
30 Long Jack Phillipus Tjakamarra, interview with John Kean, Papunya, 1987.
31 Bardon, *Papunya Tula*, p. 42.
32 RG (Dick) Kimber, 'Papunya Tula Art: Some Recollections August 1971 – October 1972', in *Dot and Circle: A Retrospective Survey of the Aboriginal Acrylic Paintings of Central Australia*, Communications Services Unit, RMIT, 1986, p. 44.
33 Laurie Owens, interview with author, Canberra, 2002.
34 ibid.
35 Bardon & Bardon, *Papunya*, p. 39.
36 Bardon, *Papunya Tula*, p. 43. See also Bardon & Bardon, *Papunya*, p. 37ff for a slightly different account of these events.
37 Owens, interview with author, Canberra, 2002. According to both Dick Kimber (in Perkins & Fink (eds), *Papunya Tula: Genesis and Genius*, p. 206) and Jeremy Long (personal communication, 2010), Cooke actively supported the Pintupi's attempts to return to their traditional homelands. Kimber also says that Cooke encouraged Owens to 'maintain his interest' in the paintings after Bardon's departure (ibid.).
38 Fred Friis, interview with author, Palmerston, NT, 2001.
39 ibid.
40 Kenneth Cook, *Wake in Fright*, Text Publishing, 2001, Melbourne, pp. 165–66. First published by Michael Joseph, 1961.
41 The title given to the film for its international release in the 1970s.
42 Bardon & Bardon, *Papunya*, p. 6.
43 Now the College of Fine Arts, University of NSW, where I worked 2005–10.
44 Ellen thought he showed commendable initiative in obtaining the best camera on campus – a Nikon – for his use as a member of the camera club. Ellen Waugh, interview with author, Sydney, 2008.
45 Viktor Lowenfeld, *The Nature of Creative Activity: Experimental and Comparative Studies of Visual and Non-Visual Sources of Drawing, Painting and Sculpture by Means of the Artistic Products of Weak-Sighted and Blind Subjects and of the Art of Different Epochs and Cultures*, Routledge & Kegan Paul, London, 1952.
46 Read lamented that Lowenfeld's evidence related to subjects of an advanced age who had been subjected to a training with a strong visual bias, speculating that 'such subjects, if urged to express themselves in abstract symbols, would have developed a plastic language of a non-representational kind'. H Read, *Education Through Art*, Cheshire, Melbourne, 1964, p. 125.

47 Bardon, *Aboriginal Art of the Western Desert*, pp. 22–23.
48 ibid., p. 22.
49 ibid., p. 23.
50 ibid.
51 Geoffrey Bardon, interview with Ulli Beier, in Ulli Beier & Colin Johnson (eds), *Long Water: Aboriginal Art and Literature*, Aboriginal Artists Agency, Sydney, p. 87.
52 Bardon & Bardon, *Papunya*, p. 37.
53 See p. 111.
54 Bardon & Bardon, *Papunya*, p. 37.
55 Sotheby's, *Important Aboriginal Art*, auction catalogue, 1997, p. 111.
56 ibid.
57 Extracts from the Minutes of the Legislative Council for the Northern Territory, 1965.
58 *Native and Historical Objects and Areas Preservation Ordinance 1955*, p. 1702.
59 Section 7(1). Section 10 of the Ordinance provided that 'A person who contravenes or fails to comply with a provision of this Ordinance ... is guilty of an offence punishable upon conviction by a fine not exceeding One hundred pounds or imprisonment for a period not exceeding three months'.
60 Report of Select Committee on the Native and Historical Objects and Areas Preservation Ordinance 1955–1960, Legislative Council for the Northern Territory, 1965, p. 4.
61 ibid.
62 P Jones, 'Objects of Mystery and Concealment: A History of Tjurunga Collecting', in Chris Anderson (ed.), 'Politics of the Secret', *Oceania Monograph* 45, University of Sydney, 1995, p. 87.
63 One of the key events in the missionaries' campaign was the desecration of the tjurunga storehouse of Manangananga Cave near Hermannsburg in 1928 (the same year as the Coniston Massacre): 'Albrecht [pastor at Hermannsburg mission] saw the symbolic value in breaking the taboo and after consulting his evangelists and other elders, arranged for the entire population of Hermannsburg to hold a Sunday service and picnic at the site. The tjurungas were taken from the cave and placed before the congregation, a fire was made under a large copper brought from the mission, and the people drank tea and sang hymns. The Aboriginal evangelist Blind Moses gave his "Churinga or Christ?" sermon in which he exhorted his people to give up their tjurunga.' (Kimber, 'Politics of the Secret', p. 86) The acquiescence of the 'cowed and battered' Aranda is unsurprising, given that the missions were their refuge from those 'killing times'.
64 ibid., p. 85.
65 See chapter 6, p. 218ff. Perhaps the Protection of Movable Cultural Heritage Act's exclusion of objects 'produced specifically for sale' had its origins in this 'fake' tjurunga trade.
66 P Hasluck, *Shades of Darkness: Aboriginal Affairs 1925–1965*,

Melbourne University Press, 1988, p. 23.
67 ibid., p. 15.
68 ibid., p. 22.
69 CD Rowley's famous trilogy on the impact of European invasion of Aboriginal Australians: *The Destruction of Aboriginal Society*, *Outcasts in White Society* and *The Remote Aborigines*, published by Australian National University Press, c. 1970, was followed in 1986 by *Recovery: The Politics of Aboriginal Reform* (Penguin).
70 Report of Select Committee on the Native and Historical Objects and Areas Preservation Ordinance 1955–1960, Legislative Council for the Northern Territory, August 1965, p. 5.
71 ibid.
72 ibid., p. 8.
73 C Jack-Hinton, 'Export of Aboriginal Artefacts', Museums and Art Galleries of the Northern Territory, Darwin, 1974.
74 Bardon & Bardon, *Papunya*, p. 37.
75 Quoted in T Rowse, *Obliged to be Difficult: Nugget Coombs' Legacy in Indigenous Affairs*, Cambridge University Press, Melbourne, 2000, p. 54.
76 Jeremy Long, interview with the author, Sydney, 2001.
77 *Wailbri and Pintubi Art*, exhibition catalogue, with introductory statement possibly by Colin Jack-Hinton, c. 1972.
78 Kimber, 'Politics of the Secret', pp. 123–42.
79 ibid., p. 126.
80 ibid., p. 128.
81 ibid.
82 ibid., p. 129.
83 ibid.
84 ibid.
85 The artists represented were Kaapa Mbitjana Tjampitjinpa, Bill Stockman Tjapaltjarri, Long Jack Phillipus Tjakamarra, Timmy Tjapaltjarri Madgera, Kingsley Tjungurrayi, Johnny Warangkula Tjupurrula, Mick Wallankarri Tjapaltjarri, Anatjari Tjakamarra, Timmy Payungka Tjapangati, Walter Tjampitjinpa and Uta Uta Tjangala whose language groups included Anmatyerr, Luritja, Warlpiri and Kukatja, as well as Pintupi.
86 Kimber, 'Politics of the Secret', p. 140.
87 ibid., p. 137.
88 ibid., p. 139.
89 ibid., p. 141.
90 ibid., p. 140.
91 ibid., p. 135.
92 See Vivien Johnson, 'How Papunya Paintings Became Art', in *Papunya Painting: Out of the Desert 1971–1981*, NMA Press, Canberra, 2007, pp. 28–46.
93 Minutes of the ninth meeting held at Council Chamber, Shepparton, Victoria, on Saturday 5 October commencing 10 am, 6 October

commencing 10 am and 7 October commencing 10 am.

94 P Fannin, Papunya Tula Artists, letter to R Edwards, 13 October 1974, AAB files, National Archives of Australia.

95 According to Dick Kimber's recollection, the Residency's curator discussed the issues with relevant Aboriginal people, removed paintings considered dangerous from the display, and put up warning signs in several Aboriginal languages (Kimber, 'Politics of the Secret', p. 130).

96 P Fannin, Papunya Tula Artists, letter to R Edwards, 13 October 1974, AAB files, National Archives of Australia.

97 'Upset tribe gets book shelved', *Australian*, 5 March 1977.

98 Bob Edwards to Dick Kimber, 24 September 1974, AAB files, National Archives of Australia.

99 ibid.

100 Not everyone had the same attitude as the Pitjantjatjara law men. In 1975 and 1976 some Western Arrente, Pitjantjatjara and Warlpiri men did attempt some acrylic paintings and though Papunya Tula's Alice Springs outlet purchased some of their work, the company had no resources (and no reliable markets either) to take on additional responsibilities. Kimber ('Politics of the Secret', p. 136) comments that 'the end result was that the original artists of Papunya appeared to control the market. This ... was to exacerbate tensions between Papunya and other communities for a number of years.'

101 Billy Stockman Tjapaltjarri, interview with John Kean, Papunya, 1987.

102 See Jo Caddy's statement, p. 12.

103 The earliest acrylic paintings in the exhibition were two small canvas boards by Clifford Possum Tjapaltjarri from 1976 (see P Sutton (ed.), *Dreamings: The Art of Aboriginal Australia*, Viking, Melbourne, 1988, p. 224). An uncontroversial 1971 circle-and-line door panel by Turkey Tolson Tjupurrula was illustrated on p. 129 of this book.

104 Christopher Anderson & Francoise Dussart, 'Dreamings in Acrylic: Western Desert Art', in Sutton (ed.), *Dreamings*, p. 129.

5 The Midas Touch

1 All prices are in Australian dollars, unless noted otherwise.

2 BBC documentary, *Desert Dreamers*, 1976. The painting was commissioned for the film. The collector was Mrs Margaret Carnegie.

3 Dick Kimber, interview with author, Alice Springs, 1992.

4 Tim Klingender, interview with author, Sydney, 2003. Bleakley was probably correct in his professional judgment. At that time, galleries and museums were the driving forces in Australian art and in 1982 all but the most far-sighted still rejected Papunya Tula paintings as neither high art nor authentic ethnographic artefacts.

5 In this, Sotheby's displayed greater perspicacity than the federal

government's cultural heritage advisers, who were in the process of amending the Protection of Movable Cultural Heritage legislation to shift Aboriginal art out of the category of Aboriginal and Torres Strait Islander heritage objects altogether and into the category of fine and decorative art – exclusively. See chapter 6.

6 *Sydney Morning Herald*, 26 January 1984, p. 2.

7 Most notably Melbourne art dealer Lauraine Diggins, *A Myriad of Dreamings: Twentieth Century Aboriginal Art*, Malakoff Fine Art Press, Melbourne, 1989.

8 Of *Songlines* fame; Bruce Chatwin, *The Songlines*, Jonathan Cape, London, 1987.

9 Sotheby's has continued to use this term, which it claims is a 'universal signifier' in preference to 'Aboriginal and Torres Strait Islander' or 'Indigenous'.

10 At the time, Purcell was Sotheby's Australia's tribal art expert.

11 *Snake Dreaming* 1972, 545.7 x 91.5 cm.

12 *Very Big Water Dreaming* 1972, 64 x 92.6 cm. See Brenda L Croft, *Indigenous Art: Art Gallery of Western Australia*, AGWA, Perth, 2001, p. 32. AGWA also acquired Kaapa Tjampitjinpa's Untitled 1971, 40.5 x 61.1 cm from this auction.

13 Sotheby's November 1993 Fine Tribal Art auction included several early Papunya works, all with scant documentation or provenance and reserves around $5000, alongside hundreds of bark paintings, shields and weapons, usually undated, unattributed and with reserves mostly under $1000.

14 Both painters, who in the early 1990s were living at Haasts Bluff, Marina Strocchi as founding co-ordinator of Ikuntji Arts. Both later worked as Papunya Tula fieldworkers, Eager being one of their longest serving officers.

15 Tim Klingender, interview with author, Sydney, 2003.

16 In fact, it was his second painting for Geoffrey Bardon. See Vivien Johnson, *The Art of Clifford Possum Tjapaltjarri*, Craftsman House/G+B Arts International, Sydney, 1994, p. 154.

17 ibid., pp. 42–46.

18 Until *Warlugulong* 1977 was sold for $2.4 million at the 2007 Sotheby's Important Aboriginal Art auction.

19 In the 1960s and 1970s, the secondary market in contemporary American art began to take off, in tandem with the US government's promotion of post-war American art as equivalent in value with European cultural achievements. The auctioning of fifty artworks belonging to US collector Robert Skull for US$2.2 million demonstrated that contemporary art was a lucrative investment. The sale made headlines when the painter Robert Rauschenberg publicly expressed his anger at how much money (US$175 000) Skull had made from a painting he had purchased from the artist fifteen years previously for US$3400 and demanded to be paid a royalty on resales.

20 Or *Red Hill*, as he called the painting, after the European name of the site of Ngarlu on Mt Allan (Yuelamu) station near Papunya which it depicts.

21 'Top artist asks for auction cut', *Sunday Territorian*, 25 June 1995.

22 Droit de suite is the concept of the artist's entitlement to a percentage of the vendor's profit when a painting is resold, also known as resale royalties.

23 The principle of an artist's entitlement to resale royalties for as long as a work is subject to copyright protection (seventy years after the artist's death) is precisely what has been advocated for European Union member states and is soon to be introduced in Australia.

24 However, the presiding judge in the 1989 T-shirts copyright action *Bulun Bulun and others vs Flash Screenprinters* (unrecorded) understood it well enough to allow the Aboriginal artists rather than the court to distribute among themselves the $140 000 damages agreed to by the company in an out-of-court settlement. Though several artists had more than one of their paintings reproduced on T-shirts without permission and others only one, the money was divided equally among the thirteen plaintiffs, on the grounds that all had suffered equally from the theft of their Dreaming designs. See Vivien Johnson, 'The Case of the Flash T-Shirts', in Vivien Johnson, *Copyrites: Aboriginal Art in the Age of Reproductive Technologies*, NIAAA & Macquarie University, Sydney, 1996, pp. 17–26.

25 Hank Ebes, quoted in 'You're not on, Possum is told', *Centralian Advocate*, 27 June 1995.

26 ibid.

27 'He will go out and buy himself a leather jacket or a good suit for $2000. The same evening he will sleep in the Todd River and next morning it will look like it's ten year's old.' Michael Hollows, 'Possum art: Sotherby's [*sic*] to bottle shop', *Alice Springs News*, 5 July 1995, p. 6.

28 ibid.

29 'Hunt is on for Centre artworks', *Centralian Advocate*, 18 July 1995.

30 Tim Klingender, interview with author, Sydney, 2003.

31 Graeme Marshall was accountant and consultant for Papunya Tula Artists in 1973–74. He remembered the 'flamboyant' Kaapa, the 'timid' Uta Uta, the 'poetic' Johnny Warangkula and the 'shy' Mick Namarari. 'During 1974 demand for large canvases increased dramatically and designs seemed to become more repetitious.' Marshall heard 'some old non-standard boards were for sale and purchased about thirty, including Turkey Tolson's first canvas'. From the archives of the NGV, which purchased several paintings from Marshall for its collection.

32 However, Anatjari Tjakamarra had the first solo exhibition of an Aboriginal artist in New York in 1990 and has a painting in the Contemporary collection of the Metropolitan Museum of Art. He passed away in 1992. See Johnson, *Lives of the Papunya Tula Artists.*

33 Tim Klingender, interview with author, Sydney, 2003.

34 ibid.
35 'Auction record for Aboriginal art', *Australian*, 18 June 1996, p. 3.
36 ibid.
37 Tim Klingender, interview with author, Sydney, 2003.
38 One of Sotheby's Australia's directors.
39 Senior Curator, Indigenous Art, NGV.
40 Melbourne-based Aboriginal art specialist.
41 Tim Klingender, interview with author, Sydney, 2003.
42 'Police check on copied artworks', *Advertiser*, 15 April 1997, p. 5.
43 ibid.
44 Mick Wallankarri Tjakamarra died in 1996. See Johnson, *Lives of the Papunya Tula Artists*, p. 14.
45 More than half of the seventeen paintings in the Tim Guthrie Collection of Early Western Desert Paintings that bore consignment numbers were from the final two consignments to the Stuart Art Centre, and most of these from the nineteenth and final consignment. The earliest consignment represented in the collection is the seventh, followed by the ninth, with just one painting from each. There were two paintings each from the fourteenth and seventeenth consignments.
46 John Wilkerson is President, Board of Trustees, American Folk Art Museum, New York City, NY.
47 The rest were stored on wire racks at the back of the Museum, amidst a jumble of plaster casts of Roman busts and other Museum paraphernalia. I saw them there when I paid a visit to the Museum in 1986.
48 He was speaking at the opening of *Icons of the Desert*, an exhibition of his collection of early Papunya boards in 2009. See chapter 8.
49 Interview with Tim Klingender, in 'Buyers are restless for natives', 'Arts on Friday', *Australian*, 20 June 1997.
50 Interview with Johnny Warangkula Tjupurrula, in 'Master painter will settle for a Toyota', *Weekend Australian*, 5–6 July 1997, p. 5.
51 See David M Bennett, 'Malangi: The Man Who Was Forgotten Before He Was Remembered', *Aboriginal History*, vol. 40, 1980, pp. 43–47.
52 Interview with Johnny Warangkula Tjupurrula, in 'Master painter will settle for a Toyota', *Weekend Australian*, 5–6 July 1997, p. 5.
53 'Artist Johnny has a lucky double-up', *Centralian Advocate*, 18 July 1997, p. 3.
54 'Old Master makes it back from "dead"', *Herald Sun*, 27 April 1998.
55 'US interest high in Aboriginal art sale', *Sydney Morning Herald*, 18 May 1998,
56 See chapter 2, p. 66ff.
57 'A nice little earner in that souvenir', *Hobart Mercury*, 19 January 1999, p. 5.
58 'Weak dollar aids boom in sales of Aboriginal art', *Canberra Times*, 19 January 1999, p. 15.

59 ibid.

60 John Kasmir, quoted in Nicholas Shakespeare, *Bruce Chatwin*, Vintage, London, 1988, p. 100.

61 ibid. The painting had been purchased directly from the artist by a theatre director who had visited Papunya in 1972 at the suggestion of Nugget Coombs to 'study comparisons between Aboriginal and Greek mythology as it is expressed in dance and ceremony'.

62 *Australian Financial Review*, 1 July 1999, p. 34.

63 Lot numbers followed by year of previous auction from which they were purchased by the 2000 vendors, from Sotheby's, 2000, *Aboriginal Art* catalogue: 35 (1996); 66 (1994); 67 (1994); 73 (1996); 107 (1997); 108 (1996); 110 (1997); 172 (1996); 173 (1996); 225 (1997); 226 (1994); 227 (1994).

64 Commission was 15% of sale price up to $50 000, 10% thereafter.

65 'Fame but no fortune for sweet dreaming artist', *Australian*, 28 June 2000, p. 3.

66 Extending native title to the mainland.

67 The year 1997 also saw the release of the federal government's *Bringing Them Home* report on the Stolen Generations of Aboriginal and Torres Strait Islander children.

68 'Buyers are restless for natives', *Australian*, 20 June 1997.

69 *Australian*, 12 February 1999, p. 16.

70 'Dots before the artist's eyes, but they're not his', *Australian*, 25 February 1999, p. 1.

71 *Weekend Australian*, 24–25 April 1999, p. 1.

72 *Art from the Heart?*, Jeremy Eccles, Australia, 1999.

73 'Dot for Dollar', *Four Corners*, ABC television, 1999.

74 'Black art signature not right', *Australian*, 24 January 2001.

75 Sotheby's, *Aboriginal Art*, catalogue for Tuesday 27 June 2000 sale, Lot 70, p. 58.

76 ibid., p. 184.

77 For example, Michael Reid, 'Aboriginal art faces a real test', *Weekend Australian*, 22–23 May 1999.

78 'Indigenous values', *Sydney Morning Herald*, 16 June 1999. Michelangelo's most famous paintings, those in the Sistine Chapel, however, were executed entirely by him. The apprenticeship system of the Renaissance masters was repeatedly invoked in an attempt to normalise the collaborative practices in traditional Aboriginal art which came to light through the 'scandals'. But why were not equally pertinent comparisons made with the contemporary practices of Postmodernism with respect to originality and authorship?

79 Brook Turner, 'An authentic market', *Australian Financial Review*, 30 July 1999, p. 12.

80 Terry Ingram, 'Aboriginal authorship no problem', *Australian Financial Review*, 1 July 1999, p. 34.

81 'How Rover found an expensive new home', *Sydney Morning Herald*, 10 July 2001, p. 3.

6 The Object of Protection

1 Held in Melbourne on 29 July 1990.
2 Bob Evans, 'Tribal art becomes our Elgin Marbles', *Sydney Morning Herald*, 14 July 1990, p. 77.
3 An Act to amend the *Aboriginal and Torres Strait Islander Heritage Protection Act 1984* to make certain provisions for the preservation of Aboriginal cultural heritage in Victoria, and for related purposes.
4 Evans appears to have confused this Act with the *Protection of Movable Cultural Heritage Act*. There is no permits process under the former legislation.
5 Bob Evans, 'Tribal art becomes our Elgin Marbles', *Sydney Morning Herald*, 14 July 1990, p. 77.
6 ibid.
7 Peter Watson, *Sotheby's: The Inside Story*, Bloomsbury, London, 1997, p. 304.
8 Tim Klingender, quoted in Susan McCulloch, 'Exports caught in the act', *Australian*, 26 June 1998, p. 16.
9 'Preamble', UNESCO Convention on the Means of Prohibiting and Preventing the Illicit Import, Export and Transfer of Ownership of Cultural Property, adopted by the General Conference at its sixteenth session, Paris, 14 November 1970.
10 Minutes of the National Cultural Heritage Committee, 23 September 1996.
11 Policies to update the National Cultural Heritage Control List September 1995, Stage 1 Report, DCITA, p. 25. The National Cultural Heritage Control List sets out the categories of objects classed as Australian protected objects and the criteria defining each of these categories.
12 Ministerial briefing on Amendments to the National Cultural Heritage Control List in Regulations under the *Protection of Movable Cultural Heritage Act 1986*, 7 May 1997.
13 *Annual Report 1997–98 on the Operation of the Protection of Movable Cultural Heritage Act*, DCITA, p. 6.
14 Susan McCulloch, 'Exports caught in the act', *Australian*, 26 June 1998, p. 16.
15 ibid.
16 ibid.
17 Sotheby's had covered itself for this eventuality with a notice to prospective buyers at the front of the catalogue, warning them that they might 'be required to obtain an export permit for certain categories of items in this sale ... under the provisions of the *Protection of Movable Cultural Heritage Act 1986*'.
18 Geoffrey Bardon, cited in Sotheby's, *Important Aboriginal Art*, 30 June 1999, p. 56.
19 Tim Klingender, quoted in Geoffrey Maslen, 'Curators seek bans to halt exodus of Aboriginal art', *Sydney Morning Herald*, 23 June 2000, p. 14.

20 *Annual Report 1999–2000 on the Operation of the Protection of Movable Cultural Heritage Act 1986 and the Administration of the National Cultural Heritage Fund*, DCITA, 2000, p. 5.

21 These include two extraordinary works from the Peter Fannin Collection at the NGA, two more from the Pat Hogan Collection at the NGV and another significant group at the Australian Museum.

22 Sotheby's, *Important Aboriginal Art*, 30 June 1999, p. 80.

23 'Reconciled to rip-offs', *Weekend Australian*, 24–25 June 2000, p. 25.

24 A fund to assist Australian institutions by providing 'matching funds' for the purchase of items whose export was banned under the legislation had been promised at the time the legislation was originally being drafted. However, an amount of $500 000 was not set aside to establish the National Cultural Heritage Account until July 1999, more than thirteen years later.

25 'Curators seek bans to halt exodus of Aboriginal art', *Sydney Morning Herald*, 23 June 2000, p. 14.

26 The following early Papunya boards from the Sotheby's 2000 auction were granted export permits:
1. *Untitled (Ceremony with Bullroarers)* 1972 by John Kipari Tjakamarra (Lot 33)
2. Untitled 1972 by Tim Leura Tjapaltjarri (Lot 34)
3. *Tingari Ceremony at Ilingawurn Gawurrng* 1974 by Shorty Lungkata Tjungurrayi (Lot 36)
4. *Water Dreaming* 1971 by Johnny Warangkula Tjupurrula (Lot 108)
5. *Water Dreaming with Emu at Kalipinypa* 1973 by Johnny Warangkula Tjupurrula (Lot 176)
6. *Water Dreaming at Mikantji* 1972 by Kaapa Mbitjana Tjampitjinpa (Lot 177)
7. *Medicine Story* 1971–72 by Shorty Lungkata Tjungurrayi (Lot 224)
8. *Untitled (Snake Dreaming)* 1971 by Long Jack Phillipus Tjakamarra (Lot 226, passed in at $7500)
9. *Emu Story* 1971 by Kaapa Mbitjana Tjampitjinpa (Lot 227)
10. Untitled 1972 by Ronnie Tjampitjinpa (Lot 229)

27 Six of these already had permits by the time of the auction (though only five needed them in the end because one did not reach the required monetary threshold).

28 Vivien Anderson, quoted in 'Reconciled to rip-offs', *Weekend Australian*, 24–25 June 2000, p. 25.

29 The following boards from the Deutscher-Menzies auction of 2001 were granted export permits before the auction:
1. Papunya Board 1972 by Old Walter Tjampitjinpa (Lot 18)
2. Papunya Board 1972 by Mick Namarari Tjapaltjarri (Lot 32)
3. Papunya Board 1972 by Yala Yala Gibbs Tjungurrayi (Lot 140)
4. Papunya Board 1972 by Shorty Lungkata Tjungurrayi (Lot 31)
5. Papunya Board 1972 by Charlie Tarawa Tjungurrayi (Lot 141)
6. Papunya Board 1972 by Johnny Scobie Tjapanangka (Lot 143)
7. Papunya Board 1972 by Mick Namarari Tjapaltjarri (Lot 142)

30 Nicolas Rothwell, 'Reconciled to rip-offs', *Weekend Australian*, 24–25 June 2000, p. 25.
31 Sotheby's, *Important Aboriginal Art*, 30 June 1999, p. 80.
32 'Money behind' is an expression in Western Desert Aboriginal English deriving from Papunya Tula's practice of giving an artist an additional payment, over and above what the artist is paid when they produce a work, if one of their works sells for an exceptionally high price. It is also applied to the cheques distributed to artist shareholders at the company's AGM as a 'dividend'.
33 Bobby West Tjupurrula, interview with author, Kiwirrkura, NT, September 2000.
34 Refusal of Export Permits, *2000–01 Annual Report on the Protection of Movable Cultural Heritage Act 1986*, p. 6.
35 Since 1 May 1999, Part 5 Objects of Fine or Decorative Art of the Control List of the Protection of Movable Cultural Heritage Act has included 5.3 (1) identifying a special class of fine and decorative art designated 'Aboriginal and Torres Strait Islander objects' which it defines as 'an object made in the indigenous tradition by an Aboriginal or Torres Strait Islander person, *other than* an object listed in the category in Part 1 of the Schedule'.
36 *Annual Report 1999–2000 on the Operation of the Protection of Movable Cultural Heritage Act 1986 and the Administration of the National Cultural Heritage Fund*, DCITA, 2000.
37 Some of these were the *Papunya Tula: Genesis and Genius* retrospective – and less obviously the 'Black Art Scandals' (see p. 172ff).
38 Terry Ingram, 'Aboriginal authorship no problem', *Australian Financial Review*, 1 July 1999.
39 'From the outback to Manhattan', *Australian Financial Review*, 30 September 2000, p. 4.
40 The others were John Kean, who worked for Papunya Tula from 1977 to 1979 and curated *East to West: Land in Papunya Tula Painting* for the Tandanya Aboriginal Cultural Institute in 1990. He now works as a producer at Museum Victoria; and Hetti Perkins, Senior Curator of Aboriginal and Torres Strait Islander art at the AGNSW and curator of *Papunya Tula: Genesis and Genius* in 2000.
41 An employee of Sotheby's was subsequently appointed to the Reference Group without the knowledge of the existing membership, who protested his inclusion on the grounds of conflict of interest when it became known.
42 Vincent Megaw, Emeritus Professor of Visual Arts and Archaeology at Flinders University; Margie West, formerly Senior Curator of Indigenous Art at MAGNT; and Kate Khan of the Australian Museum who was Bob Edwards' assistant at the AAB in the 1970s have also been members.
43 'Artworks face foreign ban', *Age*, 9 July 2001, p. 4.
44 When we dispatched this letter on 25 June 2001, the following men from the founding group of artists were still alive: John Tjakamarra

(c. 1937–2002), Long Jack Phillipus Tjakamarra (1932–), Billy Stockman Tjapaltjarri (1927–), Clifford Possum Tjapaltjarri (c. 1932–2002); Charlie Egalie Tjapaltjarri (c. 1938–2002); Dinny Nolan Tjampitjinpa (c. 1928–); Ronnie Tjampitjinpa (c. 1943–); Dr George Tjapaltjarri (c. 1940–); Turkey Tolson Tjupurrula (c. 1943–2001).

45 Wankjuk Marika, 'Copyright on Aboriginal Art', *Aboriginal News*, vol. 3, no. 1, February 1975, pp. 7–8, excerpted in Vivien Johnson, *Copyrites: Aboriginal Art in the Age of Reproductive Technologies*, exhibition catalogue, NIAAA & Macquarie University, Sydney, 1996, p. 11.

46 That is, the Papunya Permanent Collection, at that time kept in storage drawers, out of sight.

47 Tim Klingender, interview with author, Sydney, 2003.

48 Recommendation 8.11. The Ley Review had also recommended that paintings from the 'Namatjira/Hermannsburg school be explicitly included as Objects of Aboriginal Fine Art', but this alteration was deferred until 'the broader issue of the setting of different monetary values for Aboriginal and other Australian works of art as well as the historical associations of artworks' could be dealt with in Stage 2 of the process.

49 'From the outback to Manhattan', *Australian Financial Review*, 30 September 2000, p. 4.

50 See chapter 4, p. 00.

51 This criterion was included in the measures of 'cultural significance' determined by the 2000 conference.

7 Give Those Men a Real Voice

1 A fourteenth work, Tommy Lowry's 1984 *Two Men Dreaming at Kuluntjarranya*, is not an early Papunya painting and will not be considered here. An appeal before the Administrative Appeals Tribunal against the Minister's decision in this case is pending.

2 For Charlie Tarawa's *Fear* 1971, there was a reference to 'esoteric meanings of the site of Tjiturrrnga for which the artist was senior custodian'. *Water Ceremony* 1972, *Water Dreaming at Kalipinypa* 1972 and *Rain Dreaming with Ceremonial Man* c. 1971 by Johnny Warangkula were also refused permits in the first year of the Reference Group's operation. In the official reasons given for the refusal of *Water Ceremony* 1972, and *Water Dreaming at Kalipinypa* 1972, both were said to contain depictions of sacred boards with the incised designs shown in sufficient detail to 'be used by the artist's descendants to maintain and revive the associated ceremony' and, the Reference Group had argued in its reports, also 'to be used by the current owners of these Dreamings to identify the original sacred objects if they were to surface in foreign or domestic collections'. *Rain Dreaming with Ceremonial Man*'s 'explicit depiction of ritual

subject matter' was noted in the Ministerial rationale published in the Protection of Movable Cultural Heritage Act's Annual Report. The 'potent' subject matter of Mick Namarari's *Untitled (Ceremonial Designs)* 1971–72 was noted and for Anatjari Tjakamarra's *Porcupine Danger.* Men Only 1973, it was quite explicit: 'This is one of a group of early Papunya boards whose "Restricted" status sets them apart as having unequivocally the highest level of significance for the artist and members of his culture' ... and again 'its "Restricted" classification must be read as an indication of the very highest level of cultural significance.' For the five of the seven other early Papunya boards refused permits over the next seven years, there was also reference in the Ministerial rationales to 'culturally weighty subject matter relating to explicit ceremonies of the sacred/secret world of men' (Long Jack Phillipus' *Corroboree for Young Men* 1972); 'specifically secret/sacred nature and explicit depiction of items from the ceremonial life of women' (Uta Uta Tjangala's *Women's Dreaming* 1972); 'depictions of eight sacred boards' (Walter Tjampitjinpa's *Water Dreaming* 1972); 'subject matter ... is ... secret and sacred in nature for the Warlpiri people and unsuitable for public display' (David Corby, *Wild Potato Dreaming* 1972); and 'sacred secret in nature and unsuitable for public display' (Anatjari Tjakamarra, *Men's Corroboree Dreaming in a Cave* 1974).

3 See Geoffrey Bardon & James Bardon, *Papunya: A Place Made After the Story*, Miegunyah Press, Melbourne, 2004, p. 31. See also chapter 4, p. 105ff.

4 See chapter 4, pp. 127ff.

5 Bobby West was born in 1958 and left Papunya in the 1970s to live with his mother's family in Balgo. His strict attitudes to these questions may come from having spent time with the men of Balgo, who in the early 1980s when Bobby was there were not yet painting and were critical of those who were. That would soon change, but not their attitudes to the early paintings, despite few people having actually seen them.

6 Uta Uta Tjangala's *Medicine Story* 1971 is one of his very first paintings of Yumari. The Museum's former Director Craddock Morton was also Chair of the National Cultural Heritage Committee and, in accordance with the letter that had gone out under his signature, the Museum was prepared to fund a consultation with the most appropriate person to give permission for its display and publication before exhibiting it in *Papunya Painting: Out of the Desert* – and to pay whoever was consulted for this purpose. The Museum was also prepared to construct a special viewing space with a warning label if necessary and appropriate to enable the painting to be included in the exhibition. But when, with assistance from Daphne Williams, Manager of Papunya Tula Artists, 1981–1993, 1995–2003, I sought out Ronnie Tjampitjinpa, Uta Uta's older brother's son, he said that it would be 'fine' to put the work on public display.

7 When asked to recall the sequence of events over this decade, the painters' practice was to divide it up into the 'times' of the various Papunya Tula managers. In the exhibition this served to demarcate the chronology of the paintings.

8 It took courage for the Museum to organise an exhibition like *Papunya Painting* in the face of this hostility – even to the extent of using my suggestion of 'The Title Deeds' as a working title for the show, until it was eventually vetoed by the Marketing Department as too obscure for the Museum's target audience of 'ordinary Australian families'.

9 He also recommended, along the lines of the National Cultural Heritage Committee letter, though more forcefully, that cultural institutions in Australia be advised of (1) the concern among the artists and their descendants about the display and reproduction of paintings produced in Papunya in the period 1971–72; and (2) that consultation with the artists and their descendants is essential if paintings produced in Papunya in the period 1971–72 are to be included in exhibitions and publications. These consultations should inform the decisions made by any institution that wishes to display or reproduce that work.

10 John Kean, personal communication, 10 February 2010.

11 Nicolas Rothwell, 'Mystery of our art in darkness', *Weekend Australian*, 5–6 April 2008, p. 31.

8 The *Icons* Precedent

1 RG Kimber, 'Relatives of the Artists Respond to the Paintings', in Roger Benjamin & Andrew C Weislogel (eds), *Icons of the Desert: Early Aboriginal Paintings from Papunya*, Herbert F Johnson Museum of Art, Cornell University, Ithaca NY, 2009, p. 72.

2 ibid.

3 'He was absolutely emphatic that this painting and a number of others of even more elaborate nature could be openly displayed.' Dick Kimber, in Sotheby's, *Important Aboriginal Art*, June 1998, Lot 21, p. 21.

4 Kimber, 'Relatives of the Artists Respond to the Paintings', p. 72.

5 ibid., p. 74.

6 Perkins did take precautions. For example, an extraordinary painting titled *Kurumba* by Charlie Tarawa Tjungurrayi in the MAGNT collection which she had initially hoped to include was left out even though it contains no obvious secret/sacred imagery, because the MAGNT catalogue identified it as 'Restricted'.

7 Fred Myers, 'Showing Too Much or Too Little: Predicaments of Painting Indigenous Presence in Central Australia', paper presented at 'The Performance of Indigeneity' conference, University of Iowa, May 2009, and later presented as the Dean's Lecture, NYU,

17 September 2010, as part of the program for *Icons of the Desert* exhibition.

8 'No-one seemed very excited about it in Dick Kimber's essay.' J Eccles, personal communication, 2009.

9 Disruption of a ceremony remains one of the most serious offences one can commit in the artists' society. Protocol must be observed in the ceremonial context, because the ancestral power called up in such ceremonies can be 'dangerous', even fatal to the participants, if it is not. See Vivien Johnson, *Michael Jagamara Nelson,* Craftsman House, Sydney, 1997, pp. 87–89, for a discussion of Nelson's expression of these views at the opening of the new Parliament House, Canberra, in 1988.

10 Something else Bobby told us at the Steakhouse that confirms this was that he had thought the government representative had come about concerns he had raised with Dick Kimber about a tjurunga being offered for sale on eBay. He was hoping the government would intervene to stop the sale.

11 RG Kimber, 'Politics of the Secret in Contemporary Western Desert Art', in Chris Anderson (ed.), 'Politics of the Secret', *Oceania Monograph* 45, University of Sydney, 1995, p. 128, where Kimber notes that the 'very public setting' of the Alice Springs Show in 1972 'with many other exhibits and thousands of people present, *precluded potential protest*'.

12 See chapter 6, p. 218.

13 Geoffrey Bardon, *Papunya Tula: Art of the Western Desert*, McPhee Gribble, Melbourne, 1991, p. 108.

14 Works by Long Jack Phillipus, Freddy West Tjakamarra and Anatjari Tjakamarra were also censored.

15 Benjamin & Weislogel (eds), *Icons of the Desert*, p. 30.

16 ibid., p. 31.

17 'Though only performed by men, the emu corroboree can be watched by the whole family – from "across the road"'. Vivien Johnson, *The Art of Clifford Possum Tjapaltjarri*, Craftsman House/G+B Arts International, Sydney, 1994, p. 154.

18 Vivien Johnson, *Clifford Possum Tjapaltjarri*, AGSA, Adelaide, 2003, p. 64.

19 This question was raised by Richard Kelton at the 'Exhibiting the Sacred' forum for the Friends of the Fowler, part of the *Icons of the Desert* symposium program for the exhibition's tour to the Fowler Museum, UCLA, 27 May 2009.

20 'From the outback to Manhattan', *Australian Financial Review*, 30 September 2000, p. 4.

21 Pat Hogan, 'Notes and Inventory for the Early Consignments of Pintupi Paintings', in *Dot and Circle: A Retrospective Survey of the Aboriginal Acrylic Paintings of Central Australia*, Communication Services Unit, RMIT, 1986, pp. 55–57.

22 See chapter 5, p. 158ff.

23 Nicolas Rothwell, 'From the desert, artists came', *Australian*, 13 February 2009.

24 R Benjamin, 'The Fetish for Papunya Boards', in Benjamin & Weislogel (eds), *Icons of the Desert*, p. 21.

25 See chapter 5, p. 160.

26 Theodore Roosevelt, 'A Layman's Views of an Art Exhibition,' *Outlook*, vol. 103, 29 March 1913, pp. 718–20. Reprinted in Roderick Nash (ed.), *The Call of the Wild (1900–1916)*, George Braziller, NY, 1970.

27 Professor Benjamin's research interests include French Orientalist art 1880–1930, including Renoir's Algerian work; the art of Henri Matisse; and contemporary Australian painting, including Indigenous art.

28 In these ceremonies, similar designs to those which appear on the early Papunya paintings are painted on the performers' bodies and ritual objects in ochres and pipe clay – but also sculpted in the elaborate mosaics of vegetable and animal down known as ground paintings which signify both the Dreaming narratives and their associated geographies. Geography, history and ceremony are seamlessly conjoined in one visual image – as in the classical Papunya painting.

29 Johnson, *Michael Jagamara Nelson*, p. 93.

30 ibid., pp. 92–98.

31 Chris Anderson, interviewed in *Market of Dreams*, Kate Kennedy White, Kennedy White Pty Ltd, 1990, a South Australian documentary about the impact of Aboriginal Art in America.

32 Johnson, *Michael Jagamara Nelson*, p. 97.

33 ibid., p. 98.

34 'The observer is encouraged to perceive meaningfulness, but not the meaning itself. The difference is that the source of meaning exists ... not in the psychological imagination of the individual artist, but in a collective, social and religious discourse.' E Michaels, 'Western Desert Sandpainting and Postmodernism', in Warlukurlangu Artists (eds), *Kuruwarri: Yuendumu Doors*, Australian Institute of Aboriginal and Torres Strait Islander Studies, Canberra, 1987, p. 140.

35 Fred Myers, personal communication, 29 January 2010.

36 Melik Kaylan, *Wall Street Journal*, 21 October 2009.

37 Fred Myers, personal communication, 29 January 2010.

38 See chapter 4, p. 135.

39 Margo Neale, *Yiribana: An Introduction to the Aboriginal and Torres Strait Islander Collection of the Art Gallery of New South Wales*, AGNSW, Sydney, 1994, p. 11.

40 *Given: 1. The Waterfall, 2. The Illuminating Gas.*

41 'Finally it is Wandjuk's turn to speak for his people and he asks for permission to stand. And he tells of travelling to the National Gallery of Victoria, where he has seen his people's most sacred and secret paintings on public display. Although he speaks very quietly, it is

clear that he is deeply distressed … "It is very wrong. You must help me," he says, searching our faces. "These things must not be seen. If they are, my people will die." Phillip Adams, 'The Shame of the White Man', reprinted in Vivien Johnson, *Copyrites: Aboriginal Art in the Age of Reproductive Technologies*, NIAAA & Macquarie University, Sydney, 1996, p. 12.

42 Natasha Robinson, 'Minister lashes the "culture vultures" of Aboriginal art', *Australian*, 11 May 2009.

43 ibid.

44 Media release from NT Labor Party, 'Henderson's Labor Team', 29 July 2009.

45 Following Scrymgour's resignation from the Ministry, these portfolios were added to Alison Anderson's Ministerial responsibilities.

46 Lindsay Murdoch, 'Priceless Aboriginal works given an outing', *Sydney Morning Herald*, 15 May 2009.

47 ibid.

48 ibid.

49 ibid.

Bibliography

Amadio, N & Kimber, RG, *Wildbird Dreaming,* Greenhouse Publications, Melbourne, 1988.

Anderson, C & Dussart, F, 'Dreamings in Acrylic: Western Desert Art', in P Sutton (ed.), *Dreamings: The Art of Aboriginal Australia*, Viking, Melbourne, 1988, pp. 89–142.

Bardon, Geoffrey, *Aboriginal Art of the Western Desert*, Rigby, Adelaide, 1979.

—, *Papunya Tula: Art of the Western Desert*, McPhee Gribble, Melbourne, 1991.

— & Bardon, James, *Papunya: A Place Made After the Story*, Miegunyah Press, Melbourne, 2004.

Batty, Phillip (ed.), *Colliding Worlds: First Contact in the Western Desert 1932–1984*, Museum Victoria, Melbourne, 2006.

Beier, Ulli & Johnson, Colin (eds), *Long Water: Aboriginal Art and Literature*, Aboriginal Artists Agency, Sydney, 1988.

Benjamin, Roger & Weislogel, Andrew C (eds), *Icons of the Desert: Early Aboriginal Paintings from Papunya*, Herbert F Johnson Museum of Art, Cornell University, Ithaca, NY, 2009.

Caruana, W, *Aboriginal Art*, Thames and Hudson, London, 1993.

Corbally-Stourton, Patrick, *Songlines and Dreamings: Contemporary Australian Aboriginal Painting*, Lund Humphries, London, 1996.

Crocker, Andrew, *Charlie Tjaruru Tjungurrayi: A Retrospective 1970–1986*, Orange City Council, NSW, 1987.

Croft, Brenda L (ed.), *Indigenous Art: Art Gallery of Western Australia*, Art Gallery of Western Australia, Perth, 2001.

Diggins, L, *A Myriad of Dreamings: Twentieth Century Aboriginal Art*, Malakoff Fine Art Press, Melbourne, 1989.

Edwards, R, *Aboriginal Art in Australia*, Ure Smith, Sydney, 1978.

— & Stewart J (eds), *Preserving Indigenous Cultures: A New Role for Museums*, Australian Government Publishing Service, Canberra, 1980.

French, A, *Seeing the Centre: The Art of Albert Namatjira 1902–1959*, National Gallery of Australia, Canberra, 2002.

Grayden, William, *Adam and Atoms*, F Daniels, Perth, 1957.

Hardy, J, Megaw JVS & Megaw, Ruth M, *The Heritage of Namatjira*, William Heinemann, Melbourne, 1992.

Hasluck, Sir Paul, *Shades of Darkness: Aboriginal Affairs 1925–1965*, Melbourne University Press, 1988.

Henson, Barbara, *A Straight-Out Man: F.W. Albrecht and Central Australian Aborigines*, Melbourne University Press, 1992.

Hogan, Pat, 'Notes and Inventory for the Early Consignments of Pintupi Paintings', in J Maughan & J Zimmer (eds), *Dot and Circle: A Retrospective Survey of the Aboriginal Acrylic Paintings of Central Australia*, Communication Services Unit, Royal Melbourne Institute of Technology, 1986, pp. 55–57.

Isaacs, Jennifer, *Wandjuk Marika: Life Story*, University of Queensland Press, Brisbane, 1995.

—, 'Epilogue: Encounters with Geoff Bardon', in Geoffrey Bardon & James Bardon, *Papunya: A Place Made After the Story*, Miegunyah Press, Melbourne, 2004, pp. 502–04.

Jack-Hinton, C, 'Export of Aboriginal Artefacts', printed circular, Museums and Art Galleries of the Northern Territory, Darwin, 1974.

Johnson, Vivien, *The Art of Clifford Possum Tjapaltjarri*, Craftsman House/ G+B Arts International, Sydney, 1994.

—, *Copyrites: Aboriginal Art in the Age of Reproductive Technologies*, exhibition catalogue, National Indigenous Arts Advocacy Association & Macquarie University, Sydney, 1996.

—, *Dreamings of the Desert*, Art Gallery of South Australia, Adelaide, 1996.

—, *Michael Jagamara Nelson*, Craftsman House, Sydney, 1997.

—, 'The "Aboriginal Art Scandals" Scandal', *ArtLink*, vol. 20, no. 1, 2000, pp. 32–35.

—, *Clifford Possum Tjapaltjarri*, Art Gallery of South Australia, Adelaide, 2003.

—, 'How Papunya Paintings Became Art', in Vivien Johnson (ed.), *Papunya Painting: Out of the Desert 1971–1981*, National Museum of Australia Press, Canberra, 2007, pp. 28–42.

—, *Lives of the Papunya Tula Artists*, IAD Press, Alice Springs, NT, 2008.

Jones, P, 'Objects of Mystery and Concealment: A History of Tjurunga Collecting', in Chris Anderson (ed.), 'Politics of the Secret', *Oceania Monograph* 45, University of Sydney, 1995, pp. 67–96.

Kean, John, *East to West: Land in Papunya Tula Painting*, (Tandanya) Aboriginal Cultural Institute, Adelaide, 1990.

—, 'Papunya, Place and Time', in Vivien Johnson (ed.), *Papunya Painting: Out of the Desert 1971–1981*, National Museum of Australia Press, Canberra, 2007, pp. 4–15.

Kerr, Joan, 'Papunya Tula: A Great Contemporary Art Movement', *Art Asia Pacific*, no. 31: 2000, pp. 4–16.

Kimber, RG (Dick), 'Papunya Tula Art: Some Recollections August 1971 – October 1972', in J Maughan & J Zimmer (eds), *Dot and Circle: A Retrospective Survey of the Aboriginal Acrylic Paintings of Central Australia*, Communication Services Unit, Royal Melbourne Institute of Technology, 1986, pp. 43–45.

—, *Friendly Country – Friendly People: An Exhibition of Aboriginal Artworks from the Peoples of the Tanami and Great Sandy Deserts*, Araluen Arts Centre, Alice Springs, NT, 1990.

—, 'Politics of the Secret in Contemporary Western Desert Art', in Chris Anderson (ed.), 'Politics of the Secret', *Oceania Monograph* 45, University of Sydney, 1995, pp. 123–42.

—, 'Notes on the Peter Fannin Collection of Early Western Desert Paintings', National Gallery of Australia, Canberra, 1998.

—, 'Recollections of Papunya Tula 1971–1980', in Hetti Perkins & Hannah Fink (eds), *Papunya Tula: Genesis and Genius*, Art Gallery of New South Wales, Sydney, 2000, pp. 204–15.

—, 'Relatives of the Artists Respond to the Paintings', in Roger Benjamin & Andrew C Weislogel (eds), *Icons of the Desert: Early Aboriginal Paintings from Papunya*, Herbert F Johnson Museum of Art, Cornell University, Ithaca, NY, 2009, pp. 71–75.

Latz, Peter, *The Flaming Desert: Arid Australia – A Fire Shaped Landscape*, Peter Latz, Alice Springs, NT, 2007.

Leske, D (ed.), *Hermannsburg: A Vision and a Mission*, Lutheran Publishing, Adelaide, 1977.

Long, Jeremy, 'Leaving the Desert: Actors and Sufferers in the Aboriginal Exodus from the Western Desert', *Aboriginal History*, vol. 13, nos 1–2, 1989, pp. 9–43.

Maughan, J & Zimmer, J (eds), *Dot and Circle: A Retrospective Survey of the Aboriginal Acrylic Paintings of Central Australia*, Communication Services Unit, Royal Melbourne Institute of Technology, 1986.

Megaw, JVS, 'Western Desert Acrylic Painting – Artefact or Art?', *Art History*, vol. 5, no. 2, June 1982, pp. 205–18.

Mellor, D & Megaw, JVS, *Twenty-Five Years and Beyond: Papunya Tula Painting*, Flinders University Art Museum, Adelaide, 1999.

Michaels, E, 'Western Desert Sandpainting and Postmodernism', in Warlukurlangu Artists (eds), *Kuruwarri: Yuendumu Doors*, Australian Institute of Aboriginal and Torres Strait Islander Studies, Canberra, 1987, pp. 135–43.

Morphy, H & Smith Boles, M (eds), *Art from the Land: Dialogues with the Kluge-Ruhe Collection of Australian Aboriginal Art*, University of Virginia, Charlottesville, 1999.

Myers, Fred, *Pintupi Country, Pintupi Self: Sentiment, Place, and Politics Among Western Desert Aborigines*, Australian Institute of Aboriginal Studies, Canberra, & Smithsonian Press, Washington, 1986.

—, 'Truth, Beauty and Pintupi Painting', *Visual Anthropology*, vol. 2, 1989, pp. 163–95.

—, *Painting Culture: The Making of an Aboriginal High Art*, Duke University Press, Durham, 2002.

—, 'Showing Too Much or Too Little: Predicaments of Painting Indigenous Presence in Central Australia', paper presented at 'The Performance of Indigeneity' conference, University of Iowa, May 2009, and later presented as the Dean's Lecture, New York

University, 17 September 2010, as part of the program for *Icons of the Desert* exhibition, 2009.
—, with Jeremy Long, 'In Recognition: The Gift of Pintupi Painting', in Hetti Perkins & Margie West (eds), *One Sun One Moon: Aboriginal Art in Australia*, Art Gallery of New South Wales, Sydney, 2007, pp. 170–78.
Neale, M, *Yiribana: An Introduction to the Aboriginal and Torres Strait Islander Collection of the Art Gallery of New South Wales*, Art Gallery of New South Wales, Sydney, 1994.
Nicholls, Christine & North, Ian, *Kathleen Petyarre: Genius of Place*, Wakefield Press, Adelaide, 2001.
O'Ferrall, Michael, *Tjukurrpa – Desert Dreamings: Aboriginal Art from Central Australia 1971–1993*, Art Gallery of Western Australia, Perth, 1993.
Papunya School, *Papunya School Book of Country and History*, Allen & Unwin, Sydney, 2001.
Perkins, Hetti & Fink, Hannah (eds), *Papunya Tula: Genesis and Genius*, Art Gallery of New South Wales, Sydney, 2000.
Report from the Select Committee on The Native and Historical Objects and Areas Preservation Ordinance 1955–1960, Northern Territory Legislative Council, Commonwealth Government Printer, Darwin, 1965.
Rothwell, N, *Wings of the Kite-Hawk*, Picador, Sydney, 2003.
Rowley, CD, *The Destruction of Aboriginal Society*, Australian National University Press, Canberra, 1970.
—, *The Remote Aborigines*, Australian National University Press, Canberra, 1971.
—, *Recovery: The Politics of Aboriginal Reform*, Penguin, Melbourne, 1986.
Rowse, Tim, *Obliged to be Difficult: Nugget Coombs' Legacy in Indigenous Affairs*, Cambridge University Press, Melbourne, 2000.
Rubuntja, Wenten, with Jenny Green & Tim Rowse, *The Town Grew Up Dancing: The Life and Art of Wenten Rubuntja*, Jukurrpa Books, Alice Springs, NT, 2002.
Ryan, Judith, *Mythscapes: Aboriginal Art of the Desert from the National Gallery of Victoria*, National Gallery of Victoria, Melbourne, 1989.
Sotheby's, *Fine Tribal Art*, auction catalogue, Sotheby's Australia, Melbourne, 1993.
—, *Contemporary and Aboriginal Art*, auction catalogue, Sotheby's Australia, Melbourne, June 1995.
—, *Fine Contemporary and Aboriginal Art*, auction catalogue, Sotheby's Australia, Melbourne, November 1995.
—, *Fine Aboriginal and Contemporary Art*, auction catalogue, Sotheby's Australia, Melbourne, June 1996.
—, *Important Aboriginal Art*, auction catalogue, Sotheby's Australia, Melbourne, June 1997.
—, *Important Aboriginal Art*, auction catalogue, Sotheby's Australia, Melbourne, June 1998.

—, *Important Aboriginal Art*, auction catalogue, Sotheby's Australia, Melbourne, June 1999.
—, *Aboriginal Art*, auction catalogue, Sotheby's Australia, Melbourne, 2000.
—, *Aboriginal Art*, auction catalogue, Sotheby's Australia, Melbourne, 2001.
—, *Important Aboriginal Art*, auction catalogue, Sotheby's Australia, Melbourne, 2007.
Wailbri and Pintubi Art, exhibition catalogue, c. 1972.
Watson, Peter, *Sotheby's: The Inside Story*, Bloomsbury, London, 1997.

Archives

Aboriginal Arts Board papers, National Archives of Australia
Stuart Art Centre Archives

Films

Art from the Heart?, produced by Jeremy Eccles and Richard Moore, 1999.
Desert Dreamers, BBC documentary, 1976.
'Dot for Dollar', *Four Corners*, ABC television, broadcast 31 May 1999.
Market of Dreams, Kate Kennedy White, Kennedy White Pty Ltd, 1990.

Index

Aboriginal names have been entered under surname/second name when one is available, eg, 'Possum Tjapaltjarri, Clifford. In other cases they have been entered under the skin name, e.g. Tjampitjinpa, Walter. 'PS' refers to the picture section.